ENGLISH PLAYS OF THE
NINETEENTH CENTURY

ENGLISH PLAYS

OF THE

NINETEENTH CENTURY

═══

IV. *Farces*

═══

EDITED BY MICHAEL R. BOOTH

OXFORD
AT THE CLARENDON PRESS
1973

Oxford University Press, Ely House, London W. 1

GLASGOW NEW YORK TORONTO MELBOURNE WELLINGTON
CAPE TOWN IBADAN NAIROBI DAR ES SALAAM LUSAKA ADDIS ABABA
DELHI BOMBAY CALCUTTA MADRAS KARACHI LAHORE DACCA
KUALA LUMPUR SINGAPORE HONG KONG TOKYO

*Printed in Great Britain
at the University Press, Oxford
by Vivian Ridler
Printer to the University*

CONTENTS

ILLUSTRATIONS

INTRODUCTION TO VOLUME FOUR

For much of the eighteenth century, and especially after the Licensing Act of 1737, the performance of farce in London was a matter for the two or three theatres legally and regularly open. Thus the output of farce, while considerable, was not immense, and the scholar can examine it thoroughly. With the nineteenth century, however, and the enormous increase in population and the number of theatres, both in London and the provinces, the writing and performance of farce became an aspect of mass marketing. In quantity and popularity farce ranked second only to melodrama, and appeared on virtually every playbill until at least the 1870s. Like the study of any form of nineteenth-century drama, therefore, the study of farce can only be selective rather than totally comprehensive; this inevitable limitation apart, a selection of the kind contained in this volume, together with a brief introduction, should illuminate at least to some degree a form of nineteenth-century theatre that has in the past been consigned almost entirely to the outer darkness of history and criticism. On the strength of its contemporary popularity and dramatic significance nineteenth-century farce certainly deserves a volume to itself. Most of the pieces reprinted here have never been available in dramatic anthologies, and at the time this is written not one of them, to the best of my knowledge, is in print.

A discussion of the considerable change that came over farce in the nineteenth century and the nature and characteristics of that farce is best prefaced by a glance at the previous century's farce and the social factors producing such a change. Socially, the eighteenth-century patent theatre audience was remarkably stable: the fashionable aristocracy and upper middle class in the boxes, the middle class, professional and literary people in the pit, and the lower middle class, servants, journeymen, apprentices, sailors, etc. in the galleries.[1] This pattern was

preserved with little change until the next century. The content
of the one- or two-act farce afterpiece reflects the tastes and
composition of this audience. Its settings and characters are
commonly middle, upper middle, and aristocratic in class: the
father or guardian, the young lady or pair of young ladies, the
lover and his friend (who may also be a lover), the foolish rival,
the clever manservant and scheming chambermaid—a pair
necessary to keep the upper gallery interested and allow it to
identify enthusiastically with its class representatives on stage,
whose intelligence and ingenuity much exceed their masters'.[1]
These stock character types repeat themselves again and again.
The plot range is also narrow. By far the most popular plot is
that in which the favoured lover, often by the aid of his servant
or his lady's maid, or both, gulls a parent or guardian as well
as a rival out of the hand of the heroine. The rival may be a fop,
a blustery coward, or a doting old man; the father (or guardian)
may be a traditional Jonsonian 'humours' character with a
dominant eccentricity. The countryman can sometimes appear
as the rival, and also separately as a character actor; he is often
satirically treated, but sometimes his moral worth and superiority to the corruption of the town are vigorously asserted—as,
for instance, in Garrick's *Bon Ton* (1775). The general tone of
eighteenth-century farce, concerned as it is so frequently with
aristocratic and upper middle-class love intrigue, is relatively
elevated and refined, and comic physical business is not abun-
dant.[2] Well before the end of the century sentimentalism reached
farce, and plot resolutions were increasingly dictated by moral
and sentimental standards of stage behaviour.

   This kind of farce persisted into the nineteenth century,
even though it became steadily less genteel. The plot of the
successful lover outwitting his rival and the heroine's father was
still popular, as instanced by *Raising the Wind*, *Patter versus
Clatter*, and *Diamond Cut Diamond*. In Thomas Dibdin's *Past
Ten O'Clock and a Rainy Night* (1815), Harry Punctual and
Charles Wildfire deceive the guardian of two clever young
women and make off with them, thus frustrating his plans to

---

[1] Obvious examples are Fielding's *The Intriguing Chambermaid* (1734) and
Garrick's *The Lying Valet* (1741).

[2] A farce like James Cobb's *The First Floor* (1787), with its characters rushing in
and out of hiding, concealing themselves in bedrooms, and stealing to and fro in the
dark, is unusual for the century.

marry one to Punctual's father and the other to his own foppish son. The traditionalism of this plot is blended with more low comedy than an eighteenth-century farce would normally have possessed. Humour arises from the drunkenness of two servants, Dozey and Squib (the former a renowned part of Munden's) and from the physical business of the dual elopement. In the same author's *What Next?* (1816), Major Touchwood impersonates his uncle Colonel Touchwood in a complicated plot to marry the Colonel's daughter and frustrate his rival Colonel Clifford, who is, however, loved by the other lady in the case. The major is aided by his inventive servant, Sharp, who devises the intrigue, gets drunk, and enjoys himself thoroughly. All this is conventional, inherited farce machinery. In John Poole's *Deaf as a Post* (1823), Templeton makes an utter fool out of his Sophia's booby fiancé and thus persuades her father to break off the match. What humour there is in T. G. Rodwell's *The Young Widow* (1824) arises from the schemes of two servants, Splash and Lucy, to outwit each other and the opposing master or mistress. J. B. Buckstone's *A Dead Shot* (1830) displays Louisa's ingenuity in evading the command of her uncle to choose within an hour between two unattractive suitors: Timid, who seeks a quiet, domestic wife, and Wiseman, who wants a delicate and refined one. She plays the virago with the terrified Timid and the hearty, mannish sportswoman with the disgusted Wiseman; in consequence neither will marry her, and her lover Frederick wins her by pretending to have been shot in a duel and marrying her on his 'deathbed'. The farce here arises out of characterization rather than situation; it should not be thought that the nineteenth-century farce writer could only create amusing contretemps. As the farces in this volume surely testify, he was also capable of inventing excellent comic characters. Certainly the main plot ideas and much of the apparatus of eighteenth-century farce survived the turn of the new century by many years, and it took some time before love intrigue ceased to be the centre of concern. After the 1830s, however, it played a less significant role in farce's increasing variety of subject-matter and social range.

The number of minor theatres in London had been growing since the last decade of the eighteenth century, and at the time of the abolition of the patent monopolies in the Theatre

Regulation Act of 1843 there were not only several important ones in the West End, such as the Adelphi, the Strand, the Olympic, and the St. James's, but also neighbourhood working and lower middle-class theatres on the South Bank, in the East End, and on the fringes of the West End. The audience distributed over these theatres was not socially as stable as it used to be, and the concept of the same theatre for all classes of patron had disappeared. Even in the established patent theatres seat prices were lowered to attract a wider audience, and boxes were on the whole poorly attended. Managers and playwrights were appealing to a different class (or classes) of patron from that which had previously dominated the compact and ordered society of the eighteenth-century patent theatre audience. Different kinds of farce were now written for different kinds of theatres; the extent of the survival of the upper middle-class and aristocratic farce of an earlier period depended upon the particular theatre of performance and the constitution of its audience. The content and style of nineteenth-century farce, like that of other forms of contemporary drama, were largely determined by the taste of its audience—or, one should say, audiences. Changes in the social composition of these audiences ensured changes in the character of farce.

Before examining the nature and attributes of this farce—an examination that will offer an aggregate description of nineteenth-century farce in place of a general and single definition impossible to frame satisfactorily—we might find it useful to consider those areas of attitude and subject-matter that farce shares with comedy. The two forms were not remote from each other. The problem of identification and definition involved in the attempt to distinguish 'comedy' from 'drama' can also attend the effort to separate 'farce' from 'comedy'. Undoubtedly farce has special characteristics comedy does not possess—these will be discussed below—but it is surprising how much they have in common. A two-act piece called a 'farce' or 'comic drama', such as Buckstone's *A Rough Diamond* (which was called both) has all the characteristics of the *petite comédie* popular at Vestris's Olympic in the 1830s; it was in fact performed at the Lyceum under Vestris and Mathews in 1847. On the other hand, the same author's *Married Life*, played at the Haymarket in 1834 and termed a 'comedy', is much more farcical. For most of the century the standard farce was in one or two acts, and its very shortness automatically distinguishes it from the three-act comedy. However, this distinction is not helpful when one is confronted with the two-act 'comedy' as well as the two-act 'farce', not to mention the two-act 'comic drama'. Later in the century the three-act 'farcical comedy' is usually identical with the 'farce' itself. As in the muddling of the categories of 'comedy' and 'drama', contemporary nomenclature does not really assist us in framing definitions—Victorian dramatists and their publishers were not legal draughtsmen— and there is much overlapping.[1] As in the case of comedy and drama once again, it is wiser to forget about definitions and instead investigate those areas where farce resembles comedy and where they markedly differ.

Several main features of nineteenth-century comedy are apparent in farce: the blending of serious and comic material, the moral and sentimental motivation of behaviour, the glorifi- cation of the domestic ideal, and the assertion of the husband's rightful authority over his wife. Buckstone's farces are good illustrations. The heroine of *A Rough Diamond* is Margery, a simple, jolly country girl; her husband, Sir William, is reduced to despair by the failure of his repeated efforts to improve her conversation and make her into a fashionable society woman like the young wife of his uncle, Lord Plato. Audiences no doubt laughed at Margery's rustic gaucherie, country prattle, and hearty affection for her cousin Joe. However, Sir William revises his opinion when he observes the educated and sophisticated Lady Plato secretly renewing an affair with a former lover. Sir William, Lady Plato, her husband, and her lover are purely serious characters; they serve only to underline both the comedy and the moral superiority of Margery and Joe. The moral and sentimental lesson is that true virtue is resident in the country; this is reminiscent not only of the characters and sentiments of many comedies, but also directly relates to the moral dogma of melodrama, which is always contrasting rural innocence with

[1] Five of the plays in this volume are labelled 'Farce' on the title-pages of nineteenth-century editions. *Diamond Cut Diamond* is an 'Interlude', *Box and Cox* a 'Romance of Real Life', and *Tom Cobb* a 'Farcical Comedy'. *Mr. Paul Pry* is a 'Comic Sketch' on the playbill, a 'Comedy' in *Duncombe* (where, however, it is confused with Poole's comedy *Paul Pry*) and *Lacy*, and a 'Farcical Comedy' in *Dicks'*.

urban vice, the virtuous peasant with the corrupt aristocrat. The country is also idealized in Charles Selby's *Peggy Green* (1847), whose heroine sings 'Home of my Childhood' and declares, 'Oh, London, London—smoky, foggy, noisy, toiling, dissipated London, how glad I am that I have exchanged your fatiguing pleasures for the peace and quiet of this sweet paradise' —a speech that could have come out of any village melodrama between 1820 and 1870.[1] In another of Buckstone's farces, *An Alarming Sacrifice* (1849), moral and sentimental assumptions are the basis of conduct. The thoughtless and extravagant Bob Ticket discovers his uncle's will, which to his horror leaves the whole estate to the housekeeper, Susan Sweetapple. Bob struggles with his conscience as he looks in the mirror:

Now, let my face tell me what I ought to do. I'll destroy the will; I'll burn it. Susan shall never know such a document ever existed. I will— I will—and enjoy my property, and—oh, what a demon I do look! I'd no idea I could ever be so frightful. I'll try again. I'll be a man; I'll do the right thing; I'll tell the poor girl of her good fortune—put her in the possession of all. My heart will approve of my conduct, and I shall be one of the noblest works of creation, an honest man! Oh, what an angel sweetness beams in every feature; what a handsome fellow I am. Yes, and I'll behave as handsome. The struggle's over—an alarming sacrifice *shall* be made!

This struggle is comically portrayed, of course, but the moral decision arrived at is a serious one. After Susan gives Bob a place as a servant and forces him to run around waiting on table, she burns the will in a fit of conscience and good-heartedness; the now thoughtful Bob offers to marry her, partly out of gratitude and partly out of respect for her virtue.

Sentimentalism in farce was admirably suited to the character of the stage Irishman, who had been a comic and sentimental type for generations and flourished vigorously throughout the century in melodrama, drama, and comedy as well as farce. The nineteenth-century stage Irishman was a clever, improvident, hard-drinking, credible rogue with a heart of gold, despite his

---

[1] We are not, however, to take this too seriously, since she is quite happy to return to London as the wife of the dashing town gallant, Roverly. The countryside in this play is represented with more farcical truth by the booby ploughboy, Nicholas. Nevertheless, the speech, the song, and the sentiment are there all the same.

innate capacity for deception and anti-social behaviour. Primarily he was a stereotyped character mechanism for extracting laughter out of low-comedy situations. A comedian like Tyrone Power stood at the head of his profession for his ability to do just this.[1] Power played the journeyman tailor Tom Moore in Buckstone's *The Irish Lion* (1838), who is mistaken for the poet of the same name, invited to an elegant party of fawning admirers, and disports himself with singing, dancing, and whisky punch. It was Power also who made his first entrance as the valet Larry Hoolagan in T. G. Rodwell's *More Blunders than One* (1824) singing 'Oh Erin, sweet Erin, the land that we live in'. Hoolagan spends the whole play blundering out of one scrape into another, but like all Irishmen in farce is tolerated and forgiven. Both Moore and Hoolagan are used only for good-natured low comedy, but in a secondary role the Irishman could also fulfil a moral and sentimental purpose—like the low-comedy countryman in the comedies of Colman, Reynolds, and Morton. Two other characters originally performed by Power can serve as examples. In George Rodwell's *Teddy the Tiler* (1830), the workman Teddy is mistaken for the heir to Lord Dunderford and behaves ludicrously in socially elegant surroundings and dress. A fire breaks out across the street, trapping the real heir in a garret; Teddy rushes up a ladder and plunges into the flames to rescue him. The others try to stop this precipitate action, but he declares, 'If I'm not to go to a fire because I'm a nobleman, the sooner I throw up my peerage and become a commoner again the better.' 'What mean you?' asks Lord Dunderford, and Teddy replies, 'Why, I mane that if I can save a fellow creature's life, I'll do it. There's rale nobility for you!'—and dashes off. O'Callaghan, the down-at-heels scrapegrace of W. B. Bernard's *His Last Legs* (1839), impersonates a doctor in order to win a meal and a fee. At the end of a series of complications and misunderstandings he is responsible for reconciling the real doctor with his wife and making possible the engagement of O'Callaghan's erstwhile patient with his loved one. The delighted O'Callaghan tells his

---

[1] 'Power was the best Irishman I ever witnessed on the stage. He was entirely divested of those vulgarities, too often adopted by the representatives of Hibernian character, and possessed the refined and happy art of making them equally droll and amusing without resorting to such coarse material.' (Edward Fitzball, *Thirty-five Years of a Dramatic Author's Life* (1859), ii. 21–2.)

new friend that the latter sees before him 'the human mind, sir, in its finest aspect, sympathizing with the happiness of others'. Thus, in the single character type of the Irishman, that curious mixture of low comedy and sentimental morality so typical of nineteenth-century farce is strikingly apparent.

Sentimentality and moralizing would not appear to be the province of farce, but they are prominent in a great many nineteenth-century farces. Neither would one think that the often militant advocacy of domestic ideals—or indeed the upholding of any ideals—properly belonged to farce. Such is the case in the nineteenth century, however, and subject-matter of this kind is again held in common with comedy and drama. The sole purpose of Mildman, an allegorical figure in Charles Dance's *Kill or Cure* (1832), is to reconcile the perpetually quarrelling Browns. He finally does so, though not until Brown has been carried off to be stomach-pumped for drinking milk that he thought was poison; the farce passes immediately from this strongly physical incident to a final scene in which the benevolent Mildman, a true fairy godfather, orchestrates an ecstasy of domestic reconciliation. The Browns soon intrude their bickering upon *Kill and Cure*, but many farces begin with a picture of apparently ideal domestic bliss, proceed to shatter it, and conclude by reaffirming it. One such farce is Charles Mathews's *My Wife's Mother* (1833). The opening lines are spoken by the husband, Bud, and reflect an exclusively male conception of domestic felicity: 'My dear Ned, I'm the happiest of men. You must see I am yourself; how comfortable everything is about me! Arm chair, dressing gown, and slippers—well ordered breakfast table, good fire, clean room—everything cheerful and smiling. There's nothing like a wife for managing these matters, and I flatter myself there are not many like my Ellen. Ah, you bachelors are wretched dogs.' However, his contentment is soon destroyed. Bud's mother-in-law, the fearsome Mrs. Quickfidget, arrives to stay and completely disrupts the household: she persuades Mrs. Bud that her husband is unfaithful, disturbs the regular habits of old Uncle Foozle, and antagonizes the servants into giving notice. Finally she is asked to leave and peace is restored. Bud's bachelor friend Waverly, wondering whether or not to marry, acts as chorus and comments enthusiastically or dispiritedly on the married state. Similarly, the happiness of the Southdowns in Tom Taylor's *To Oblige Benson* (1854)—a play from the French labelled a 'comedietta' and possessing the characteristics both of farce and of *petite comédie*—is marred by their attempt 'to oblige Benson' and awaken Mrs. Benson to her folly in corresponding secretly with Meredith. Moral pronouncements and a general elegance of tone and setting are mingled with comic business in Southdown's pretended rage at his wife—acted at her prompting for Mrs. Benson's benefit—that turns into a real furniture-smashing tantrum when he comes to believe that Meredith's letter was meant for Mrs. Southdown. The play ends in perfect domestic harmony for both couples, and all characters indulge in dreadful warnings of the possible consequences of a wife's indiscretions; little slips are not to be condoned.

The expression of the domestic ideal in farcical terms meant that the wife, of necessity subordinate to her husband since such subordination was essential to the ideal, can be either a sweet insubstantial being like Mrs. Bud, who doubts her husband only because of misunderstanding and the suspicions of her nasty mother, or a seemingly strong-willed woman with her own weaknesses and indiscretions who sees the light before the final curtain and crumbles into submission.[1] Husbands and wives frequently quarrel in farce, but such quarrelling is easily patched up and never destructive. The wives only temporarily resent the sort of treatment typified by Mr. Mammoth's declaration in Douglas Jerrold's *Law and Lions* (1829) that 'we of the better sort of creation only associate wives with household affairs, connubial love and a shoulder of mutton'. More often than not in domestic squabbles it is the wife who confesses to error, like Mrs. Hussey in Thomas Bayly's *The Culprit* (1838), who after discovering that her husband's secret infatuation is with a Turkish pipe (she abhors smoking) rather than another woman admits that 'when I married, I expected

---

[1] In many farces a wife was not needed at all. Of the nine farces in this volume, only *The Magistrate* contains a wife in a leading role, and *Tom Cobb* is the only other to number a wife in the *dramatis personae*. Such an absence of wifely representation is coincidental and not truly characteristic of the general domestic scene in farce, especially Victorian farce, which like Victorian melodrama, 'drama', and comedy is much more domestic than the drama of the first part of the nineteenth century.

too much. I required my husband to give up an innocent indulgence which long habit had rendered essential to his comfort.' The exonerated Hussey triumphantly installs the hookah in his own home. On a more serious note, the wife in J. P. Wooler's *A Model Husband* (1853) confesses her weakness in being tempted by the attentions of a flashy young man: 'No more jaunts without my husband—no more amusement but *with* my husband—no more care but *for* my husband.' 'You are master and shall be,' she tells him, 'and I will try to be a good and dutiful wife.' Even in farce, therefore, the stage doctrine of the husband's marital superiority—no matter how much of a fool he might look in the midst of comic domestic confusion—goes basically unchallenged.

Attitudes toward marriage and the domestic ideal expressed in farce are held with undoubted conviction. The nearest a nineteenth-century farceur comes to placing these subjects schematically on a plane of thematic significance is Buckstone. *Second Thoughts* (1832), *Married Life* (1834), and *Single Life* (1839) are described as comedies on their title-pages, but they are strongly farcical. In *Second Thoughts* the impulsive Sudden quickly resolves to marry Mrs. Trapper, has his usual second thoughts when he thinks that she has poisoned her first husband, withdraws, is sued for breach of promise, decides to flee England, and is caught by Mrs. Trapper and her bailiffs. His problems are solved by the timely arrival of the very much alive Mr. Trapper from America. This plot is entirely farcical; Sudden is a 'humours' character with an obsession about 'second thoughts', and his eccentric and gossipy friend Jabber makes a living imitating musical instruments at society parties. However —and unusually for a two-act farce—there are two sub-plots, and here serious matters are introduced. Mrs. Trapper tries to find husbands for her three daughters, who have pleasant but useless hobbies hardly calculated to improve their marital chances: reading novels, collecting autographs, making knick-knacks. In the other sub-plot Sudden attempts to prevent his ward from marrying an attractive young man, Cecil. Underneath the farcical events and eccentric characterization in which the theme of marriage is initially developed is a current of seriousness and pathos, at first evident only in the second sub-plot, in which Cecil and Sudden's ward are quite devoid of humour, but dominant in the second act with the discovery that Cecil is Sudden's long-lost nephew and the suffering of Mrs. Trapper's now married daughters. Because of her insistence on husbands for the sake of being married, the daughters make unfortunate matches: one marries a footman, one a rich business-man who is exposed as a fraud and sent to Newgate, and one a poor miniature-painter struggling with poverty. In so far as *Second Thoughts* was written to express a serious theme, Buck-stone appears to be saying that the borderline between comedy and disaster in marriage is a narrow one, and that what seems to be merely amusing in marital complications may mask wrong attitudes toward marriage that if persisted in lead to serious harm and personal sorrow.

Married Life and *Single Life* are early examples of the three-act farce popular in the last quarter of the century. The former contains four comic couples who fall out for various reasons: Coddle complains of the cold and draughts; Mrs. Coddle is always too hot; the Younghusbands perpetually contradict each other; Dismal is rude and surly to his wife; Dove, a former footman, irritates his middle-class wife by forgetting his elevated station and running to answer the door whenever he hears the bell; Mrs. Dove annoys Dove by continually correct-ing his footman's vocabulary and pronunciation. The farcical climax of the play comes when five spouses rush out of the room, one after another, after each has had a vigorous altercation with his or her partner. The fifth couple, the Lynxes, are intense and melodramatic characters, and their part in the plot and the sequence of misunderstanding and marital discord is entirely serious.[1] Mrs. Lynx is obsessed with suspected infidelity on her husband's part, but not in a comic way, and utters powerful and disordered speeches on the subject. Lynx is protecting the identity and honour of a mysterious young girl who turns out to be his dead sister's daughter. The emotional scenes between them come from melodrama, not farce, as does Lynx's rescue of his wife from the assault of an off-stage villain. The potentially

---

[1] A practical explanation of their presence in a farce might be that Mrs. Lynx was played by Helen Faucit, whose forte was not comedy, and who, being in the Haymarket company at the time, presumably had to be employed. A theatrical reason might be the answer, or part of it, in this particular case, but nevertheless the inclusion of purely serious characters in comedy and farce was a characteristic of the age.

tragic treatment of marriage in the Lynx relationship parallels the purely comic but nevertheless full development of the same theme in relation to the other couples. Mrs. Lynx is reconciled to her husband; both confess faults and agree to let 'mutual confidence henceforth secure to us that happiness to which we have so long been strangers'. Miserable, repentant wives are reunited with miserable, repentant husbands, and Coddle delivers a final harangue to the audience on the principal subject of the play, a speech so solemn in content and so glowing with domestic idealism that it is worth quoting in its entirety. It is prefaced by a piece of comic though none the less idealistic stage business. Coddle addresses the assembled married couples:

CODDLE. Whenever a disagreement breaks out among you in future, recall the memory of those inducements which first led you to think of each other, and you will find it to be a wonderful help to the restoration of peace. Do you all agree to this?

ALL. Yes, yes!

CODDLE. Then follow my example, and ratify the agreement by a hearty conjugal embrace; I will give the word of command. Make ready! [*As* CODDLE *puts his arm round his wife's waist, each of the husbands do the same to their wives.*] Present! [CODDLE *takes his wife's chin between his fingers and thumb, and prepares to kiss her; all the husbands do the same.*] Fire! [*They all kiss and embrace at the same moment.*] There, this is the way that all matrimonial quarrels should end—and if *you* are of the same opinion [*To the audience.*] then, indeed, will our conjugal joy be complete, and our light lesson not have been read in vain. You have seen the result of perpetual jealousy in the case of Mr. and Mrs. Lynx; of continual disputes and contradiction in that of Mr. and Mrs. Younghusband; of a want of cheerfulness in Mr. and Mrs. Dismal; of the impolicy of public correction in the instance of Mrs. Dove; and of the necessity of assimilating habits and tempers in the singular case of Mr. and Mrs. Coddle; and though these may not be one half the causes of quarrel between man and wife—yet even their exposure may serve as beacon lights to avoid the rocks of altercation when sailing on the sea of matrimony. So think of us, all ye anticipating and smiling single people; for you *must*, or *ought* all to be married, and the sooner the better—and remember us ye already paired; and let our example prove to you that to mutual forbearance, mutual confidence, mutual habits, mutual everything, must we owe mutual happiness. And where can the *best* of happiness be found, but in a loyal and affectionate married life?

It would seem that Buckstone deliberately exceeded both the usual length and the ordinary moral proprieties of the comic tag —the one that ends *Married Life* must be the longest in any nineteenth-century play—in order to emphasize his theme.

In *Single Life*, which Buckstone intended as a companion piece to *Married Life*, five bachelors, all with different attitudes to marriage, are eventually united to five spinsters. Niggle desperately wants a wife, but has always been prevented from marrying, sometimes forcibly, by his misogynist friend Damper, who despite himself is attracted to a professed man-hater, Miss Macaw. Pinkey loves Miss Skylark, but is too bashful to propose and instead copies love letters for her from *The Complete Letter Writer*. The elegant Narcissus Boss, who spends much time admiring himself in a mirror, becomes engaged to the equally self-admiring Miss Snare. The serious interest, slighter than in *Married Life*, is provided by Chester and Miss Meadows, each afraid of being married for money, each pretending to poverty and concealing wealth. The play opens with an excellent and truly farcical scene in which Niggle, in a feverish hurry to slip away to church for a secret marriage with Miss Coy, is prevented from doing so by a steady stream of callers. Scenes in which marriage is a subject for irony are followed by scenes in which it is considered beautiful and romantic; on the whole, as in *Married Life*, marriage is more praised than derided, even though, as in the earlier play, all five couples quarrel and are reconciled. Together with *Second Thoughts*, *Married Life* and *Single Life* constitute the fullest and most 'serious' examination of marriage and the domestic ideal undertaken by any single author of nineteenth-century farce. And clearly, farce and seriousness are not entirely incompatible.

The basically sentimental outlook of nineteenth-century farce, despite its necessary plot machinery of intrigue, deception, misunderstanding, and coincidence, is closely allied to the overwhelming domesticity of this and other kinds of nineteenth-century drama. The best farce is the disciplined expression of moral and domestic anarchy, the plausible and logical presentation of a completely crazy world that all the characters take with the greatest seriousness, a world in which extraordinarily

absurd and fantastic pressures on the ordinary individual drive
him to the very extremity of his resources and his senses, a world
in which he can survive only by pitting the ingenuity of his own
insanity against the massive blows of hostile coincidence and a
seemingly remorseless fate. Such a world is the world of the
best French farce, the world of Labiche and Feydeau, whose
undoubted domesticity is uncompromisingly ruthless, savage,
and anti-familial, whose very chaos and controlled violence is a
kind of inverse moral order of great rigidity. Labiche and
Feydeau are not sentimental, nor do they write on that level of
domesticity concerning the trivia of home, hearth, and daily
living that cram the English farce to bursting. One might say
the domesticity of French farce is hard and sharp-edged, the
domesticity of English farce soft and well-disposed. The
difference occurs because the farce of Labiche and Feydeau is
anti-idealistic and satirical in aim, whereas the purpose of its
far less aggressive Victorian counterpart is to amuse in a jolly
and properly moral way, to cast a friendly, avuncular eye on the
minor vicissitudes of home and family.[1] The ideals of love,
marriage, and household that enervate so much serious nineteenth-century drama also debilitate nineteenth-century farce,
yet simultaneously give it a sort of homey charm that the French
farce eschews.

Charm, sentiment, and a sense of fun, all expressed in the
proper moral spirit, are distinctively characteristic of nineteenth-
century English farce, but of course that is not all this farce had
to offer. One must also take note of those characteristics that
separate it from comedy and other forms of theatre, those
seemingly more appropriate to its peculiar province than the
ones already discussed.

Several major techniques of farce—the repetition and accumu-
lation of misunderstanding and coincidence, the reversal of
normal expectation, the surprise entrance, the bringing together of characters who at all costs should remain apart, the
extreme eccentricity of a minority of characters, the truncation
of time so that comic events follow one another with ludicrous
rapidity—are too familiar to require elaboration and are part of

---

[1] The Examiner of Plays and public opinion prevented Victorian farceurs from
writing—even if they had wished to, which is most doubtful—as witheringly
about love and marriage and as openly about adultery as the French playwrights did.

the conventional machinery of all farce; they are much in evidence in this volume. One could also mention another aspect of technique illuminating not only the way in which nineteenth-century farce works but also the nature of the world it creates. All farce is fantasy; all farce must involve its audience in this fantasy as well as indicate clearly that it *is* fantasy. Nineteenth-century farce does this through technique as well as subject-matter.

One of the ways in which the farce author involved his audience was by addressing it directly, confiding in it, appealing for approval, and frankly stressing the non-realistic nature of his genre by directing attention to the strings on which his puppets dance. Soliloquies and informational asides are standard procedure in nineteenth-century drama, but farce goes much further than this. A common device is a speech near the beginning, sometimes opening the play, sometimes of great length, relating to the audience the events that have happened already, the precise situation in which the character speaking finds himself, and how he got there. The longest speeches of this type were assigned to comedians of great skill who could hold their audiences with such narrations. For example, J. M. Morton's *Grimshaw, Bagshaw, and Bradshaw* (1851) begins with a two-page rambling account from Grimshaw—originally played by Buckstone—stating how sleepy he is, how early he has to get up, what his employer is like, that he must put on dressing-gown and slippers, how he went to Cremorne (a Victorian pleasure-garden in Chelsea) three weeks ago to watch a man go up in a balloon with a donkey, how it rained, how he met the delightful Fanny and took her home, that he had better go to bed. Similarly, Charles Mathews in *Little Toddlekins* (1852) wrote a three-page speech for himself as Brownsmith, explaining his whole history and particularly how he came to be the father of a daughter eighteen years older than himself. Brownsmith appeals directly to the audience for assistance ('Is there anybody who'll take her off my hands?') and sympathy ('There, now you've seen her! Well, what do you say?') Muddlebank in W. E. Suter's *Our New Man* (1866) swears the audience to secrecy before providing it with an involved explanation of how he came to be at Cremorne without his wife and how he had tea with a charming young lady. Such speeches are simple and naïve in intention and effect; there is no attempt to develop exposition by the frequently clumsy device resorted to in other forms of contemporary drama whereby two characters ignore the audience and carry on an opening dialogue that conveys necessary information which both characters usually know anyway. The peculiar flavour of the longer expository speeches in farce—they can scarcely be called soliloquies, since their speakers are not engaged in self-communion—can be gathered from *Going to the Dogs* (1865), by William Brough and Andrew Halliday, in which Fidge explains to the audience how it is that he is afraid of being arrested as an accessory in the crime of dog-stealing:

The other day, just as I was leaving the quoit ground at the Welsh Harp, the landlord, Mr. Groggins, comes up to me and tells me a confounded story about a dog—hang Groggins and his stories! It seems my friend Captain Lightfoot bought a dog of a man in Regent-street. Well, one day, walking along with the animal, up comes one Boodle, a cowkeeper, and claims the dog as one that has been stolen from him. Lightfoot refuses to give up the dog, and Boodle gives him into custody for the theft. Magistrate discharges Lightfoot, of course, but orders dog to be given up to Boodle. Then, what does Lightfoot do but go and bribe the fellow of whom he first bought the dog, to steal dog back again from Boodle. . . .

and so on, for as many lines again.

Shorter speeches of this kind were more common than longer ones. To give only one example, in *More Blunders than One* the maid Susan opens the play by admiring herself in the glass, declares that 'I'm in momentary expectation of the arrival of Mr. Larry Hoolagan, valet de chambre to my mistress's intended', and praises him rapturously. Henry Melbourne begins the second scene with 'Now I am alone, let me again read my uncle's letter', which he does; the uncle shortly arrives with 'Well, here I am, once more in my native land, and under the very roof, too, with the only relation I have in the world.' Just before his entrance the bailiff Trap comes on and says, 'I've gammon'd 'em so far, however. How lucky I happened to hear of the expected arrival of old Melbourne from India. In this disguise of his uncle I shall bring him down.' In the third scene Hoolagan enters with 'So, here I am once more under the same roof with my little darling. I've sneaked in this after-noon to wish her good morning. My master sent me some-where else, but I preferred coming here because it was more agreeable.' The fourth scene opens with a speech from the now tipsy Hoolagan beginning 'My master discharged me, but I won't go.' To cut summary short, there are nine-teen speeches like this in the one-act farce, apart from the ordinary confidential asides when more than one person is on stage.

More Blunders than One ends with Larry Hoolagan asking the audience to bestow their favours 'on poor Larry's "More Blunders than One" ' so that the piece can continue its run. A final brief speech or tag, addressed directly to the audience, usually by the principal comic actor, with the rest of the cast on either side of him straight across the front of the stage, or dis-posed in a semicircle, was the ritualistic conclusion of virtually every farce acted until the 1870s. This tag commonly begged the audience's blessing and often included the title of the play. Such an ending was frankly artificial and made the same appeal to the house as the prologue and epilogue of an earlier age. Sometimes the tag was ingeniously varied in a way that made the audience even more aware of the workings of a comic mechanism. When the curtain rises upon J. M. Morton's *Slasher and Crasher* (1848), the characters are lined up across the stage and Blowhard is about to deliver the tag to a play presumably just finished, in which Slasher and Crasher have been successful suitors for Blowhard's sister and her niece. He is then handed a letter informing him that Slasher and Crasher are really cowards. He goes no further with the tag, orders them out of the house, and the farce proper begins. When Slasher and Crasher have been successful at last and the play ends, the characters resume their opening positions and the interrupted tag proceeds to its con-clusion. Slasher and Crasher were played by the Adelphi's low comedians, Wright and Bedford; the same actors took the parts of the Intruder and Snoozle in the same author's *A Most Un-warrantable Intrusion* (1849), whose full title is *A Most Un-warrantable Intrusion Committed by Mr. Wright to the Annoyance of Mr. Paul Bedford*. This kind of theatricality is emphasized at the end of the piece when Wright as the Intruder repeats a cue for Bedford as Snoozle, and Bedford as himself declares that

he has no more in his part; Wright as himself replies that
neither has he. The prompter is summoned and asked where the
tag is; he explains that the author did not write one because
'Wright always spoke his own'. Wright then does speak 'his
own' and the curtain comes down. The conclusion of Blanchard
Jerrold's *Cool as a Cucumber* (1851) is equally inventive. Old
Barkins refuses to support the young lovers if they marry without his consent. The comic lead, Plumper, angrily orders the
curtain down behind him, cutting off the other characters from
the auditorium; he then abuses Barkins to the audience. From
behind the curtain Barkins cries out that he relents; Plumper
orders the curtain raised, pronounces the piece properly finished,
and calls for red fire and a tableau as the young couple kneel
before Barkins in a parody of a conventional melodramatic
finale. J. S. Coyne's *Binks the Bagman* (1843) concludes with
Binks, a commercial traveller, distributing among the audience
cards announcing that his business will continue at the Adelphi
every night at nine o'clock. As the weary Dabchick of William
Brough's *How to Make Home Happy* (1853)—a title typical of
contemporary domestic farce—persecuted by his wife's ground-
less jealousy but now reconciled with her, steps forward to
speak the tag, Mrs. Dabchick asks, 'Who is that lady in the dress
circle you are looking at?' and becomes jealous again, especially
when Dabchick says that he hopes to see the audience again
tomorrow night at the same time. 'An appointment! Before my
very face!' she cries. In such ways the farceur involved his
audience by placing it in communion with his characters and
establishing a direct and sympathetic bond between stage and
auditorium. Simultaneously he distanced this audience by making
it aware of the wheels and cogs of his own ingeniously con-
structed comic machinery. In a rather Pirandellian way, too,
actors sometimes played actors playing characters. Nineteenth-
century farce is not as utterly simple and artless as it might
appear.

The attention to physical business is another technique of
farce taken for granted: one vaguely assumes that all farce
actors run in and out, knock each other over, hide in closets, and
make a great deal of noise. As far as the nineteenth century is
concerned, this assumption contains some truth. Farce of this
type exists. However, although uproarious moments and

situations where comic effects depend upon physical business occur frequently, they dominate few farces, and many are without them entirely. Of the plays in this volume, *Mr. Paul Pry* is the only one with a fair amount of what might be loosely termed knockabout comedy, in which a number of unfortunate physical things happen to the inquisitive Pry. In *Raising the Wind* a glass of water is thrown in somebody's face; in *Patter versus Clatter* Parker suffers agonies at the hands of the pretended barber Patter; in *Box and Cox* food is thrown out of the window, bell-ropes pulled, and boxing positions assumed. One could go on and describe the physical situations in each selection, but the story would be much the same: although each situation is comically important and vigorous physical climaxes are not uncommon (as in *Mr. Paul Pry, How to Settle Accounts with your Laundress*, and Act II of *The Magistrate*), clearly this is only one aspect of farce technique, and one that is not in constant use. Physical comedy is more prevalent in the farce of the last quarter of the century, but it is not absolutely essential to the genre.

Comic business arising out of the preparation, serving, and consumption of food is very noticeable in nineteenth-century farce, especially in the twenty years around the middle of the century. The connection between low comedy and food and drink is an old one on the stage, and is particularly strong in nineteenth-century pantomime as well as farce. (One also remembers the comic uses of food in the silent film.) There are many comic inebriates in eighteenth-century farce—the stage Irishman of the eighteenth and nineteenth centuries could hardly have existed without his bottle—but it rarely resorted to the extended comedy of cooking, serving, and eating as represented in *Box and Cox, How to Settle Accounts with your Laundress, The Area Belle, The Magistrate*, or in a great number of their contemporaries. The funniest scene of *Deaf as a Post*, an early example of 1823, is that in which Templeton, pretending to deafness, intrudes upon his stingy rival's private dinner party, takes his rival's place at table, eats his way unheedingly through his rival's capon, drinks his port and madeira, and blissfully departs. The best scene of *An Alarming Sacrifice* also occurs at table. Bob Ticket, in his new capacity of unwilling servant to his uncle's housekeeper, suffers the indignity of being forced to wait on what was a few minutes ago his own table:[1]

> [DEBORAH *appears with a tray on which are three dishes, one of hashed mutton, one of hot potatoes, and the third roast duck.* PUGWASH *takes cover off the dish before him.*

PUGWASH. Here, young man, take this cover.   [BOB *takes it.*

MISS WADD. Bob, some bread!

SKINNER. Bob, some ale!

PUGWASH. Bob, some pepper!

SUSAN. Bob, some butter!

MISS GIMP. Bob, some vinegar!

MISS WADD. Bob, some mustard!

SUSAN. Hot plates, Bob!

> [BOB *brings the articles, as they are called for, from a table at the back.* DEBORAH *enters with hot plates;* BOB *takes them, burns his fingers, and drops them.*

Similarly, in Mark Lemon's *The Railway Belle* (1854), Greenhorne, so infatuated by the barmaid in a station refreshment room that he sits there every day ordering endless bowls of vile and undrinkable soup, seizes the chance to take the waiter's place when the need arises but is horrified to find himself waiting, quite incompetently, upon his fiancée and her hot-tempered father. The low-life Irish tinker of Samuel Lover's *Barney the Baron* (1857) is supposed to be amusing because in a German castle that he has won in a lottery he demands 'plenty of tripe and onions, and liver and bacon, and cabbage, and a big bowl of praties'. Peeled potatoes infuriate him, however; he throws them at the servants and is disgusted by a dish of sauerkraut. He carves clumsily, looks forward to breakfast on 'a few butter rolls and some boiled praties with the skins on them', and as a matter of course retires to bed to get drunk on a bottle of wine.

As can be seen, then, the use of food in farce is not general or suggestive, but extremely explicit. Detail is piled upon detail,

---

[1] The reversal of roles and the degradation of the 'master' is a common feature of nineteenth-century farce, e.g. Widgetts serving at his own table in *How to Settle Accounts with your Laundress*, Mr. Posket's battered humiliation in Act III of *The Magistrate*, and the Dean of St. Marvell's imprisonment in the village jail in Pinero's *Dandy Dick*.

and a piece of business can be so fully elaborated that it completely dominates the scene or even the whole farce. An example occurs in Charles Selby's *Hotel Charges* (1853), in which the waiters of a hotel, worried by the campaign 'A. Biffin' has been running in *The Times* against extortionate hotel charges, give extra-special food and service, at an incredibly low price, to a Captain Fitzchizzle whom they mistake for Biffin. The headwaiter, Sminker, is simultaneously concerned for the hotel's reputation and enraged to see his fiancée, the chambermaid Mary, flirting with Fitzchizzle. In the business that follows, seven waiters and a page are concerned in serving Fitzchizzle's meal:[1]

> *A* WAITER *brings on a covered dish supposed to be the boiled fowl, and another the partridge; two others bring covered vegetable dishes which they place on the table; then* ROBERT *brings on haunch of mutton, which is passed from one* WAITER *to the other and placed on the table;* SMINKER *takes from sideboard a large carving knife and steel, and sharpens knife, looking ferociously at* FITZCHIZZLE, *who is coqueting with* MARY.
>
> SMINKER. [*Flourishing knife.*] Oh, shouldn't I like to have a cut at him! [*Advancing.*] Mutton, sar! [*He takes hold of the shank of the mutton, cuts with savage flourishes two very small slices and puts them with some gravy, which he takes from dish with a large spoon, on a plate which* JAMES *holds. At this moment* SMINKER *sees* FITZCHIZZLE *offering* MARY *a glass of wine, and in his rage strikes the plate so violently with the spoon that it breaks;* JAMES *gives another plate and takes up the slice of mutton and places it before* FITZCHIZZLE; *the* PAGE *brings currant jelly from sideboard, taking by the way a sly spoonful, and gives it to* MARY, *who helps* FITZCHIZZLE *and returns it to* PAGE, *who eats the whole of it.* SMINKER *stamps and waves his hand;* JAMES *takes away the mutton and passes it to the other* WAITERS, *who pass it off; the* PAGE *takes away the fowl and* JAMES *the partridges, and as they are running off with them, meet, and the* PAGE *falls—a scramble and a bustle.* SMINKER *beats the* PAGE, *who goes off bellowing, pushed about by the* WAITERS. FITZCHIZZLE *takes advantage of the bustle to put his arm round* MARY'S *waist;* SMINKER *turns and sees him, and takes* MARY *up in his arms and carries her off.* WAITERS *enter and clear table.*

[1] A note in the text relating to the initial serving of the bread, soup, wine, and cruet, before the main meal begins, says that 'the whole of this business must be managed with great precision and rapidity, the idea being to show the division of labour practised in hotels'. An interesting anticipation of the stage business, if not the point of view, of Arnold Wesker's *The Kitchen*.

Comic business in farce, although a significant aspect of technique, cannot be easily separated from subject-matter and setting, even for the purpose of discussion. By the 1840s it arose directly out of the domesticity and materiality of early Victorian farce. A strong argument could be advanced for the contention that, aside from the farces of Pinero in the 1880s, the golden age of nineteenth-century farce was the forties, fifties, and sixties; that is, when the tide of domesticity engulfed farce as well as other forms of drama, and finally swept aside the farce traditions inherited from the eighteenth century. When one examines plays like *Box and Cox*, *How to Settle Accounts with your Laundress*, and *The Area Belle*—all performed between 1847 and 1864—one can see that what happened to farce in these years and did not happen to comedy was a substantial infusion of lower middle- and working-class material,[1] and therefore the appearance of comic techniques inseparable from this material. One has only to compare the settings, characters, and comic styles of these three farces with the same elements in *Raising the Wind*, *Patter versus Clatter*, and *Diamond Cut Diamond* to notice the change. The earlier farces have middle- and upper middle-class settings (except for the inn scene in *Raising the Wind*), protagonists of social and financial standing, and comic situations developed through intrigue, deception, and misunderstanding. Of course all farce is dependent to some extent upon intrigue, deception, and misunderstanding, but the world of the later farces mentioned above is markedly different from that of the earlier. Their protagonists—journeyman printer, journeyman hatter, lodging-house keeper, tailor, laundress, hairdresser, ballet dancer, policeman, soldier, milkman, housemaid—work for a living in relatively humble positions; the settings in which they move, like their occupations, are in that border area between working- and lower middle-class life: *'decently furnished'* lodgings, a tailor's showroom, a kitchen. Comic business is inextricably involved with *things*: a gridiron, a chop, a rasher of bacon, a penny roll, a water-butt, a tailor's dummy, a kidney, a laundry copper, a joint of mutton, a table-cloth. This materiality is overwhelmingly domestic, and omnipresent in mid-century

[1] The 'below stairs' farces of the eighteenth century come to mind here, but these are a very small minority, and the world of servants is always juxtaposed with a higher world of masters and mistresses.

farce. When the commercial traveller of *Binks the Bagman* opens his heart to Mrs. Crimmins, his expression of romantic sentiment in the metaphor of mercantile and domestic materialism is utterly characteristic of the period: 'Has not your lovely image been printed in fast colours on the heart that beats beneath this Marcella waistcoat, never to be washed out, Mrs. C. ? . . . Embrace the present favourable opportunity—take advantage of the opening that now offers, and invest your valuable stock of charms in the arms of your faithful Binks.' Such a content and such a style tells us much about the taste of mid-century farce audiences,[1] and the result of all this is a farce whose healthy vulgarity, comic invention, naïve domesticity, and endearingly eccentric humanity make it one of the finest products of the nineteenth-century stage.

An important characteristic of farce is, for want of a better name, philosophical rather than technical, although developed through appropriate technical devices. This is the harassment of the ordinary individual beyond the bounds of reason, his entrapment in an incomprehensible and absurd situation, his unwilling involvement in an apparently mad world; in short, the farce of the preposterous and desperate predicament. To some degree, these things occur in all farce, especially in that of Labiche and Feydeau. In English farce of the nineteenth century they find characteristically homely expression, and their effect is softened by sentiment and friendly domesticity.

A failure to communicate is one of the first steps on the road to bewilderment and isolation. Templeton in *Deaf as a Post* reduces the stupid Sappy to sputtering rage by pretending deafness, eating Sappy's diner, and occupying Sappy's bed. There is no point of contact between the two; what Sappy takes as outrageously intrusive and anti-social behaviour the 'deaf' Templeton engages in as a matter of pleasant social intercourse

---

[1] Buckstone pointed out to the parliamentary Select Committee of 1866 that 'I can only keep on the Haymarket as a legitimate comedy theatre; and that class of entertainment is not so suited to the galleries.' (*Report of the Select Committee on Theatrical Licenses and Regulations* (1866), p. 126.) Comedy as such was not popular in the neighbourhood working- and lower middle-class theatres of the East End and South Bank, the taste of whose public ran mainly to farce, melodrama, and pantomime. The fact that the afterpiece farce of a West End theatre was usually calculated to begin at half-price time (9 p.m.) and thus attract an audience with a different character from the full-price patrons who had already seen a comedy or a drama, is also significant in any attempt to assess audience taste.

between amicable gentlemen of a like mind. In Buckstone's *Shocking Events* (1838), Puggs, mistaken (unbeknown to him) for a dumb man from whom the horse doctor Griffinhoof expects to make his fortune by discovering a remedy for dumbness, assumes the affliction for the sake of protection from an angry pursuer. Griffinhoof tries every means within his power to 'cure' Puggs, and since these means comprise a series of shocks calculated to make even the dumb cry out, Puggs finds himself inexplicably assaulted by a seeming maniac. The situation worsens when Griffinhoof decides that Puggs is a woman in disguise, addresses him without warning as 'dear Mrs. Perkins', and tells him to 'put on apparel more suitable to your sex'. 'It is a private mad-house,' declares Puggs, 'and that old fellow is one of the lunatics.' Griffinhoof continues planning to subject Puggs to a variety of shocks; at one point he *'comes from his room on tiptoe, produces a pistol which he discharges near* PUGGS' *ear.* KITTY *screams without, and a crash of china is heard. . . .* PUGGS, *stunned with the report, falls into a chair.'* Despite its apparent insanity, *Shocking Events* is anchored to normality and good humour by the solidity and plebeian matter-of-factness of Puggs; indeed, the more normal and down-to-earth is Puggs, the more insane the world in which he finds himself—which is how this kind of farce works. Alfred Highflyer's erroneous belief in Thomas Morton's *A Roland for an Oliver* (1819) that Sir Mark Chase's pleasant country estate is actually a lunatic asylum and Sir Mark a lunatic leads to similar complications, if not to the same sort of domestic rough and tumble. Jacob Earwig, the deaf boots of Selby's *The Boots at the Swan* (1842) is the cause of much misunderstanding and confusion in the first act, when the angry Higgins is simply unable to communicate with him. It is not surprising that the deaf or dumb character recurs; his affliction, pretended or real, represents the ultimate breakdown in communication and the damaging lack of comprehension at the centre of so many farce plots.

Truly farcical also is the situation which the central character may or may not understand, but which makes increasingly impossible demands upon him; a vain attempt to satisfy them may exhaust his physical and mental powers. Sometimes the situation is so extreme that he can be reduced to mindless and quivering helplessness, scurrying willy-nilly like a rat in a trap.

On the level of minor domestic harassment this is what happens to Perkins Pocock in J. M. Morton's *An Englishman's House is his Castle* (1857), who resolves to be master of his own house in Bloomsbury Square but is besieged by a variety of extraordinary lodgers: the jealous inventor Dr. Bang, whose experiments involve innumerable explosions and who, even while talking to Pocock, walks about '*producing a number of explosions*', the fearful Mrs. Bang, the blustering Captain Connaught, the ever-complaining maid-of-all-work, and Pocock's eccentric nephew. Other lodgers make their presence felt by noises off: thumps, a piercing bosun's whistle, 'God Save the Queen' practised on a flageolet. Everything in the house goes wrong, including the kitchen range. In Thomas Williams's *Ici on Parle Français* (1859), Mr. and Mrs. Spriggins are forced by the sudden departure of their overworked maid to wait upon their lodgers, who request boots polished, stays laced, steak cooked, and coffee made. More serious is the problem of Brownsmith in Mathews's *Little Toddlekins* (1852). On the point of escaping from Amanthis, a large and ugly stepdaughter eighteen years older than himself, to a quiet marriage in Devon, he is horrified by the arrival in his own house of the Babicombes, his fiancée and her father, who wish to stay with him and transfer the marriage ceremony to London. In a fever of anxiety Brownsmith tries to conceal Amanthis's existence from them (they hear of his former marriage and, believing Amanthis an infant—Toddlekins—bring her toys and a baby's bonnet) and then, when the secret is out, desperately attempts to marry her off, since his fiancée angrily refuses to be called 'mother' every day by a woman twice her age. Brownsmith's seemingly intractable difficulty is resolved by Babicombe himself agreeing to marry Amanthis, and the play ends in complete bewilderment as the characters ponder the precise nature of their relationships once the two couples are married. The main character's ordinariness, emphasized by his name—John Robinson Brownsmith—and complete conventionality are set against a grotesquely ludicrous but thoroughly domestic situation of extreme pressure; the tensions engendered by the comic interplay between the two constitute farce.

One of the best farces treating the situation of the placid individual invaded and imposed upon by an incomprehensible outside force that pushes him to the limits of his sanity is Morton's *A Most Unwarrantable Intrusion* (1849), adapted like so many others of its time from the French, but domesticated, also like so many others, in a peculiarly English and Victorian way. Snoozle, relaxing quietly at home with his wife, daughter, niece, and servants out for the day, sees someone about to throw himself into the fishpond. He rushes out, drags him back inside—and finds him a perfect nuisance. The intruder sits in Snoozle's favourite easy chair, fiddles with the breakfast things, stirs the fishbowl with a toasting fork, sneezes into Snoozle's handkerchief, criticizes his clothes, puts on his dressing-gown, rearranges his furniture, decides to stay with his benefactor forever, abuses the portrait of his wife, touches up a picture of Snoozle standing on an easel, knocks over the book-case, accompanies himself on the piano, singing loudly and out of tune, snatches the cap off Snoozle's head and places it on his own, rummages through his drawers, hears his womenfolk come home and resolves to make love to them all. All this drives the frantic Snoozle—who has been rushing about trying to stop him, urging him to leave, and persuading him to drown himself—to distraction. Finally it transpires that this is a stratagem on the part of a rejected suitor for the niece's hand to force Snoozle's consent to the match. The despairing and baffled fury of the dazed, peace-loving Snoozle, fruitlessly expended against a situation quite out of his control, places him in the category of the quintessential farce victim, a placatory sacrifice to the household gods of a malicious universe.

Continual stress can make a farce hero doubt his own reality. Gilbert's Tom Cobb does this; a much earlier character, Colonel Touchwood in Dibdin's *What Next?* (1816) is impersonated by a nephew whom he closely resembles. The Colonel's lawyer claims that he was summoned, post-horses are brought that he has not ordered, a dentist arrives unbidden to draw his teeth, and he is arrested for fighting a duel he knows nothing about. Touchwood, totally bewildered by the chaos around him, believes that his house and family are bewitched. Grimshaw of J. M. Morton's *Grimshaw, Bagshaw, and Bradshaw* (1851), is mistaken for Bradshaw as well as Bagshaw and subjected to an inexplicable sequence of events in which he is turned out of his lodgings and various unknown people, popping in and out of doors and a secret panel, keep appearing and disappearing. When finally asked, 'Who the devil are you, sir?' he replies, 'Whoever you like, my little dear. The fact is that I'm in such a state of confusion that I neither know nor care who I am; but to the best of my belief I'm not Bradshaw—and I think I can take upon myself that I'm not Bagshaw, tho' I *have* paid his tailor's bill.' Like Tom Cobb and Colonel Touchwood, Grimshaw is reacting to a situation that questions his very identity, a situation that is the philosophical heart of farce.

The acting of nineteenth-century farce appears to have embodied its two main principles: the active and the passive, restlessness and stolidity, the frantic energy that was one way of coping with farce problems and the grave, incredulous stillness at the centre of a fevered world that was the other possible reaction. Examples of the first principle can be found in the acting of Lewis, Munden, and Buckstone. According to Leigh Hunt, Munden over-reacted to comic situations:

Almost the whole force of his acting consists in two or three ludicrous gestures and an innumerable variety of as fanciful contortions of countenance as ever threw woman into hysterics: his features are like the reflection of a man's face in a ruffled stream, they undergo a perpetual undulation of grin, every emotion is attended by a grimace, which he by no means wishes to be considered as unstudied, for if it has not immediately its effect upon the spectators, he improves or continues it till it has.[1]

In a later generation Buckstone's acting seems in some respects to have been remarkably similar to Munden's. In the farces already discussed, it was Buckstone who created the roles of Box, Grimshaw, Bob Ticket of *An Alarming Sacrifice*, Coddle of *Married Life*, and Cousin Joe of *A Rough Diamond*. Certainly his acting personified the active principle of farce:

Buckstone, in all his characters, was metaphorically the trombone-player, calling attention to his humour by salient and very effective appeals to the audience, demonstrative, various, gesticulatory . . . His genial people were ultra-genial, his cowards thorough poltroons, his mischief-makers revelled in their sport; but it is quite true to say that characterization with him was quite subordinate to mirth . . . Never was there a face more fitted to excite mirth . . . the chief drawback from this favourite actor's striking merit was his love of exaggeration.

[1] *Critical Essays on the Performers of the London Theatres* (1807), p. 82.

He was accused by some critics of violating taste in certain characters by the breadth of his illustrations. This occasional fault was the result of the same animal spirits and enjoyment of frolic to which he was indebted for much of his success.[1]

On the other hand, the acting of Liston and Keeley was in some roles interpretative of the passive principle, of bewilderment and resignation on the part of the victim of farcical circumstance and the maleficence of fate. It was Liston who played Sappy in *Deaf as a Post* and Brown in *Kill or Cure*. According to Westland Marston, 'in almost every character he evinced quiet, intense self-satisfaction, and ludicrous gravity in absurd sayings and doings. His humour was often to seem insensible to the ludicrous, and a look of utter unconsciousness on his serene and elongated face would accompany the utterance of some absurdity or sly jest, and rouse shouts of laughter, while he stood monumentally calm.'[2] Keeley—the Puggs of *Shocking Events* and Jacob Earwig of *The Boots at the Swan*—'was usually phlegmatic, impassive, and pathetically acquiescent in the droll inflictions which fate had in store for him'.[3] The first kind of acting conveyed the vigour, bustle, pace, exaggeration, and not uncommon frenzy of farce; the second the puzzled incomprehension and fundamental helplessness of the farce hero who finds himself at the centre of an absurd world. The two kinds complemented each other; both were necessary to express the style and meaning of farce.

Many characteristics of the earlier farce can be found later in the century. There is less sentimentality and overt moralizing, less intrusion of serious matter and pathetic emotion, less direct addressing of the audience, less use of working- and lower middle-class material, and less insistence on the marital superiority of the husband; in fact he becomes even more of a comic butt than before. However, the basic machinery of misunderstanding, deception, intrigue, coincidence, and the inordinate rapidity of events is unchanged, and this machinery continues to operate in a cozy domestic setting, a setting that is socially elevated as the century progresses.

One aspect of farce intensified and elaborated in the later period is the use of physical comedy and comic business. The

---

[1] Westland Marston, *Our Recent Actors* (1888), ii. 88–91.
[2] Ibid., p. 292. [3] Ibid., p. 88.

physical excess of J. M. Morton's *Drawing Room, Second Floor, and Attics* (1864) can hardly be found in the first half of the century. A plot summary is necessary to indicate the extent of the business, which indeed constitutes the whole play. Triptolemus Brown, a chemist's assistant, flees in terror from the violent pursuit of the jealous Captain Hardaport (whom he has never met); he is aided by his true love, the servant Phoebe. The play begins in an attic: Bunny, a retired furrier, enters and Phoebe's uncle accidentally knocks his hat over his eyes with the broom; Bunny then falls downstairs. Brown is perceived climbing out of a chimney-pot on the roof—where he took shelter during his first flight from Hardaport—and, exhausted and black with soot, gets through the attic window, wipes his face with clean linen, which is blackened, then clambers on to the roof again and hides in the other chimney-pot to avoid discovery by Phoebe's uncle. In the second scene he struggles to free himself as he hangs kicking above the fireplace a floor lower down, in the apartment of Arabella, Hardaport's sister; in this struggle he knocks the fire-irons over and does not succeed in dropping into the grate until a fire has been lit beneath him. When Hardaport tries to enter the room, Brown quickly puts on a dress of Arabella's over his torn and now even blacker clothes, and pretends to be a charwoman. In a fury Hardaport bursts open the locked door and struggles with Brown—someone carrying a tray of plates, glasses, and food is knocked over—who crashes through the window to the balcony below. In the next scene Brown emerges in the drawing-room looking more battered than ever and drenched with rain. He disguises himself in a ridiculous costume at an elegant party—other characters also appear in exaggerated dress—tries to avoid his drunken uncle, attempts to rush out when discovered, and in the ensuing scuffle pulls the cloth off a table loaded with '*pastry, cakes, decanters, wine glasses, &c.*' The precise character of the comic business is evident from a stage direction occurring when the wrathful Captain Hardaport finds Brown in Arabella's room:

TRIPTOLEMUS *here makes a sudden bolt, but is stopped by the* CAPTAIN. *In the struggle* TRIPTOLEMUS *slips out of his gown, which remains in* CAPTAIN's *hands, and leaves* TRIPTOLEMUS *his trousers and waistcoat, with a very ample crinoline over them. He then makes a rush to the door, meeting* LUKE SHARP *as he enters carrying a tray, on which are a pie, plates, and glasses, upsets him and the contents of the tray. The* CAPTAIN *again seizes* TRIPTOLEMUS, *who retreats backwards struggling with the* CAPTAIN; *when close to the window,* TRIPTOLEMUS *loses his balance and falls backward through the window with great smash of glass.* ARABELLA *and* PHOEBE *each scream with all their might, and fall into different chairs.* LUKE SHARP *shouts 'Police', &c. &c.*

With its lower middle-class emphasis and jolly bouncing vulgarity, *Drawing Room, Second Floor, and Attics* belongs to the older variety of nineteenth-century farce. But its heavy indulgence in physical comedy is a mark of the newer farce. The banal dialogue and awful jokes of Charles Hawtrey's immensely popular *The Private Secretary* (1883) are accompanied by an enormous amount of violently physical business.[1] The unfortunate private secretary, Spalding—a timid, bewildered, uncomprehending character—is, among the innumerable physical indignities he suffers, pushed around, tripped up, shoved under tables, tied to a chair, hit by an umbrella, sat on, and stuffed into a chest. This kind of farce humour was much on the increase in the last quarter of the century, despite the refining influence of writers like Pinero and the gradual sophistication of other aspects of farce. One possible explanation is that, as the low comedian who could skilfully create character and a range of human eccentricities became rarer on the stage, his kind of comedy had to be replaced by one that did not require such powers of personal artistic creativity but could emphasize instead the much more easily attainable humour of general stage business and physical knockabout, a group effect rather than the power of an individual talent. Whatever the reason,

---

[1] Two examples of the quality of Hawtrey's jokes can be cited.

Gibson, a tailor, is talking to Cattermole:

GIBSON. That coat was made by an ijyot.

CATTERMOLE. It was not 'made in Egypt'. It was made in Calcutta.

GIBSON. What cutter?

CATTERMOLE. Calcutta.

GIBSON. I don't know him!

Douglas is showing the girls books in the library:

DOUGLAS. First of all, here's *The Vicar of Wakefield* . . . . .

EDITH. Oh, we know that—by heart.

DOUGLAS. No, by Goldsmith!

such farces abounded. Brandon Thomas's *Charley's Aunt* (1892) is one well-known example; its reliance on obvious physical effects—all carefully noted in stage directions—is extreme. Shaw recorded his disgust at this kind of farce when he reviewed *Never Again* (1897), an anonymous adaptation from the French:

In this play everyone who opens a door and sees somebody outside it utters a yell of dismay and slams the door to as if the fiend in person had knocked at it. When anybody enters a room, he or she is received with a roar of confusion and terror, and frantically ejected by bodily violence. The audience does not know why; but as each member of it thinks he ought to, and believes his neighbour does, he echoes the yell of the actor with a shout of laughter; and so the piece 'goes' immensely. It is, to my taste, a vulgar, stupid, noisy, headachy, tedious business.[1]

By 1897, plays of the general description of *Never Again*, adapted from the contemporary French boulevard farce, had been popular in the West End for twenty years. As in melodrama, drama, and comedy, adaptation from the French had been so widespread in farce, particularly since about the 1830s, that there is little point in treating it separately. The French farce that attracted English dramatists in the 1870s, however, was rather specialized, a farce that commonly dealt in bourgeois adultery or near-adultery, often involving both wife and husband, and placing the guilty parties in a series of compromising situations from which it would seem impossible to extricate them without the fatal discovery of the truth. To these ends the considerable abilities of the French farceur were directed, and the best results resemble precision machinery operating with inexorable and smoothly oiled inevitability. *The Wedding March* (1873), Gilbert's version of *Un Chapeau de Paille d'Italie* (1851), by Eugène Labiche and Marc Michel, really began the vogue of adaptation from this type of French farce. However, the major impetus to the movement on the English stage was *Les Dominos Roses* (1876), by Alfred Hennequin and Alfred Delacour, which spawned numerous English progeny over the next thirty years. The best of the immediately contemporary ones were Dion Boucicault's *Forbidden Fruit* (New York 1876, London 1880) and James Albery's direct adaptation, *Pink Dominos* (1877).

[1] *The Saturday Review*, lxxiv (16 October 1897), p. 417.

Both plays share the basic plot and comic complications of *Les Dominos Roses*. Two husbands plan a night out with ladies of doubtful character; the rendezvous is a restaurant of equally doubtful character at Cremorne, with a farcically convenient number of private rooms and doors opening onto the stage. By coincidence or design their wives appear in the same restaurant, to the confusion and horror of all. The pattern of development in farces of this kind is generally similar: in the first act a slow buildup of plots and counterplots; in the second (or third in the case of *Forbidden Fruit*) a fast pace with everybody arriving at the restaurant amid growing comic tension, and a climax with characters running in and out and hiding from each other; in the third act, set once more in the home, a painful unravelling of the tangled plot skein, a profusion of explanations and consequences, and peace made between all parties. In *Forbidden Fruit* Dove and Buster scheme to get away from their wives, and Dove invents a trip to Nottingham on business. Of course everything goes wrong: Dove's wife and her brother arrive at Cremorne when Dove is there, and Dove, not knowing the brother, suspects her of infidelity; Mrs. Buster discovers her husband with Mrs. Dove. Finally the brother intervenes to rescue Dove's reputation and the play ends happily. As in all farces of its type the plot is elaborate and complex; a full summary would occupy considerable space. In *Pink Dominos* Charles Grey-thorne, a quiet businessman from Manchester, and his friend Sir Percy Wagstaffe make assignations at Cremorne with two unknown ladies in pink dominos. The ladies are actually their wives engaged in testing their character. All four, as well as an old friend, Tubbs, his *'bright little lady'*, and Mrs. Tubbs's nephew with the Wagstaffe maid, gather in couples at the restaurant, whose head waiter is the unscrupulous Brisket. Many complications ensue: there is a steady stream of entrances and exits through the four doors to private rooms; partners are interchanged; the maid is involved with three men consecutively. Once again, in the third act, the characters extricate themselves with great difficulty from the consequences of their actions.

Without doubt this was a new farce on the English stage. Comic business concerning men and women hiding in bedrooms and closets had long been traditional, and examples could be offered from scores of comedies and farces. In the late eighteenth century and the first seventy years of the nineteenth century, however, such business was merely amusing and rather innocent; the naïveté of whatever sexual suggestion there was rendered it innocuous. Several critics of the 1870s, however, found the new farce alarming.[1] E. L. Blanchard, at first objecting to *Pink Dominos* on the grounds that the marriages depicted in French farce did not truly reflect 'the present conditions of domestic life in any capital where the slightest regard is paid to the "humanities" or where friendship, love, and truth have any distinct significance', finally made his protest specifically moral:

It is yet right to assume that conjugal infidelity has not yet become recognized as a trait in the national character, and that husband and wife are not, in this country at least, passing their existence in trying to deceive, dishonour, and detect each other. . . . Of the very nature of the story it would hardly be excessive prudishness to withhold a description, for the same reason that no one in a family circle would think of explicitly detailing the plots of the plays of the Restoration.[2]

C. P. Newton suggested that English dramatic taste might have been 'depraved by a too close study of the dramatic works of our French neighbours and their views of domestic life', a taste that indulged itself in 'the worthless side of life' and 'the attempted invasion of married life and its obligations'.[3]

Nevertheless, even Blanchard had to admit that in English adaptations of the 'by no means squeamish' Palais Royal school 'a kind of deodorizing process has been usually deemed necessary before presentation to a London public of a theatrical dish compounded of such ingredients'.[4] Joseph Knight noted of French farces that 'complaint has been heard of the licence in which authors indulge in pieces of this class. As a rule, on the English stage at least, farcical comedy is skittish rather than indecent, and frequenters of the modern theatre have little of which to complain.'[5] Indeed, although the English adaptations had many more sexual implications than earlier farce, they were in all sorts of ingenious ways bowdlerized, sentimentalized, and generally rendered far less 'offensive' than the French originals.

[1] Before 1870 there was an almost total absence of critical comment upon farce.
[2] *The Daily Telegraph*, 5 April 1877.
[3] 'Frivolous Comedy', *The Theatre* (November 1881), pp. 268–9.
[4] *The Daily Telegraph*, 5 April 1877.
[5] *Theatrical Notes* (1893), p. xiii.

At the end of *Forbidden Fruit* the repentant Dove was made to say, 'I have tried the taste of forbidden fruit. I don't like it! A fast life looks charming to those who see it as spectators look at a play, but you have introduced me behind the scenes, and I prefer the illusion to the reality.' The *demi-mondaine* Foedora of *Les Dominos Roses*, picked up at the Variété and taken to the restaurant, became the virtuous Miss Barron of *Pink Dominos*, who innocently danced with Tubbs, could not find her friend afterwards, and 'promised ma to be home by one'.

The process of adaptation from the French and the adapter's methods of 'deodorizing' can be observed from a comparison of *Bébé* (1877), by Hennequin and Émile de Najac, with *Betsy* (1879), the English version by F. C. Burnand. In the French play Gaston, the son of Baron D'Aigreville, is treated as a baby by his parents; actually he is socially and sexually quite sophisticated, having had affairs with *cocottes* and the maid, Toinette. At present he is trying his best to seduce the wife of a family friend, De Kernanigous. One of the *cocottes* who come to visit him in his private part of the house, Aurelie, is also a mistress of De Kernanigous. From then on women are hidden in rooms, misunderstandings and misidentifications proliferate, Gaston's sexual proclivities are discovered, but De Kernanigous is talked out of suspecting his wife, who was on the point of surrendering to Gaston. Finally Gaston reluctantly agrees to marry a distant relative, Toinette is frustrated, and the play ends on a note of uneasy calm and hasty patchings up. The plot of *Betsy* is very similar; many of the same incidents and some of the same dialogue are used. But that is where the similarity ends. Characterizations and relationships between characters are fundamentally altered. The maid Betsy wants Adolphus (Gaston) to *marry* her, and Adolphus wants to *marry* the now perfectly respectable girl who was a *cocotte* in *Bébé*. The whole business of *cocottes* and sexual infidelity is excised from the English. Aurelie becomes Madame Polenta, a singing teacher, and McManus (De Kernanigous) takes private lessons from her. No doubt on stage this was made suggestive of McManus's intentions, but their relationship is totally innocent compared to the French. The only suggestion of impropriety between Adolphus and Mrs. McManus is contained in the following passage:

ADOLPHUS. If you call me dear child and little boy, and treat me as you used to, I'll treat you as I used to, and call you auntie, and give you a kiss. [*Kisses her.*

MRS. MCMANUS. Oh, for shame!

ADOLPHUS. Am I a boy now?

Not only are their relations and Gaston's intentions much more explicit in the French, but the same scene is much fuller, and passionate rather than playful:

GASTON. C'est de vous seule qu'il s'agit — de vous, si jolie, si bonne et si bien faite pour être adorée —

DIANE. Ah! Gaston, s'il rentrait!

GASTON. Mais puisqu'il est au couvent, votre mari. Ne parlons donc pas de ça! De vous que la cruelle destinée a unie à un être incapable de vous apprécier, de vous comprendre. [*Il la reprend dans ses bras.*

DIANE [*Voulant se dégager.*] Encore une fois, je vous en supplie!

GASTON. Oui! Incapable. [*Il l'embrasse.*] Tandis que moi! [*Il l'embrasse.*] Oh! Moi! [*Il l'embrasse.*

DIANE. [*À part.*] Ah, mon Dieu!

In *Betsy* McManus tells his wife that 'a flame of Dolly's' is hidden behind the door; the French is 'sa maîtresse', and translation of this kind is a matter of course in the English version. In *Bébé* Gaston's tutor discovers that Aurelie is the wife from whom he separated and to whom he pays an allowance that he cannot afford; he is delighted to find her a *cocotte* because he then possesses legal proof of her infidelity and will not have to pay the allowance. His English equivalent, Dawson, is happily reconciled with his wife at the end of the play. Adolphus eagerly rushes out for a marriage licence so that he can be speedily united with his beloved Nellie; Gaston has no desire to marry at all. Finally, the social tone and setting of the English version is lower than that of the French original, and although *Bébé* is full of characters rushing around to conceal themselves it does not contain in its stage directions the sort of traditional nineteenth-century English farce business specifically required in *Betsy* and exemplified by these two quotations:

MCMANUS. You keep my secret and I'll keep yours. [*Nudges him.*

ADOLPHUS. [*Nudging* MCMANUS *violently.*] I think I got the best of him that time.

Adolphus and his friend Dick are talking to Dawson:

ADOLPHUS. Ah, you've been a gay dog in your time.   [*Nudging him.*
DICK. A slyboots, eh?
     [*Both dig him in the ribs till he falls; they pick him up, apologizing.*

Farces in which a married man is discomfited by a sequence
of domestic contretemps, misconceived by all about him, and
everybody's antagonist in turn, until the pressures of cumulative
harassment build up to a comically explosive climax involving
the whole household, remained popular. Whether original or
adapted from French or German, their pattern was similar.
The *Pink Dominos–Forbidden Fruit* plot was also popular, but
not ubiquitous. Two examples of the former plot are *The
Snowball* (1879) and *The Arabian Nights* (1887), both by Sydney
Grundy. In *The Snowball*, Felix Featherstone, resolved to
teach his wife a lesson for going to see *Pink Dominos* without
his knowledge, writes her a note signed 'Pink Dominos'
appointing a rendezvous. The wife discovers his plot, and,
equally determined to chastise him for going to the same play
on the same evening without *her*, manages it so that he believes
he has actually given the note to the maid, Penelope. Terrified
of his wife finding out, he tries to escape from Penelope, and
when that fails attempts to bribe her into silence. She, however,
is also bribed by Mrs. Featherstone to threaten him with dis-
closure. Utterly bewildered and very frightened, Featherstone
has no idea that his wife is playing a trick on him or that
Penelope is unaware of the contents of the note. Domestic
complications multiply, and from all sides he is browbeaten
into a state of panic and despair. The Act II curtain finds five
people chasing him several times across the stage in order to
deliver notes to him. Ultimately all is happily resolved when he
decides to make a clean breast of it and tell the truth—a rare
occurrence in French farce. Arthur Hummingtop of *The Arabian
Nights* gets himself into just as much trouble as Featherstone.
Inspired by the example of Harun al-Rashid, he goes disguised
into the streets where he meets a pretty girl lost in the fog and
gallantly escorts her to a theatre. To his horror the girl—a
circus performer—turns up at his house the next day and will
not leave. Under the grim eye of his mother-in-law he intro-
duces her as his niece just arrived from New York, hurries the

real niece off to a hotel, is of course suspected by his wife, and sweats his way through further twists and turns of the plot. At the Act II curtain five women faint successively upon recognizing each other or receiving damaging information; by Act III Hummingtop is the helpless victim of a situation completely out of control, a situation not only injurious to himself but also, because of his wild inventions, to everyone in the house.

To the kind of drama that presented the comic agonies of such as Felix Featherstone and Arthur Hummingtop, Shaw took the strongest exception:

> To laugh without sympathy is a ruinous abuse of a noble function; and the degradation of any race may be measured by the degree of their addiction to it . . . we find people who would not join in the laughter of a crowd of peasants at the village idiot, or tolerate the public flogging or pillorying of a criminal, booking seats to shout with laughter at a farcical comedy, which is, at bottom, the same thing— namely, the deliberate indulgence of that horrible, derisive joy in humiliation and suffering which is the beastliest element in human nature.[1]

What alarmed Shaw was not farce at all, but that part of human nature which enjoys farce as a means of sadistic gratification not available in ordinary life. Certainly, physical and mental humiliation is an essential aspect of farce, and it can be found abundantly in English farce of the nineteenth century. Both the comedy of physical business and the comedy of the despairing imprisonment in unrelenting circumstance—much intensified in the farce of the last quarter of the century—can be directed to this end. Yet despite the sufferings of its protagonists and the powerful influence of late-century French farce, the English farce of the nineteenth century, taken as a whole, remains essentially innocent of malice and destructive anarchy. Its homely domesticity, its fondness for ideals, morality, and sentiment, its seemingly naïve charm, its bumbling aggression, its friendly contact with its audience—all these things effectively and cheerfully keep at bay the darker devils of farce.

[1] *The Saturday Review*, lxxxi (9 May 1896), pp. 473–4.

RAISING THE WIND

A FARCE IN TWO ACTS

BY

JAMES KENNEY (1780–1849)

———

First performed at Covent Garden Theatre
5 November 1803

———

CAST

JEREMY DIDDLER	Mr. Lewis
PLAINWAY	Mr. Blanchard
FAINWOULD	Mr. Simmons
SAM	Mr. Emery
WAITER	Mr. Atkins
RICHARD	Mr. Abbot
JOHN	Mr. Harley
MESSENGER	Mr. Truman
MISS DURABLE	Mrs. Davenport
PEGGY	Mrs. Beverly

———

SCENE

A Country Town

PREFACE TO *RAISING THE WIND*

Raising the Wind was the first of Kenney's plays to be performed, the first of over fifty melodramas, farces, comedies, comic operas, and the occasional tragedy and burlesque. His last recorded piece, a comedy, *Infatuation*, was acted in 1845. Apart from *Raising the Wind*, whose immediate success was owing to Lewis's Jeremy Diddler (a part played by many leading actors, including Henry Irving), Kenney's best-known plays in his own time were the melodramas *Ella Rosenberg* (1807) and *The Blind Boy* (1807)—the former being one of the earliest domestic melodramas, albeit with a foreign setting—a farce, *Love, Law, and Physic* (1812), a comic opera, *Sweethearts and Wives* (1823), and a comedy, *The Irish Ambassador* (1831). *Sweethearts and Wives* was not only popular when it first appeared, with Madame Vestris in a light-hearted singing role and Liston as a cockney servant obsessed with romances, but also enjoyed a long stage life. In *Love, Law, and Physic* Liston played the booby Lubin Log, who has inherited a fortune but is cheated out of the woman he is going to marry by the tricks of Flexible, a fast-talking barrister. Humour arises chiefly from the utter stupidity of Log, his appearance as an elegant with his hair powdered, and the unquestioning way he falls into the traps set for him—in short, from the problems of coping with a world quite beyond his limited understanding into which he is violently precipitated, problems common enough in nineteenth-century farce.

Love, Law, and Physic has the same general framework—the standard one of eighteenth-century farce—as *Raising the Wind*: the deception of both the family and a rival, and the lover's ultimate success in winning the heroine. In the case of *Raising the Wind* the basic plot is complicated by the necessity of also imposing on a credulous and man-hungry spinster; as a result Diddler is forced to the usual extremities of farce in order to carry through his deception and win. The atmosphere of *Raising the Wind* is still that of the genteel world of the upper middle class and their comic servants which is so prevalent in the farce of the previous century; even the down-at-heels hero is restored to £10,000 and his proper station in life by the end of the play.

It is instructive in this respect to compare *Raising the Wind* to a farce of 1838, Buckstone's *Weak Points*, in which the plausible and attractive Jemmy Wheedle insinuates himself into the Docker family with the intention of marrying their well-off boarder, Miss Pump, and for his own ends plays on the weak points of all the other characters. Except that Wheedle, who closely resembles Diddler, is unsuccessful and finally arrested for forgery, the two plays are remarkably similar in intention. What is interesting is the precise nature of the differences. Firstly, the settings of *Weak Points*—the shop in which Wheedle learns about the Dockers, and the Docker house itself—as well as its characters are distinctly lower in class level than those of *Raising the Wind* (one must except the inn scene that was almost a necessity in farces dealing with travellers). Secondly, there is more low comedy and physical business in *Weak Points*: when in the final scene Wheedle tries to run away with Miss Pump, characters pop in and out of bedrooms, bump together in the dark, hide from each other, and become completely confused. (Compare Diddler's relatively simple elopement with Miss Plainway.) Thirdly, the physical business, the low comedy, and the *dramatis personae* function in a context now thoroughly and materially domesticated: for instance, in the scene where Wheedle meets Docker for the first time there is a discussion of domestic expenditure and how it could be reduced; such items as lamb, sherry, coals, and bonnets are mentioned. *Raising the Wind* is essentially an eighteenth-century farce; *Weak Points* belongs firmly to the world of early Victorian farce, and there is a great deal of difference between them.

Raising the Wind was performed thirty-six times before the close of the 1803–4 Covent Garden season; Kenney received £150 for it, a good sum for an afterpiece at that time. The text printed here is a conflation of the first edition of 1803, the text in vol. i of Inchbald's *A Collection of Farces and Other Afterpieces* (1815), and the first acting edition, *Cumberland's British Theatre*, v. 19. The play had been slightly cut by the time it appeared in Inchbald, and further cuts were made for the *Cumberland* and for *Lacy's Acting Edition of Plays*, supplementary v. 2. A later acting edition is *Dicks' Standard Plays*, no. 208. The Lord Chamberlain's manuscript copy, entitled *How to Raise the Wind*, was also used in collation; it is very close to the 1803.

ACT I

SCENE I. *The Public Room in an Inn. Two tables and three chairs; bell rings.*

SAM. [*Without.*] Coming, I'm a coming!

Enter WAITER *and* SAM, *meeting.*

WAITER. Well, Sam, there's a little difference between this and hay-making, eh?

SAM. Yes, but I get on pretty decent, don't I? Only, you see, when two or three people call at once, I'm apt to get flurried, and then I can't help listening to the droll things the young chaps say to one another at dinner—and then I don't exactly hear what they say to me, you see. Sometimes too I fall a laughing wi'em, and that they don't like, you understand——

WAITER. Well, well, you'll soon get the better of all that.

[*A laugh without.*

SAM. What's all that about?

WAITER. [*Looking out.*] Oh, it's Mr. Diddler, trying to joke himself into credit at the bar. But it won't do; they know him too well. By-the-bye, Sam, mind you never trust that fellow.

SAM. What, him with the spy-glass?

WAITER. Yes, that impudent short-sighted fellow.

SAM. Why, what for not?

WAITER. Why, because he'll never pay you. The fellow lives by spunging—gets into people's houses by his songs and his bon-mots. At some of the squires' tables he's as constant a guest as the parson or the apothecary.

SAM. Come, that's an odd line to go into, however.

WAITER. Then he borrows money of everybody he meets.

SAM. Nay, but will anybody lend it him?

WAITER. Why, he asks for so little at a time that people are ashamed to refuse him; and then he generally asks for an odd sum to give it the appearance of immediate necessity.

SAM. Damma, he must be a droll chap, however.

WAITER. Here he comes; mind you take care of him.   [*Exit.*

SAM. Never you fear that, mun. I wasn't born two hundred miles north of Lunnun to be done by Mr. Diddler, I know.

Enter DIDDLER.

DIDDLER. Tol lol de riddle lol. Eh! [*Looking through a glass at* SAM.] The new waiter—a very clod, by my hopes! An untutored clod. My clamorous bowels, be of good cheer. Young man, how d'ye do? Step this way, will you? A novice, I perceive. And how d'ye like your new line of life?

SAM. Why, very well, thank ye. How do you like your old one?

DIDDLER. [*Aside.*] Disastrous accents! A Yorkshireman! [*To him.*] What is your name, my fine fellow?

SAM. Sam. You needn't tell me yours, I know you, my—fine fellow.

DIDDLER. [*Aside.*] Oh, Fame, Fame, you incorrigible gossip! But *nil desperandum*—at him again. [*To him.*] A prepossessing physiognomy, open and ruddy, importing health and liberality. Excuse my glass, I'm short-sighted. You have the advantage of me in that respect.

SAM. Yes, I can see as far as most folks.

DIDDLER. [*Turning away.*] Well, I'll thank ye to—oh, Sam. you haven't got such a thing as tenpence about you, have you?

SAM. Yes. [*They look at each other—*DIDDLER *expecting to receive it.*] And I mean to keep it about me, you see.

DIDDLER. Oh—aye—certainly. I only asked for information.

SAM. Hark! there's the stage-coach comed in. I must go and wait upon the passengers. You'd better ax some of them—mayhap they mun gie you a little better information.

DIDDLER. Stop! Hark ye, Sam! You can get me some breakfast first. I'm devilish sharp set, Sam; you see I come from a long walk over the hills, and——

SAM. Aye, and you see I come fra—Yorkshire.

DIDDLER. You do; your unsophisticated tongue declares it. Superior to vulgar prejudices, I honour you for it, for I'm sure you'll bring me my breakfast as soon as any other countryman.

SAM. Aye: well, what will you have?

DIDDLER. Anything—tea, coffee, an egg, and so forth.

SAM. Well now, one of us, you understand, in this transaction mun have credit for a little while; that is, either I mun trust you for t'money, or you mun trust me for t'breakfast. Now, as you're above vulgar preju-prejudizes, and seem to be vastly taken wi'me, and as I'm not so conceited as to be above 'em, and a'n't at all taken wi'you, you'd better give me the money, you see, and trust me for t'breakfast—he, he, he!

DIDDLER. What d'ye mean by that, Sam?

SAM. Or mayhap you'll say me a bonn mo.

DIDDLER. Sir, you're getting impertinent.

SAM. Oh, what—you don't like they terms? Why, then, as you sometimes sing for your dinner, now you may whistle for your breakfast, you see—he, he, he!   [*Exit.*

DIDDLER. This it is to carry on trade without a capital. Once I paid my way, and in a pretty high road I travelled; but thou art now, Jerry Diddler, little better than a vagabond. Fie on thee! Awake thee, rouse thy spirit! Honourably earn thy breakfasts and thy dinners too. But how? My present trade is the only one that requires no apprenticeship. How unlucky that the rich and pretty Miss Plainway, whose heart I won at Bath, should take so sudden a departure that I should lose her address and call myself a foolish romantic name that will prevent her letters from reaching me. A rich wife would pay my debts and heal my wounded pride. But the degenerate state of my wardrobe is confoundedly against me. There's a warm old rogue, they say, with a pretty daughter, lately come to his house at the foot of the hill. I've a great mind—it's d—d impudent; but if I hadn't surmounted my delicacy I must have starved long ago.

Enter WAITER; *crosses in haste.*

George, what's the name of the new family at the foot of the hill?

WAITER. I don't know; I can't attend to you now.   [*Exit.*

DIDDLER. There again. Oh! I mustn't bear this any longer—I must make a plunge—no matter for the name. Gad! perhaps it may be more imposing not to know it. I'll go and scribble her a passionate billet immediately—that is, if they'll trust me with pen and ink. [*Exit.*

Enter SAM, *showing in* FAINWOULD *and* RICHARD.

FAINWOULD. Bring breakfast directly. [*Exit* SAM.
Well, Richard, I think I shall awe them into a little respect here, though they're apt to grin at me in London.

RICHARD. That you will, I dare say, sir.

FAINWOULD. Respect, Richard, is all I want. My father's money has made me a gentleman, and you never see any familiar jesting with your true gentlemen, I'm sure.

RICHARD. Very true, sir. And so, sir, you've come here to marry this Miss Plainway, without ever having seen her.

FAINWOULD. Yes, but my father and hers are very old friends. They were school-fellows. They've lived at a distance from one another ever since, for Plainway always hated London. But my father has often visited him, and about a month ago at Bristol they made up this match. I didn't object to it, for my father says she's a very pretty girl; and besides, the girls in London don't treat me with proper respect by any means.

RICHARD. At Bristol? Then they're new inhabitants here. Well, sir, you must muster all your gallantry.

FAINWOULD. I will, Dick; but I'm not successful that way—I always do some stupid thing or other when I want to be attentive. The other night, in a large assembly, I picked up the tail of a lady's gown, and was going to present it to her for her pocket-handkerchief. Lord, how the people did laugh!

RICHARD. It was an awkward mistake, to be sure, sir.

FAINWOULD. Well, now for a little refreshment, and then for Miss Plainway. Go and look after the luggage, Richard.
[*Sits down at table. Exit* RICHARD.

Enter DIDDLER, *with a letter in his hand.*

DIDDLER. Here it is, brief but impressive. If she has but the romantic imagination of my Peggy, the direction alone must win her. [*Reads.*] 'To the beautiful maid at the foot of the hill.' The words are so delicate, the arrangement so poetical, and the *tout ensemble* reads with such a languishing cadence, that a blue-stocking garden-wench must feel it! 'To the beautiful maid at the foot of the hill.' She can't resist it!

FAINWOULD. I am very hungry; I wish they would bring my breakfast.

DIDDLER. Breakfast! Delightful sound! Oh, bless your unsuspicious face; we'll breakfast together. [DIDDLER *goes to the table, takes up a newspaper, and sits.*] Sir, your most obedient. From London, sir, I presume?

FAINWOULD. At your service, sir.

DIDDLER. Pleasant travelling, sir?

FAINWOULD. Middling, sir.

DIDDLER. Any news in town when you came away?

FAINWOULD. Not a word, sir. [*Aside.*] Come, this is polite and respectful.

DIDDLER. Pray, sir, what's your opinion of affairs in general?

FAINWOULD. Sir? Why, really, sir—[*Aside.*] nobody would ask my opinion in town, now.

DIDDLER. No politician, perhaps? You talked of breakfast, sir; I was just thinking of the same thing—shall be proud of your company.

FAINWOULD. You're very obliging, sir, but really I'm in such haste.

DIDDLER. Don't mention it. Company is everything to me. I'm that sort of man, that I really couldn't dispense with you.

FAINWOULD. Sir, since you insist upon it—waiter!

SAM. [*Without.*] Coming, sir.

FAINWOULD. Bless me, they're very inattentive, here—they never bring you what you call for.

DIDDLER. No—they very often serve *me* so.

Enter SAM.

FAINWOULD. Let that breakfast be for two.

DIDDLER. Yes, this gentleman and I are going to breakfast together.

SAM. [*To* FAINWOULD.] *You* order it, do you, sir?

FAINWOULD. Yes, to be sure; didn't you hear me?

SAM. [*Chuckling.*] Yes, I heard you.

FAINWOULD. Then bring it immediately.

SAM. Yes. [*Still chuckling.*]

FAINWOULD. What d'ye mean by laughing, you scoundrel?

DIDDLER. Aye, what d'ye mean by laughing, you scoundrel?
[*Drives* SAM *out, and follows.*

FAINWOULD. Now, that's disrespectful, especially to that gentleman, who seems to be so well known here; but these country waiters are always impertinent.

Enter DIDDLER, *his letter in his hand.*

DIDDLER. A letter for me? Desire the man to wait. That bumpkin is the most impertinent—I declare it's enough to—. You haven't got such a thing as half-a-crown about you, have you, sir? There's a messenger waiting, and I haven't got any change about me.

FAINWOULD. Certainly—at your service.
[*Takes out his purse and gives him money.*

DIDDLER. I'll return it to you, sir, as soon as possible. Allo! Here!

Enter WAITER.

Here's the man's money. [*Putting it into his own pocket.*] And bring the breakfast immediately.

WAITER. Here it is, sir.   [*Exit.*

Enter SAM, *with breakfast.*

DIDDLER. There we are, sir. Now, no ceremony, I beg, for I'm rather in a hurry myself. [*Exit* SAM, *chuckling.* DIDDLER *pours out coffee for himself.*] Help yourself, and then you'll have it to your liking. When you've done with that loaf, sir, I'll thank you for it. [*Takes it out of his hand.*] Thank ye, sir.

FAINWOULD. [*Aside.*] That's not quite so respectful, though.

DIDDLER. Breakfast, sir, is a very wholesome meal.

[*Eats fast.*

FAINWOULD. It is, sir; I always eat a good one.

DIDDLER. So do I, sir, [*Aside.*] when I can.

FAINWOULD. I'm an early riser, too; and in town the servants are so lazy that I am often obliged to wait a long while before I can get any.

DIDDLER. That's exactly my case in the country.

FAINWOULD. And it's very tantalizing, when one's hungry, to be served so.

DIDDLER. Very, sir—I'll trouble you once more.

[*Snatches the bread out of his hand again.*

FAINWOULD. [*Aside.*] This can't be meant for disrespect, but it's very like it.

DIDDLER. Are you looking for this, sir? You can call for more if you want it. [*Returns a very small bit.*] Here, waiter!

WAITER. [*Without.*] Sir?

DIDDLER. Some more bread for this gentleman. You eat nothing at all, sir.

FAINWOULD. Why, bless my soul, I can get nothing.

SAM *enters with rolls.*

DIDDLER. Very well, Sam—thank ye, Sam—but don't giggle, Sam; curse you, don't laugh.   [*Following him out.*

SAM. Ecod! you're in luck, Mr. Diddler.   [*Exit.*

DIDDLER. [*Again taking his letter out of his pocket.*] What, another letter by the coach. Might I trouble you again? You haven't got such a thing as tenpence about you, have you? I live close by, sir; I'll send it to you all the moment I go home. Be glad to see you any time you'll look in, sir.

FAINWOULD. You do me honour, sir—I haven't any halfpence, but there's my servant; you can desire him to give it you.

DIDDLER. You're very obliging. [*Puts the rolls* SAM *brought, unobserved, into his hat.*] I'm extremely sorry to give you so much trouble. I will take that liberty. [*Aside.*] Come, I've raised the wind for to-day, however.   [*Exit.*

FAINWOULD. That must be a man of some breeding, by his ease and his impudence.

Enter SAM; *he crosses.*

Who is that gentleman, waiter?

SAM. Gentleman!

FAINWOULD. Yes; by his using an inn I suppose he lives upon his means—don't he?

SAM. Yes, but they're the oddest sort of means you ever heard of in your life. What, don't you know him?

FAINWOULD. No.

SAM. Well, I thought so.

FAINWOULD. He invited me to breakfast with him.

SAM. Aye; well, that was handsome enough.

FAINWOULD. I thought so myself.

SAM. But it isn't quite so handsome to leave you to pay for it.

FAINWOULD. Leave me to pay for it!

SAM. [*Looking out.*] Yes, I see he's off there.

FAINWOULD. Poh! He's only gone to pay for a letter.

SAM. A letter! Bless you, there's no letter comes here for him.

FAINWOULD. Why, he's had two this morning; I lent him the money to pay for 'em.

SAM. No; did you, though?

FAINWOULD. Yes; he hadn't any change about him.

SAM. [*Laughing.*] Dam' if that a'n't the softest trick I ever knowed. You come fra' Lunnun, don't you, sir?

FAINWOULD. Why, you giggling blockhead, what d'ye mean?

SAM. Why, he's had no letters, I tell you, but one he has just been writing here himself.

FAINWOULD. An impudent rascal!

SAM. Well, sir, we'll put t' breakfast all to your bill, you understand, as you ordered it.

FAINWOULD. Psha! Don't tease me about the breakfast.

SAM. Upon my soul, the flattest trick I ever heard of.

[*Exit, laughing.*]

FAINWOULD. Well, this is the most disrespectful treatment.

Enter RICHARD.

RICHARD. I lent that gentleman the tenpence, sir.

FAINWOULD. Confound the gentleman and you too.

[*Exit, driving off* RICHARD.]

SCENE II. *The Outside of* PLAINWAY's *House.*

Enter PLAINWAY, PEGGY, *and* MISS DURABLE.

MISS DURABLE. Dear cousin, how soon you hurry us home.

PLAINWAY. Cousin, you grow worse and worse. You'd be gaping after the men from morning till night.

MISS DURABLE. Mr. Plainway, I tell you again I'll not bear your sneers; though I won't blush to own, as I've often told you, that I think the society of accomplished men as innocent as it is pleasing.

PLAINWAY. Innocent enough with you it must be. But there's no occasion to stare accomplished men full in the face as they pass you, or to sit whole hours at a window to gape at them, unless it is to talk to them in your famous language of the eyes; and that I'm afraid few of 'em understand, or else you speak very badly; for whenever you ask 'em a question in it they never seem to make you any answer.

MISS DURABLE. Cousin Plainway, you're a sad brute, and I'll never pay you another visit while I live.

PLAINWAY. I'm afraid, cousin, you have helped my daughter to some of her wild notions. Come, knock at the door. [MISS DURABLE *knocks at door of house.*] Well, Peg, are you any better prepared to meet your lover?

PEGGY. [*In a pensive tone and attitude.*] Alas! Cruel fate ordains I shall never see him more.

[*The door opens.* MISS DURABLE *goes into the house.*]

PLAINWAY. There—she's at her romance again. Never meet him more! Why, you're going to meet him to-day for the first time.

PEGGY. You speak of the vulgar, the sordid Fainwould; I of the all-accomplished Mortimer.

PLAINWAY. There! that Mortimer again. Let me hear that name no more, hussey; I am your father, and will be obeyed.

PEGGY. No, sir; as Miss Somerville says, fathers of ignorant and grovelling minds have no right to our obedience.

PLAINWAY. Miss Somerville! And who the devil is Miss Somerville?

PEGGY. What, sir! Have you never read the Victim of Sentiment?

PLAINWAY. D—n the Victim of Sentiment! Get in, you baggage —Victim of Sentiment indeed!   [*They go into the house.*

Enter DIDDLER.

DIDDLER. There she dwells. Grant, my kind stars, that she may have no lover, that she may be dying for want of one; that she may tumble about in her rosy slumbers with dreaming of some unknown swain, lovely and insinuating as Jeremy Diddler. Now, how shall I get my letter delivered?

MISS DURABLE. [*Appearing at the window.*] Well, I declare, the balmy zephyr breathes such delightful and refreshing breezes, that in spite of my cousin's sneers I can't help indulging in them.

DIDDLER. [*Looking up.*] There she is, by my hopes! Ye sylphs and cupids, strengthen my sight, that I may luxuriate on her beauties! No—not a feature can I distinguish—but she's gazing on mine, and that's enough.

MISS DURABLE. What a sweet-looking young gentleman—and his eyes are directed towards me. Oh, my palpitating heart! What can he mean?

DIDDLER. You're a made man, Jerry. I'll pay off my old scores, and never borrow another sixpence while I live.

MISS DURABLE. [*Sings.*] 'Oh! listen, listen to the voice of love'——

DIDDLER. Voice indifferent But d—n music when I've done singing for my dinners.

Enter SAM, *with a parcel.*

Eh, Sam here—he shall deliver my letter. My dear Sam, I'm so glad to see you. I forgive your laughing at me. Will you do me a favour?

SAM. If it won't take me long, for you see I've gotten a parcel to deliver in a great hurry. By the bye, how nicely you did that chap——

DIDDLER. Hush, you rogue. Look up there—do you see that lady?

SAM. Yes, I see her——

DIDDLER. Isn't she an angel?

SAM. Why, if she be, she's been a good while dead, I reckon; long enough to appearance to be t' mother of angels.

DIDDLER. Sam, you're a wag, but I don't understand your jokes. Now, if you can contrive to deliver this letter into her own hands, you shall be handsomely rewarded.

SAM. Handsomely rewarded! Aye, well let's see. [*Takes the letter.*] 'To the beauti——'

DIDDLER. Beautiful——

SAM. 'Beautiful maid at the foot of the hill.' [*Looks up at the window.*] Damma it now, you're at some of your tricks. [*Aside.*] The old toad's got some money, I reckon. Well, I can but try, you know—and as to the reward, why it's neither here nor there.   [*Knocks at the door.*

DIDDLER. Thank ye, my dear fellow. Get an answer if you can, and I'll wait here for you.

[*The door opens;* SAM *nods and enters.*

MISS DURABLE. A letter to deliver. Oh, dear! I'm all of a flutter. I must learn what it means.

[*Retires from the window.*

DIDDLER. Transport! She has disappeared to receive it. She's mine. Now I shall visit the country squires upon other terms. I'll only sing when it comes to my turn, and never tell a story or cut a joke but at my own table. Yet I'm sorry for my pretty Peggy. I did love that little rogue, and I'm sure she never thinks of her Mortimer without sighing. [SAM *opens the door, holds it open, and beckons.*]. Eh Sam! Well, what answer?

SAM. Why, first of all she fell into a vast trepidation.

DIDDLER. Then you saw her yourself?

SAM. Yes, I axed to see she that were sitting at the window over the door.

DIDDLER. Well——

SAM. Well, you see, as I tell you, when she opened the letter she fell into a vast trepidation, and fluttered and blushed, and blushed and fluttered—in short—I never see'd any person play such comical games i' my days.

DIDDLER. It was emotion, Sam.

SAM. Yes, I know it was a motion, but it was a devilish queer one. Then at last, says she, stuttering as might be our potboy of a frosty morning, says she, 'Tell your master'— she thought you was my master—he, he, he!

DIDDLER. My dear Sam, go on.

SAM. Well, 'tell your master', says she, 'that his request is rather bold, but I've too much—too much confidence in my own—diss—dissension——'

DIDDLER. Discretion.

SAM. Aye, I fancy you be right—'in my own discretion, to be afraid of granting it'. Then she turned away blushing again—

DIDDLER. Like the rose——

SAM. Like the rose, he, he, he! Like a red cabbage.

DIDDLER. I'm a happy fellow.

SAM. [*Smiling.*] Why, how much did you ax her for?

DIDDLER. Only for an interview, Sam.

SAM. Oh! Then you'd better go in, I han't shut the door.

DIDDLER. I fixed it for to-morrow morning, but there's nothing like striking while the iron's hot. I will go in, find her out, and throw myself at her feet immediately. I'll reward you, Sam, depend upon it. I shall be a monied man soon, and then

I'll reward you. [SAM *sneers.*] I will, Sam, I give you my word.   [*Goes into the house.*

SAM. Come, that's kind, too, to give me what nobody else will take.   [*Exit.*

SCENE III. *A Room in* PLAINWAY'S *House.*

Enter DIDDLER, *cautiously.*

DIDDLER. Not here. If I could but find a closet now, I'd hide myself till she came nigh. Luckily, here is one. Who have we here?   [*Retires into a closet and listens from the door.*

Enter FAINWOULD *and* JOHN.

JOHN. Walk in, sir; I'll send my master to you directly.
          [*Exit.*

FAINWOULD. Now let me see if I can't meet with a little more respect here.

DIDDLER. [*Approaching and examining him.*] My cockney friend, by the lord! Come in pursuit of me, perhaps!

FAINWOULD. Old Plainway will treat me becomingly, no doubt; and, as he positively determined with my father that I should have his daughter, I presume she's prepared to treat me with proper respect, too.

DIDDLER. What! Plainway and his daughter! Here's a discovery! Then my Peggy, after all, is the beautiful maid at the foot of the hill, and the sly rogue wouldn't discover herself at the window on purpose to convict me of infidelity. How unlucky! And a rival arrived, too, just at the unfortunate crisis.

Re-enter JOHN.

JOHN. He'll be with you immediately, Mr. Fainwould. [*Exit.*

DIDDLER. Mr. Fainwould, eh! Now, what's to be done? If I could but get rid of him, I wouldn't despair of excusing myself to Peggy.

FAINWOULD. I wonder what my father says in his letter of introduction. [*Takes a letter out of his pocket.*

DIDDLER. A letter of introduction! Oh, oh! The first visit, then. Gad, I have it! It's the only way; so impudence befriend me! But first I'll lock the old gentleman out. [*Goes cautiously and locks the door*, R., *then advances briskly to* FAINWOULD, *as if he had entered by that door.*] Sir, your most obedient.

FAINWOULD. He here!

DIDDLER. So you've found me out, sir. But I've sent you the money—three-and-fourpence, wasn't it? Two-and-six, and ten——

FAINWOULD. Sir, I didn't mean——

DIDDLER. No, sir, I dare say not—merely for a visit. Well, I'm very glad to see you. Won't you take a seat?

FAINWOULD. And you live here, do you, sir?

DIDDLER. At present, sir, I do.

FAINWOULD. And is your name Plainway?

DIDDLER. No, sir, I'm Mr. Plainway's nephew. I'd introduce you to my uncle, but he's very busy at present with Sir Robert Rental, settling preliminaries for his marriage with my cousin.

FAINWOULD. Sir Robert Rental's marriage with Miss Plainway!

DIDDLER. Oh, you've heard a different report on that subject, perhaps. Now, thereby hangs a very diverting tale. If you're not in a hurry, sit down, and I'll make you laugh about it.

FAINWOULD. [*Aside.*] This is all very odd, upon my soul.
[*They sit down.*

DIDDLER. You see, my uncle did agree with an old fellow of the name of Fainwould, a Londoner, to marry my cousin to his son, and expects him down every day for the purpose; but a little while ago Sir Robert Rental, a baronet with a thumping estate, fell in love with her and she fell in love with him. So my uncle altered his mind, as it was very natural he should, you know, and agreed to this new match. And as he never saw the young cockney, and has since heard that he's quite a vulgar, conceited, foolish fellow, he hasn't thought it worth

his while to send him any notice of the affair. So if he should
come down, you know, we shall have a d——d good laugh at his
disappointment. [*Slaps him on the thigh*—FAINWOULD *drops
his letter, which* DIDDLER *picks up unseen.*] Ha, ha, ha! Capital
go, isn't it?

FAINWOULD. Ha, ha, ha! A very capital go, indeed. [*Aside.*]
Here's disrespect. [*To him.*] But if the cockney shouldn't be
disposed to think of the affair quite so merrily as you?

DIDDLER. Oh, the puppy! If he's refractory I'll pull his nose.

FAINWOULD. [*Aside.*] Here's an impudent scoundrel! Well, I
shall cheat 'em of their laugh by this meeting, however.

DIDDLER. [*Aside.*] A shy cock, I see.

FAINWOULD. Oh, you'll pull his nose, will you?

DIDDLER. If he's troublesome, I shall certainly have that
pleasure. Nothing I enjoy more than pulling noses.

FAINWOULD. Sir, I wish you a good morning. Perhaps, sir,
you may——   [*A knocking at the door*, R.

DIDDLER. [*Aside.*] Just in time, by Jupiter! [*Aloud.*] Be quiet
there. Damn that mastiff! Sir, I'm sorry you're going so soon.
[*Knocking again.*] Be quiet, I say. Well, I wish you a good
morning, sir. Then you won't stay and take a bit of dinner?

FAINWOULD. Perhaps, sir, I say, you may hear from me again.

DIDDLER. Sir, I shall be extremely happy, I'm sure.
          [*Exit* FAINWOULD, *door* L.
Bravo, Jeremy! Admirably hit off. [*Knocking repeated.*] Now
for the old gentleman.   [*Opens the door*, R.

Enter PLAINWAY.

PLAINWAY. My dear Mr. Fainwould, I'm extremely happy to
see you. I beg pardon for keeping you so long. Why, who the
deuce could lock that door?

DIDDLER. He, he, he! It was I, sir.

PLAINWAY. You? Why, what——

DIDDLER. A bit of humour, sir, to show you I determined to
make free and consider myself at home.

PLAINWAY. [*Aside.*] A bit of humour! Why, you must be an inveterate humorist indeed to begin so soon. [*To him.*] Well, come, that's merry and hearty.

DIDDLER. Yes, you'll find I've all that about me.

PLAINWAY. Well, and how's my old friend and all the rest of the family?

DIDDLER. Wonderfully well, my old buck. But here, here you have it all in black and white.   [*Gives the letter.*

PLAINWAY. So, an introduction.

DIDDLER. [*Aside.*] It's rather unlucky I don't know a little more of my family.   [*Struts familiarly about.*

PLAINWAY. [*Reads.*] 'This will at length introduce to you your son-in-law. I hope he will prove agreeable, both to you and your daughter. His late military habits, I think, have much improved his appearance, and perhaps you will already discern something of the officer about him.' Something of the officer; [*Looking at him.*] damme, it must be a sheriff's officer, then. 'Treat him delicately, and above all avoid raillery with him.' So then, I suppose, though he can give a joke he can't take one. 'It is apt to make him unhappy, as he always thinks it levelled at that stiffness in his manners, arising from his extreme timidity and bashfulness. Assure Peggy of the cordial affection of her intended father and your faithful friend—Francis Fainwould.' A very pretty introduction, truly.

DIDDLER. But where is my charming Peggy? I say—couldn't I have a little private conversation to begin with?

PLAINWAY. Why, I must introduce you, you know—I desired her to follow me. Oh, here she comes.

DIDDLER. [*Aside.*] Now, if she should fall in a passion and discover me!

Enter PEGGY.

PLAINWAY. My dear, this is Mr. Fainwould.

DIDDLER. Madam, your most devoted.

[*She screams; he supports her.*

PEGGY. [*In a low tone.*] Mortimer!

DIDDLER. [*Aside to her.*] Hush! Don't be astonished—you see what I'm at—keep it up.

PLAINWAY. What ails the girl? Oh, I see, she's at her romance
again. Mr. Fainwould, try if you can't bring her about while
I go and fetch my cousin Laury to you.

DIDDLER. No fear, sir; she is coming about. [*Exit* PLAINWAY.]
My dear Peggy! After an age of fruitless search, do I again
hold you in these arms?

PEGGY. Cruel man! How could you torment me with so long an
absence and so long a silence? I've written to you a thousand
times.

DIDDLER. A thousand unlucky accidents have prevented my
receiving your letters, and your address I most fatally lost
not an hour after you gave it to me.

PEGGY. And how did you find it out at last?

DIDDLER. By an accidental rencontre with my rival. I've
hummed him famously, frightened him away from the house,
contrived to get his letter of recommendation, and presented
myself in his stead.

PEGGY. It is enough to know that you are again mine, and now
we'll never part.

DIDDLER. Never if I can help it, I assure you.

PEGGY. Lord, Mortimer, what a change there is in your dress!

DIDDLER. Eh? Yes—I've dressed so on purpose—rather in the
extreme, perhaps—but I thought it would look my vulgar
rival better.

PEGGY. Well thought of; so it will. Here's my father coming
back. I'd better seem a little distant, you know.

DIDDLER. You're right.

Enter PLAINWAY, DIDDLER *not seeming to notice him.*

Do, my dear lady, be merciful. But perhaps it is in mercy that
you thus avert from me the killing lustre of those piercing
eyes.

PLAINWAY. [*Aside.*] Well done, timidity. [*To him.*] Bravo! Mr.
Fainwould, you'll not be long an unsuccessful wooer, I see.
Well, my cousin's coming to see you the moment she's a little
composed. Why, Peg, I fancy the old fool has been gaping out
at window to some purpose at last. I verily believe somebody,

either in jest or in earnest, has really been writing her a billet doux, for I caught her quite in a fluster reading a letter, and the moment she saw me she grappled it up, and her cheeks turned as red as her nose.

DIDDLER. [*Much disconcerted, aside.*] Oh, Lord, here's the riddle unfolded! Curse my blind eyes! What a scrape they've brought me into! A fusty old maid, I suppose. What the devil shall I do? I must humour the blunder or she'll discover me.

PLAINWAY. Here she comes.

DIDDLER. [*Aside.*] Oh Lord! Oh Lord!

Enter MISS DURABLE.

PLAINWAY. Mr. Fainwould, Miss Durable. Miss Durable, Mr. Fainwould.

[MISS DURABLE *screams, and seems much agitated.*

DIDDLER. [*Advancing to her.*] My dear lady, what's the matter? [*Aside to her.*] Don't be astonished. You see what I'm at— keep it up.   [*Continues whispering to her.*

PLAINWAY. Why, what the devil! This fellow frightens my whole family. It must be his officer-like appearance, I suppose.

PEGGY. [*Aside.*] Well, I declare Laurelia means to fall in love with him and supplant me.

MISS DURABLE. [*Aside to* DIDDLER.] Oh, you're a bold adventurous man!

DIDDLER. [*To her.*] Yes, I am a very bold adventurous man, but love, madam——

MISS DURABLE. Hush.

PLAINWAY. Why, Fainwould, you seem to make some impression upon the ladies.

DIDDLER. Not a very favourable one, it would seem, sir.

MISS DURABLE. I beg Mr. Fainwould's pardon, I'm sure. It was merely a slight indisposition that seized me.

PLAINWAY. Oh, a slight indisposition, was it?

PEGGY. [*Aside.*] Yes, I see she's throwing out her lures.

DIDDLER. Will you allow me, madam, to lead you to the air?

PLAINWAY. Aye, suppose we show Mr. Fainwould our garden. A walk will do none of us any harm.

MISS DURABLE. Unless Mr. Fainwould is fatigued with his journey.

DIDDLER. Not in the least, I assure you. Miss Plainway, give me leave. [*Aside, in taking her hand.*] Did you observe that old fool? I believe she has a design upon me.

PEGGY. [*Aside.*] That she has, I'll be sworn.

DIDDLER. [*Aside.*] I'll hum her. Miss Durable, here's the other arm at your service.

MISS DURABLE. [*Taking it.*] Dear sir, you're extremely obliging.

DIDDLER. Don't say so, madam; the obligation is mine. [*Nodding.*] Plainway, you see what a way I'm in.
[*Exeunt* DIDDLER, PEGGY, *and* MISS DURABLE.

PLAINWAY. Bashfulness! Damme, if ever I saw such an impudent dog!   [*Exit.*

ACT II

SCENE I. *The Inn.*

Enter FAINWOULD *and* RICHARD.

FAINWOULD. In short, I never met with such disrespectful treatment since I was born. And so the rascal's name is Diddler, is it?

RICHARD. So I heard the waiters call him.

FAINWOULD. As to the disappointment, Richard, it's a very fortunate one for me, for it must be a scrubby family indeed when one of its branches is forced to have recourse to such low practices. But to be treated with such contempt! Why, am I to be laughed at everywhere?

RICHARD. If I was you, sir, I'd put that question where it's fit it should be answered.

FAINWOULD. And so I will, Richard. If I don't go back and kick up such a bobbery—I warrant I'll—why, he called me a vulgar, conceited, foolish cockney.

RICHARD. No, sure?

FAINWOULD. Yes, but he did—and what a fool my father must have been not to see through such a set—a low-bred rascal with his three and fourpence. But if I don't—I'll take your advice, Richard: I'll hire a postchaise directly, drive to the house, expose that Mr. Diddler, blow up all the rest of the family, Sir Robert Rental included, and then set off for London and turn my back upon 'em for ever.   [*Exeunt.*

Enter SAM, *with a letter, followed by a* MESSENGER.

SAM. Why, but what for do you bring it here?

MESSENGER. Why, because it says to be delivered with all possible speed. I know he comes here sometimes, and most likely won't be at home till night.

SAM. Well, if I see him, I'll gi't to him. Most likely he'll be here by and by.

MESSENGER. Then I'll leave it.   [*Exit.*

SAM. Mr. Jeremiah Diddler. Dang it, what a fine seal, and I'll
be shot if it don't feel like a bank-note. To be delivered wi' all
possible speed, too—I shouldn't wonder, now, if it brought
him some good luck. Ha, ha, ha! wi' all my heart. He's a
droll dog, and I like him vastly.   [*Exit.*

———

SCENE II. *A Room in* PLAINWAY's *House. Four chairs. Wine,
with glasses and dessert, on a table.*

PLAINWAY, DIDDLER, PEGGY, *and* MISS DURABLE *discovered
at table.*

PLAINWAY. Bravo, bravo! Ha, ha, ha!   [*They laugh.*

MISS DURABLE. Upon my word, Mr. Fainwould, you sing
delightfully; you surely have had some practice?

DIDDLER. A little, madam.

MISS DURABLE. Well, I think it must be a very desirable
accomplishment, if it were only for your own entertainment.

DIDDLER. It is in that respect, madam, that I have hitherto
found it most particularly desirable.

MISS DURABLE. But surely the pleasure of pleasing your
hearers——

DIDDLER. I now find to be the highest gratification it can
bestow, except that of giving me a claim to a return in kind
from you. [*Aside to* PEGGY.] I lay it on thick, don't I?

MISS DURABLE. You really must excuse me; I can't perform to
my satisfaction without the assistance of an instrument.

PLAINWAY. Well, well, cousin, then we'll hear you by and by;
there's no hurry, I'm sure. Come, Mr. Fainwould, your glass
is empty.

MISS DURABLE. Peggy, my love.
          [*The* LADIES *rise to retire. Exit* MISS DURABLE.

PLAINWAY. Peg, here, come back; I want to speak with you.

PEGGY. [*Returns.*] Well, papa.

PLAINWAY. Mr. Fainwould, you know I told you of a billet-doux that old Laury had received.

DIDDLER. Yes, sir.

PLAINWAY. Coming through the passage to dinner, I picked it up.

PEGGY *and* DIDDLER. No!

PLAINWAY. Yes; I have it in my pocket—one of the richest compositions you ever beheld. I'll read it to you.

DIDDLER. [*Aside.*] How unlucky! Now if she sees it, she'll know the hand.

PLAINWAY. [*Reads.*] 'To the beautiful maid at the foot of the hill.' Ha, ha, ha!

DIDDLER *and* PEGGY. Ha, ha, ha!

    [DIDDLER *endeavours to keep* PEGGY *from overlooking* PLAINWAY *while he reads.*

PLAINWAY. [*Reads.*] 'Most celestial of terrestrial beings! I have received a wound from your eyes which baffles all surgical skill. The smile of her who gave it is the only balsam that can save it. Let me therefore supplicate admittance to your presence to-morrow, to know at once if I may live or die. That if I'm to live, I may live your fond lover; And if I'm to die, I may get it soon over. Adonis.'

    [*They all laugh.* DIDDLER *appears much disconcerted.*

PLAINWAY. Why, this Adonis must be about as great a fool as his mistress, eh, sir? Ha, ha, ha!

DIDDLER. Yes, sir; he, he, he! [*Aside.*] They've found me out, and this is a quiz.

PEGGY. Or more likely some poor knave, papa, that wants her money—ha, ha, ha!

PLAINWAY. Ha, ha, ha! Or perhaps a compound of both, eh, sir?

DIDDLER. Very likely, sir; he, he, he! [*Aside.*] They're at me.

PLAINWAY. But we must laugh her out of the connection and disappoint the rogue, however; though I dare say he little thought to create so much merriment. So short-sighted is roguery.

DIDDLER. [*Aside.*] Short-sighted! It's all up, to a certainty.

PLAINWAY. So, she's returning, impatient of being left alone, I suppose. Now we'll smoke her——

DIDDLER. [*Aside.*] I'll join the laugh, at all events.

Enter MISS DURABLE.

MISS DURABLE. Bless me, why, I'm quite forsaken among you all——

PLAINWAY. Forsaken, my dear cousin! It's only for age and ugliness to talk of being forsaken; not for a beautiful maid like you—the most celestial of terrestrial beings!

[*All laugh but* MISS DURABLE.

MISS DURABLE. [*Aside.*] I'm astonished—*he* laughing, too!

DIDDLER. [*Aside to her.*] Excuse my laughing; it's only in jest.

MISS DURABLE. In jest, sir?

DIDDLER. Yes.   [*Whispers and winks.*

PLAINWAY. Well, but my dear cousin, I hope you'll be merciful to the tender youth. Such a frown as that, now, would kill him at once.

MISS DURABLE. Cousin Plainway, this insult is intolerable. I'll not stay in your house another hour.

PLAINWAY. Nay, but my dear Laury, I didn't expect that truth would give offence. We'll leave Mr. Fainwould to make our peace with you.

DIDDLER. [*Aside.*] Leave me alone with her! Oh, the devil!

PEGGY. Aye, do, Mr. Fainwould, endeavour to pacify her— pray induce her to continue a little longer the beautiful maid at the foot of the hill.

[*Exeunt* PLAINWAY *and* PEGGY. MISS DURABLE *and* DIDDLER *look sheepishly at each other.*

DIDDLER. [*Aside.*] I'm included in the quiz, as I'm a gentleman. [*To her.*] My dear madam, how could you——

MISS DURABLE. How could I what, sir?

DIDDLER. Wear a pocket with a hole in it?

MISS DURABLE. I wear no pockets, which caused the fatal accident. But sir, I trust it is an accident that will cause no change in your affection.

DIDDLER. [*Aside.*] Damn it! Now she's going to be amorous. [*To her.*] None in the world, madam. I assure you, I love you as much as ever I did——

MISS DURABLE. I fear my conduct is very imprudent. If you should be discovered——

DIDDLER. It's not at all unlikely, madam, that I am already. [*Aside.*] Now she'll be boring me for explanations—I must get her among them again. [*To her.*] Or if I am not, if we don't take great care, I soon shall be: therefore I think we'd better immediately join——

MISS DURABLE. Oh, dear sir! So soon? I declare you quite agitate me with the idea.

DIDDLER. Ma'am!

MISS DURABLE. It is so awful a ceremony, that really a little time——

DIDDLER. My dear ma'am, I didn't mean anything about a ceremony.

MISS DURABLE. Sir!

DIDDLER. You misunderstand me; I——

MISS DURABLE. You astonish me, sir! No ceremony, indeed! And would you then take advantage of my too susceptible heart to ruin me? Would you rob me of my innocence? Would you despoil me of my honour? Cruel, barbarous, inhuman man! [*Affects to faint.*]

DIDDLER. [*Supporting her.*] Upon my soul, madam, I would not interfere with your honour on any account. [*Aside.*] I must make an outrageous speech; there's nothing else will make her easy. [*Falls on his knees.*] Paragon of premature divinity! What instrument of death or torture can equal the dreadful power of your frowns?

Enter PEGGY, *listening.*

Poison, pistols, pikes, steel-traps and spring-guns, the thumb-screw or lead-kettle, the knout or cat o' nine-tails, are impotent compared with the words of your indignation! Cease, then, to wound a heart whose affection for you nothing can abate, whose——

PEGGY. [*Interrupting him, and showing his letter.*] So, sir, this is your fine effusion, and this is the fruit of it. False, infamous man!

DIDDLER. [*Aside to* MISS DURABLE.] I told you so. You'd better retire, and I'll contrive to get off. My dear Miss Plainway——

PEGGY. Don't dear me, sir—I've done with you.

DIDDLER. If you would but hear——

PEGGY. I'll hear nothing, sir; you can't clear yourself. This duplicity can only arise from the meanest of motives, Mr. Mortimer.

MISS DURABLE. Mr. Mortimer! Then I am the dupe, after all.

PEGGY. You're a mean——

MISS DURABLE. Base——

PEGGY. Deceitful——

MISS DURABLE. Abominable——

DIDDLER. [*Aside.*] Here's a breeze! This is raising the wind with a vengeance. My dear Miss Plainway, I—a—my dear Miss Durable, [*Aside.*] pray retire; in five minutes I'll come to you in the garden and explain all to your satisfaction.

MISS DURABLE. And if you don't——

DIDDLER. Oh, I will; now do go.

PEGGY. And you too, madam; aren't you ashamed——

MISS DURABLE. Don't talk to me in that style, miss; it ill becomes me to account for my conduct to you, and I shall therefore leave you with perfect indifference to make your own construction. [*To him.*] You'll find me in the garden, sir.
                                                            [*Exit.*

DIDDLER. [*Aside.*] Floating in the fish-pond, I hope. [*To* PEGGY.] My dear Peggy, how could you for a moment believe——

PEGGY. I'll not listen to you—I'll go and expose you to my father immediately. He'll order the servants to toss you in a blanket, and then to kick you out of doors.

DIDDLER. [*Holding her.*] So, between two stools, poor Jeremy comes to the ground at last. Now, Peggy, my dear Peggy, I know I shall appease you.

PEGGY. If you detain me by force I must stay; and if you will talk I must hear you; but you can't force me to attend to you.

DIDDLER. That's as you please—only hear me. That letter— [*He takes her hand.*] I did write that letter. But as a proof that I love you, and only you, and that I will love you as long as I live, I'll run away with you directly.

PEGGY. Will you, this instant?

DIDDLER. I'll hire a postchaise immediately. [*Aside.*] That is, if I can get credit for one.

PEGGY. Go and order it.

DIDDLER. I'm off. [*Going.*] Nothing but disasters! Here's the cockney coming back in a terrible rage, and I shall be discovered.

PEGGY. How unlucky! Couldn't you get rid of him again?

DIDDLER. Keep out of the way, and I'll try.   [*Exit* PEGGY.

Enter FAINWOULD.

FAINWOULD. So, sir——

DIDDLER. How do you do, again, sir? Hasn't my servant left you three-and-fourpence yet? Bless my soul, how stupid!

FAINWOULD. Sir, I want to see Mr. Plainway.

DIDDLER. Do you, sir? That's unlucky—he's just gone out—to take a walk in the fields. Look through that window and you may see him; there, you see, just under that hedge; now he's getting over a stile. If you like to follow him with me, I'll introduce him to you, but you'd better call again.

FAINWOULD. Sir, I see neither a hedge nor a stile, and I don't believe a word you say.

DIDDLER. [*With affected dignity.*] Don't believe a word I say, sir!

FAINWOULD. No, sir.

DIDDLER. Sir, I desire you'll quit this house.

FAINWOULD. I shan't, sir.

DIDDLER. You shan't, sir?

FAINWOULD. No, sir—my business is with Mr. Plainway. I've a postchaise waiting for me at the door, and therefore have no time to lose.

DIDDLER. A postchaise waiting at the door, sir?

FAINWOULD. Yes, sir; the servant told me Mr. Plainway *was* within, and I'll find him too, or I'm very much mistaken.

[*Exit.*

DIDDLER. A postchaise waiting at the door! We'll bribe the postboy, and jump into it. Now, who shall I borrow a guinea of to bribe the postboy?

Enter JOHN.

JOHN. Has that gentleman found my master, sir?

DIDDLER. Oh yes, John, I showed him into the drawing-room. [JOHN *is going.*] Stop, John, step this way. Your name is John, isn't it?

JOHN. Yes, sir.

DIDDLER. Well, how d'ye do, John? Got a snug place here, John?

JOHN. Yes, sir, very snug.

DIDDLER. Aye—good wages, good vails, eh?

JOHN. Yes, sir, very fair.

DIDDLER. Um—you haven't got such a thing as a guinea about you, have you?

JOHN. No, sir.

DIDDLER. Aye—that's all, John, I only asked for information. [*Exit* JOHN.] Gad—I said a civil thing or two to the gardener just now. I'll go and try him; and, to prevent all further rencontres, make my escape through the garden-gate.

[*Going.*

Enter MISS DURABLE.

Oh, Lord! Here is old innocence again.

MISS DURABLE. Well, sir, I'm all impatient for this explanation. So you've got rid of Miss Peggy.

DIDDLER. Yes, I have pacified her, and she's retired to the—drawing-room. I was just coming to—you haven't got such a thing as a guinea about you, madam, have you? A troublesome postboy that drove me this morning is teasing me for his money. You see, I happened unfortunately to change my small——

MISS DURABLE. Oh, these things will happen, sir. [*Gives a purse.*] There's my purse, sir; take whatever you require.

DIDDLER. I'm robbing you, ma'am.

MISS DURABLE. Not at all—you know you'll soon return it.

DIDDLER. [*Aside.*] That's rather doubtful. [*To her.*] I'll be with you again, madam, in a moment.   [*Going.*

MISS DURABLE. What, sir! So even your postboys are to be attended to before me.

DIDDLER. Ma'am!

MISS DURABLE. But I see through your conduct, sir. This is a mere expedient to avoid me again. This is too much.

DIDDLER. [*Aside.*] What the devil shall I do now? Oh! Oh, dear! Oh, Lord!

MISS DURABLE. What's the matter?

DIDDLER. Your cruelty has so agitated me—I faint—a little water—a little water will recover me. [*Falls into a chair.*] Pray get me a little water!

MISS DURABLE. Bless me, he's going into hysterics! Help—help—John, Betty, a little water immediately!
                              [*Exit.* DIDDLER *runs off.*

Enter FAINWOULD.

FAINWOULD. Nowhere to be found. So Mr. Diddler is gone now. They've found me out by my letter, and avoid me on purpose. But I'll not stir out of the house till I see Mr. Plainway, I'm determined; so I'll sit myself quietly down. [*Sits down in the chair* DIDDLER *has left.*] I'll make the whole family treat me with a little more respect, I warrant.

Enter MISS DURABLE, *hastily, with a glass of water which she throws in his face. She screams; he rises in a fury.*

FAINWOULD. Damnation, madam! What d'ye mean?

MISS DURABLE. Oh, dear sir! I took you for another gentleman.

FAINWOULD. Nonsense, madam! You couldn't mean to serve any gentleman in this way. Where is Mr. Plainway? I'll have satisfaction for this treatment.

Enter PLAINWAY.

PLAINWAY. Hey-dey! Hey-dey, cousin! Why, who is this gentleman, and what is all this noise about?

MISS DURABLE. I'm sure, cousin, I don't know who the gentleman is. All that I can explain is that Mr. Fainwould was taken ill in that chair; that I went to get some water to recover him; and the moment after, when I came back, I found his place occupied by that gentleman.

FAINWOULD. Madam, this is no longer a time for bantering. You found Mr. Fainwould's place occupied by me, who am Mr. Fainwould; and you found him suffering no illness at all, though you wanted to give me one.

PLAINWAY *and* MISS DURABLE. You Mr. Fainwould!

FAINWOULD. Yes, sir; and you've found out by this time, I suppose, that I'm perfectly acquainted with all your kind intentions towards me—that I know of your new son-in-law, Sir Robert Rental—that I am informed I am to make merriment for you—and that, if I am refractory, your nephew Mr. Diddler is to pull my nose.

PLAINWAY. Sir Robert Rental, and my nephew Mr. Diddler! Why, Laury, this is some madman broke loose. My dear sir, I haven't a nephew in the world, and never heard of such people as Sir Robert Rental or Mr. Diddler in the whole course of my life.

FAINWOULD. This is amazing!

PLAINWAY. It is, upon my soul! You say your name is Fainwould?

FAINWOULD. Certainly!

PLAINWAY. Then nothing but the appearance of the other Mr. Fainwould can solve the riddle.

FAINWOULD. The other Mr. Fainwould!

PLAINWAY. Yes, sir: there is another gentleman so calling himself now in this house, and he was bearer of a letter of introduction from——

FAINWOULD. My letter of introduction! The rascal picked my pocket of it in this very house this morning—I see through it all! I dare say your house is robb'd by this time.

PLAINWAY. A villain! Why, where is he, cousin? Here, John— where are all the servants?

Enter JOHN.

PLAINWAY. Where is Mr. Fainwould?

JOHN. What, the other, sir?

PLAINWAY. The other, sir? Then you knew this gentleman's name was Fainwould, and you never told me he was here this morning.

JOHN. Yes, sir, I did; I sent you to him.

PLAINWAY. You sent me to the other fellow.

JOHN. No, sir, I did not let in the other.

PLAINWAY. I suppose he got in at the window, then. But where is he now?

JOHN. I'm sure I don't know, sir, but I thought that gentleman was gone.

FAINWOULD. Why did you think so, sir?

JOHN. Because, sir, the chaise is gone that you came in.

PLAINWAY. What!

FAINWOULD. Gone!

JOHN. Yes, sir.

PLAINWAY. Why, then, the rascal's run off in it—and Peg— where is she? Where is my daughter?

MISS DURABLE. Gone with him, cousin.

JOHN. Here they are, sir.   [*Exit.*

Enter DIDDLER, PEGGY, *and* SAM. DIDDLER *dancing and singing.*

PLAINWAY. Sing away, my brave fellow; I'll soon change your note.

DIDDLER. Thank'ye, sir; but it is chang'd already. Sam, pay my debts to that young man, three-and-fourpence, [*Pointing to* FAINWOULD.] and give him credit for a breakfast on my account. Ah, my dear old innocence! [*To* MISS DURABLE.] There's your purse again. When I'm at leisure, you shall have your explanation.

MISS DURABLE. Oh, false Adonis!

PLAINWAY. And now, sir, what have you to answer to——

DIDDLER. I plead guilty to it all. I've been a sad rogue, but as a proof I've some conscience left, here's your daughter, just as I found her. Don't give her to me unless you like.

PLAINWAY. Give her to you! And pray, sir, what claim have you to her?

DIDDLER. 'Not my desserts, but what I will deserve.' My resolution to lead a new life, with the trifling collateral recommendation of ten thousand pounds in my pocket——

PLAINWAY. Ten thousand pounds in *your* pocket!

DIDDLER. In brief, sir, you shall hear my case. Idle habits, empty pockets, and the wrath of an offended uncle made me the shabby dog you see before you. But my angry uncle has on his death-bed relented. This fine fat-headed fellow arrested our flight through the town to put into my hand this letter, announcing the handsome bequest I have just mentioned, and enclosing me a hundred-pound note as earnest of his sincerity.

SAM. Yes, I'm witness to the truth of all that, and——

DIDDLER. [*Stopping his mouth.*] That's enough, Sam—the less we say the better. I shall be steady now, Plainway, I shall indeed; I've felt too much my past degradation not to make the best use of my present good fortune.

PLAINWAY. Um! I imagine you are the Mr. Mortimer she sometimes sighs about.

DIDDLER. The same, sir. At Bath, under that name, and under somewhat better appearances, I had the honour to captivate her. Hadn't I, Peggy?

PEGGY. And isn't that your name, then?

DIDDLER. No, my dear, my legitimate appellation is Mr. Diddler.

PEGGY. What! And am I to have a lover of the name of Diddler?

SAM. I'm sure Mrs. Diddler's a very pretty name.

DIDDLER. Don't be rude, Sam.

PLAINWAY. Well, sir, your promises are fair, there's no denying; but whether it would be fair to attend to them depends entirely upon that gentleman.

FAINWOULD. As to me, Mr. Plainway, if your daughter has taken a fancy for another, I can't help it. Only let her refuse me respectfully, and I'm satisfied.

DIDDLER. You are a very sensible fellow, and we have all a very high respect for you.

FAINWOULD. I'm satisfied.

DIDDLER. But I shall not be satisfied without the hope that all such poor idle rogues as I have been may learn by my disgraceful example——

> Howe'er to vice or indolence inclin'd,
> By honest industry to RAISE THE WIND.

[*Curtain.*

MR. PAUL PRY

OR I HOPE I DON'T INTRUDE

A COMIC SKETCH IN THREE ACTS

BY

DOUGLAS WILLIAM JERROLD (1803–1857)

———

First performed at the Coburg Theatre
10 April 1826

———

CAST

PAUL PRY	Mr. Davidge
OLDBUTTON	Mr. Rowbotham
SIR SPANGLE RAINBOW	Mr. E. L. Lewis
CAPTAIN HASELTON	Mr. Hemmings
POMMADE	Mr. Young
BILLY	Mr. Buckstone
TANKARD	Mr. Goldsmith
LAURA	Mrs. Young
CRIMP	Mrs. Davidge

———

SCENE

Dover

PREFACE TO *MR. PAUL PRY*

O F the farces in this volume *Mr. Paul Pry*—as it was entitled on the Coburg playbills—is only one of two to have been originally performed outside the West End. Before 1843 doubts about whether farce was part of the 'legitimate' drama—directly contrary opinions were advanced—compelled some of the West End minor theatres (in delicate proximity to the patent houses) to add a few songs to them and call them 'burlettas'; even the Coburg called *Mr. Paul Pry* a 'Comic Sketch', although it was in three acts. The character of the Coburg itself and of the drama performed there was different from that of Drury Lane, Covent Garden, and the Haymarket. The West End minor theatre it most resembled in repertory was the Adelphi; the fondness for physical business in Jerrold's farce—unusual in the West End at the time—can also be found in Adelphi farces of the 1830s and 1840s.

When he wrote *Mr. Paul Pry*, Jerrold was house dramatist for Davidge at the Coburg and was completely unknown. In 1829 he moved over to Elliston at the Surrey for £5 a week, where *Black-Eyed Susan*, though an enormous success there, in the rest of London, and all over the country, brought Jerrold himself only £60. At the Coburg Davidge paid him little, and he could not have made much out of *Mr. Paul Pry* additional to his salary. Davidge declared that the largest sum he had ever given a dramatist (and not Jerrold) was fifty guineas; his average payment for a new piece was about £20.[1] In fact Jerrold could never make an adequate living from playwriting, either at the Coburg or the Surrey or from the plays he later wrote for Covent Garden, Drury Lane, the Haymarket, and other theatres. He eventually left dramatic authorship for journalism, where the remuneration was higher.[2]

Mr. Paul Pry is a version of a comedy by John Poole, *Paul Pry*, performed at the Haymarket in 1825. In comparing the two plays it is interesting to see how a dramatist went about

---

[1] *Report from the Select Committee on Dramatic Literature* (1832), p. 78.
[2] For Jerrold see also Volume One, p. 155.

turning a comedy into a farce, and how within the framework of the same basic idea the two genres do indeed differ sharply when this idea is developed with different comic objectives in view. To begin with, Jerrold did not use all of Poole's plot material. In the latter's play Witherton's housekeeper Mrs. Subtle schemes to marry her master, who has become dependent on her. Grasp, Witherton's steward, in past collusion with Mrs. Subtle in suppressing the affectionate letters of their master's nephew, struggles with her for control over Witherton. However, the nephew, Willis, whom his uncle has disinherited for marrying without permission (the letters requesting permission were also intercepted), and his wife have been living incognito with Witherton as companion and deputy housekeeper respectively, observing the machinations of Mrs. Subtle at first hand. The other plot concerns the plans of the blustery and authoritarian Captain Hardy to marry his daughter Eliza to a man whom he refuses to name. Eliza's true love arrives, pretends to be a nephew whom Hardy has never seen, and plans an elopement, aided by her clever maidservant Phoebe. It turns out that Hardy all along intended Eliza for her lover. The more serious plot is concluded by the exposure of Grasp and Mrs. Subtle. Paul Pry himself is a character with the same qualities as in Jerrold's farce, but, despite the fact that he is the principal comic figure, has no real plot function. He intrudes comically in both plots, but becomes significantly involved only at the end of the play when he fishes up Willis's letters from a well where Mrs. Subtle hid them; the proof of their existence leads to her downfall. Jerrold discarded the Subtle–Witherton plot, simplified and lightened the Colonel Hardy–Eliza plot, and centred his farce firmly on Paul Pry. All Jerrold's characters except Laura and perhaps Oldbutton are comic, but of Poole's characters Grasp and Mrs. Subtle are villains, Witherton, Willis and his wife are entirely serious. Captain Haselton's foppish, cowardly rival, Sir Spangle Rainbow and his French valet—both low-comedy parts—are not in the cast of *Paul Pry*. The setting of the comedy is much more refined than that of the farce, the action taking place largely in the houses and gardens of two country gentlemen, with only two short scenes laid in the inn. Most of the action in the farce is set in the inn. Pry dominates the farce, and the eccentric character he possesses in the comedy is coloured even further: he is more curious; he 'intrudes' more often, and the soliloquies in which he ponders everybody's affairs are longer and more numerous. His part is enlarged and he is much more of a comic butt. In the comedy Pry is only once mixed up in physical business (which happens off stage), arriving in Hardy's house out of breath with his clothes torn, having been chased by dogs. But in the farce he is sat on, jabbed in the rear by a red-hot poker, pitched through a transom, blown up by fireworks, discovered hiding in a cradle, and stuck in the face with a foil while peeping through a keyhole—all these incidents occurring on stage. Finally, in Poole's play Eliza's lover merely hides in her bedroom to avoid Hardy; in Jerrold's his equivalent is disguised as a washerwoman. In these ways Jerrold made a fast-paced farce out of a rather slack comedy. Comically he much improved his original; the only thing that could not be improved was the acting of Liston as Poole's Paul Pry.

Mr. Paul Pry played six consecutive weeks for a total of thirty-seven performances during the Coburg summer season. The text printed is that in *Duncombe's British Theatre*, v. 1, the earliest and most authoritative acting edition. *Lacy's Acting Edition of Plays*, v. 47 and *Dicks' Standard Plays*, no. 982, identical except for punctuation, alter, subtract from, and add to the *Duncombe*, as well as fitting its three acts and seven scenes into two acts and five scenes. Since the Coburg was outside the Lord Chamberlain's licensing authority, there is no manuscript of *Mr. Paul Pry* in the Lord Chamberlain's collection.

ACT I

SCENE I. *Dover. Room in the Golden Chariot.*

Enter TANKARD *and* BILLY.

TANKARD. Now, Billy, as this is the first week of your service, you must stir about you—look well to the customers, and see they want nothing.

BILLY. I warrant me, sir, though the folks says I look harmless, I'm sharp; I carry my wits about me in a case, as my grandmother carries her scissars: but sir, when I like I can draw and cut, I assure you.

TANKARD. Well, this is to be proved. Now you know what you have to do to-day?

BILLY. First there's to attend to Captain Hawkesley in the blue room, he that locks himself up all day and only comes out with the stars. Then there's to look to the fire-works when the company arrives. Then there's to get ready the room that you call the Elephant for the new company, Mr. Oldbutton and his ward; and—and the last of all——

TANKARD. To get rid of that Paul Pry.

BILLY. I'll do it, sir.

TANKARD. Will you? It's more than I can. I have only taken this inn six months, and he's been here every day. First he asked me where I got the money to take the house; then if I was married, whether my wife bore an excellent character, whether my children had had the measles—and as I wouldn't answer any of these questions, he hoped he didn't intrude, but begged to know how many lumps of sugar I put into a crown bowl of punch.

BILLY. Oh, sir, that's nothing to what he asked me last night— he asked me whether you gave me good wages.

TANKARD. Well, and I hope you gave him an answer.

BILLY. Yes I did, sir.

TANKARD. What did you say?

BILLY. Why, I told him my wages were like his good manners, very little of 'em; but I hoped they would both soon mend.

TANKARD. Well, Billy, only rid me of this infernal Paul and your wages shall mend. Here has this Mr. Pry, although he has an establishment of his own in the town, been living and sleeping here these six days; but I am determined to get rid of him, and do you instantly go, Billy, and affront him. Do any thing with him, so as you make him turn his back upon the house. Eh, here's a coach driven up—it is surely Mr. Old-button! Run, Billy, run! [*Exit* BILLY.] Roaring times, these.

Enter CRIMP *and* BILLY, *showing in* OLDBUTTON *and* LAURA.

TANKARD. Welcome, sir—and welcome, ladies, to the Golden Chariot.

OLDBUTTON. Landlord, let the lady be shown to her room. I have some letters to answer, which will engage me a short time; I will afterwards rejoin you. [BILLY *shows off* LAURA *and* CRIMP.] Now, landlord, which is my apartment?

TANKARD. Why, sir—. [*Aside.*] Confound that Paul Pry, he has the gentleman's room, and I can't get him out of it! Why, sir, I did not expect you some hours yet; if you'll have the kindness to step into this apartment for a few minutes, your own room shall be properly arranged. I really beg ten thousand——

OLDBUTTON. No compliments, Mr. Landlord; and when you speak to me in future, keep yourself upright—I hate tradesmen with backs of whalebone.

TANKARD. Why, civility, Mr. Oldbutton——

OLDBUTTON. Is this the room?
  [TANKARD *bows, and* OLDBUTTON *goes through door in flat,* L.C.

TANKARD. Now such a customer would deeply offend a man if he had not the ultimate satisfaction of making out his bill.

Enter BILLY.

Oh, you've just come in time. Ask no questions—there's Mr. Pry's room: if you get him out of the house, I'll raise your

wages; if you do not, you shall go yourself. Now you know
the terms.   [*Exit.*

BILLY. Then it's either you or myself, Mr. Pry, so here goes.
[*As* BILLY *is running towards the room, he sees* PAUL *with
his head out of door in flat,* R.C., *listening.*

PAUL. Hope I don't intrude. I say, Billy, who are these people
just come in?

BILLY. People! Why, there's nobody come in.

PAUL. Don't fib, Billy; I saw them.

BILLY. You saw them! Why, how could you see them when
there's no window in the room?

PAUL. I always guard against such an accident, and carry a
gimblet with me. [*Producing one.*] Nothing like making a
little hole in the wainscoat.

BILLY. Why, surely you haven't——

PAUL. It has been a fixed principle of my life, Billy, never to
take a lodging or a house with a brick wall to it. I say—tell
me, who are they?

BILLY. [*Aside.*] Well, I'll tell him something. Why, if you must
know, I think he's an army lieutenant on half-pay, and that
young lady is his ward—or niece—or something——

PAUL. An army lieutenant—half-pay! Ah, that will never afford
ribbons and white feathers.

BILLY. Now, Mr. Pry, my master desires me to say he can't
accommodate you any longer. Your apartment is wanted;
and really, Mr. Pry, you can't think how you'd oblige me by
going.

PAUL. To be sure, Billy; I wouldn't wish to intrude for the
world. Your master's doing a great deal of business in this
house—what did he give for the good-will of it?

VOICE. [*Without.*] Billy!

BILLY. There now, I'm called—and I've to make ready the
room for the Freemasons that meet to-night: they that
wouldn't admit you into their society.

PAUL. Yes, I know—they thought I should intrude.

VOICE. [*Without.*] Billy!

BILLY. Now you must go—good bye, Mr. Pry—I'm called.

PAUL. Oh, good bye—good morning. [*Exit.*

BILLY. He's gone. I'm coming, sir! [*Exit.*

Re-enter PAUL PRY.

PAUL. An army lieutenant! Who can it be? I shouldn't wonder if it's Mrs. Thomas's husband, who she says was killed in India. If it should be it will break off her flirting with Mr. Cinnamon, the grocer: there's pretty doings in that quarter, for I caught the rheumatism watching their frolics in a frosty night last winter. An army lieutenant! Mrs. Thomas has a daughter. I'll just peep through the key-hole and see if there's a family likeness between them. [*Goes to the door and peeps.*] Bless me, why, there certainly is something about the nose— eh! he's writing.

[*The door is suddenly opened by* OLDBUTTON, *who discovers* PAUL.

PAUL. Hope I don't intrude—I was trying to find my apartment.

OLDBUTTON. Was it necessary to look through the key-hole for it, sir?

PAUL. I'm rather short-sighted, sir—sad affliction: my poor mother was short-sighted, sir—in fact, it's a family failing— all the Prys are obliged to look close.

OLDBUTTON. Whilst I sympathize with your distresses, sir, I trust to be exempt from the impertinence which you may attach to them.

PAUL. Would not intrude for the world, sir. What may be your opinion, sir, of the present state of the kingdom? How do you like peace? It must press hard upon you gentlemen of the army; a lieutenant's half-pay now is but little to make both ends meet.

OLDBUTTON. Sir!

PAUL. Especially when a man's benevolent to his poor relations. Now, sir, perhaps you allow something out of your five and sixpence a day to your mother, or a maiden sister. Between you and me, I must tell you what I've learnt here.

OLDBUTTON. Between you and me, sir, I must tell you what I have learnt in India.

PAUL. What, have you been in India? Wouldn't intrude an observation for the world, but I thought you had a yellowish look—something of an orange-peeling countenance. You've been in India? Although I'm a single man I wouldn't ask an improper question, but is it true that the blacks employ no tailors or milliners—if not, what do they do to keep off the flies?

OLDBUTTON. That is what I was about to inform you—they carry canes. Now, sir, five minutes conversation with you has fully convinced me that there are flies in England as well as in Hindostan, and that a man may be as impertinently inquisitive at Dover as at Bengal. All I have to add is—I carry a cane.

PAUL. In such a case, I'm the last to intrude—I've only one question to ask. Is your name Thomas, whether you have a wife, how old she is, and where you were married?

OLDBUTTON. Well, sir, a man may sometimes play with a puppy, as well as kick him; and if it will afford you any satisfaction, learn my name is Thomas——

PAUL. Oh, poor Mr. Cinnamon! This is going to India. Mr. T., I'm afraid you'll find that somebody here has intruded in your place—for between you and me—[OLDBUTTON *surveys him contemptuously, and walks into his room.*] Well, it isn't that I interfere much in people's concerns; if I did, how unhappy I could make that man. This Freemason's sign puzzles me: they wouldn't make me a member—but I've slept six nights in the next room to them, and thanks to my gimblet, I know the business. There was Mr. Smith, who was only in the Gazette last week, taking his brandy and water; he can't afford that, I know. Then there was Mr. Hodgkins, who makes his poor wife and children live upon baked potatoes six days out of the week (for I know the shop where they are cooked), calling like a lord for a Welch rabbit: I only wish his creditors could see him—but I don't trouble my head with these matters—if I did——eh! Why there's one of the young Joneses going again to Mr. Notick, the pawnbroker's—that's the third time this week. Well, I've just time enough to run to Notick's and see what he has brought before I go to enquire at the Post-office who in the town has letters.   [*Exit.*

SCENE II. *A Room in the Inn. A Fire-place in back. A Sofa, upon which is a large Scarf.*

Enter LAURA *and* CRIMP.

LAURA. You surely must be mistaken, Crimp.

CRIMP. Never trust me, then, madam. I saw Captain Haselton at the window as we drove up, and he looked almost as amiable as he used to appear when he paid me for planning assignations and back-staircase escapes.

LAURA. But you know, Crimp, Mr. Oldbutton, who is a very odd sort of a man, has destined me for Sir Spangle Rainbow.

CRIMP. For Sir Spangle Rainbow! Now, if he were the last man in the world I wouldn't have him!

LAURA. You wouldn't?

CRIMP. No, I—eh! The last man, did I say—why, perhaps that's promising too much. But lord, madam, talking about being designed for Sir Spangle—I've no notion of such designing indeed. It's having a wife per order—it's likening us dear little women to so many parcels of grocery in thus packing us up, labelling, and sending us home to one particular customer. Do you take my advice, madam—run away with Captain Haselton, and get married at once.

LAURA. Married! I declare, Crimp, I'm terrified at the idea.

CRIMP. Why, the idea is shocking to be sure, but I've heard say that marriage is like bathing in cold water; we stand shivering a long time at the edge, when it's only one plunge, and all is over.

LAURA. Then you know that Mr. Oldbutton, as uncle to Captain Haselton, is highly incensed with him for having gambled away his fortune.

CRIMP. No matter; as I know you wish to see the Captain, I will endeavour to decoy him hither.

LAURA. Not for the world! Should we be discovered——

CRIMP. Leave that to me. Do you retire within your chamber, and I'll go and reconnoitre. Oh, how fortunate you ought to think yourself in having so prudent and clever a person as myself! Now don't stir till I come back.

[CRIMP *goes off. Exit* LAURA *into room,* R.

Enter PAUL PRY, *at back.*

PAUL. Nobody here? I wouldn't wish to intrude, but——. [*Sees scarf upon sofa.*] Oh, ho! This is the apartment of Mr. Thomas's young lady. Eh! Something smuggled about this, I've no doubt—they can't afford to dress in this manner, I know. Eh! Somebody coming, bringing a young man in here—Miss does deal in smuggled articles indeed. I'll just crouch down and listen.

[*He throws himself along the sofa, entirely covering himself with the scarf.*

Enter CAPTAIN HASELTON *and* CRIMP.

HASELTON. My dear Crimp, I can't express how much I am indebted to you, and if I were not brought to my last five pounds——

CRIMP. You'd give me the whole; as it is, I suppose I must only hope for half.

HASELTON. Crimp, you have but one error—you are too fond of money.

CRIMP. My dear sir, that's the only fault I find in you. These things, sir, are merely the little perquisites of office: a young lady in love is as profitable to her chambermaid as a consumptive patient to the physician. All we have to do, sir, is to take the fees and let the malady work its own cure. But here, sir, is Miss Laura, and now for raptures.

Enter LAURA.

LAURA. Captain Haselton, my surprise at finding you here is——

HASELTON. Let me hope but equal to your pleasure; believe me, my charming love——

CRIMP. Oh! I suppose I may go now, madam. You see the advantage of having an intelligent waiting-woman; I know when 'loves' and 'doves' begins to fly about, the presence of a third person acts as a scarecrow. I wouldn't spoil the precious minutes; I am a woman of experience, and have my own feelings on these occasions—I'll go watch.   [*Exit.*

LAURA. Is this true, Haselton? Have you sacrificed your wealth and good name to the monster—gaming?

HASELTON. Aye, Laura, of my wealth every doit past redemption. My good name I may yet recover with my sword; but, alas! instead of having a soldier's laurels around my brow——

PAUL. [*Aside.*] You may have the hangman's hemp about your neck. I've just popped in here in time.

LAURA. Nay, away with sad reflection; we must by some means amend your fortune. What can I do?

PAUL. [*Aside.*] I shouldn't wonder if he was to ask her to buy a lottery-ticket, or to go him halves in a Little-Go.

HASELTON. My generous Laura, nothing. I yet trust my uncle will restore me to his favour when——

   [HASELTON *and* LAURA *are, during the foregoing, drawing up to the sofa, and at length both sit upon* PAUL.

PAUL. [*Jumping up.*] I hope I don't intrude.   [LAURA *shrieks.*

HASELTON. [*Seizing* PAUL.] Scoundrel! Your life shall answer——

CRIMP runs in.

CRIMP. Oh, ma'am, Captain——ah! [*Screams at seeing* PAUL.] My master! My master's coming!

HASELTON. My uncle! Now then, I cannot delay. [*To* PAUL.] Dare to follow me, and I'll pin you to the earth!   [*Exit.*

PAUL. I'm afraid I've intruded here.

OLDBUTTON. [*Without.*] Crimp! Crimp, I say!

CRIMP. [*To* PAUL.] Oh, go along—go along—we shall be ruined!

PAUL. But where am I to go? Am I to die the death of a cockchafer, and have cold iron run through my bowels? Eh! the chimney.

   [PAUL *goes into the chimney, and places the board before him.*

CRIMP. Now, madam, you must faint.

LAURA. Faint!

CRIMP. If you don't scream and faint too, we are ruined. Oh, oh!   [CRIMP *screams for her, and puts* LAURA *in a chair.*

Enter OLDBUTTON.

OLDBUTTON. What—what is the matter?

CRIMP. Oh, sir—my poor mistress—she has fainted.

OLDBUTTON. Fainted! From what cause?

CRIMP. The—the—that's it, sir.

OLDBUTTON. What's it?

CRIMP. The room's so hot, sir. My dear madam, pray compose yourself.

OLDBUTTON. Hot!

CRIMP. I mean so cold, sir.

OLDBUTTON. Well, we'll have a fire. Waiter!

Enter BILLY.

CRIMP. No, sir—no fire for the world.

OLDBUTTON. Never tell me. Light a fire here directly.

BILLY. Yes, sir, the fire is laid—so I've only to put a red-hot poker to it.   [*Exit.*

OLDBUTTON. How do you find yourself, Laura?

CRIMP. Oh, she's quite well, sir.

Re-enter BILLY, *with a red-hot poker.*

BILLY. I'll light the fire directly.
   [*Runs up, takes away the chimney-board, and without observing* PAUL, *who has his back turned to the audience and his head up the chimney, thrusts the red-hot poker against him.*

PAUL. Damme, but you intrude! Oh, Lord!
   [*The women scream*—BILLY *chases* PAUL *round the stage with the poker*—TANKARD *comes in—there is a general shout of* 'Paul Pry.' *Picture, and Act closes.*

ACT II

SCENE I. *View of Dover.*

Enter SIR SPANGLE RAINBOW *and* LA POMMADE.

SIR SPANGLE. Pommade, what do you think of Dover—is it not a beautiful place?

POMMADE. Oh, qu'oui, c'est belle—it is ver handsome.

SIR SPANGLE. And yet it is not altogether so elegant.

POMMADE. Oh, 'tis damn bad.

SIR SPANGLE. You know, Pommade, I have journeyed here to gallant my future wife. I don't admire this sort of thing; it is like making one play with the halter before one is hanged. Besides, these matters are by no means novel to me.

POMMADE. Assurément, non; you have played so long vid de halter dat, be gar, it is vonder you vas not hanged long ago.

SIR SPANGLE. Have you any meaning in what you say, rascal?

POMMADE. Meaning! I never have no meaning in dat que je dis, vat I say.

SIR SPANGLE. You had better not, for in the first place, sir, it would be doing what I never presume to do.

POMMADE. Chevalier—vous me payez des gages; you pay me de vages, and veder you mean ever so much, or not noting at all, I sall be as like you as two—two—vat dey give de pigeons à manger, to eat—two peas.

SIR SPANGLE. A good servant.

POMMADE. Chevalier, did you ever see de tings a top of de house—did you ever see de—de—de—cock of de veather?

SIR SPANGLE. The weather-cock you mean.

POMMADE. C'est égal, de vedercock. Vell, ven it blow east it stand—so, vest—so, north—so, south—so, and ven it no blow one vay, it swing about all vay. Now, I am de vedercock, and you are de vind; I stand before you mouth, and turn vich vay you speak; and ven you only visper, I swing about too.

Enter PAUL PRY.

PAUL. Hope I don't intrude. Fine day, sir.

SIR SPANGLE. Very fine, though much warmer than yesterday.

PAUL. Excuse me, I must say that, than yesterday, I never felt it warmer in all my life. Frenchman that, you have with you. Hope I don't intrude, but is that the way in which all Frenchmen dress?

POMMADE. The way—c'est la mode; it is de fashion.

PAUL. Just the way we treat the poodle dogs, I declare: make them discard their long coats and only wear spencers. You see, monsieur, I'm a very plain man.

POMMADE. Yes, damned plain.

PAUL. I am quite John Bull, eh?

POMMADE. No, you are not, you are not yet old enough.

PAUL. Not old enough?

POMMADE. No, you are not Jean *Bull* yet; you are now only Jean *Calf*.   [*Exit.*

PAUL. Between you and me, sir, that's a sharp youth.

SIR SPANGLE. He is now, sir, though it's all owing to me; he was quite a rusty nail at first, but long intercourse with me has——

PAUL. Oh, I see; the nail has rubbed so long against brass that it has at length gained a polish: hope my remarks don't intrude. [*Aside.*] Wonder who he is? Must know—excuse me, sir—bless me, I've a sudden pain in my head—have popped out without my handkerchief; could you lend me yours, just to apply to my forehead? I'd take it very kind of you.

SIR SPANGLE. [*Aside.*] Rather an odd request—certainly, sir.
    [*Gives him handkerchief.*

PAUL. Much obliged. [*Looks at corner of handkerchief and reads.*] 'S. R. No. 10.' S. R.! Who can that be? I shouldn't wonder if it's Samuel Robinson, Esq., the new member. [*Returns it.*] Thankee, sir; the pain has quite left me. You are come down to canvass, Mr. Robinson, I presume. Between you and me, there is Mrs. Wilkins, the grocer's wife; she always makes her husband vote as she likes, and if——

SIR SPANGLE. Come to canvass? No, sir, I am come here for a wife.

PAUL. What, a married man?

SIR SPANGLE. No, sir, only contracted.

PAUL. Oh, half-done, like a parboiled turkey.

SIR SPANGLE. A parboiled turkey! Damme, sir, what do you mean? I suppose next you'll compare me to a roasted pig.

PAUL. No, nothing like it—never compare you to a roasted pig. No, never, never.

SIR SPANGLE. And why not?

PAUL. A great reason to the contrary. Because when we roast a pig——

SIR SPANGLE. Well, sir?

PAUL. We always put his brains in a plate—now there you'd puzzle us.

SIR SPANGLE. Sir, I have a sword.

PAUL. I've only a pen-knife—so you've the long odds against me.

SIR SPANGLE. When I am married I shall have more time to quarrel with you.

PAUL. Don't you think the lady will keep your hands employed?

SIR SPANGLE. Well, we won't quarrel—I see you are a clever fellow, so I can ask your advice. Have you seen anything of a Captain Hawkesley about here?

PAUL. Hawkesley? What kind of a man is he—tall?

SIR SPANGLE. Yes.

PAUL. Dark complexioned?

SIR SPANGLE. Yes.

PAUL. Something of an aquiline nose?

SIR SPANGLE. Exactly.

PAUL. Stoops a little in the shoulder?

SIR SPANGLE. The same.

PAUL. Has a mole upon his cheek, and an odd twist of the hand?

SIR SPANGLE. The very man!

PAUL. Then I haven't seen any body like him.

SIR SPANGLE. Can you give me no intelligence?

PAUL. Why, there's a gentleman in the house—I hope I don't intrude—but will you tell me every thing about this business?

SIR SPANGLE. Every thing. There's an officer who owes me an immense sum of money—would you believe it, there's a bailiff very near at hand.

PAUL. Yes, I can very easily believe it, seeing you so close— but do you intend to arrest?

SIR SPANGLE. Assuredly—he shall touch the iron bars—he shall peep through a grating.

PAUL. But how did he owe you all this money?

SIR SPANGLE. At the gaming table—he had not the ready cash, so I made him sign a bond—a bond; you see I always preserve sheep-skin before any thing else.

PAUL. And yet it strikes me, if you were in personal danger, you would preserve ass's skin before any thing else.

SIR SPANGLE. Did you speak?

PAUL. Who?

SIR SPANGLE. You!

PAUL. When?

SIR SPANGLE. Now!

PAUL. No!

SIR SPANGLE. Oh!   [*Exeunt.*

SCENE II. *Another room in the Inn.*

Enter OLDBUTTON *and* CRIMP.

OLDBUTTON. Very mysterious, all this, Mistress Crimp.

CRIMP. Very, sir. But how the man got into the room, I assure you, sir, upon the word and honour of a single young woman, I can't imagine——you don't suspect me, I hope?

OLDBUTTON. Well, I shall not stay long here, so it matters but little—yet I must confess there are strange freaks carried on in this house.

CRIMP. Freaks, sir, I think you may call 'em—it's quite dangerous, sir—men here in sofas and chimneys—law, Mr. Oldbutton, a young woman never knows when she's safe— her feelings are always in a flurry; you would not believe how I tremble now, sir.

OLDBUTTON. Oh, I dare say you have, with all ladies'-maids, your due share of sensibility: you are a very clever girl, Crimp, and I've no doubt, to serve your own or your mistress's turn, would go into hysterics on the shortest notice. I am going into my room, and do not let me be disturbed. I expect Sir Spangle Rainbow every minute, and only by him can I be seen. As soon as he arrives he shall marry Laura, and——

CRIMP. Marry Miss Laura, sir! You don't mean it!

OLDBUTTON. But I do mean it—I have promised her to my nephew, but he has turned out a gamester, and I discard him. Now I don't believe Sir Spangle ever touched a dice-box in his life.

CRIMP. Yes, sir, but he's not half such a nice man as Captain Haselton.

OLDBUTTON. A nice man, Mrs. Topknot; what do you know about men?

CRIMP. What do I know about them, sir? Why, I think it's time I—that is—I know nothing about them—nothing about them—nothing at all—only you should consider, sir, we of the gentler sex have our little preferences.

OLDBUTTON. Well, and who can object to Sir Spangle?

CRIMP. Why, sir, to speak plainly, in the first place he is something of a puppy.

OLDBUTTON. That's true, but I shouldn't have thought that would have formed any objection with your sex; if a man be not a puppy before he's in love, it's a chance but he is one directly afterwards.

CRIMP. Yes, sir, but then you know he's of one's own making, and that's all the difference. Then Sir Spangle pays so much attention to himself that he'll have no time to attend to his wife.

OLDBUTTON. All the better for her; she'll be able to play the fool with greater liberty.

CRIMP. Then, sir, he's a man of no conversation.

OLDBUTTON. All the better still—she'll have the whole of the talk to herself.

CRIMP. Then, sir, he's an ugly man.

OLDBUTTON. His wife's beauty will appear to greater advantage. The more he approaches to a devil, the greater her chance of appearing a goddess. There are two sides to a card, Mistress Crimp, and your mistress will be the painted one.

CRIMP. A side that will bear no heart, depend upon it, sir. Now, sir, for all you look so sober and discreet, you don't know but you may be married yet.

OLDBUTTON. What, married! Crimp, if I was asked where I considered was the greatest mischief in the smallest compass, where do you think I should answer?

CRIMP. In a superannuated bachelor, perhaps.

OLDBUTTON. No, in a woman's tongue. I married! I do not like to hear the sharpening of saws—I have no great relish for a dustman's bell—the ungreased wheel of a waggon is by no means agreeable to me—a parliament of parrots would put me into a fever—and half a dozen children each with the hooping cough, would, I believe, make me call for my pistols. Yet, any one, nay, all of these would I sooner endure than be subjected to that terror of the world—that concord of thunder and shrillness—that only perpetual motion yet discovered—a woman's tongue. Ah, women of modern times!

CRIMP. Ha, ha, ha! Why, sir, don't you believe women were always alike?

OLDBUTTON. All, except one, and she was Eve.

CRIMP. Oh, then she was not so terrible?

OLDBUTTON. No, not till after she fell; then she changed her tongue for the tail of a rattle-snake, which has come down to the whole sex. Now I'm going to my room, and take care I am not disturbed. Mind that I have no flirting; when your mistress is married, there is one good thing: I shall get you off my hands—and when once rid of you women, I shall be light and buoyant again.   [*Exit into room* R.

CRIMP. Yes, as a shuttlecock without feathers.

Enter PAUL PRY.

PAUL. Hope I don't intrude—just popped in.

CRIMP. Why, I declare, you are the man that was hid in the fire-place.

PAUL. Yes—I—I thought the chimney smoked. But I saw no smoke at all.

CRIMP. No smoke, sir! But I hope you enjoyed the fire—you had justice done you there, I think.

PAUL. Justice! Yes, damn it—*Burn's* Justice. Almost enough to make a man swear that he'd never do another good-natured thing again. Between you and me, that poker is not settled for yet. Mr. Tankard here cuts a great dash, but I waited about the door yesterday for two hours to waylay the tax-gatherer—don't let it go any further, but the poor's rates are not paid for the last quarter. It's no business of ours, you know.

CRIMP. Certainly not, but you seem to know every body's business.

PAUL. It isn't that I ask—can't help hearing it. There! [*Pointing off.*] You see Mr. Figgins there in the bar; he appears a monstrous blade, don't he? It's all collar and wristbands. I know his washerwoman.

CRIMP. Indeed!

PAUL. Yes; he hasn't a shirt for every day in the year, I can tell you.

CRIMP. Really!

PAUL. No, indeed. In fact, all the people here are in a bad way; there's no bills being paid by anybody.

CRIMP. How do you know?

PAUL. Why—don't let it go any further, but there are only two shops in the town that sell receipts: they've neither of them— for I made it my business to enquire—sold a single stamp this fortnight. That's a proof: folks can't pay bills without stamps, or if they do it's against the law—but it's no business of ours. I dare say your master has his tailor's bill for the last twelve month with paid at the bottom of it.

CRIMP. I dare say he has. Pray, is such a thing a curiosity to *you?*

PAUL. It is to some people here, I assure you. You've a tolerable place here; you are lady's-maid.

CRIMP. No, indeed, not exactly a lady's-maid; I attend on my lady certainly, but my master being a single man——

PAUL. Oh, ah! I see, you are lady's maid, and make yourself generally useful.

CRIMP. What do you mean, sir?

PAUL. Mean! Oh, I wouldn't intrude—but you tuck the old man up.

CRIMP. Tuck him up!

PAUL. Ah, carry a warming-pan. Between you and me, he looks a wicked old chap. He's a man of fortune, I dare say. Shouldn't wonder if he has a thousand a year. West Indian property, perhaps. I thought he was in the army. It's nothing to me of course, you know.

CRIMP. That's just what I was thinking; for being so curious is like——

PAUL. Like! Talking about being like—between you and me— now, upon any account, don't let this go any further, or I'll never do another good-natured thing. Talking about like— you know Mrs. Tankard has a little baby—a fine little boy certainly. You see Mr. Nohops, the brewer, inside the bar there—don't you think there is an astonishing resemblance between them—eh? The double chin I'd swear to. I'm told he has given the child a coral and half a dozen lace caps: very kind of him, isn't it, eh? Poor Mr. Tankard! But it's no business of mine. Do you stay long here?

CRIMP. Now what can it be to you?

PAUL. Oh, nothing. I wouldn't intrude. There are some people who would put their noses anywhere. Now I'll tell you what I heard as a little bit of scandal. I don't put any truth in it myself, but it is said that Mrs. Hawkins, whose third husband, by-the-bye, is just dead—and certainly that woman does get rid of her husbands most astonishingly quick—well, it is said that in the course of the week she intends to—to—[*Looks round and discovers that he is by himself,* CRIMP *having stolen off during the speech.*] Well, I'll never do another good-natured thing again. Umph, these people are no great matters. Eh, here comes Tankard; no, it isn't. I must keep out of his way.

Enter SERVANT, *with a letter.*

Ah, got a letter?

SERVANT. Yes; it's for a gentleman here called Mr. Oldbutton.

PAUL. Oldbutton! Ah, I'm just going to him. I'll deliver it, depend on me. [*Exit* SERVANT.] Umph, I don't know the seal; it can't be any body belonging to the town—eh! and yet there is a similitude to Mrs. Yellowcap's hand; that woman is after all the men. She's a very curious woman—will see everything. I know she went to see the Living Skeleton when he was here, unknown to Mr. Y. She went in company with Mr. Camphor the doctor, in order to have the benefit of his remarks on the exhibition. Ah, I know all these things. How unhappy I could make half the husbands in this town, if I liked, but it's no business of mine. It certainly is Mrs. Yellowcap's hand: I am most assured of it. 'Oldbutton'—there's her 'Old', I'm convinced, and I'd swear to her 'button'. I'll venture a peep just to satisfy myself. [*Opens it.*] Eh! It's from Sir Spangle Rainbow, the gentleman I met here; what does he say? 'My dear sir—I should have staid at your inn, but a most inquisitive puppy so annoyed me —' now who can he mean?—'so annoyed me, that I was compelled to move to the George. I will, however, wait upon you in a few minutes.' Now, who can he mean? An inquisitive puppy! I shouldn't wonder if it was that Henry Dixon; he's in every body's business, and yet I didn't see him. Eh, how shall I get this into his room? [*Goes to door.*] I'll see what he's doing. Eh! Why, he's stuffed paper into the keyhole. Now there's something very mysterious in that. Ah, there's a window above the door; I know where they put the fire-ladder.

[*Runs off, and brings a ladder; climbs, and whilst he is peeping in at the window the door bursts open.* PAUL *is thrown in.* OLDBUTTON *springs from the table, and presents a pistol to his head.*

I hope I don't intrude.

OLDBUTTON. Pest!

PAUL. Just popped in——

OLDBUTTON. Consider: this pistol is within an inch of your
head——

PAUL. And between you and me, don't let it go any further.

OLDBUTTON. Inquisitive scoundrel! [*He drags* PAUL *to the
front of the stage.*] Landlord! Landlord!

PAUL. Murder!

TANKARD, BILLY *and* SERVANTS *run in, followed by* SIR
SPANGLE.

SIR SPANGLE. My dear Mr. Oldbutton—confound it, there is
that rascal again!

OLDBUTTON. A pretty house you keep—this prying scoundrel——

PAUL. Between you and me, Mr. Tankard, I slept here last
night—I just popped in—I've left my tooth-brush—I hope
I don't intrude—this letter I was going to——

OLDBUTTON. [*Shaking him.*] Why, this letter is directed to me.
How dare you open it?

PAUL. Open it! I—why, so it is, and no wonder: the tumble I had
was enough to break a man's neck, much less the seal of a letter.

BILLY. Now, Mr. Pry, you must go; and if I catch you here
again I'll ferret you out of the house with a gun, or a pistol,
or a poker.

PAUL. A poker! Don't mention it; I wouldn't wish to intrude
for a minute. Good morning. [*Exit; returns. To* TANKARD.]
I've just one question to ask. How is Mrs. Tankard and the
baby—quite well? I wish you a good day. [*Exit; returns.*] Beg
pardon—forgot my umbrella.   [*Exit.*

TANKARD. And I'll take care you don't forget any thing else.
Billy, go and see Mr. Pry to the door.

BILLY. I will, sir; and you may depend, sir, if I catch him here
again, I'll settle him.
                [*Exeunt all but* OLDBUTTON *and* SIR SPANGLE.

OLDBUTTON. And now, Sir Spangle, I suppose you are rather
impatient to see Laura.

SIR SPANGLE. Impatient, sir! You know I never say the thing
that is not, but I may safely affirm that I am dying every

minute until I—eh! surely I caught a view of her precious flounce—it must be! Now you'll excuse me, Mr. Oldbutton, I'll do the business myself. I want no introduction; my face is always my letter of recommendation. Ah, there she is. Excuse me.   [*Runs off.*

OLDBUTTON. His face a letter of recommendation! It's written in a very bold hand. However, this marriage puts an end to my troubles, and it must even be with this knight of powder and pomatum.   [*Exit.*

SCENE III. *The Kitchen at the Golden Chariot. A Cradle on the Stage.*

Enter PAUL PRY.

PAUL. Just popped in here the back way—resolved to see it out. The Freemasons meet here again to-night. There's something very mysterious about them; must find out the sign. If I can but creep up the back stairs and—eh, somebody coming! Where shall I hide? Ah, the cradle —no young one here, else I wouldn't intrude—here I'll wait till the danger is over.
                    [*Gets into cradle and covers himself up.*

Enter CRIMP *and* BILLY.

CRIMP. La, Billy, I never thought to see you again.

BILLY. I dare say you didn't; I shouldn't wonder now if you haven't changed away for a new thimble the silver two-pence I gave you. But I declare, Crimp, you are grown quite a woman—and there's another thing, Crimp.

CRIMP. And what's that?

BILLY. I'm grown quite a man. I never thought I should see you again when you left the village to go to service in London, but now we've met once more——

CRIMP. Aye, now we've met once more, you must do as I tell you. In the first place you know that Captain Hawkesley, as you call him, is Captain Haselton, my master's nephew; he's in love with my mistress, and you must let them have an interview here, for fear of detection.

BILLY. What, in the kitchen! Aye, but so it is; this love, you see, will make folks creep into a coal-hole.

CRIMP. Why, this is not a very elegant place for an assignation, certainly; so full of lumber. Billy, what is that ugly looking box for?

BILLY. Oh, that's of great consequence; that's what we keep our fire-works in.

CRIMP. The fire-works—what for?

BILLY. What for? Why, to illuminate when any great folks land here at Dover. But your mistress and the Captain can come here very well. But I say, Crimp, don't that [*Pointing to the cradle.*] remind you of something?

CRIMP. What?

BILLY. Why *that*—you know you said we should be married.

CRIMP. Well, and what has that to do with marriage?

BILLY. What? Why—he, he! Only to think now of having a little Cupid in long clothes—he, he! I say——

CRIMP. Oh, nonsense!

BILLY. Pretty, won't it be?

CRIMP. I don't know.

BILLY. Oh yes, you do; and then, Crimp, when I come home to dinner—if we have any dinner to eat—and there, you know, will be the little angel without wings——

CRIMP. What are you talking about?

BILLY. And you'll say 'Billy, won't you look at the child?' and I dare say I shall say, 'I don't care if I do,' and then, you know, you'll just draw me up to the cradle in this manner, and then, you know, I shall fancy its little face like a bunch of red and white roses; and you'll just take hold of the clothes, and draw them down, and I shall say——. [*He acts the whole of this speech, and pulling down the clothes, discovers* PAUL.] Who the devil brought you here?

PAUL. Hope I don't intrude; just popped in——
                              [CRIMP *screams and runs off.*

BILLY. I'm hanged if I don't have you up for burglary; what do you do here?

PAUL. Why, I lent the little baby my watch-key to play with; I thought perhaps it might have dropped it in the cradle.

BILLY. Oh, nonsense; there was never any thing belonging to you in that cradle, I know, or if there were, you'd better not let my master hear you say so. Now, you'd better go.

PAUL. Oh, I'm going; I can't think where my watch-key is— I'm going; I wouldn't intrude for the world—good morning.
[*Exit.*

BILLY. Well, he's gone—[PAUL *re-enters behind.*] and now to go and lay this plan with Crimp.   [*Exit.*

PAUL. Well, this is strange—queer people—I must see this out. It's no business of mine to be sure. They are coming— where shall I go—the cradle—no, that won't do again. Oh, in this box—there is nothing in it but some rolls of paper. [*Gets into the box among fire-works.*] Here I can watch them. This is nothing—I once suffered myself to be turned up in a bedstead for a whole day, on purpose to worm out a secret.

Enter LAURA *and* CAPTAIN HASELTON.

HASELTON. If you suffer this opportunity to pass, we must for ever be lost to each other. Mr. Oldbutton is intent on your marriage, and there is no other mode of escaping it but by flight. I will have a ladder at your chamber window tonight; say but the word and——

Enter CRIMP *and* BILLY.

CRIMP. My master—my master—he has watched you here, miss.

HASELTON. The devil! What shall I do?

CRIMP. Oh here, dress yourself up, quick, quick.
[*They throw at* HASELTON, *from a basket of clothes, an old woman's gown, apron, and bonnet, which he puts on.*

Enter OLDBUTTON, SIR SPANGLE, *and* TANKARD.

TANKARD. I'm sure, sir, you must be mistaken.

OLDBUTTON. Nay, I'm convinced I saw her—and here she is. Pray, madam, is this preference for a kitchen to be attributed to your humility, or has another motive——

CRIMP. La, sir, what a fuss—she came here to see the washing.
[BILLY *has, during the foregoing, been peeping through the lid
of the box, and runs off.*

SIR SPANGLE. Washing! Lady Rainbow, that is to be, overlooking blue bags and dimities!

OLDBUTTON. Washing!

CRIMP. Yes, sir. I'm getting up some small linen for my lady—
nobody can do it to her fancy like me.

LAURA. Indeed, sir, this suspicion is unworthy of you.

OLDBUTTON. I see no signs of washing—if you are washing,
you are in very good order.

CRIMP. La, sir, we were just going to begin.

Re-enter BILLY, *with light.*

BILLY. Oh, master, I've got him!

TANKARD. Who?

BILLY. Mr. Paul Pry—he's in that box—and only say the word
—you consent, eh? Well, then, here goes.
[BILLY *sets fire to some paper hanging from the box. It
is blown up*—PAUL *rolls out. Tableau.*

ACT III

SCENE I. *The Inn.*

Enter SIR SPANGLE *and* LA POMMADE.

SIR SPANGLE. True, Pommade, it is evident there is no time to be lost.

POMMADE. Point du tout, not none at all, mi lud.

SIR SPANGLE. I'm certain Captain Hawkesley is in the house, and I am determined to call him out. I did think of arresting him, but it is too mechanical; so like a tradesman, these arrests—therefore I shall call him out like a man of honour.

POMMADE. Ah, ma foi, de man of honour is bien semblable, ver like yourself.

SIR SPANGLE. Yes, Pommade, [*Using his box.*] this pinch has decided it. I'll cut his throat—he dies. I always follow two plans on great occasions—I first take a pinch of snuff to arouse my valour, and then a cigar to compose it.

POMMADE. Ah, ha! So your valour begins in sneezing, and ends in smoke.

SIR SPANGLE. What, puppy!

POMMADE. Mi lud, I say you tak de tabac—de snuff to clear your head—[*Aside.*] and a deal you must tak to do it.

SIR SPANGLE. Get me my foils, Pommade. I shall touch him with cold steel. I don't like these unmannerly bullets—they might blow my brains out before I knew it.

POMMADE. Oui, mi lud—[*Aside.*] but dey must find before dey blow.

SIR SPANGLE. You know with the sword I am inimitable. You remember in my last duel but six, when I knocked off the waistcoat button of Sir Harry Filagree, pierced his clothes, and with the point of the weapon scratched out one of the lovely blue eyes of Lady Violet's miniature suspended at his breast. Was not that something?

POMMADE. Something, chevalier—I know no man so worthy to knock out a lady's eye as yourself.

SIR SPANGLE. And don't you remember how, at the humane request of the Dowager Duchess of Duckspool, with one pass I pinned with my sword the leg of a spider against her grace's bureau? And don't you remember, he, he, he! the epigram I made on it? The—the point that was in it, Pommade—the point, you know, he, he, he! I have point.

POMMADE. Oh, you all point—you'd make a ver good finger-post.

SIR SPANGLE. You brute. Quit the apartment; you make a compliment as Lord Slamerkin's tailor makes a coat; to adopt either is to render oneself a savage. Where are the foils?

POMMADE. In your room, my lord. And now I shall go faire l'amour, make love to de littel girl Anglaise—I will put aside de English bumpkin vid one touch of my chapeau.   [*Exit.*

SIR SPANGLE. I am rather out of practice—but an hour or two will set all right again. [*Gets foils from room in flat,* R.] Now I shall make a few passes at the key-hole—one—two—a hit.
    [*He enters the room, shuts the door, and the foil is seen at intervals protruding through the key-hole.*

Enter PAUL PRY.

PAUL. Well, it's no business of mine—but this is a precious house—just met Mr. Goinggone the auctioneer, and I said to him, says I, the folks at the inn there will soon have a job for your hammer. I hope he won't let it go any further—but I know how it will be. I've got in the back way. These Free-masons haven't met yet—there must be something very strange in all this—couldn't admit me—I'll have it—eh, who's that stamping in the next room? I must look. [*Looks in at the key-hole.*] Why, it's that fellow with a drawn sword—I shouldn't wonder if he was going to stab himself—perhaps he's committed forgery—it's no business of mine. I have a great mind to give an alarm—I'll peep again. Eh, there he is —eh! [*The foil is pushed through.*] Oh, Lord, I'm stabbed! I'm murdered! Oh, dear!

Enter SIR SPANGLE, OLDBUTTON, *and* CRIMP.

ALL. What's the matter?

PAUL. I'm the matter! But I hope I don't intrude. Between you and me, I'm dead.

SIR SPANGLE. Have I scratched you, sir?

PAUL. Scratched! You've killed me nicely.

OLDBUTTON. I am the last person, Mr. Pry, to taunt any man in the hour of danger with his infirmities—I would not add a pang to any miserable wretch in the agonies of death, but you really are very much to blame.

PAUL. I take all this very kind of you—you talk like a parson, sir; and by-the-bye—speaking of parsons—between you and me—don't let this go any further—there's our clergyman; you wouldn't think—it's no business of mine—but you wouldn't believe—oh, dear—I'm dying—I——

OLDBUTTON. Pray then compose yourself, Mr. Pry; it's an awful moment—consider your latter end.

PAUL. It's my stomach, my stomach. Oh, Sir Spangle, if I die, you may depend upon it, my ghost will intrude very often.

OLDBUTTON. But Mr. Pry, you must have some assistance—is there no doctor at hand?

CRIMP. Oh, yes, there's one over the way.

PAUL. Oh, don't mention him—between you and me, he contracts with an undertaker—I could tell you a long story about that.

Enter BILLY.

BILLY. What, Mr. Pry, you here again?

CRIMP. Silence, Billy; the gentleman is in his last moments.

BILLY. Well, it mustn't be in this room—it's wanted.

PAUL. Don't intrude, Billy—between you and me, I'm dying.

BILLY. Dying! Well, will you be longer than ten minutes, because they hold the lodge in this room, and the Freemasons are coming?

PAUL. Oh, dear, and I shall go off at last without knowing the secret. I'll stay in the horse-trough; lead me off, Billy. I'll strive to live if I can; if not—oh!

OLDBUTTON. How could you be so imprudent, Sir Spangle, as to exercise with a foil without a button.

PAUL. A button! You've buttoned me up for another world. Oh, dear! I shall not intrude much longer here—Billy, between you and me, this is much worse than the poker. If I die, I hope the jury will bring in a verdict, 'Died of Natural Curiosity!'
                              [BILLY *and* CRIMP *lead* PAUL *off*.

SIR SPANGLE. And now, Mr. Oldbutton, we had perhaps better settle this marriage without delay.

OLDBUTTON. It is my wish, sir; and here, fortunately, comes the lady herself.

Enter LAURA.

SIR SPANGLE. Dear Miss Laura, I was just breathing my fondest aspirations for—for—it's not often that I trouble myself to make compliments, but——

LAURA. Perhaps, sir, you use them ready-made.

OLDBUTTON. Laura, be assured; Mr. Spangle speaks his mind.

LAURA. And that's the reason, sir, he says so little.

SIR SPANGLE. You are pleased, madam, to be merry. I was about to remark that my love for you was as pure as——

LAURA. You need not tax your ingenuity for similies, Sir Spangle, for I must declare at once——

Enter PAUL PRY.

PAUL. Hope I don't intrude.

OLDBUTTON. What, Mr. Pry, in your state——

PAUL. Just popped back to tell you—I'm much better.

OLDBUTTON. But is your wound dressed?

PAUL. Yes; Mrs. Tankard did that—she was rather squeamish at first, but I looked at her in this manner—and I said in my usual cutting way, 'Mrs. Tankard,' says I, 'how is Mr. Nohops the brewer?' She did it directly. I could tell you such a story about that.

LAURA. But they told me, Mr. Pry, that you bled very much.

PAUL. Yes, so I thought, but you see it was only this: you broke

· my bottle of red ink that I always carry about me to take little notes down about the women.

ALL. About the women?

PAUL. Yes, always carry a note-book and two bottles of ink— one black for the gentlemen, and the red one for the ladies; so, you know, I can tell where to pop upon a name in a minute. Oh, I could show you such an exhibition! I have the whole of the town upon paper—but don't let it go any further.

LAURA. A very amiable occupation, Mr. Pry.

PAUL. Oh, it's the delight of my heart—though it's no business of mine. Now there's the widow Crowsfoot; everybody thought that she wore her own hair before I undeceived them —now all the town know it's a wig.

OLDBUTTON. And pray, Mr. Pry, how did you achieve such a meritorious discovery?

PAUL. Ah, that was it. You know there's some poplar trees growing at the back of Mrs. Crowsfoot's garden—I mounted one of them, and there I stayed till Mrs. Crowsfoot came home from a rout at four o'clock in the morning. Well, I could look quite into her bedroom and there I discovered the fact; you can't think how all the folks tittered at church the next Sunday. Now what do you think of me?

OLDBUTTON. Why, sir, I'll give you my opinion. Of all failings, that of an idle curiosity is the most abject and contemptible: it is generally found in those whose utter littleness of mind prevents their engaging in any useful or honourable pursuit, and who, thus incapable of action themselves, seek to be distinguished by meddling in the affairs of others. A curious man is, in my opinion, a species of thief. Men are so branded who enter our abodes and abstract our property; and is not the individual who violates every law of decency and social life, and seeks to clandestinely possess himself of the secrets of another, only a robber in a different degree? Such a man I think you, Mr. Pry, and I should feel as little compunction in throwing you over the bannisters were I to catch you in my dwelling-place, as I should a swindler or a house-breaker.

PAUL. Well! I have often thought it; I have even dreamt it; and I have a thousand times said it, that I never would do another good-natured thing again. Mr. Oldbutton, between you and me, you'll believe that I consider myself extremely insulted; and mark me, sir, another thing—[OLDBUTTON *lifts his cane.*] I—that's all. [*Exit.*

OLDBUTTON. And now, Laura, I'll leave you with Sir Spangle; remember, he has my word, and must have your hand.
[*Exit.*

SIR SPANGLE. You hear, madam, the injunction of Mr. Old-button?

LAURA. Perfectly well, sir, and I have only to tell you, were it possible that he could constrain me to marry you, my heart could not accompany my hand: both are irrevocably promised to another.

SIR SPANGLE. Another! What, and I in the world—impossible!

LAURA. Very true, sir; and that you may not charge me with the least duplicity, his name is—is—Hawkesley.

SIR SPANGLE. Hawkesley! Captain Hawkesley!

LAURA. The same, sir. Having, I trust, perfectly understood each other, any further comment is unnecessary. [*Exit.*

SIR SPANGLE. Captain Hawkesley! I swear by musk and laven-der, if he were now within my reach I'd annihilate him; I'd tattoo him like a South Sea Indian. He should be a mere jelly in uniform.

Enter HASELTON *from room in flat,* L.

HASELTON. I believe, sir, you wished to see Captain Hawkes-ley? Now, sir, your business?

SIR SPANGLE. [*Retreating from him.*] My business, why— Captain—I—you know we have met before——

HASELTON. I will not allow that any man can blush more deeply at his acquaintance with you than myself.

SIR SPANGLE. Captain Hawkesley, some men would take that as an affront. I only hope, sir, you'll not mistake my temper on this occasion for want of courage; you know, sir, that I do not want daring.

HASELTON. No man has more at the gambling-table. A bravado with a dice box, a poltroon with a sword; why, what a scandal is it to manhood that such an abject outline of humanity should wear steel by its side! Pshaw, your sword rattles in its scabbard!

SIR SPANGLE. If it does rattle, it's with anger, sir, with anger! I'd have you to know, sir, that my ancestors wore steel.

HASELTON. I don't doubt it; about the wrists and ankles, particularly.

SIR SPANGLE. Damn it, sir—[*After looking at him to see if he is armed.*] draw, draw, draw——

HASELTON. But I have nothing to draw——

SIR SPANGLE. Draw—draw—— [*Following him up.*

HASELTON. [*Taking out a pair of pistols.*] Stop; these will make us equal.

Enter PAUL PRY.

PAUL. Hope I don't intrude.

HASELTON. By no means; you come very opportunely.

PAUL. Don't intrude! Well, I take that very kind of you.

HASELTON. You will serve for a second to both parties.

PAUL. What, going to fight? Well, it's no business of mine. Have you made your wills—can I be an executor?

HASELTON. Come, sir, choose—choose—choose. [*Forces* SIR SPANGLE *to accept a pistol.*] Now, Mr. Pry, walk over the ground: six paces.

SIR SPANGLE. Stop, Captain; this is taking an unfair advantage. You know I'm short-sighted; I couldn't fight without my spectacles, and as I haven't them about me——

PAUL. I wouldn't intrude for the world, but here's a pair that I think will just fit. [*Offers a pair.*

HASELTON. Aye, now we shall do.

SIR SPANGLE. Stop, stop, sir; I'm obliged to you for the offer, but it would be against my conscience to avail myself of it.

PAUL. Would you just favour me—how?

SIR SPANGLE. Why, since I once lost a pair belonging to a dear friend, I took an oath I'd never wear any man's spectacles but my own.

HASELTON. Evasive miscreant!

SIR SPANGLE. Miscreant! Damn it, sir, this is not to be borne!

HASELTON. Well then, fight. Come, Mr. Pry, do you give the signal for firing.

PAUL. What signal shall I give? Stop, I have it; I'll take a pinch of snuff, and at the first sneeze both fire away.

HASELTON. Come, sir, are you ready?

SIR SPANGLE. Captain Hawkesley, I am surprised at you. What are these weapons? Would you wish to degrade me in the eyes of the world? What are these weapons?

HASELTON. What new objection? Why, pistols.

SIR SPANGLE. Pistols! Precious pistols, indeed. Do you take me, gentlemen, for a horse or an ass?

PAUL. For something between both, I think.

SIR SPANGLE. Do you suppose, sir, that a man of my blood and family would stand up to such things as these? You've injured me by the supposition, sir.

HASELTON. What other shift, Sir Spangle?

SIR SPANGLE. Why, sir, do you imagine I would so irreparably disgrace the family of the Rainbows by fighting with any thing but hair-triggers?

HASELTON. Contemptible coxcomb!

SIR SPANGLE. Sir, some men are punctilious about trifles. I have as great a value of my honour as any body; but, sir, any thing less than hair-triggers I despise. I leave you, sir, to eschew as you may the affront you have put upon me in endeavouring to draw a man of my family into a quarrel, and then producing weapons only fit to despatch a hypochondriacal dog or a spavined horse. Hair-triggers, sir, and I'm your man.

[*Exit.*

PAUL. Well, it's no business of mine—but I never saw—will you allow me to ask you one question?

HASELTON. Pshaw!   [*Exit.*

PAUL. Very mysterious all this! It's no business of mine—I've often said it, but now I'll stand to it—I'll never do another good-natured thing again as long as I live. I must see this

out. What excuse shall I make to get into the Captain's room.
It looks into the Freemason's lodge. I know—I'll go and
return him his pistol. It's no business of mine—but I'm
determined to find out these Freemasons.   [*Exit.*

———

SCENE II. *Night. Outside of the Golden Chariot. A Watchbox
at the side.*

Enter LA POMMADE *and two* BAILIFFS.

POMMADE. Now you know vat you sall do.

BAILIFF. Aye, aye, we know—touch and carry, touch and carry.

POMMADE. C'est vrai, you sall tak dis Capitaine Hawkesley to
de place where dey use de lock and key—you will keep him
safe.

BAILIFF. Aye, aye, we know. Only you show us the pigeon, and
we'll cage him.

POMMADE. Ah vell, I'll go and push him down here, and den
you stick your claw into him. But you go off, and when you
see a man steal out do you seize him.

BAILIFF. We'll be ready, only don't be long.
                                        [*Exeunt* BAILIFFS.

POMMADE. Now I sall go and push him out, and after I will go
again and make a little more l'amour.   [*Exit into inn.*

Enter BILLY *and* CRIMP.

CRIMP. Now, Billy, no mistake.

BILLY. I know—I've got the ladder just at hand. Miss sleeps
there in the front room—Captain Hawkesley has only to
climb up there, get out here, and we'll all go off together. I'll
go and see if the chaise is all ready.

CRIMP. And I'll go back to prevent suspicion. Now, be cautious.
          [CRIMP *goes into house. Exit* BILLY *at wing.*

Enter PAUL PRY, *drest as a watchman, with lantern, &c.*

PAUL. They turned me out of the house—but I'm resolved to
discover the secret. I gave Tim Wilkins the watchman half-a-

crown to let me take his place to-night. Now he don't know what I want—but he's a Freemason, and when the Freemasons break up at the inn, they always shake hands with him and give him the sign. That's how I shall get it; they'll be too drunk to know me. Besides, I shall be able to watch the out-goings of my friend the baker there—they say he smuggles a little, but it's no business of mine. [*Goes into box.*] Here I can have a nice look out.

Enter BILLY *and* HASELTON, *with ladder.*

HASELTON. Hush, my fine fellow—the watchman!

BILLY. Oh, never mind that Tim Wilkins; he's always asleep.

HASELTON. Now then to venture——

PAUL. Hollo, a robbery! [*Aside.*] This is business of mine.

HASELTON. Do you hold the ladder firm. [HASELTON *ascends to the window, which is opened by* LAURA *and* CRIMP.] Where are your boxes?

PAUL. [*Running from box, springs his rattle, lays hold of* BILLY, *and presents a pistol at* HASELTON, *who is thus kept on the ladder.*] Robbers! Housebreakers! Mr. Tankard! Robbers!
[*The inn door is opened.*

Enter OLDBUTTON, TANKARD, SIR SPANGLE, LA POMMADE, SERVANTS, *and* BAILIFFS, *who seize* OLDBUTTON.

BAILIFF. You are our prisoner!

OLDBUTTON. Prisoner!

TANKARD. What is all this? Robbery!

HASELTON. I am the only culprit—my crime, an attempt to steal this inestimable prize.   [*To* LAURA.

OLDBUTTON. My nephew—Haselton!

SIR SPANGLE. Your nephew! You mistake; this is Captain Hawkesley. Here—officer, this is your man; this is my debtor.

POMMADE. Ma foi—ah, there is he!

OLDBUTTON. Debtor to Sir Spangle, sir; how is this—and why the name of Hawkesley?

HASELTON. All the result, sir, of a vice which I have for ever relinquished. The amount due to Sir Spangle is a gambling debt which——

OLDBUTTON. A gambling debt! Why, I thought, Sir Spangle, you never played.

SIR SPANGLE. Never played! Sir, I'm a man of fashion.

HASELTON. To Sir Spangle I may attribute the whole of my indiscretion—yet, sir, at the very zenith of my delusion I was resolved not to compromise the name of your brother, and hence my assumption of the title of Hawkesley.

SIR SPANGLE. A very good name to play under. But Mr. Oldbutton, your promise to me——

OLDBUTTON. Is annulled, sir, for it was made to one whom, if I knew him not to be overburthened with wit, had at least, I thought, some principle. I find him destitute of both, and bestow the lady where circumstances incline me to believe she will be better valued.   [*Gives* LAURA *to* HASELTON.

PAUL. Now I take that very kind of you.

ALL. Paul Pry! A watchman!

PAUL. Hope I don't intrude—I just want to ask——

ALL. No, no questions!

PAUL. Well, I never will do another good-natured thing again. I'll not ask another question, I'm determined. I'll take an oath—I'll—ladies and gentlemen, I hope I don't intrude—but I have just one thing to tell you. Perhaps Paul Pry may be here again to-morrow night—now don't let this go any further. I take all this very kind of you—and wish you all a very good evening.   [*Curtain falls.*

PATTER VERSUS CLATTER

A FARCE IN ONE ACT

BY

CHARLES JAMES MATHEWS (1803–1878)

———

First performed at the Olympic Theatre
21 May 1838

———

CAST

CAPTAIN PATTER	Mr. Charles Mathews
MR. PEPPER PARKER	Mr. Wyman
PIERRE PYTTER	Mr. Ireland
PETER PERKER	Mr. Kerridge
PERCY POUTER	Mr. Connell
MISS PATTY PARKER	Miss Beresford
POLLY PILFER	Miss Jackson

PREFACE TO *PATTER VERSUS CLATTER*

CHARLES MATHEWS, the son of a famous comic actor, singer, entertainer, mimic, and monologuist, went on the stage in 1835 following a training as an architect, married Madame Vestris in 1838 after three seasons in her Olympic company, and partnered her in the management of Covent Garden from 1839 to 1842 and of the Lyceum from 1847 to 1855. After her death and his withdrawal from the financial disasters of management, he acted until the end of his life, and won success and further reputation in tours to India, America, and Australia. Not only was he the most distinguished light comedian of his day, but also the author of some thirty burlettas, farces, comedies, and entertainments, and collaborator in several others; many of these were written to display his own acting talents, such as *The Hump-backed Lover* (1835), *He Would Be an Actor* (1836), *Used Up* (1844), *Little Toddlekins* (1852), and *My Awful Dad* (1875).[1] Mathews was also responsible for *Paul Pry Married and Settled* (1861), in which he took the part of Pry.

One of the most popular of these pieces was *Used Up*, by Mathews and Boucicault, adapted from the French. Mathews played the elegant and wealthy Sir Charles Coldstream, thoroughly bored with life and unable to feel any emotion but world-weariness. The blacksmith Ironbrace, believing him the seducer of his own wife, physically attacks him; the excited Sir Charles, delighted that at least some feeling is aroused in him, grapples with Ironbrace and the two of them topple through a window into the river below. In the second act Sir Charles, assumed to be dead, disguises himself as a ploughboy and goes into the service of a farmer to avoid arrest for the murder of Ironbrace. A second emotion is by now awakened in him: he falls in love with the farmer's niece. Ironbrace, of course, is not dead; Sir Charles casts off the company of his sycophantic acquaintances, who had been manœuvring to benefit under his will, and by now quite aroused to the joys and pleasures of living marries the niece. Towards the end of his life Mathews adapted *My Awful Dad* from the French to create another leading part

[1] See the Appendix on Mathews's acting, pp. 145–53 below.

for himself, and this proved as popular as the other mainstays of his repertory. Here he played Adonis Evergreen, the gay, sprightly father of a solemn young barrister who proceeds to involve his son in all kinds of legal, financial, and amatory embarrassment. Putting on barrister's robes over a Punch costume, he pretends to be his son, advises an attractive young widow about a will, and is taken for his son in various adventures. Finally he wins the widow for himself, and his very dull son is snapped up by a wealthy young woman attracted to him because she believes that he is responsible for the exciting things his father has actually done. Like all pieces in which Mathews starred, *My Awful Dad* was tailored exclusively to his abilities and depended entirely for its effects upon his acting. No other actor could come near him in his own repertory.

Mathews was not a low-comedy actor, and *Patter versus Clatter* shows that low comedy was not absolutely essential to farce.[1] The part of Captain Patter—a successful lover who tricks father and rival in the tradition of eighteenth-century farce—is a virtual monologue, and displayed the younger Mathews at the height of his powers. He was still playing it in his seventies.[2] On its first appearance *Patter versus Clatter* was performed ten times in the few days remaining before the season ended; in the following season of 1838–9 it received thirty-five more performances after Mathews's return from America.

The text is that of *Lacy's Acting Edition of Plays*, v. 118, the earlier acting edition, collated with the only other edition, *Dicks' Standard Plays*, no. 660, which is almost identical. It seems that Mathews developed the text and the songs as he continued to perform the play; the *Lacy*, published after Mathews's death, probably records the final state of both. In the Lord Chamberlain's copy the play runs along precisely the

---

[1] Farce without low comedy was most unusual, however. *Patter versus Clatter* is the only farce in this volume from the first seventy years of the century without at least one low-comedy role.

[2] His most curious performance of Patter must have been in Honolulu in February 1871, by command of Kamehameha V, King of the Sandwich Islands. After a vivid description of the setting, the theatre, and the audience, Mathews concluded: 'And it was nothing to see a pit full of Kanakas, black, brown, and whitey-brown (till lately cannibals), showing their white teeth, grinning, and enjoying "Patter v. Clatter" as much as a few years ago they would have enjoyed the roasting of a missionary or the baking of a baby.' (*The Life of Charles James Mathews*, ed. Charles Dickens, jun. (1879), ii. 228.)

same lines, but between manuscript and acting edition there are many alterations, additions, and subtractions in the dialogue. The three songs in the Lord Chamberlain's copy are all different from and much shorter than the printed songs; one song is missing in manuscript, although a space has been left for it. The three songs before the finale that appear in the printed texts are listed by their titles in the Olympic playbills from December 1838, when Mathews reappeared; they may have been in their final form by that date. The first and finale songs (especially the former) in the acting editions are obviously corrupted, and emendations had to be made on the basis of internal evidence.

SCENE I. *A plain chamber in* CAPTAIN PATTER'*s house.*

Enter PETER.

PETER. Well, this is a happy moment for me. I haven't opened my mouth these three days, for where my master the Captain is he lets nobody talk but himself, and I shouldn't be able to say a word now if he hadn't just stepped down stairs to stop the tongues of three antiquated aunts, piping hot from Yorkshire.

CAPTAIN. [*Sings without.*]

> Tag rag
> Merry, derry
> Perriwig and hat band
> Hic hoc horum
> *Genitivo.*

PETER. There he is again. When he gets married, he'll rob his wife of one of the first privileges—that of talking.

Enter CAPTAIN PATTER.

CAPTAIN. The deuce take the women! I never heard anybody talk at such a rate in my life! It's impossible to get in a word edgeways. I'm a pretty good hand at talking myself, but really they don't give me a chance. I never saw anything to equal it in the whole course of my life. Now Peter, half-past ten o'clock; another hour and a half, and my fate will be decided!

PETER. What, sir, is the——

CAPTAIN. Yes, to be sure it is. I know what you mean—a letter by the London mail, that's it—the result of the law suit—long-pending—never-ending—Patter *versus* Clatter—Consistorial Court——

PETER. Why, sir, I thought that Clatter——

CAPTAIN. Exactly, you can't convince the lawyer. Yes, Clatter takes possession of the family estates left by my father, the late Colonel Patter, of Parrot Hall, Patterdale, pretending to claim as next of kin.

PETER. But ain't you——

CAPTAIN. Of course I am. My father never doubted I was his son; therefore why should he? But Clatter being a villain, and having no other plea to go upon, throws a slur on the regularity of my birth, takes possession of the family estate left by my father, the late Colonel Patter of Parrot Hall, Patterdale, thereby gaining nine points of the law, and sets me at defiance.

PETER. Well, I——

CAPTAIN. No, I am sure you never did , nor anybody else; the thing is perfectly preposterous—my father, who was regularity itself! No matter, twelve o'clock will bring the London mail—the London mail will bring the decision of the Court. By-the-bye, Peter, did you send the porter to watch for its arrival?

PETER. Oh, yes, not a——

CAPTAIN. Not a moment ago—that's all right. Now, Peter, I'll let you into a secret. Now don't answer, but listen.

PETER. Certainly.

CAPTAIN. Will you hold that chattering tongue of yours at once? Well, Peter, you know old Mr. Pepper Parker next door?

PETER. Of course I——

CAPTAIN. Of course you do—now don't interrupt. Well, Peter, I love pretty Patty Parker, his daughter, and Patty Parker loves me. Now, what can I do?

PETER. Oh, why——

CAPTAIN. Yes, I knew you'd say that—marry her, my master. So I would if I could find out the way.

PETER. Ha, ha, ha!

CAPTAIN. What's the matter? What are you giggling at? Don't I tell you I'm half mad with anxiety? That old Parker refuses his consent, refuses even to see me.

PETER. You don't say so——

CAPTAIN. Don't I? But I do. You want to know all about it? Your curiosity is natural, I must admit that. Well then, Peter, you must know for your private and peculiar satisfac-

:tion that old Mr. Pepper Parker, the father of my pretty
Patty, is a very respectable old pump with but two failings in
the world—one is an unconquerable love of talking, and the
other an inveterate aversion to me.

PETER. But why should he——

CAPTAIN. I'll tell you if you'll allow me; your interruptions are
not to be borne.

PETER. Sir, I——

CAPTAIN. I didn't say you did, sir. I don't know whether you
mean it or not, but it sounds like impertinence, which is the
same thing.

PETER. In future, sir, I'll——

CAPTAIN. Well, then do—do. I don't know what I'm talking
about—you quite put me out. Oh yes, I know—I know—old
Parker, it seems, has conceived the very worst opinion of my
extravagance. [PETER *shakes his head and sighs.*] Now will
you hold that chattering tongue of yours? When once you begin
the vocabulary of my misdemeanours, I know I shall never
hear the end of it. Yes, old Parker, it seems, has got hold of an
infernal report that I borrowed one thousand pounds of one
Pierre Pytter, a German Jew, a dabbler in discount, and that
having hitherto failed in wiping off the debt, I have failed in
wiping off the disgrace. Now that report, at all events, must
be refuted, and I think I have hit on the means.

PETER. Indeed!

CAPTAIN. Yes. Old Parker has sent off to London for this same
Pierre Pytter, that he may himself examine him, touching
the subject in question.

PETER. I see.

CAPTAIN. No you don't, but you will, if you have a little
patience and listen. No sooner shall he have satisfied himself
as to the truth of the report, than he delivers over the hand of
my pretty Patty Parker to my ridiculous rival, Mr. Percy
Pouter, a man he has never even set eyes on.

PETER. Surely he can't——

CAPTAIN. Can't! But he will, I tell you, and why? Because I am
poor and Percy Pouter is rich. How came he so? The money

was all made behind the counter; not a drop of good blood in his veins.

PETER. And who is this——

CAPTAIN. A merely mechanical monkey. Dumb as a Dutchman. Child of a cheesemonger. His father was a respectable tradesman enough, cut his way on through the world with his knife, but wanted rank, so bought a commission in the double Gloucester—in the North Wiltshire Militia, I mean. He was called captain in consequence. A comical captain, eh? However, he cut himself on with his sword. At last he died. Cut his stick, and cut up into as many pounds as his cheeses did.

PETER. But his son——

CAPTAIN. Oh, his son, Percy Pouter, my ridiculous rival, immediately cut his shop in the New Cut, which he was originally cut out for, took a short cut from the East End, and, to cut the story short, has come here to cut me out of my wife.

PETER. But how do you——

CAPTAIN. Nothing more easy. Twelve o'clock will bring the London mail, the London mail the decision of the Court in the long-pending, never-ending Patter *versus* Clatter. Now, if decided in my favour, which I doubt not, I at once throw my name and fortune at the feet of pretty Patty Parker; pay Pierre Pytter his paltry one thousand pounds, and pelt Percy Pouter out of possession of the place.

PETER. But if——

CAPTAIN. Ah, if! Quite right. I know what you're going to say. If he decides against me I'll run away with pretty Patty Parker to Paris, and leave the rest to fate.

PETER. But will she——

CAPTAIN. Will she? To be sure she will. You take her that little note. It contains an account of my scheme. The most adorable angel that ever tickled the fancy of a languishing lover. Just eighteen years old. Lovely eyes, all fire and animation, her teeth twin rows of pearl in beds of coral. Isn't that delicious? Eh, Peter? [PETER *smacks his lips.*] Ah, ah! You never spoke a truer word than that in all your life.

Wouldn't a man fly to the top of Etna, to the bottom of the Bay of Biscay, dig, delve, swim, run, fly, or dive, to possess her—he would. So do you run and tell her from me that she's a second Venus, a tenth Muse, a fourth Grace. Tell her that—now I recollect, you needn't tell her anything of the sort. I've told her myself five hundred and ninety times before, and for the five hundred and ninety-first have repeated my irrevocable opinion in that little note, so run away as if you'd half-a-dozen bailiffs at your heels.

PETER. But sir——

CAPTAIN. Don't stand chattering there, but get along. [*Exit* PETER.] He's a deuced good servant that, if he wouldn't talk so much. Loquacity in a servant is the very devil, to be sure. So then, eleven o'clock at last; only another hour to wait, and if I can't contrive to keep old Parker in tow for so short a time, I deserve to lose my pretty Patty Parker for ever. He refuses to see me, does he? He shall see me whether he will or no, for I have it all here; so I'll run and attack him at once, that is, if I can get in a word, for really it is wonderful how people can chatter at the rate I understand he does; there's nothing so detestably unpleasant as one person engrossing the whole conversation. Stop, though; I must give Peter time to take the note to pretty Patty. How slowly the time passes—it never will be twelve o'clock. Oh ye fates, be propitious! Patter *versus* Clatter, be favourable to my wishes! But at all events if I can't get her father's consent I've got hers, so I'll run away with her at once, and then hey for a journey to Paris.

SONG.

When a man travels he mustn't look queer
If he gets a few rubs that he doesn't get here,
And if from Calais to Paris he stray
I'll tell him the things that he'll meet on his way.

      Dover heights
      Men like mites
      Skiffery-cliffery-Shakspeare.
      Can't touch prog
      Sick as a dog

Sackenem-rackenem makes pier.
Calais clerks
Custom House sharks
Searchery-lurchery-fee-fee.
On the pavé
Cabriolet
Crackery-backery-oui-oui.
Abbeville
Off went a wheel
Habbery-dabbery-tub-tub.
Montreuil
Look like a fool
Hickery-dickery-shut-shut.
Mowing-bowing-snoozing-poozing
Crattery-battery-mummery-flummery.
　　　　　When a man travels, &c.

Ding dong!
Lost bags throng
Swackery-crackery-gaze-gaze.
Soups and ragouts
Messes and stews
Hashery-crashery-pshaw-pshaw.
Beggars' woes
Give quelque-chose
Howling-growling-sou-sou.
Crawling calf
Post and a half
Huggery-sluggery-shoe-shoe.
St. Denis
Custom House fee
Lacery-tracery-non-non.
Silver tip
Fingers on lip
Zee-en-em-bow-wow.
Skiffery-cliffery
Sackenem-rackenem
Searchery-lurchery
Crattery-battery
Habbery-dabbery

Hickery-dickery
Swackery-crackery
Hashery-crashery
Huggery-sluggery
Lacery-tracery
Fee-em-free-en-em.
         When a man travels, &c.

When a man travels if he has the good luck,
To Paris he strays, like a pig that is stuck,
And as he must look for a key to Paris,
He'd better be silent and listen to me.

Montagne-russe,
Down like a sluice
Dizzery-wizzery see-saw.
Catacombs
Ghosts and gnomes
Granery-dranery fee-faw.
Mille colonnes
Queen on a throne
Mummery-flummery-charmant.
What's to pay
Beau-villiers
Suttle'em-guttle'em-gourmand.
Saint Cloud
Fête de St. Love
Showeram-boweram-jets d'eau
Bastile-waterwork-wheel
Elephant-belephant-wet toe.
Walking-stalking
Drinking-winking
Higgledy-piggledy
Gad about-mad about.
         When a man travels, &c.

Sol-da-fa
Grand Opera
Shinkery-squinkery-strum-strum.
Louis d'or
Haven't got more

Packery-quackery-glum-glum.
Call for his bill
Worse than a pill
Largery-chargery-oh-oh.
Diligence
Less in expense
Waggon'em-draggen'em-dow-dow.
Glad to get back
Shuttery-fluttery-sea sick.
Now we steer
Right for the pier
Over'em-Dover'em-quick-quick.
Skiffery-cliffery
Sackenem-rackenem
Searchery-lurchery
Crattery-battery
Habbery-dabbery
Hickery-dickery
Swackery-crackery
Hashery-crashery
Howlery-growlery
Lacery-tracery
Fee-on'em-free-on'em
Dizzery-wizzery
Mummery-flummery
Suttle'em-guttle'em
Showeram-boweram
Walking-stalking
Drinking-winking
Higgledy-piggledy
Shinkery-squinkery
Packery-quackery
Largery-chargery
Waggon'em-draggen'em
Shuttery-fluttery
Over'em-Dover'em
Gad about-mad about.
       When a man travels, &c., &c.

                 [*Exit.*

PLATE 1

Patter versus Clatter. Charles Mathews and his four roles

SCENE II. PARKER's *dressing-room. Sofa,* L.C., *against flat. Fireplace,* C., *with fire burning. Window,* L. PARKER *discovered at dressing-table,* R., *in a powdering jacket, no neckcloth, powdered wig in disorder. On the back of his chair a white neckcloth hangs; on another chair,* L., *a dressing gown.* POLLY, *dusting room, also discovered.*

P. RKER. Well, Polly, no signs of Mr. Soapsuds yet. Upon my word, eleven o'clock and no barber. Polly, go and find me someone else, then. I've a particular appointment with a gentleman I am to see for the first time to-day, my future son-in-law, Mr. Percy Pouter. I can't present myself un-shaved, undressed, so, d'ye hear, get me the first barber you can find, and as quickly as you can. [*Double knock.*] There, someone come to call. Polly, go and see who it is; stop, child, ake off your apron; it's a double knock. [POLLY *puts her apron on sofa and exit.*] If instead of teaching me mathematics, my ather had taught me to shave myself, it would have been much more service to me.

Enter POLLY.

POLLY. Sir, here's a foreign gentleman wants to see you, and he is chattering at such a dreadful rate that——

PARKER. Oh, Mynheer Pierre Pytter, I suppose. Give me my morning gown. [POLLY *gives him his dressing-gown, and puts his powdering jacket on the chair, instead of it.*] Show him in. I should like to hear a man talk. I never found one that could beat me at it yet.

Enter CAPTAIN PATTER *as* MYNHEER PIERRE PYTTER.

CAPTAIN. Mynheer Pepper Parker, I dravelled down from town agreeably to that letter you wrote to me, respecting that little business of that devilskin, Captain Patter. I've always the greatest pleasure in obliging mine friends, for dere is none at all dat I respec and approve so much as mine vara coot and charrnink friend ze Captain.

PARKER. Eh? Why, you are very civil about the Captain.

CAPTAIN. Not at all, I want no tanks. I've my own heart vat tank me more zan twenty tousand pound, or hundred tousand pound, so vizout circumlocution I'll open de buziness. Mine very coot and—eh! amiable friend—eh, eh, eh! I cannot help from laughin' when I think of his comical ways— the Captain have a very great wish to marry wiz your beautiful daughter, Miss Patty Parker. Oh mine Got, mine Got, when I tink of zat bewitching Miss Parker! I never see nozing zo beautiful in Germany in all my days; all ze other young girls, if you gompare dem togezer, dere is not gom- parison at all; they're like so many painted images at top of de board, what goes niddles, noddles all about ze streets.

PARKER. [*Getting angry.*] Well, but you're quite going away from the business.

CAPTAIN. Not at all, not at all, or perhaps you think I've gome to make love to her myself. Not at all. No more, though I dare say she would have no objection, ha, ha! for without vanity I'm a devil amongst ze women! Donner und blitzen! Vat viz ze twinkle of mine eye and ze twirl of my petite moustache, I play de very tifel viz dem all.

PARKER. Very likely! I don't want to hear anything about it.

CAPTAIN. I want none of your compliment. But to return to ze business. Mine very goot and charminte friend that devilskin ze Captain—ha, ha, ha! Excuse my laughin'; I cannot help from laughin' when I think of his comical way—the Captain have been very ill spoken of in various ways; ze people say that he borrow a thousand pound of me, and it's nine hundred to one that I never gets mine money. Now with all due respect, Mynheer Parker, that is one damn lie—

PARKER. Eh! What's that you say!

CAPTAIN. The Captain he come to me one day, and he say, 'My very coot friend Pierre Pytter'—that's my name—he say, 'My very coot friend Pierre Pytter'—he always calls me his very coot friend—indeed I always was his very coot friend— he say 'My very coot friend, will you be paid your moneys?' Then I say, 'Eh! My dear Captain, viz all my heart, I have no objection,' and then the Captain counted down on the mahog- any table which was in my gompting house, one thousand two hundred and twenty-two pounds, seventeen shillings and eleven pence three farthings, which was the principal and the interest of mine moneys, as it is always my principle and my interest to act right in ze world.

PARKER. But I should like to know——

CAPTAIN. I will hear you by-and-bye—there's no getting in one word for you. All I want to say is this, that this is that only you're so very vexing you won't listen to my words; that if you marry your bewitching daughter Miss Patty Parker to that vagabond Mr. Percy Pouter, marry her, marry her—that is all, and I will prosecute him for twenty thousand pounds vat he owe me.

PARKER. Indeed! Does he owe you so much?

CAPTAIN. Not another word—not another word. You know my determination. [*A double knock.*] Oh the devil, what's here! [*Aside in his own voice.*

Enter POLLY.

POLLY. If you please, sir, here's Mr.——

CAPTAIN. Mr.—Mr.—what the teifel you mean by Mr.—all alike—chatter-chatter-chatter-gabble-gabble-gabble.   [*Exit* POLLY. [For all ze world like as on de Stock Exchange, vizout knowing vat ve talks about. Nevare gonsider me for one single moment, Mr. Parker, if you want to go to your friend, only bear this in mind what I tell you, and do what I bid you, and, den— den— [*Pushes* PARKER *off.*] then you'll be as great a fool as I could wish. Pierre Pytter himself! Now what's to be done? No other way out and no means of another disguise. I can't stop to confront him, but I won't abandon the field, I'm deter- mined—I'll try another scheme. At all events, if I fail in deceiving him I shall gain time by the pretence, and that's something. Hallo! Here he comes again—oh, this is too rapid. [*During the finish of this speech he buttons up his coat close to his throat and tucks the shirt collar into his stock, which is a high old fashioned one.*

Re-enter PARKER; *he looks about for* PIERRE.

CAPTAIN. [*Assuming the voice and manner of* PERCY POUTER *with a very bad cold.*] How d'ye do, sir? Mr. Parker, I presume —hope I have the pleasure of seeing you well, sir. You're looking charmingly, how you look generally, because I never had the pleasure of seeing you before, but I should say, if I might be allowed a remark, that you are looking better than usual! Eh? I thought you were speaking, but I have such a cold I can hardly——hardly——   [*Sneezes.*

PARKER. Confound you——

CAPTAIN. Eh? I thought you spoke. I beg you ten thousand million pardons for my abrupt intrusion; to be thus in-delicately introduced without an introduction is like publish-ing a book without—[*Sneezes.*] a title page, or a table of its contents. Eh? I thought you were speaking. I hope my irrelevant deviation from the consistency of fashionable behaviour will be sufficiently expiated by the spontaneous asseveration of enthusiastic contrition, for really I am unable to offer an apology sufficiently material to abrogate or exonerate me from censure—or—[*Sneezes.*] eh? I thought you spoke.

PARKER. Amazement!

CAPTAIN. I perceive by the vacuity of your ocular powers that you are yet scarcely aware of the name and title of your obsequious friend. In me you behold——eh? Eh?
                                        [*About to sneeze.*

PARKER. Pray who?

CAPTAIN. [*Sneezes.*] Your future son-in-law, Mr. Percy Pouter.

PARKER. [*Bowing and shaking hands.*] Oh, my dear sir, I'm delighted to see you. Allow me to welcome you here.

CAPTAIN. Eh? I thought you were speaking. I've got such a cold in my head, I can hardly hear or see anything else. I caught it serenading by moonlight. We romantic young chaps—we troubadours are very apt to catch a cold in the head. If you won't tell your daughter, Mr. Parker, I'll relate to you how it happened. It was a little flirtation. [*Sneezes.*] Ah, you may well pity me. It's very bad, very bad indeed; one of the worst I ever had. A flirtation of mine, with a little girl in my neighbourhood. Quite a romantic incident. I made a song about it; shall I sing it to you?

PARKER. No, sir. I don't wish to hear it.

CAPTAIN. So you shall.

SONG.

I once fell in love with an old woman's daughter,
But the old one soon guessed what we young ones were
   after;
With arms stuck akimbo in quarrelsome mood,
She vowed that she'd settle our loves if she could.
But she couldn't.
Down, down, down, derry down.

She put to the shutters, and bolted the door,
And barred up her cottage behind and before;
For she thought that by slamming the door in my face,
I should take to my heels and abandon the chase.
But I didn't.
Down, down, &c., &c.

She called in a farmer my plans for to puzzle,
Who loaded his blunderbuss up to the muzzle;
But when I came next, only judge of my fright,
Whizz, bang! Lord, I thought I was murdered outright.
But I wasn't.
Down, down, &c., &c.

So believe me, I didn't go many times more,
I'd watch in the night at this old woman's door;
And as telling my tale hasn't taken me long,
Perhaps you think there's another verse more to my song.
But there isn't.
Down, down, &c.

PARKER. Rubbish and stuff!

CAPTAIN. Well, I'm very glad you like it, I'm sure; but don't attempt to praise my voice, execution, or modulation, for 'tis a mere waste of breath, and I hate a superabundance of words as I do the devil. Therefore if you'll only condescend to listen, and not run on at the violent rate you—[*Double knock.*] eh? I thought you spoke, but I've got such a cold.

Enter POLLY.

POLLY. If you please, sir, here's Mr.——

CAPTAIN. Who, who? If you will all talk together! That girl,

she walks into the room, and walks out again, and says Mr.—
and no human being can make out another syllable of any sort
or kind. Go to your friend, but there's no earthly hurry. I'm
here for the day, only the sooner you come back the more
agreeable it will be to me, for I'm naturally anxious to—
[*Sneezes, talking* PARKER *off.*] Ah, now let's see—[*Looks out.*]
Percy Pouter *in propria persona*! Now I'm regularly hemmed
in. What's o'clock? A quarter to twelve—only a quarter of an
hour; so near the victory, and yet defeated. Forbid it, Love!
If there was anything in the world—what's here? A jacket.
[*Takes up the powdering jacket which* PARKER *took off.*] I
heard old Parker bawling for a barber as I came in; if I could
contrive—[*Puts it on.*] With his own jacket too! Luckily it's
a white one; he won't recognise it. Here's the girl's apron
left providentially as if for the very purpose—[*Puts it on.*]
That will do capitally. [*Looking in glass.*] Oh, hang it, he will
know that head again; if I had but a night cap—what's this?
A neckcloth—that's better than nothing. Here he comes
again. 'Pon my life, he does not consider how little time he
gives me to make preparation.

Turns wig and appears as PAUL POUTERPUFF. *Re-enter* PARKER.
CAPTAIN *bows to him.* PARKER *looks about for* PERCY

CAPTAIN. Mr. Parker, I presume? I hope I have the pleasure of
seeing you well. I'm Paul Pouterpuff at your service—Paul
Pouterpuff, Mr. Parker; Mr. Parker, Paul Pouterpuff. Hope
I haven't kept you waiting; if I have let's make amends by
expediting the business in hand.

PARKER. [*Looking round for* PERCY.] But where the devil is
Pouter?

CAPTAIN. I don't know what you allude to, Mr. Parker,
otherwise I should not have forgotten—I never forget anything. I am Paul Pouterpuff, the chronological barber,
because I recollect everything. Shall we commence, Mr.
Parker?

PARKER. By all——

CAPTAIN. Don't say another word—pop yourself down in this
chair—make yourself quite at home, Mr. Parker; you're in
your own house—don't stand upon any ceremony. I presume

you have the requisite utensils—[*Pushes table down.*] for really I came out in such a hurry I quite forgot—that is to say, not forget, for I never forget anything. Allow me to insinuate this under your chin. [*Puts cloth over his mouth.*] I beg your pardon; I didn't know your chin was so low down. Head up. This is indeed a remarkable day for me—one I must not forget. Let me see. [*Takes razor and strop from table, and placing the strop on* PARKER'S *shoulder commences to sharpen it.* PARKER *exhibits alarm.*] 21st May, A.D., 1838, half past eleven a.m., called in to shave and dress strange gentleman. Turn your face a little more this way. Thank you. [*Takes up lather box and prepares lather.*] One good turn deserves another, as the attorney said when he indicted his friend for sending him game without being qualified. Any news from London this morning, Mr. Parker? Always like to hear the news, that I may register it in my mind.

PARKER. Why, I really haven't seen a newspaper——

CAPTAIN. [*Stops his mouth with shaving brush.*] That's rather a remarkable fact you were mentioning, Mr. Parker. Excuse my jocularity, it's a way I've got. First cut a joke the moment I was born. First saw the light in the year '90. Remarkable year that. Earl Howe lathered the Spaniards. Soap very dear in consequence. Great fire at Wapping. Great treat on the Thames. Warm work on the ice. Trade and the Salamander frozen to death. Very sharp, very sharp indeed. Where's your razor?

PARKER. On the table.

CAPTAIN. I've got it. I remember I took my first man by the nose, August 19th, '98, at twelve o'clock a.m. Was taken by the nose myself at five o'clock on the same day for laughing at the crier. Great scarcity that year, I remember. We were all obliged to shave very close.

PARKER. Oh!   [*Winces.*

CAPTAIN. Don't be alarmed, Mr. Parker, don't be alarmed. Never made a mistake of that kind. I recollect everything, as if I were quite an annual register.

PARKER. Will you get on?

CAPTAIN. I should say you were between fifty-two and

fifty-three, Mr. Parker. Old Body, the butcher, about the same age. Cut his throat with a cleaver in St. Mary Axe.

PARKER. Oh!   [*Winces.*

CAPTAIN. [*Takes lather brush from table and brushes his chin.*] If you'll allow me, I'll just replenish this. They say he did it for love of Alderman Gobble's black cook, Agrippa. The wound was only skin deep.

PARKER. Oh!   [*Winces.*

CAPTAIN. Mr. Parker, I shall be under the necessity of cutting you if you waggle about in that manner. He ate three pounds and a half of lamb chops immediately afterwards, and said he never felt better in the whole course of his life. There you are, Mr. Parker. I flatter myself chin as smooth as a razor strop, not a hair upon it, with the exception of that on the tip of the nose.   [*Cuts hair from nose with razor.*

PARKER. Good! Now my head.

CAPTAIN. I beg your pardon; I didn't know you wanted your head shaved.   [*Takes up lather-box.*

PARKER. Head, sir? No, sir.

CAPTAIN. No. I see it only wants a little judicious dressing. Doesn't even want cutting. Talking of cutting, I remember I made my début on the head of a tailor. Wanted his mop turned into a Brutus. Borrowed his shears for the occasion. Cut off the tip of his ear while listening to Dick Goacher's story of catching a hare. Swore he'd make me remember. I never forgot it. [*Fetches basin.*] Pop your head into that. [*Puts basin under his chin, then washes it.*] Old File, the saw-maker, saw me as he was cutting his teeth. Allow me. [*Appearing to wash his chin.*] Set all mine on edge to hear him. Permit me. [*Wipes chin with towel.*] The comb, I think you were saying. Yes, here it is—the tongs, you were observing.

PARKER. The tongs are there.

CAPTAIN. [*Taking tongs from table, going to fire, and putting them in.*] Quite right; you never made a truer observation in the whole course of your life. I remember old Forge, the smith, recommended me not to have too many irons in the fire. Gave me my first pair of tongs to set me up in business, curled his wig out of gratitude. Set it on fire, I remember; made the poor fellow positively light-headed.

PARKER. Zounds! You're burning my ear off.

CAPTAIN. [*Unconcerned and warming the tongs.*] I beg your pardon, Mr. Parker; you must allow me to be the best judge whether I'm burning your ear off or not. Rather too much practice for that, I flatter myself. Got all my eye-teeth—I remember, cut my first tooth at the churchwardens' dinner. The parish met to provide against the scarcity of provisions— four aldermen died of over-eating. Swallowed my coral by mistake, and fell in the water butt the very day I was christened. When old master died took possession of the shop; left me heir to all his wigs.

PARKER. Oh!

CAPTAIN. I beg your pardon; mistook the curl of your ear for the curl of your wig—left me heir to all his wigs and bear's grease. Got any pomatum, Mr. Parker?

PARKER. There, by the looking glass.

CAPTAIN. Don't move.   [*Pulls his hair with curling tongs.*

PARKER. [*Roars out.*] You're murdering me!

CAPTAIN. What a face you're making to be sure; bad as Red Cotton, the costermonger, who won a gold lace hat last June by grinning through a horse collar. Made his mouth a yard and a half wider than any one else's. Oh, here's the bear's grease. [*Taking it from table, smells it.*] Very good, though it was not bought at my shop. I remember that same month poor Bob Cruikshank fell off the York waggon—poor fellow broke his leg in three places. Luckily it was his wooden one. Sam Splinter, the carpenter, set it for him, charging him five shillings for making a new one. Got drunk at the Blue Moon and Porridge Pot the same night through sorrow. Lost his rule, made poor Bob's leg a foot too short, and the poor fellow went on crutches for a year afterwards.

PARKER. Will you make an end?

CAPTAIN. Sir, I'll make an end of you before you'll even know there's a beginning. If you will allow me to insinuate this

under your chin, it may materially save your property from
the effects of the powder—[*Puts large cloth round him.*] Like
your head inside or out, sir? Great fall of rain that month.
Parson's barn blown down in a tempest. Government very
much put to it to raise the wind. Lots of new taxes levied,
fresh duty on powder—got the puff, sir? [*Takes powder puff
from table.*] Take this to keep the dust out of your eyes.
[*Gives mask.*] I remember strange things. I don't know what
I don't remember. I'll tell you what I do remember.

SONG

I remember the days
When in one-horse chaise
You could take your wife with a neighbour to dine,
And not think it low, if he didn't give you French wine;
When a joint and a pudding were the summit of your
    wishes,
And we'd never tasted any French dishes;
When it wasn't thought a bore
To go to dinner at four,
When supper was a solid meal;
Where a smoking fillet of veal
Was back'd by that powerful coadjutor,
A well froth'd pot of porter in its native pewter,
And tables groan'd so amply loaded.
But now when your friend asks you to dine
You go as he asks you at six, but get no dinner till nine,
And then if you have any appetite at all
You must be content with pâté or forced meat ball,
For solid joints are quite exploded.
After which with a twist of your moustache, and a touch of
    your cravat,
You pull on your kid gloves, and move off towards your
    home,
Elegantly half fed, and as sober as a monk,
For you really are not allowed the necessary time to get
    drunk,
A thing to put one in a passion.
After which you go to a ball
Where there's the greatest change of all;

For as now it's no longer genteel
To kick about in a country dance or a reel,
If to dance at all you're willing
You must be content with melancholy quadrilling,
Look down gravely at your shoes
And glide about like so many Methodist kangaroos.
And instead of a jolly supper of oysters and bottled porter
You must be content with a tooth pick and a glass of water.
For eating now is out of fashion;
For there's an alteration, a very wonderful alteration;
For those were days when little boys of ten
Didn't fancy they were men,
And young ladies of fourteen
Didn't go a courting,
But till eighteen could be tarrying
Without thinking of marrying,
And grew up all the faster
For not having a music master,
Or learning to play on the piano very badly;
When farmers' wives wore pattens
Instead of silks and satins;
When many an honest butcher's wife
Had never heard of Rossini in all her life,
And could live perfectly easy
Without seeing Grisi,
And shopmen were not so double refined
As to complain of being too much confined,
To allow them to improve their mind,
A hardship which now afflicts them sadly;
When toy shops weren't turned into bazaars,
And little boys didn't smoke cigars,
And we should have thought it a hoax
To have seen apprentices in moustache and cloaks;
And tradesmen thought of knowledge they'd no scarcity,
And didn't want a London University
To teach them to speak Latin and Greek in a week;
For ignorance bound us so strongly with its fetters,
That housemaids couldn't read their masters' letters,
Which now they can, and do do every minute;
When you couldn't come, with your fingers and thumbs,

> And turn tea tables like tea-totums,
> And make hats spin round like tops,
> Sending your friend round whirling after them like a
>   whirligig till he drops.
> Though I don't mean to pretend
> That we never turn the tables on a friend,
> Or have any difficulty in sending the hat round.
> The only difficulty I ever found
> Was in getting anybody to put anything in it,
> For there's an alteration, a wonderful alteration.
>
>   [*Coach horn sounds.*

CAPTAIN. Victory—victory! Twelve o'clock—the London mail! Ten thousand thanks, Mr. Parker, for the use of your jacket and Polly's apron, which I here resign to their respective places.   [*Putting apron and jacket on sofa.*

PARKER. Why, who the devil are you?
           [CAPTAIN *turns his wig, and assumes* PERCY.

CAPTAIN. [*As* PERCY.] I beg you ten thousand pardons, my dear Mr. Parker, but I really have got such a cold!

PARKER. Eh! [*Struck with the idea of fetching the real* PERCY, *who is in the house, to confront him.*] Stop a minute, my fine fellow.   [*Exit.*

CAPTAIN. What, he's got Percy Pouter to confront me! Then I must foil him at his own weapons.

Enter PARKER, *bringing* PERCY.

PARKER. Now, sir——   [CAPTAIN *assumes* PIERRE.

CAPTAIN. Not a word, monsieur, you vant dat tiefelskin ze Captain.

PARKER. Oh, that's it, eh? Stop a minute.   [*Runs off.*

CAPTAIN. What, he's got Pierre Pytter too to confront me? Then I must slip my skin once more, and for the last time. As the London mail has arrived, I care for neither Percy Pouter nor Pierre Pytter; therefore as soon as he likes to come, I am only quite ready to receive him.
       [*During this speech he takes off the disguise of* PIERRE.

Enter PARKER, *bringing on* PIERRE.

CAPTAIN. Gone, all gone except your humble servant Captain
Patter of Parrot Hall, Patterdale.

PARKER. Why, didn't I forbid you my house?

CAPTAIN. Quite true, but I found I couldn't exist without your
adorable daughter Patty. Patty has an equal attachment to
me, and as to my commission——

PARKER. Damn your commission!

CAPTAIN. Don't damn my commission. [*Bell.*] Here comes the
welcome news which makes or mars me.

Enter PATTY, *followed by* PETER *with a letter.*

Now my darling Patty, speak, quick, what is it?

PATTY. Peter has——

CAPTAIN. That's it. Peter has——. [*Goes to* PETER *and takes
letter.*] Nothing like a letter. Says so much, and yet says
nothing. My lawyer's hand—the result of my law suit.
Patter *versus* Clatter, Consistorial Court. [*Opens letter.*]
Verdict for plaintiff. I was certain of it. How I should like to
have heard my counsel's opening speech. I drew his brief
myself. My lud and gentlemen of the jury: plaintiff in this case,
who I shall prove to you upon undoubted authority is in-
contestably the son of his father and mother, consequently
entitled to whatever property they left, of which defendant
would unjustifiably dispossess him. There can be no doubt,
gentlemen of the jury, of the antiquity of my client's family.
His father and mother must have had their father and mother,
and their father and mother must have had their fathers and
mothers too; in short, my lud and gentlemen of the jury, to
say at what particular period the first of my client's ancestors
existed, who was born without father and mother, I leave to
my learned friend on the other side to tell you. My learned
friend on the other side, no doubt, simply replied by saying
that if one man was the son of his father, another man must
necessarily be so too; that though not in a condition to prove
the marriage of defendant's mother, that was not to prove
that he was not the son of his father; that in the whole course

of his professional experience it had never been his lot to hear so absurd a plea as that trumped up by the plaintiff. He should, however, leave it in the hands of an impartial jury, who would, no doubt, bring in such a verdict as would effectually put an end to the proceedings. The learned judge, of course, merely summed up by stating that it was a wise child that knew his own father, and wiser still the father who knew his own child; that a son and heir was one thing, and that an heir and son was another; that there were many sons without being heirs, and many heirs without being sons; there were fathers with heirs, and fathers without heirs. These were the legal points. The jury, however, would consult their own judgment, and if they found one party right, they might very safely pronounce the other party wrong. The verdict, of course, was given for the plaintiff. Judge expressed his satisfaction, jury pocketed their fees, counsel put their briefs in their bags, and everybody departed satisfied, except the defendant, and finally reinstated that lawful heir to thirty thousand pounds, the fine estate of Parrot Hall, Patterdale, as decided by the judge in the cause long-pending, now ending, Patter *versus* Clatter, Consistorial Court.

PETER. Huzza!

CAPTAIN. You noisy, chattering scoundrel, get out! [*Drives* PETER *off.*] Mynheer Pierre Pytter, congratulate me, or rather congratulate yourself, for now the thousand pounds I owe you shall be forthwith paid, and if any forfeiture is due to Mr. Percy Pouter, I'll pay it out of the thirty thousand pounds of which I've been in full possession—let me see: eighteen seconds and a half exactly. Come, Mr. Parker, what can be your objection?

PARKER. Well, I hardly know what to say.

CAPTAIN. Thirty thousand reasons have occurred to-day to make you change your opinion, so let's shake hands and there's an end of the matter.

PARKER. Well, but you won't give me time.

CAPTAIN. Now do let me get in one word if only for the novelty of the thing. I deceived you this morning, I own— that's bad, but consider the motive—that's good. I ask your

pardon—that's well; you give it me—that's better. Percy
Pouter loses a wife—that makes him very melancholy; I win
the girl of my heart—that makes me very merry. Pierre
Pytter is a money-lender without principle—that's very
common; I pay him a thousand pounds with interest—that's
very uncommon. I wish to marry your lovely daughter—
that's very natural; she consents—that's very obliging; you
agree to our union—that's very politic. I step forward to
crave indulgence—that's very proper; and if you, ladies and
gentlemen—now don't speak—if you only grant your
approving signs, that will be very agreeable.

FINALE.

[CAPTAIN *leads forward* PATTY *as if to sing.*

CAPTAIN. I hope my blushes you'll excuse,
    And that my boon you'll not refuse.
      Kind friends, be lenient pray,
      Kind friends, be lenient pray.
    Papa has joined our hands at last,
    If you'll join yours, our fears are past.
    That's what you meant to say—isn't it?

PATTY. Yes!

CAPTAIN. That's what she meant to say.
      [PARKER *advances to sing;* CAPTAIN *stops him.*

    Well, since I've given my consent
    I hope to make us quite content,
      That you will not say nay,
      That you will not say nay.
    I want no answer—words are weak,
    So only with your fingers speak.
      That's what you meant to say.

PARKER. Yes!

CAPTAIN. That's what he meant to say.
      [PIERRE *advances;* CAPTAIN *stops him.*

    If any vants a tousand pounds,
    My friends I'm always to be found.
      But I shall make you pay,
      But I shall make you pay.

Yet do not, pray, misunderstand,
I only want your note of hand.
   That's what you meant to say.

PIERRE. Yes!

CAPTAIN. That's what he meant to say.

                   [PERCY *advances;* CAPTAIN *stops him.*

I've lost a wife but never mind,
I really could not prove unkind,
   On such a happy day,
   On such a happy day.
I tried to catch a wife with gold,
Instead of which I caught a cold,
That's what you meant to say.

PERCY. Yes!

CAPTAIN. That's what he meant to say.
   Now chorus.   [*All advance.*
The only object we've in view,
Kind friends, is that of pleasing you,
   Smile on our little play,
   Smile on our little play.
A trifle 'tis, but we would earn,
From you a trifle in return,
   That's what they mean to say,
   That's what they mean to say.

                        [*Curtain.*

APPENDIX

THE ACTING OF CHARLES MATHEWS

It is obvious from a perusal of *Patter versus Clatter* that the attributes of Captain Patter are not those of Paul Pry in *Mr. Paul Pry*, or of Box and Cox, or of Widgetts in *How to Settle Accounts with your Laundress.* In fact Davidge, Buckstone, Harley, and Wright, who created those parts, were low comedians; Charles Mathews was a light comedian[1]— Captain Patter's brother in spirit is Jeremy Diddler, the creation of another famous light comedian, William Lewis—and the two styles were embodied in two distinct lines of business. A stock company would contain a first light comedian and a first low comedian, each specializing in his own line. Mathews, however, never regarded himself as the practitioner of a traditional line of comic business; neither did he think himself a farce actor, although he appeared in many farces. He told a Boston audience in 1858 that 'I do not pretend to be a physical farce actor, my only aim is the agreeable and natural.'[2] In Philadelphia he complained about the size of the theatre in which he was appearing: 'it is by expression of countenance, propriety of delivery, and delicacy of by-play that I seek to produce effect, all of which are necessarily more or less lost in the magnitude of the house. . . . My aim has always been to keep comedy within its true limits, and represent society to the best of my ability.'[3] Commenting upon his début at the Olympic in 1835, Mathews said that he was attracted only by 'the lighter phase of comedy, representing the more natural and less laboured school of modern life, and holding the mirror up to nature without regard to the conventionalities of the theatre', and in a well-known passage distinguished himself from the light comedian then in possession of the stage with his 'claret-coloured coat, salmon-coloured trousers with a broad black stripe, a sky-blue neckcloth with a large paste brooch, and a cut-steel eye-glass with a pink ribbon'.[4] Writing to Mathews in 1875, J. R. Planché recalled how different was his style from the 'artificial exuberance of the first light comedian.

---

[1] A light comedian who played caricatures of the English gentleman, with extreme mannerisms of dress and behaviour, was also known as an eccentric comedian; this latter term, however, was not generally employed until after 1850.

[2] *The Life of Charles James Mathews*, ii. 261.

[3] Ibid., ii. 262.

[4] Ibid., ii. 76. Eccentricity of dress was not, however, expelled from the comic stage by Mathews; it was a marked feature of the light comedian of the 1860s and 1870s.

. . . Nature was altogether ignored. Prevailing fopperies of dress or manner were imitated with Chinese fidelity; but "Soul was wanting there." You are the first actor I have seen in the course of my exceptionally long life who has realized on the stage the peculiarities of English gentlemen, giving "the very age and body of the time its form and pressure".'[1]

In one of his earliest parts, George Rattleton in his farce *The Humpbacked Lover* (1835), Mathews established the distinctive performing style that remained peculiarly his own. Rattleton is a gay dashing fellow who pretends to the supposed hump of his rival to further his suit with Louisa and deceive her uncle. George Daniel noted that 'Mr. Mathews played the young spark with great mental, as well as physical, vivacity. His manner is sprightly and unembarrassed; he treads the stage with the ease and confidence of a practised professor, and speaks and looks like a man of sense and a gentleman. His singing, which is aided by a rapid and clear enunciation, (the family peculiarity!) is excellent.'[2] The resemblance to his father, who was on stage from 1794 to 1834, was generally observed: Mathews Sen. was probably the only major influence in the formation of his son's style—unless Mathews Jun. came to this style naturally and instinctively, as some critics claimed. Contemporary reviews of *Patter versus Clatter* also mention the similarity between the two, and give a clear impression of Mathews's Patter. One critic termed the play 'a monopololologue [*sic*] for Mr. Charles Mathews, with smart dialogue and clever songs . . . delivered with an astonishing degree of ease and rapidity'.[3] Another was more detailed:

Charles Mathews . . . utters an infinite deal of agreeable nonsense, and with life, spirit, and volubility, the last being the quality of all in such a character; the effect of the whole is not merely whimsical but amusing. He not only talks but sings for all the other characters with ease and *vraisemblance*, changing his costume, &c. without leaving the stage, and, finally, carries the piece through and the audience along with him, with spirit to the last. All this is amply sufficient to prove his versatile talent, and indicates, too, a larger share of the ability for which his father was distinguished than has hitherto been allowed him.[4]

The Times is also helpful in reconstructing Mathews's acting in the part:

Captain Patter, enacted by Mr. C. Mathews, unites with the talents of a

---

[1] *The Life of Charles James Mathews*, ii. 277–8. Planché began going to the theatre in the first decade of the century.

[2] 'Memoir of Mr. Charles Mathews' attached to *The Hump-backed Lover* in *Cumberland's British Theatre*, xii.

[3] *The Athenaeum*, no. 522 (26 May 1838), p. 380.

[4] *The Satirist*, 27 May 1838.

personifier those of the parleur eternel, and though he successively changes himself into a Jew moneylender, a man with a cold, and a barber, he preserves his eternal chattering throughout, and talks every one of the other characters into literal silence. Not satisfied with interrupting them through the piece, and allowing them to speak only broken sentences, he sings for them their respective solos in the finale, and when, after the fall of the curtain, Wyman comes forward to announce the piece for repetition, he rushes forth, stops him, and delivers the announcement himself. . . . The piece is smartly written, an uninterrupted briskness sustained throughout, and three capital comic songs are sung by Mathews. This gentleman scarcely ever (if ever) appeared to so much advantage; his fast manner of enunciating his words, his rapid transition from one character to another, the changes being effected on the stage by the mere altering the hair, and slipping on a few light articles of costume, his happy personation of the parts, were altogether so excellent, that the high praise of a close approximation to his father may justly be awarded him, especially as the character was one of those which the late Mr. Mathews would have selected.[1]

Remembering Mathews's Patter—which he played for forty years—and similar 'personation pieces', John Coleman said that 'his changes were not only unique and perfect, but they were totally independent of tremolo accompaniments, or a darkened stage, or any other adventitious aids to illusion. These remarkable metamorphoses were effected in a single instant in the full blaze of foot- and float-light.'[2]

Like the reviews of *Patter versus Clatter*, general summations of Mathews's acting tend to be similar and repetitive because the main characteristics of their subject were few and evident. Phrases such as 'exquisite airiness and sprightliness', 'vivacity, ease, artistic finish', 'nonchalance, cool impudence', 'airy gracefulness', and 'gentlemanly ease of manner' are scattered generously through the obituary notices that appeared upon his death in 1878. The precise enunciation of every syllable of his torrential speeches and breakneck patter songs was much admired:

His utterance was clearness itself, and with his winning charm of manner was allied extraordinary incisiveness in speaking. Every word was finished, and every sentence was delivered with a crispness that brought its full meaning home at once to the mind of the listener . . . No one who knew him in the old days can forget his pleasant glibness, his extraordinary volubility and his most remarkable distinctness of articulation. . . . Rapidity of delivery or pronunciation was, in his case, allied with a distinctness that has been very rarely equalled, and certainly not in our time.[3]

Almost all critics agreed that although Mathews excelled in parts

[1] *The Times*, 22 May 1838.
[2] *Players and Playwrights I Have Known* (1888), i. 233.
[3] *The Morning Advertiser*, 29 June 1878.

in his own range, this range was a narrow one, that he could not play parts requiring the expression of powerful emotions, and that even in the characters of the older comedy—such as Charles Surface—he was out of place and lacked courtliness and the formal grace dictated by the social modes of a past age. Mathews was at his best in characters like Patter, Plumper in Blanchard Jerrold's *Cool as a Cucumber* (1851), Sir Charles Coldstream in *Used Up*, and Affable Hawk in G. H. Lewes's *The Game of Speculation* (1851)—a more serious part than most—characters which displayed all his talents and did not extend his range beyond the amiable manipulative cunning, the cool detachment, and the carefree ruthlessness that were important aspects of the Mathews stage *persona*. Plumper does not require the impersonations of Patter, but it was ideally suited to Mathews. Claiming to be a friend of Barkins's son (which is untrue), Plumper invades Barkins's house, rearranges the furniture and pictures, orders wine, invites himself to lunch, makes love to the maid, makes love to Barkins's niece, overwhelms Barkins with endless chatter, and generally behaves with supremely energetic insouciance. A good description of Mathews as Sir Charles Coldstream has been left by Westland Marston, who much admired him in the part:

Sir Charles Coldstream, first as the victim of ennui, and then as the man who recovers the zest of life, presents a very diverting contrast, enriched with various touches so suited to Mathews, that the part might have been written for him. The sense of boredom was capitally expressed by the actor—not too strongly insisted on, for that would have betrayed interest, but with a careless lassitude that showed its genuineness. The man who, from Dan to Beersheba, had found all barren, was no longer surprised, and his despondency had in it a sort of listless resignation. Very droll, it seems, was the manner between hope and fear in which he sees in the notion of marriage a possible excitement, and yet distrusts it, like a disheartened patient who has tried many remedies in vain. His prompt attempt to carry out the notion by proposing to Lady Clutterbuck, who solicits him for a charity, then his forgetfulness that he had meant to propose to her, and his way of calling her back and offering her his hand, as if presenting her with a forgotten glove, were full of effortless humour in which he excelled. Excellent, too, was the air of dispassionate politeness in which he ran through the statistics of his property, and placed himself at her disposal. Matrimony might arouse him to interest, and he courteously hid his doubts. The first act gave scope to his languor and *nonchalance*, the second to his vivacity and enjoyment of the absurd. A suspected murderer, disguised as a ploughboy, because he has accidentally fallen with his adversary into the river—restoration of Sir Charles to hearty interest in life by this too stimulating position was capitally handled. His forgetfulness of his disguise before the master who had hired him, and his sudden correction of himself; the delighted voracity with which he gulped down his soup; his aside comments on his ungrateful legatees, who, believing him also drowned, abused their benefactor; his horror at seeing the man he was supposed to have murdered half emerge from a trap; his frantic efforts to keep him down, and his final exultation at finding the suspected ghost still flesh and blood, gave countless chances for displaying his colloquial ease, quiet irony, his sense of farcical terror and boundless spirit.[1]

There are many summations of the acting of Mathews. Among the most illuminating are those by G. H. Lewes, John Hollingshead, Dutton Cook, and the editor of Mathews's *Life*, Charles Dickens Jun. Lewes devoted a chapter to Mathews in his book on acting, but a few sentences admirably express the actor's qualities:

Charles Mathews was eminently vivacious: a nimble spirit of mirth sparkled in his eye, and gave airiness to every gesture. He was in incessant movement without ever becoming obtrusive or fidgety. A certain grace tempered his vivacity; an innate sense of elegance rescued him from the exaggerations of animal spirits. 'He wanted weight', as an old playgoer once reproachfully said of him; but he had the qualities of his defects, and the want of weight became delightful airiness. Whether he danced the Tarentella with charming Miss Fitzpatrick, or snatched up a guitar and sang, he neither danced like a dancer, nor sang like a singer, but threw the charm of a lively nature into both.[2]

Hollingshead was particularly impressed by an art that concealed art:

His acting was something that was born and died with him. It was the perfection of what appeared to be unstudied ease and spontaneous and rapid brilliance. There must have been art in it—much and elaborate art—but no microscopic critic could discover it. It attained Horace's standard of excellence—it was the perfection of concealment. Whatever part he played, the gentleman shone through it, and his wildest impudence would have delighted an archbishop.[3]

Cook also believed that Mathews achieved his technique independently:

His method as an actor was not founded upon the method of any other actor. He was essentially a light comedian—the lightest of light comedians; but it was difficult to classify his art in relation to the art of others or to established technical conventions. He was distinguished for an extraordinary vivacity, an airy grace, an alert gaiety that exercised over his audience the effect of fascination. Elegance and humour so curiously combined can hardly have been seen upon the stage except in this instance.[4]

Like Hollingshead, the editor of the *Life* stressed the apparent effortlessness of Mathews's acting and his originality:

In truth, Mathews came of no school, and founded none. The light and

---

[1] *Our Recent Actors*, ii. 164–6.
[2] *On Actors and the Art of Acting* (1875), pp. 61–2.
[3] *Gaiety Chronicles* (1898), p. 327.
[4] *Hours with the Players* (1881), ii. 135.

airy manner, the brisk incisiveness, the delicate attention to by-play, the voluble but distinct delivery, the careful observation of character, the watchfulness in all points of detail—so well concealed that every action seemed to spring spontaneously from the requirements of the moment—all these are matters difficult to describe, but easily and vividly recalled to the minds of those who saw this admirable artist. . . . There was, as it were, a personal quality about his acting, which, one felt instinctively, belonged to the man, and could not be caught by anyone else. In a word, he was Charles Mathews, and his style, born with him, died with him.[1]

In 1841 Macready wrote to Henry Compton for his opinion of a light comedian in Dublin who was seeking employment at Drury Lane. He asked several questions: 'Is he vivacious on the stage? Is he bustling? Is he light, elastic, and nimble in his movements? Has he a hearty and a ready laugh? Has he humour? Does he make his effects with care and judgment? Does he give evidence of genius, or seem likely to do so? Or is he merely even, level, unoffending, and thus far agreeable?'[2] Mathews obviously possessed these requirements and considerably more; Macready's ideal was neither the 'even, level, unoffending' light comedian nor the garishly dressed and extravagantly mannered light comedian whose style Mathews rejected when he went on stage and whose 'artificial exuberance' displeased Planché.

The whole subject of light-comedy acting and low-comedy acting in the nineteenth century, their development, their similarities and differences, their relationship to and effect upon those aspects of characterization and the drama to which they gave life, has never been properly explored and is too large for the scope of this brief Appendix. It is clear, however, that in both areas of acting there was until about 1880 a continual struggle by a minority of actors to impose restraints upon a strong inclination to comic excess. Clearly, also, Mathews was among this minority. Attempts by less talented actors to imitate him, like the attempts of an earlier generation to reproduce the light-comedy skills of Lewis, who retired in 1809,[3] merely resulted in a coarsening and debasement of his inimitable style. Writing in *The Illustrated Times* in the early sixties, Tom Robertson gives a picture—no doubt satirically coloured, but probably valid—of the common run of light comedians:

The Light Comedian is the actor who represents the characters of young patricians, volatile lovers, voluble swindlers, well-dressed captains, swells in and out of luck, and the upper classes generally on this side of forty years of age. He is purely and entirely the creation of the dramatist; for

---

[1] *The Life of Charles James Mathews*, ii. 257–8.

[2] *Memoir of Henry Compton*, ed. Charles and Edward Compton (1879), pp. 98–9.

[3] See the Appendix on the acting of early-nineteenth-century comedy in Volume Three, pp. 145–53.

neither in nature nor in society was the like of this bustling, talkative creature ever seen, for which let nature and society be thankful; for, not excepting neuralgia, snakes, or earnest men with missions, the presence of a high-spirited, high-voiced, highly-dressed hero of comedy is the most intolerable nuisance.

Conceive a boisterous, blatant fellow in a green coat and brass buttons, buckskin breeches and boots, or in a blue frock, white waistcoat, and straw-coloured continuations, always talking at the top of his voice, slapping you heavily on the back, laughing for five minutes consecutively, jumping over the chairs and tables, haranguing a mob from your drawing-room window, going down upon his knees to your daughter or your wife, or both, kissing your servant-maid, borrowing your loose cash, and introducing a sheriff's officer to your family as an old college friend, and you form some idea of the type of animal the dramatic writers of the last century forced upon the public as the beau-ideal of a gentleman, a blood, and 'A fine fellow, sir, by Gad!'[1]

By the 1880s the light or eccentric comedian with this exaggerated style was passing away. Dutton Cook, indeed, complained about the underplaying of the new generation of light comedians, a generation that in England sprang from E. A. Sothern's Lord Dundreary (in Taylor's *Our American Cousin*) in 1861 and developed through the modern fops of Robertson and Byron to the drawing-room elegants of the eighties and nineties:

Restlessness and bustle upon the boards are less in vogue than once they were. The light comedian, wont to run or trip lightly on to the stage, waving his hat, or flourishing his cane, laughing and chattering in a breathless way, and for ever doing something: contemplating his reflection in the pier-glass, arranging his chair, or his cravat, or his wristbands, plunging jocosely at the ribs of his interlocutors—a performance known professionally as the 'sly dog business'—dusting his boots with his handkerchief, odious practice!—never still an instant, toying with all the properties and furniture of the scene, meddling with the trappings, and patting and haling hither and thither the other characters in the play—this animated and frisky performer is rarely seen nowadays. It is the fancy of our players of the present that they are necessarily lifelike because they are dull. They act in a numb sort of way; torpidity characterises their speeches, they speak with drawling deliberation, they pause long in their intervals of utterance, lethargy and languor oppress their every movement.[2]

Cook may have been thinking of Mathews, for his description more closely resembles that actor's style than does Robertson's account, which represents everything in light comedy that Mathews reacted against. Another critic of the 1880s compared the present-day light

---

[1] Quoted in *The Life and Writings of T. W. Robertson*, ed. T. Edgar Pemberton (1893), pp. 92–3. [2] *On the Stage* (1883), i. 235.

comedian with his counterpart in the 1840s, and his description is much like Robertson's:

The light-comedy gentleman of forty years ago was as unlike the light-comedy gentleman of the present day as the exaggerated zinc ornaments on a stage-make-believe monarch's crown are unlike the real jewels in that of a genuine sovereign. The stage representatives of dashing young swelldom, in those days, rejoiced in the assumption of costumes that now can only be found among the ''Arrys and Charlies' who, on Bank and other holidays, adorn the trains and steamboats; splendid specimens of genus 'toff', snob or 'cad' . . . Fashion by those who could afford it was carried to the verge of caricature. Crimson and peacock blue stocks, three layers of different coloured under-waistcoats, pantaloons so tightly strapped under the wellington boots it gave one the idea that should the said straps by any accident give way, the wearer, like a released sky-rocket, would disappear through the roof of the theatre; Union breast pins, large enough to hobble a mustang, cable (gilt) watch guards, massive enough to anchor the Great Eastern, and paste rings . . . were then necessary 'props' in a stage-gentleman's outfit. As may naturally be supposed, the acting of the stage-gentleman was as 'loud' and outré as his outward adornments. The dashing young swell was never at rest. He rushed on the stage like a rocket, and rushed off like a meteor. He spoke as rapidly as he could, used his cane on the unfortunate shoulders of all beneath him, jumped over tables and chairs with an astonishing agility, smashed all the crockery the property-man placed in the way, dug his jokes into the audience, to whom, especially the gods, he always acted, and prided himself on being what was then called by the press—and applauded and patronised by the play-going public—'a dashing and spirited' representative of whatever part he appeared in.[1]

With this kind of acting we are on the borderline between light comedy and low comedy, the same borderline as that between comedy and farce. The question of the appropriateness of an acting style to the form and content of the drama it seeks to express is always a vital one in any consideration of that style, which cannot possibly be judged until this question is answered. How appropriate to the plays in which they appeared was the acting of several generations of nineteenth-century light and low comedians can only be decided after a careful examination of surviving records of their performances, of the characters they played, and of the plays themselves; one can then go on to the related question of how good the acting was. It would not be surprising if such an examination revealed that on the whole, especially among the better performers, acting style adequately and sometimes perfectly expressed form and content,[2] for I have found this true of the only two

[1] H. P. Grattan, 'Mr. Byron', *The Theatre* (June 1882), pp. 347–8.

[2] Critics mainly objected that an exaggerated comic style was untrue to life, not to the drama—a very different subject.

investigations of this kind that I have undertaken: into the acting of early nineteenth-century comedy and into melodramatic acting.[1] With the acting of Charles Mathews there can be no doubt whatever concerning both appropriateness and quality. A reading of his parts and his plays shows that his kind of light comedy was absolutely right for the subject matter, characters, and style of the pieces that formed his own distinctive repertory for so many years.

[1] For the latter, see the Appendix on the acting of melodrama in my *English Melodrama* (1965), pp. 190–210.

DIAMOND CUT DIAMOND

AN INTERLUDE IN ONE ACT

BY

WILLIAM HENRY MURRAY (1790–1852)

———

First performed at the Adelphi Theatre, Edinburgh
2 October 1838

———

CAST

MR. HEARTLEY, guardian to Charlotte	Mr. Redford
CAPTAIN SEYMOUR ⎫ officers in the same	Mr. Euston
CAPTAIN HOWARD ⎬ regiment, and both	Mr. Griffiths
⎭ in love with Charlotte	
TRAP, servant to Captain Seymour	Mr. Murray
TRICK, servant to Captain Howard	Mr. Lloyd
CLAY, a brick-maker	Mr. Johnson
SERVANTS	Messrs J. and H. Saunders
CHARLOTTE DOUBTFUL, an heiress	Miss Vining

PREFACE TO *DIAMOND CUT DIAMOND*

WILLIAM MURRAY was best known in Scotland as an actor and as manager of the Adelphi Theatre and Theatre Royal, Edinburgh. He was one of many dramatists to adapt Sir Walter Scott for the stage; half his dramatic work consists of melodramas made out of Scott's novels, such as *Rob Roy*; *The Antiquary*; *Montrose*; *George Heriot*; *The Heart of Midlothian*; *Ivanhoe*; *Mary, Queen of Scots*; *Redgauntlet*; and *The Two Drovers*, all performed between 1818 and 1828. At the end of his playwriting career he turned to Harrison Ainsworth with *Jack Sheppard* (1840), and to Dickens with *Oliver Twist* (1840). Of the twenty plays attributed to Murray, at least sixteen were first seen in Edinburgh; he had little to do with the London stage after his first Edinburgh appearance as an actor in 1809.

Besides *Diamond Cut Diamond*, Murray is the identified author of only two other farces, *What! The Devil Again* (1833), which does not survive in print or manuscript, and *No* (1826), adapted from the French, which after its Edinburgh performance was given at London minor theatres and at Drury Lane. It is a slight piece, with an elegant setting in the garden of a country house. Sir George Doubtful, mistakenly thinking that Frederick is in love with his wife and wishing him to be kept away from his house, lays a wager with Lady Doubtful that the whole household, including the servants, will be unable to speak only the one word 'no' to all callers at the gate until four o'clock that afternoon. In spite of certain difficulties Lady Doubtful wins her bet, and to Sir George's delight his wife's sister is revealed as the object of Frederick's love. The most comic scene occurs when the irascible Commodore Hurricane calls at the gate and can get nothing but 'no' out of the servant in answer to his questions. A truly farcical situation develops in which Hurricane's bewilderment turns to fury at the maddening incomprehensibility of the whole business.

Diamond Cut Diamond was based upon an anonymous two-act farce of 1812, *How to Die for Love*, which in turn was taken from a one-act piece by August von Kotzebue, *Blind Geladen*

(1811). *How to Die for Love* is more formal and genteel than
Diamond Cut Diamond; the latter's sense of farcical briskness,
climax, and anti-climax, with its series of rapid entrances and
exits essential to develop the comic situation, is much stronger,
and the neat symmetry of plot and counterplot in Kotzebue's
basic idea is more marked in Murray's version than in *How to
Die for Love*. It is worth noting that both versions parody
melodramatic situations and sentiments: in *Diamond Cut
Diamond*, Trick's declaration of his own virtue—the sort of
moral platitude frequently on the lips of the melodramatic hero
—followed by his immediate acceptance of a bribe; the comic
deflation of the momentarily pathetic scene in which Trap
brings Seymour the news that his mother lies on her deathbed
asking for her son; Howard's pronouncements on the heroic
virtues of saving the innocent and helpless from the flames—
pronouncements counterpointed by the knowledge that the 'fire'
is another subterfuge to get rid of him; and the final duel that
results in the grievously stricken Seymour urging Howard
with his 'dying' breath to flee the wrath of the law. Parodies of
melodrama occur in burlesque from the beginning of the nineteenth century, but they can also be found in farce. *Diamond Cut
Diamond* is not the only farce in which comedy is obtained from
a parody of melodramatic conventions and machinery.

  Diamond Cut Diamond was played at least four times in
Edinburgh in the short After Season of 1838, and opened in
London at the Strand on 19 June 1843, where it was given nine
performances before the end of the season in October. In the
Strand cast were Romer as Heartley, Craven as Seymour,
Walton as Trick, Alfred Wigan as Trap, and Miss Granby as
Charlotte. Since neither the Adelphi in Edinburgh nor the
Strand in London needed to submit plays to the Examiner of
Plays, there is no copy of *Diamond Cut Diamond* in the Lord
Chamberlain's collection. The text is that of the first acting
edition, *Lacy's Acting Edition of Plays*, v. 7, corrected for mis-
prints and punctuation, and collated with the only other text
of the play, *Dicks' Standard Plays*, no. 372, which is virtually
identical.

SCENE. *The Gardens of a Country Mansion. Hedges, trees, statues, bowers, &c.*

HEARTLEY. Really, Charlotte, you must come to the point and decide for yourself; I have announced to your two lovers that you will this day choose between them.

CHARLOTTE. Then, my dear Guardy, you have done very wrong. To speak in your own language, matrimony is a joint stock in which it is easier to buy a share than sell it; and as a husband is a very serious speculation, I should prefer waiting till——

HEARTLEY. These young men have waited long enough, and must have an answer to their proposals. Howard is a man of honour.

CHARLOTTE. So is Seymour.

HEARTLEY. Howard is a pleasant fellow.

CHARLOTTE. So is Seymour.

HEARTLEY. Howard is a man of property.

CHARLOTTE. So is Seymour.

HEARTLEY. Well then, marry Seymour.

CHARLOTTE. But then I lose Howard.

HEARTLEY. What! Would you marry both?

CHARLOTTE. The Fates forbid! As many lovers as you please, but one husband will be quite sufficient.

HEARTLEY. Well then, choose that one.

CHARLOTTE. In truth I can't. They are both handsome, both accomplished, both agreeable, and both qualified to make a woman happy. One day I prefer this, the next I prefer the other, and the third I am puzzled between both. Could they arrange the matter between themselves——

HEARTLEY. Have a care—your trifling may lead to serious results, and terminate a friendship which has existed between them from boyhood. Educated at the same school, they have served in the same regiment, bled in the same fields, and——

CHARLOTTE. Dancing in the same ball-room, very foolishly fell in love with the same woman. Now, my dear Guardy, to come to the point, he who prevails upon his rival, either by argument or stratagem, to pass the bounds of your estate and leave me, shall win me; and to avoid those 'serious results' you fear, we must forbid all fighting. Now, Guardy, there's the Bill that shall regulate the disposal of my hand. You are an M.P., so lay it before their Lordships—but mark me: no amendments, no conferences—I'll have '*the* bill, the *whole* bill, and *nothing* but the bill.'

Enter TRAP.

TRAP. My master, Captain Seymour, and his friend, Captain Howard, are just returned, and beg to know if they may see you and Miss Doubtful.

HEARTLEY. Where are they?

TRAP. In the great parlour.

HEARTLEY. I'll go to them. [TRAP *bows and retires up.*] I fear me that no good will come of this scheme of yours; but I will communicate your decision, caring little how the matter ends so it does end.   [*Exit.*

CHARLOTTE. I am not sorry to give Fortune some small share in this choice, for I am sorely puzzled between the men. Howard is certainly every thing that a woman ought to approve, though Seymour is as certainly every thing that— [*Observing* TRAP, *who is watching her.*] But I must be on my guard—there's his servant. What can he linger here for?

TRAP. [*At back, aside.*] I should like to find out which of the Captains she prefers.

CHARLOTTE. [*Aside.*] I guess his motive, and will pay him in his own coin. [*To* TRAP, *who advances.*] I hope Captain Seymour is well today.   [*Sighing deeply.*

TRAP. As well as can be expected, ma'am. [*Aside.*] Seymour's the man.

CHARLOTTE. And *dear* Captain Howard, I hope he is well too.
                                            [*Sighing more deeply.*

TRAP. [*Puzzled.*] That's a pozer—quite, ma'am.

CHARLOTTE. Pray present my best regards—respects, I mean, to them, and say—'How happy could I be with either.' [*Speaking between each line ad lib.*] Good morning, Mr. Trap, &c. 'Were t'other dear charmer away.' Good morning, Mr. Trap. 'But when they both teaze me together.' Good morning, Mr. Trap. 'To neither a word will I say.' Good morning, Mr. Trap. [*Exit, laughing.*

TRAP. That woman bothers me. She's a pitty-mee of the sex. She's as difficult to understand as an Act of Parliament, or a Railway Guide, or a Weather Almanack. When you expect rain she smiles, or blows a hurricane when she ought to be 'set fair'. Does she love either, or neither, or both?

Enter CAPTAIN HOWARD.

HOWARD. Trap.

TRAP. Sir.

HOWARD. A word with you. You know that your master and myself are in love——

TRAP. With the same lady.

HOWARD. Now, Trap, I am going to pay you a great compliment.

TRAP. Not more than I deserve, I dare say sir.

HOWARD. Time will show, for though you are the servant of my rival, I am going to prove my confidence in you by bribing you.

TRAP. Your honour does my honour great honour, and I'll return the compliment by at once accepting whatever your honour pleases to offer above ten pounds.

HOWARD. Agreed, and now you must help me to make your master pass the boundaries of this estate.

TRAP. Lord, sir, he can surely do that without either your help or mine.

HOWARD. Listen: the adorable Charlotte has declared that while Seymour and myself both remain here she will wed neither, but if one can be induced to leave, she takes the man who stays.

TRAP. I understand. Take one from two, and she marries the remainder. But isn't this a plot against my master?

HOWARD. No! A coalition with me.   [*Holding up a purse.*

TRAP. [*Taking it.*] That's another thing. I am satisfied.

HOWARD. Of course you are acquainted with all your master's secrets?

TRAP. Why, sir, though only in his service three weeks, I have kept my ears and eyes open.

HOWARD. The concerns of his family, for instance?

TRAP. Oh, certainly. [*Aside.*] For money, I'll pretend to know all his relations. [*Aloud.*] But surely, sir, you ought to know them; you told Mr. Heartley that you and my master were school-fellows.

HOWARD. Pshaw! Three months ago, I knew no more of Seymour than I do of Hebrew; about that time he exchanged into our regiment—he admired the cut of my coat, I liked the shape of his boots, and over a bottle of wine we vowed eternal friendship. That night I saw Charlotte at the race-ball, and fell over head and ears in love with her. Her guardian, old Heartley, knowing my family; invited me—I, fool-like, couldn't come without my friend, so inventing a cock and bull story about boyish days—long service—mutual dangers, &c. &c., Seymour was included in the invitation, and has very naturally fallen in love with the girl too.

TRAP. 'What great events from trifling falsehoods spring!'

HOWARD. You speak from experience, no doubt—but follow to my room, and I'll put your abilities to the test.

TRAP. You will find I have great talents.

HOWARD. For roguery?

TRAP. Oh no—politics.

HOWARD. The same thing. But where's my rascal? I told him to wait. Trick!

Enter TRICK.

TRICK. Here, sir.

HOWARD. Remain here, and observe what passes in my absence.

I have but a few words to say to my worthy friend, Mr. Trap,
and shall return immediately. Trap, this way.

[*As* HOWARD *goes off he winks significantly at* TRAP, *who
returns it, and looks with an affected air of superiority on*
TRICK.

TRAP. 'Only a few words to say to his worthy friend, Mr.
Trap.'   [*Struts off.*

TRICK. 'His worthy friend, Mr. Trap.' There's some villainy
going on, and my master has bribed that rascal to assist it.
And shall I submit to such wickedness—allow my perquisites
to be abstracted by a wretch like that—permit the Secret
Service money of the Home Department to swell the pockets
of a stranger? Never! May I lose place, character, wages—
all, ere I bend to such interference.

SEYMOUR. [*Without.*] Trap, Trap! Where the devil are you—
that fellow is always out of the way—continually minding his
own affairs, and neglecting mine.

Enter SEYMOUR.

Ah, Trick—quite alone.

TRICK. The virtuous man is never alone. Honour, conscience,
morality, integrity, and sobriety, are his constant associates.

SEYMOUR. Indeed—then I shouldn't think you kept much
company—at least of that class, but are you indeed so
virtuous?

TRICK. Terribly.

SEYMOUR. I am sorry for that, for it interferes with a little plot
which I have arranged, and in which your assistance would
have been of service.

TRICK. Might I be permitted to know it?

SEYMOUR. Oh! No—your terrible virtue has induced me to
give it up.

TRICK. Sir, if the weakness of your nature has induced you to
form any idea of offering me a bribe, relieve your mind, and
declare it at once.

SEYMOUR. Perhaps you would relieve my pocket, and take it.

TRICK. If the weight is at all unpleasant.

SEYMOUR. Try it.   [*Giving him a purse.*

TRICK. You would feel lighter without it.

SEYMOUR. Worthy fellow—I see you would sacrifice your own feelings to relieve mine. I blush for my conduct. Keep the money, and never let me see it more.

TRICK. [*Much overpowered by his feelings.*] Not a farthing of it, depend upon it.

SEYMOUR. Trick, I'll reward your generosity. Your master's in love—wants to marry. If he does, ten to one you lose your place. Now aid me to induce him to give up the lady and leave the estate, and I double that sum.

TRICK. Say no more—but mum—here's your man.

Enter TRAP, *running*.

SEYMOUR. Well, sir. Where have you been all this time?

TRAP. The mail, sir, has just gone through the village; the guard left this letter for you.

SEYMOUR. Indeed! Give it me.

[SEYMOUR *opens and reads letter, during which* TRAP *and* TRICK, *unseen by each other, count the bribes they have severally received, then put them in their pockets, and make faces at each other.*

SEYMOUR. Strange! This letter informs me that my poor mother lies on her death bed, and anxiously desires to see me.

TRAP. Alas, poor lady!

SEYMOUR. It adds, if I wish to see her alive I have not a moment to lose.

TRAP. I'll saddle your horses immediately.

SEYMOUR. But love—all powerful love—bids me stay.

TRAP. But filial duty bids you go.

SEYMOUR. [*Much agitated.*] That's true.

TRAP. Methinks I hear the dear old lady cry, 'My child! Where is my little one?' The noise of your horse's feet is heard rattling up the avenue—you rush to her bedside and while she tenderly exclaims, 'Bobby, my boy, how are you?' you faintly utter, 'How's my mother?'

SEYMOUR. You rend my heart with the pathetic scene. One thought alone restrains me.

TRAP. What, under such circumstances, can restrain a son?

SEYMOUR. The recollection that my mother died ten years ago.
[TRICK *laughs heartily.*

TRAP. Are you sure it wasn't your father, sir?

SEYMOUR. Quite! It was my dear respected mother, who bequeathed you a sound horse whipping.

TRICK. Generous woman!

SEYMOUR. And filial duty makes me pay it.

TRAP. Don't hurry yourself, sir.

SEYMOUR. Rascal! You have been bribed by my rival, but tell Captain Howard I despise such petty arts! [TRICK *coughs—* SEYMOUR *turns to* TRICK *each time he coughs.*] Be quiet! I say, the man that bends to tamper with the fidelity of a servant— [TRICK *coughs.*] silence!—is unworthy the name of—[TRICK *coughs.*] s'death, you put me out! Trap, I blush for you. Trick, follow me. [*Exit.*

TRICK. [*In affected grief.*] 'You rush to her bedside, and while she tenderly exclaims, "Bobby, my boy, how are you?" you faintly utter, "How's my mother?" ' [*Exit.*

TRAP. I understand; Trick has sold himself too. We're a couple of rogues, and have been knocked down to the best bidder.

Enter HOWARD.

HOWARD. [*Looking around.*] So the coast is clear! Well, Trap, have we succeeded?

TRAP. We should have done—but for one circumstance.

HOWARD. What was that?

TRAP. Mamma took the liberty of dying ten years ago.

HOWARD. The deuce take her; that was mal-apropos certainly! But s'death, sirrah, you told me she was alive!

TRAP. She never told me she was dead.

HOWARD. Well, nil desperandum. He is but a fool indeed who has but one string to his bow. We must change our ground.

TRAP. *I* must, for some one approaches, and it won't answer our purpose to be seen much together.

HOWARD. Away to my apartment. I will join you there, and plot new mischief. [*Exit* TRAP. Who have we here?

> [*Goes up stage, paying no attention to* CLAY's *entrance or dialogue.*

Enter CLAY, *somewhat intoxicated.*

CLAY. Charming ten guineas! I'm a gentleman for life. How odd to give a man ten guineas for leave to burn an old shed not worth two! Well, I'll up to the Hall—pay the steward what I owe him, and then to the Blue Lion with the rest, and keep out of the way as I promised. [*Red fire off.*

HOWARD. What do I see—a fire?

> [*Voices without calling* 'Fire, fire', &*c.*

CLAY. I'm off. [*Staggers off.*

Enter HEARTLEY *and several* SERVANTS.

HEARTLEY. As I live, there's a fire in the village—run lads, and give every assistance. [*Exeunt.*

SEYMOUR *and* TRICK *rush on.*

SEYMOUR. Quick, quick! Saddle every horse—raise the house—send for the fire engines! The village is in flames. Howard, lose not a moment! Follow me and let us save the innocents, or perish in the attempt! [*Exit.*

HOWARD. Fly—order my horses, and return on the instant!

> [TRICK *runs off, rubbing his hands.*

Enter TRAP, *running.*

TRAP. Be on your guard; 'tis a trick of your rival's. I learnt it all from a drunken booby who has received ten guineas for burning an old shed not worth two. Mum—here's Trick. [*Exit.*

Re-enter TRICK, *running.*

TRICK. All's right. The horse is ready, sir. Captain Seymour's off already.

HOWARD. Generous fellow, he'll immortalize himself! Trick, how constantly the newspapers teem with the noble conduct of the military at fires!

TRICK. Yes, sir! Let us haste and distinguish ourselves.

HOWARD. True! If not for the sake of the newspapers—for
humanity.   [*Going.*

TRICK. True, sir! For humanity and the newspapers.
[*Following.*

HOWARD. It is so sweet, to assist the afflicted.

TRICK. Dinner's nothing to it.

HOWARD. To save a child from the flames.

TRICK. To restore it to its raving mother.

HOWARD. To hear her thanks.

TRICK. But sir, if you don't make haste, mothers, fathers,
children, cows, cocks, hens, and chickens will all be burned to
cinders.

HOWARD. True! As Hamlet says, 'Lead on, I'll follow thee.'
[*Rushes off, followed by* TRICK.

Enter SEYMOUR.

SEYMOUR. Victoria, victoria, he's caught, the day is won, and
the lovely prize is mine!

TRICK *runs on.*

TRICK. All's safe; I gave him the slip as he was preparing to
mount his horse, [HOWARD *enters at back.*] and ran back to
bring you the joyful tidings—ere this he will have passed the
boundary, and the day's your own.

SEYMOUR. Trick, thou prince of valets, come to my arms, and
be my friend for ever.
[*As* SEYMOUR *embraces* TRICK, HOWARD *advances behind
his rival, and looks* TRICK *full in the face, who immediately
disengages himself from* SEYMOUR *and runs off.*

HOWARD. Precious scoundrel!

SEYMOUR. Howard!

HOWARD. [*Bowing.*] In propria persona.

SEYMOUR. Why, I thought you were at the fire.

HOWARD. Oh no, I waited for you.

SEYMOUR. The fact is, my mare slipped her shoulder.

HOWARD. And my horse lost a shoe. In short, my noble rival,
I am sorry for the ten guineas you have so gallantly lost, but
were all the brick-sheds in England in a blaze, I have a flame

here [*Pointing to his heart.*] before which they would pale
their ineffectual fires. And so farewell, my noble Ephesian.
You must fire more temples ere you win this war's garland.

> The strength of love alone to me's a host,
> And may he win the prize who loves it most!

[*Exit, laughing.*

SEYMOUR. Confound your poetry!

Enter CHARLOTTE.

But I care not. Antæus-like, each overthrow but renews my
ardour, and the order of the day shall be, Death or Victory!

CHARLOTTE. 'Death or Victory!' Very fine, indeed! Do you
really think, Captain Seymour, that a woman's heart is to be
carried like a castle, by fire and sword, that you thus burn
your way to my affections? This late conflagration was a
notable proof of your gallantry. A brick-shed sacrificed at the
Shrine of Love!

SEYMOUR. I would have sacrificed an empire for such a prize!

CHARLOTTE. An empire? Pshaw! For such a divinity as
Charlotte Doubtful you should have set a world on fire, and
Phæton-like

> Snatch from Apollo's hands the reins, and learn
> To see a universe around you burn!

Now do that, and should I escape unsinged I'll——

SEYMOUR. What?

CHARLOTTE. Think about it.

SEYMOUR. Adorable girl! Thus, on my knees, I swear——

CHARLOTTE. Attention, Captain, some one approaches.

CHARLOTTE *retires quickly to arbour, unseen by* TRAP *as he runs
on breathless.*

SEYMOUR. S'death and the devil! What brought you here?

TRAP. I'm a lost man!

SEYMOUR. That's no loss.

TRAP. Ah, sir, but such a dreadful thing has happened!

SEYMOUR. What, is my mother dead again?

TRAP. No, sir. No, but Captain Howard——

SEYMOUR. What of him?

TRAP. He's off.

SEYMOUR. Dead?

TRAP. No, sir—fled with Miss Charlotte.

SEYMOUR. You don't say so!

TRAP. Fact, sir. Mount your horse, and you may overtake them, sir—there goes the chaise. [*Pointing off.*

SEYMOUR. [*Looking through his eye-glass.*] I see four capital greys. And did you see all this yourself?

TRAP. With my own eyes. Anxious to regain your good opinion, which I saw the mistake this morning respecting your respected mother had somewhat shaken, I dogged Captain Howard like his very shadow. Miss Doubtful was taking her afternoon walk by the road-side, the Captain lurking behind. Suddenly he rushed upon her, popped her into the carriage, and set off full gallop.

SEYMOUR. And were you a quiet spectator of all this?

TRAP. What could I do, sir, against a chaise and four? I halloed out; he threatened to shoot me, so I ran to you. [CHARLOTTE *begins to advance.*] Follow instantly, my dear master; your horse is ready, and there's not a moment to lose!

SEYMOUR. [*Pretending to exit, stops short.*] And did the lady make no resistance?

TRAP. Not the least. I should be sorry to take away a lady's character, but indeed it appeared to me a settled thing between the parties.

SEYMOUR. What, not a struggle—not a scream?

TRAP. Not one.

CHARLOTTE. [*Who has advanced behind* TRAP.] Not one, Mr. Trap?

TRAP. [*Horror-struck.*] Oh yes, ma'am—I recollect one scream, so unlimited, so tremendous, so terrific, that the Captain was compelled to—to——

SEYMOUR. To what, sir?

TRAP. To bring the lady back again.

CHARLOTTE. Ha, ha, ha! I am extremely obliged to you, Mr. Trap, for remembering that scream, so essential to my character; but I cannot thank you sufficiently at present for the fatigues of the journey—and above all, that terrific scream has so exhausted me, that I must retire and repose. Farewell, Captain Seymour; good evening, Mr. Trap. Ha, ha, ha!   [*Exit.*

SEYMOUR. And now, you rascal, what do you deserve?

TRAP. Nothing sir. Virtue is its own reward.

SEYMOUR. Virtue?

TRAP. Yes, sir. As the black man says in the play, I have done all in honour. With bitter grief did I see that you bribed Trick, and placed no confidence in my abilities. This roused my honour—for honour is my failing—and I immediately got myself bribed, to convince you of your error.

SEYMOUR. This time I pardon you, but beware how you offend again. Go and inform your suborner how it has fared with you, and say I wish to speak to him particularly.

TRAP. I will, sir. What will be the next contrivance, I wonder?
                                                      [*Exit.*

SEYMOUR. The rascal's right. When we bribe the servants of others we little think, by so doing, we undermine the fidelity of our own.

Enter HOWARD.

HOWARD. Seymour, you sent for me. Is it to resign the girl?

SEYMOUR. Never but with life!

HOWARD. Well then, I'll relieve you from so painful an alternative by giving up my pretensions.

SEYMOUR. Some new manœuvre?

HOWARD. No. When we first vowed eternal friendship, I was in love with a very beautiful girl who returned my passion, but her father, being opposed to mine in politics, refused consent. We parted with the usual vows of constancy, but after a time, looking upon my passion as hopeless, and seeing Charlotte——

SEYMOUR. I understand. Oh, you faithless Adonis!

HOWARD. Although the first love may sleep, it is a slumber that a breath may disturb.

SEYMOUR. Has yours risen, then, like a giant refreshed?

HOWARD. Joking apart. I have just received this letter [*Gives letter to* SEYMOUR.] from Caroline. Her father is dead—she is still true—and rich and lovely, awaits me with impatience.

SEYMOUR. I see. [*Returns letter.*

HOWARD. Now Charlotte here is rich and lovely, but she leaves me to chance. Caroline prefers me to all others—I have therefore determined to resign the contest and quit the field.

SEYMOUR. I'll believe it when I see you cross the boundary.

HOWARD. Well then, see me across the boundary.

SEYMOUR. I will.

HOWARD. I ask it as a favour. Night approaches—my chaise is ready—and as Charlotte's charms might yet unsettle me, I shall avoid the pain of an adieu and start immediately. Will you go with me?

SEYMOUR. I will.

HOWARD. You will make my excuses to Charlotte and her guardian, for I'll not see her again, but throw myself into the carriage—shut the blinds—and not look back till out of danger.

SEYMOUR. Quite right.

HOWARD. [*Sighing.*] I shall be bad company—therefore spare me all conversation. Wrapt in my cloak and lost in thought, a nod or a mutter will be all you can expect.

SEYMOUR. Oh, be as stupid as you please; but remember, when we reach the land-mark, you get out and pass it before me— then I go where you please.

HOWARD. Still mistrustful! Well, be it so. The evening draws on, and time presses—I'll fetch my cloak, and rejoin you instantly. [*Exit.*

SEYMOUR. Is this a trick or not? He seems sincere, but it is as well to be cautious, for hang me if I think that a girl like Charlotte is to be parted with so easily as my rival pretends! So no standing at ease yet—I'll seek my ally, the sapient Mr. Trick, and hear what he says. [*Exit.*

Enter TRAP, *muffled up in* HOWARD's *cloak and hat.*

TRAP. I wish this joke was over—I'm afraid it will prove a dear frolic for me. When we reach the land-mark, I get out and fasten the door—Captain Seymour is driven rapidly across the boundary—and then, legs befriend me!

Enter SEYMOUR, *unobserved by* TRAP.

SEYMOUR. So, there's Howard. His manner is very suspicious— and why has he muffled himself up so mysteriously?
                           [*Conceals himself in arbour.*

TRAP. My courage is evaporating——

SEYMOUR. Where can Trick loiter? Oh, here he comes.

Enter TRICK, *muffled up in* SEYMOUR'*s hat and cloak.*

TRICK. If I am discovered. Heaven have mercy upon my bones! And I am so much accustomed to get *behind* a carriage, I don't think I shall have courage to get *into* one.   [TRAP *coughs.*

TRICK. [*Alarmed.*] What's that? As I live, it's the Captain! Needs must, when his majesty drives.
    [*Pointing below. They mutually salute each other with great formality.*

TRAP. [*Fearfully putting his hand out of the cloak, and taking that of* TRICK'*s.*] Hem, hem!

TRICK. [*Shaking* TRAP'*s hand.*] Hem, hem!

TRAP. [*Makes signs to offer to go to the carriage.*] Hem, hem!

TRICK. [*Nods assent.*] Hem, hem!
    [*They compliment each other as to priority; at last* TRAP *passes off quickly, followed as quickly by* TRICK.

SEYMOUR. [*Advancing from the arbour.*] Excellent! They are getting in—now they're seated. Drive off, my boy. That's it —off they go, and in less than ten minutes they pass the boundary, and Charlotte's mine!

Enter HOWARD; *by remaining up the stage and looking off, he does not see* SEYMOUR.

HOWARD. Bravo, bravo! There they go—and now to my charmer!   [*They mutually turn, and run against each other.*

HOWARD. Seymour!

SEYMOUR. Howard!

HOWARD. This is beyond all patience. Trick!

SEYMOUR. He's in the chaise. Ha, ha, ha!

HOWARD. With your Trap. Precious scoundrels!

SEYMOUR. Captain Howard, you have insulted me—bribed my servant.

HOWARD. [*Quietly.*] And you mine.

SEYMOUR. Disguised him as an officer.

HOWARD. And you mine.

SEYMOUR. It seems that I was to have been the laughing-stock of my own valet. I shall expect satisfaction.

HOWARD. We have promised Charlotte not to fight.

SEYMOUR. Not to fight for her, certainly; but this is a different question, though you seem inclined to make it an excuse for sneaking out of a duel.

HOWARD. Captain Seymour, nobody has yet dared to say thus much to me.

SEYMOUR. That surprises me, for one don't venture much by it.

HOWARD. S'death and fire! Name your weapons!

SEYMOUR. Pistols.

HOWARD. Mine are at the gun-maker's.

SEYMOUR. Mine are in my pocket. [*Producing them.*] Take your choice.

HOWARD. Either. [*Takes one.*]

SEYMOUR. Eight paces?

HOWARD. Eight paces.
    [*They measure four paces each from back to back, and then turn.*

HOWARD. Seymour, must this be?

SEYMOUR. It must. Fire, or I brand you with the name of coward!
    [*They fire together—*SEYMOUR *falls—*HOWARD *runs to him.*

HOWARD. Seymour, are you hit?

SEYMOUR. Right through the breast. All's over!

HOWARD. Accursed passion!

HEARTLEY. [*Without.*] Here, John! Philip! Thomas!

SEYMOUR. Fly, fly! The family is alarmed. Should you be taken, this duel, without seconds, would be certain death. My horse —fly for your life!

HOWARD. I will not leave you!

SEYMOUR. Nay, nay, they will bring me aid. Howard, I forgive you—and when I am dead, Charlotte shall be yours——
            [*Voices without,* 'This way,' *&c., and trampling of feet.*

HOWARD. Generous Seymour! They come, and I must fly; forgive, and pity me!   [*Exit* HOWARD *hastily.*

Enter HEARTLEY *and* CHARLOTTE, *followed by two* SERVANTS
with lights.

CHARLOTTE. Good Heavens! Seymour! And dead!

HEARTLEY. Impossible! Not five minutes ago I beheld him in conversation with Captain Howard.

CHARLOTTE. [*Observing pistol on stage.*] Oh! They have fought; and Seymour, the man I now feel I loved, has fallen the victim of my fatal project!

HEARTLEY. [*Looking off.*] It must be so; for see where Howard gallops like a madman, and is now passing the boundary.

SEYMOUR. [*Jumping up.*] Huzza! Huzza! The day is mine!
                                          [*General surprise.*

CHARLOTTE. For Heaven's sake, explain!

SEYMOUR. He thinks he has killed me. In short, suspecting his last trick, I determined to end all by forcing him to a duel. I knew his pistols were not at hand and brought mine, loaded only with powder. He has passed the boundary, and the prize, I trust, is mine.

Noise behind. Enter TRICK *and* TRAP, *both intoxicated, and singing*

        'See the conquering hero comes'.

SEYMOUR. So, rascals, which kept his countenance longest?

TRICK. Oh, we acted our parts beautifully, until discovering a bottle of brandy in the chaise we became so mutually attentive that at last we forgot which was not to be the other, and have come back to enquire.

SEYMOUR. Ah, you pair of rascals!

TRAP. My dear friend, where's the bottle?

TRICK. Here, most estimable man.

> [TRAP *takes the bottle, and finding it empty, respectfully returns it to* TRICK. SEYMOUR, CHARLOTTE, *and* HEARTLEY, *who have retired while* TRAP *asks for the bottle, now advance.*

SEYMOUR. All shall be explained to Howard. I know his friendship, and the knowledge of my safety will, if anything can, atone for his disappointment.

CHARLOTTE. Well, as I believe you are the only man that ever died for love, I pardon the duel, and surrender on honourable terms.

> Thus I resign the spinster's merry life,
> For the more solemn duties of a wife.
> Cheer my adventurous path with one kind ray
> And your petitioners shall ever pray.

HOW TO SETTLE ACCOUNTS
WITH YOUR LAUNDRESS

AN ORIGINAL FARCE IN ONE ACT

BY

JOSEPH STIRLING COYNE (1803–1868)

———

First performed at the Adelphi Theatre
26 July 1847

———

CAST

WHITTINGTON WIDGETTS, a West-end tailor   Mr. Wright
BARNEY TWILL, Widgetts's page and light porter
                                            Mr. Ryan
JACOB BROWN, a hairdresser at the opera   Mr. Munyard
POSTMAN   Mr. Lindon
WAITER   Mr. Mitchenson
MLLE. CHERI BOUNCE, an opera dancer   Miss E. Harding
MARY WHITE, a young laundress   Miss Woolgar

812466X   **N**

PREFACE TO
HOW TO SETTLE ACCOUNTS WITH YOUR LAUNDRESS

LIKE John Maddison Morton, Coyne was an author of that sort of mid-century farce that dealt in the comedy of the material and domestic, the tradesman's counter and the suburban parlour, the shop assistant and his sweetheart, the public house and the homely fireside, the delights of grilled sausages and the extra-special pint of champagne. Coyne was an active journalist as well as a dramatist, and one of the first contributors to *Punch*; he was also drama critic of the *Sunday Times*. He wrote a book on the scenery and antiquities of Ireland (illustrated by W. H. Bartlett) and in 1856 became secretary of the Dramatic Authors' Society. Coyne's plays were performed between 1835 and 1869, and half his output of some seventy pieces consisted of farces; like most dramatists of his time he also wrote comedies, extravaganzas, burlesques, and melodramas. Many of his farces were performed at the Adelphi, which meant catering specially for Adelphi audiences and their enjoyment of working- and lower-middle-class characters, physical business, and the low-comedy talents of Wright and Bedford. These farces are perhaps Coyne's most interesting work.

Aside from *How to Settle Accounts with your Laundress*, the best of Coyne's farces, his writing for the Adelphi is well characterized by two pieces, *Binks the Bagman* (1843) and *Did You Ever Send your Wife to Camberwell?* (1846). The former is thoroughly plebeian: the setting is an inn at Dover and the *dramatis personae* include the innkeeper and his wife, the chambermaid, a sailor, and a commercial traveller from Whitechapel, Binks, who pays marked attention to the land-lord's wife. The sailor, Robinson, owns a tame bear and is determined to revenge himself upon his wife's admirer, whom he takes to be Binks. The unwitting bagman finds himself in the same bedroom as Robinson (a situation rather like that of Morton's *The Double-Bedded Room*) and overhears him talk of cutting the bear's throat and selling its skin. Believing that he is the subject of this speech, the terrified Binks rushes about the room pursued by Robinson; the climax is purely physical.

Did You Ever Send your Wife to Camberwell? is worth summarizing to illustrate the manner in which Coyne manipulates subject-matter and technique to produce the comic effects that constituted 'screaming farce', a term used on Adelphi playbills in the forties. To get his wife out of the way so that he can keep a rendezvous with another woman, Honeybun, a poor attorney's clerk, sends her to Camberwell with a note to his rich but estranged aunt, begging for financial assistance. His eccentric neighbour Crank calls in from next door and leaves his hat; Mrs. Crank, searching for her husband and believing Honeybun's apartment to be his, enters carrying her baby, sees Mrs. Honeybun's bonnet, concludes that Crank is living with another woman, leaves the baby and her umbrella, and dashes out in despair. Crank returns to retrieve his hat, discovers the umbrella, believes that Honeybun is his wife's lover, and rushes off, furiously vowing revenge. Honeybun enters, finds the baby, hides it behind the chest of drawers when he hears a knock at the door, and conceals himself in fear and trembling. Aunt Jewell arrives to forgive the Honeybuns their marriage, sees the baby, thinks it is theirs, coos over it, and takes it away to be looked after properly.[1] Honeybun comes out of hiding; Crank rushes in, attacks him, and rushes out again to procure pistols. In the struggle the chest of drawers is knocked over; the horrified Honeybun believes that the baby has been squashed flat, puts on his wife's bonnet and cloak, and hides on the roof in the pouring rain. Crank runs in and out again without finding him; Mrs. Crank enters, having been unable to discover her husband, feels tired, gets into bed, and draws the curtains around her. Honeybun climbs back through the window, soaking wet; his suspicious wife returns to discover Mrs. Crank in the bed; she promptly asks for her child, thus further enraging Mrs. Honeybun and terrifying her helpless husband. The still furious Crank comes back, but his mistake is revealed; Aunt Jewell returns with the baby and her forgiveness; the contrite Honeybun tears up his rendezvous note and, addressing the audience,

---

[1] Aunt Jewell's first speech is the fourth consecutive soliloquy; before her Mrs. Crank, Crank, and Honeybun have individually informed the audience of their problems and intentions.

declares his intention of sending his wife to Camberwell every evening despite the difficulties. All this is good vigorous stage business, very domestic, apparently artless and naïve but really carefully calculated, with entrances, exits, concealments, mis-identifications, and misunderstandings cleverly arranged in a sequential pattern of comic climaxes.

For the Haymarket and not the Adelphi Coyne wrote *Box and Cox Married and Settled* (1852), which like the original makes comic use of food as the two couples bicker over a large breakfast while energetically eating it. The play also cleverly catches *Box and Cox*'s symmetry and dialogue rhythms, as in the passage which occurs after Mrs. Box has swooned into Cox's arms and Mrs. Cox into Box's because Cox has discovered and made public an affectionate note that Box wrote to Mrs. Cox before either couple was married:

cox. Hah, Box, you're a villain!

box. Cox, you're another!

cox. Drop my wife this instant, sir!

box. I shan't, until you relinquish my better half.

cox. Miserable subterfuge! As husband of that lady I demand your card, sir.

box. You'll find it in my left-hand trousers' pocket—come and take it.

cox. I regret that the affair I have on hand prevents my availing myself of your polite offer.

box. Nothing but the pressing nature of my present engagement could make me think of putting you to so much trouble.

cox. Don't mention it. Will you allow me to make one observation?

box. Certainly, Cox, with pleasure.

cox. Well, then; I had no idea Mrs. Box was so ponderous.

box. And I assure you I am quite overpowered by the solidarity of Mrs. Cox.

How to Settle Accounts with your Laundress was given 109 performances before the Adelphi closed for two months in the summer of 1848. In addition to its popularity in England, the play was also performed in French and German. The authoritative text is in the *National Acting Drama*, v. 14; the much later *Dicks' Standard Plays*, no. 1006 is almost identical. The Lord Chamberlain's copy—with the title of *Settling Accounts with your Laundress*—was also used in collation; the acting editions amplify the manuscript text considerably.

SCENE. *A Tailor's Show-room, Jermyn-street, handsomely fitted up with cheval-glass, large round table in centre, fashionable chairs, &c. A dummy figure, dressed in the extreme mode, near window. Articles of gentlemen's attire exhibited in window,* L. *Door of entrance to street,* L. *Fire-place and chimney glass,* R. *Door to* WIDGETTS's *chamber,* R. *Large pair of folding-doors,* C., *opening towards the stage; beyond these doors a passage to the kitchen, in which stands a stillion, with a water-butt standing on it. At the end of this passage, the door of the kitchen. A round table,* C., *with writing materials and lighted candle upon it. A print of the fashions and tailor's patterns cut in brown paper on the wall. Table at back,* L., *on which is a table lamp. Another table at back,* R., *on which is a bottle of brandy and glasses.* TWILL *discovered brushing the coat on the dummy figure, and singing a verse of an Irish song. A postman's knock at door,* L.

TWILL. Whist! I'll bet a pinny that's the post. [*Runs to door and opens it;* POSTMAN *appears.*]

POSTMAN. Mr. Widgetts. [*Gives letter to* TWILL.]

TWILL. Thank you, sir. Maybe you've got a bit of a letter for me, from my poor mother in Ireland? I'm not particular—the first that comes to hand in the bundle will do.

POSTMAN. No, I haven't one for you.

TWILL. Thank you, sir. Maybe you'd have one the next time. Good-bye, sir. [POSTMAN *goes away.* TWILL *reads the address on the letter.*] 'Whittington Widgetts, Esquire.' Ow wow! Esquire! The devil a ha'porth less. 'Whittington Widgetts, Esquire, Hierokosma, Jarmyn Street.' Hierokosma! That's French for a tailor's shop. By the Attorney-General, 'twould give a man a headache in his elbow to write such a cramp word. [*Smells the letter.*] Why then, it smells elegant intirely. [*Goes to door* R. *and enters while speaking.*] Mr. Widgetts, here's a letter for you, sir.
    [*Returns immediately from the room, re-commences his song, and begins to brush the figure again. A church clock in the neighbourhood strikes eight.*

WIDGETTS. Twill!   [*Speaking from the door of chamber.*

TWILL. There, listen to that row. That master of mine will persist in calling me Twill, though he knows my name is Barney Toole, because Twill, he says, is genteeler.

WIDGETTS. What o'clock is that, Twill?

TWILL. Eight o'clock, sir.

WIDGETTS. Put up the shutters.

TWILL. What the devil can he mean? We never shut until nine o'clock.

Enter WIDGETTS *from chamber, kissing a note which he holds.*

WIDGETTS. Well, don't you hear me? Put up the shutters and close the establishment, directly.

TWILL. Of coorse, sir; never say it twice.
   [TWILL *runs out and is seen putting up the window shutters outside.*

WIDGETTS. This night I devote to the tender union of love and lobsters. The adorable Ma'amselle Cheri Bounce, the ballet dancer, at last consents to partake a little quiet supper with me here this evening. I must read her charming note once more. 'Ma'amselle Cheri Bounce presents compliments to Mr. Whittington Widgetts, will feel happy to sup with Mr. W. W. this evening. Ma'amselle C. B. fears that female notions don't correspond with supping with a single gent, but lobsters is stronger than prudence, therefore trusts to indulgence; at nine o'clock precise. P.S. I'll come in my blue *visite* and my native innocence, and hopes you'll treat them with proper delicacy.' Glorious! Angelic creature! [*Kisses the letter and puts it in his waistcoat pocket.*] Oh, Widgetts, you lucky rascal, to have the happiness of a private and confidential supper with that magnificent girl, whose image has never left my mind since the evening I danced with her at the Casino! Twill!
                          Enter TWILL.

TWILL. Sir?

WIDGETTS. You must run directly to the tavern over the way, and order them to send a roast fowl and lobster in the shell, here at nine o'clock.

TWILL. Roast fowl, sir?

WIDGETTS. And lobster. He—hem! I expect a particular party to sup with me.

TWILL. Coorse you'll want cigars, sir?

WIDGETTS. No. The party, Twill, is a lady and don't smoke.

TWILL. A lady! Tare my agers, sir. Does the lady bring the lady's maid with her?

WIDGETTS. Don't be impertinent, Twill, but listen to me. The party I expect is Ma'amselle Cheri Bounce, a splendid creature, who dances on a limited income, with the strictest regard to propriety, at the Opera House, and gives lessons to private pupils in the *pokar* and the waltz *ah do tongs*.

TWILL. Whoo! She must be a switcher. [*Going.*] I'll run directly, sir!

WIDGETTS. Stay; I must make myself attractive for the interesting occasion. Give me the coat that has just been finished for Sir Chippin Porrage, and the waistcoat that's to be sent home to-morrow morning for the Honourable Cecil Harrowgate's wedding. [TWILL *hands a dress coat and waistcoat from the table,* L.] I'll give them an air of gentility by wearing them this evening. That will do. There, be off now.

TWILL. Ha, ha! By the powers o' war, when you get them on your back, sir, you'll be like Mulligan's dog; your own father wouldn't know you.

WIDGETTS *carries the coat and waistcoat into his bed-room.* TWILL *is going towards door, when* MARY WHITE *enters, carrying a basket of clothes under her arm.*

MARY. Here, Twill, take my basket, good chap. Is master at home?

TWILL. [*Takes basket.*] Yes, he *is* at home. [*Aside.*] Take my basket—good chap—well, there's no bearing the impidence of the lower orders. [*Sets down basket, and calls at door,* R.] Please, sir, here's the laundress come for your clothes. [*Aside.*] Good chap! [*Exit.*

Enter WIDGETTS.

WIDGETTS. [*Aside.*] She always comes at an awkward crisis. Mary, my dear, you're rather late this evening.

MARY. Oh dear, yes. I've been half over the town for my

customers' washing and I'm almost tired to death, but I left yours for last, that we might have a comfortable chat together. Stop a minute though, till I take off my clogs.

[*She goes into the kitchen passage through the folding-doors.*

WIDGETTS. The poor creature loves me to distraction, but she's painfully familiar; she forgets that our positions are materially altered since I was a journeyman tailor in a two pair back, struggling to make love and trowsers for the small remuneration of fifteen shillings a week. Mary White is an uncommon nice girl—as a laundress, but my sentiments is changed respecting her as a wife.

Re-enter MARY.

MARY. Now, Widgy dear—oh, good gracious, what a love of a waistcoat you've on! Let me look at it, do! Well, it's a real beauty.

WIDGETTS. Stylish, eh? The last Paris touch.

MARY. You used not to wear such waistcoats as that when you lived in Fuller's Rents.

WIDGETTS. Oh no, no! Ha, ha! [*Aside.*] I wish she'd cut Fuller's Rents.

MARY. Do you know, Widgy, I don't think you're at all improved since you fell in for that fortune by a legacy you never expected. When you lived in Fuller's Rents you used to walk out with me on a Sunday; you never walk with me at all now.

WIDGETTS. Walking's vulgar, my dear.

MARY. And you sometimes used to take me at half-price to the theatres.

WIDGETTS. Theatres is low, my dear.

MARY. And you remember how we used to go together to Greenwich, with a paper of ham sandwiches in my basket, and sit under the trees in the park, and talk, and laugh—law, how we used to laugh to be sure—and then you used to talk of love and constancy and connubial felicitude in a little back parlour, and a heap of beautiful things.

WIDGETTS. [*Aside.*] A heap of rubbish.

MARY. And you know, Widgy dear, when we enter that happy state—

WIDGETTS. What state do you allude to, Miss White?

MARY. The marriage state, of course.

WIDGETTS. Oh, indeed. Ah!

MARY. You don't forget, I hope, that I have your promissory note on the back of twenty-nine unpaid washing bills to make me your lawful wife. [*Produces several papers.*] There they are —and there's the last of them. 'Six months after date I promise to marry Miss Mary White.' There, sir, you're due next Monday.

WIDGETTS. Am I! Then I'm afraid I shan't be prepared to take myself up. I'll let myself be protested.

MARY. No, you shan't; you've been protested often enough. I can't be put off any longer, and understand me, Mr. Widgetts, I *won't* neither.

WIDGETTS. [*Aside.*] There's a savage hymeneal look in her eye that makes me shiver in my Alberts. I must soothe her a little or I shall have a scene. Why, Mary my dear, now don't be angry; you know it's one of my jokes.

MARY. Well, you'd better not try any more of them, for I don't like them. No woman does.

WIDGETTS. No, of course, no woman does. Ha, ha, ha! Quite proper too, my dear.

MARY. Well, now that matter's settled, I'll go and collect your soiled things, for it's getting late.

WIDGETTS. Do so, Mary; you'll find them in my room as usual. I'll make out the list as you call them out. [MARY *enters room*, R., *and* WIDGETTS *prepares to write.*] She's resolved to make me her victim and I don't know how to get rid of her. I'd give—

MARY. [*Inside.*] Four shirts.

WIDGETTS. [*Writes.*] Four shirts. She's a perfect treasure at shirt buttons, but what is shirt buttons to a bosom that beats for another?

MARY. [*Inside.*] One false front.

WIDGETTS. [*Writes.*] One false front. She'd make a comfortable little wife if she only had——

MARY. [*Inside.*] A pair of white trowsers.

WIDGETTS. [*Writes.*] A pair of white trowsers. Ah! I wore those ducks at the Casino last Wednesday, and Ma'amselle Cheri Bounce observed, while I was handing her a glass of champagne—ecod, 'tis well I recollected it—I've forgotten to order champagne for my supper. I must run over to the tavern myself and tell them to send some.

[*Snatches up his hat and exit.*

Enter MARY, *with the white waistcoat worn at first by* WIDGETTS, *and a note in her hand.*

MARY. Well, you're a pretty careless fellow, to leave your letters in your waistcoat pocket. Where is he gone to? [*Examines the note curiously.*] 'Whittington Widgetts, Esq.' It's a woman's hand. I've a good mind to read it. I've no secrets from him and he has none from me—or at least he oughtn't to; so it can be no harm. [*Opens note and reads hastily.*] 'Ma'amselle Cheri Bounce'—ah!—'compliments— happy to sup with Mr. W. W. this evening—female notions —single gent—lobsters is stronger than prudence—therefore trusts to indulgence, at nine o'clock precise.' Oh, the minx! 'P.S. I'll come in my blue *visite* and my native innocence.' Oh, Widgetts, the false deceitful wretch! To deceive me and wash out all his promises; to wring my heart and mangle my affections like that. [*Sobbing.*] But I—I—don't care not a pin's point, no—I despise him and hate him worse than poison, and I'll—I'll—I'll—tell him so. [*Sobbing.*] I'll—I'll—

Enter JACOB BROWN.

BROWN. [*Angrily.*] Where's Widgetts! I want to see Widgetts.

MARY. Then you want to see a good-for-nothing fellow.

BROWN. Exactly, and I shouldn't mind adding that I consider him an humbug.

MARY. A wretch!

BROWN. Most decidedly.

MARY. A puppy!

BROWN. Not a doubt of it. You see we're unanimous in our
verdict. That man, ma'am, has been a *reptile* in my path, a
wiper to all my hopes, and an *adder* to all my woes; he has
lacerated my heart and singed the tender buds of young
affection here.   [*Lays his hands on his bosom.*

MARY. Ah! What has he done?

BROWN. He has *done me*, ma'am, *me*, Brown; that's what he's
done. Cut me out with Ma'amselle Cheri Bounce.

MARY. Cheri Bounce! Ah! [*Aside.*] She that's to sup tonight with
Widgetts.

BROWN. I'm an 'airdresser, ma'am; my name's Brown, and I've
a professional engagement at the Opera House, where I
cultivate romance and ringlets amongst the ladies of the
ballet. There I first beheld the lovely Cheri Bounce, the very
image of the wax Wenus in my shop window. I loved her, not
for her foreign grace, but for her native hair. Oh, she had such
a head of real hair, and, oh, the showers of tears and the bottles
of Macassar oil that I've poured upon it nobody would
believe! Well, I toasted her for two years regularly, and at
length she consented to become *Brown*. Well, we were to
have been married; I had bought my wedding suit, when this
fellow Widgetts came to take the curl out of my happiness.
We quarrelled about him last Saturday, and grew so warm
that we've been cool ever since. But that's not all. This very
day I heard that she had accepted an invitation to sup with
him to-night, but I'll prevent *that*; he shall fight me—one of
us must fall—let him choose his own weapons—curling irons
if he likes.

MARY. Don't be rash, Brown. Widgetts has deceived *me* and
wronged *you*; we must take a better way of being revenged
on him.

BROWN. How? What way? Tell me! I'll do anything to be down
on Widgetts.

MARY. Then you must assist me in a scheme I've just thought of.
Here, carry this stuffed gentleman into the kitchen there.
                         [*Pointing to dummy figure.*

BROWN. This chap! Come along, old fellow. [*Takes him up.*] Why,
he's a regular railway speculator—nothing but a man of straw.

MARY. [*Taking a gown and other articles of female attire out of her basket.*] Aye, here's a gown, petticoat, and stockings, [*Takes a pair of green boots out of her pocket.*] and a pair of green boots. Now, Brown, you must dress the figure in these clothes.

[*Gives him clothes.*

BROWN. Dress him in these! Why, bless you, I don't know how. I'm not a lady's maid.

MARY. Oh, never mind; you'll manage very well. There, make haste, and do as I tell you.

BROWN. Well, I'm only made to order, so I'll try and do my best.

[*Exit through the folding-doors into the passage and then through the door beyond into kitchen.*

MARY. Now to write to Widgetts and tell him of my melancholy end. [*Writes and reads.*] 'Base man—I have discovered the truth of your falsity, and know all about the lobsters and the creetur that's to sup with you to-night. Oh, Widgetts! Once, you swore to love none but Mary *White*—but now your vows is *blew* to the winds. I shan't trouble you no more with my *mangled* feelings, for I'm going to drown myself in the water-butt in your kitchen, where you'll find me. Adieu, Widgetts— I forgive you, but I know that my ghost and them lobsters will sit heavy on your stomach to-night; so no more at present from your departed—MARY WHITE.'

Enter BROWN.

BROWN [*Showing the figure dressed in the clothes given him by* MARY.] Here she is; will she do?

MARY. Oh, beautifully! Ha, ha, ha, ha! I can't help laughing at the droll figure I cut. [*Folds and directs the letter.*] There lies the train that's to blow up Widgetts. Now, Brown, we must pop her head-downwards into the water-butt.

BROWN. Well, that's easily done.

MARY. [WIDGETTS *heard singing in the street.*] Hark! I hear Widgetts coming—quick, we must get out by the back door quietly.

[*Exeunt into the passage, closing the folding-doors after them.*

PLATE 2

How to Settle Accounts with your Laundress. Widgetts discovers a 'suicide'.
British Museum

Enter WIDGETTS *by street door.*

WIDGETTS. I've ordered the champagne—these opera girls all
drink champagne, when they can get it. I wonder is *she* here
still. [*Looks into chamber.*] Ah, bravo! She's gone. [*Sees the
letter on table.*] Ah, a letter—for me! [*Opens it carelessly, starts
and reads to himself.*] Oh, oh, oh! What? 'MaryWhite—I'm
going to drown myself in the water-butt, where you'll find
me.' Gracious powers! 'Adieu, Widgetts, I forgive you.' Poor
dear soul. 'But my ghost and them lobsters will sit heavy on
your stomach to-night.' Horrible idea! It can't be true—she'd
never go to commit such a catastrophe in my establishment.
Make a coroner's inquest of herself in my private water-butt,
when the Thames is open to all! No, she's only said so to
frighten me. [*Throws letter on the floor and goes to folding
doors.*] Why, Mary, Mary, my dear, don't be foolish, ha, ha,
ha, ha! I know it's one of your jokes, ha, ha! Little rogue—
ha, ha, ha, ha! [*Throws open folding doors and discovers the
dummy figure, which has been dressed in female garments, with
the legs and part of the dress sticking out of the water-butt, a pair
of women's green boots on the feet of the figure.* WIDGETTS
totters back, horrified at the sight.] Oh, oh, oh! She's done it;
she's there, with her legs sticking out of the water-butt, and
her green Sunday boots on her feet—and the vital spark
extinct! Oh! It's too dreadful a sight for human feelings: them
legs, and them green boots. [*Returns and closes the folding
doors.*] What an awful sensation 'twill make when its found
out; they'll have my *head* in all the print-shops and my *tale* in
all the newspapers—I shall be brought out at half the theatres
too. They'll make *three* shocking acts of one fatal act at the
Victoria, and they'll have the real water and water-butt at the
Surrey. What's to be done? I'm in a desperate state of mind,
and feel as if I could take my own measure for an unmade
coffin.

Enter TWILL, *at the last words.*

TWILL. I've ordered it, sir, for nine precisely.

WIDGETTS. [*Starts.*] Ordered it? What?

TWILL. The fowl and the lobster in the shell.

WIDGETTS. Oh! Ha! I was thinking of another *shell*. Ha, ha, ha, ha! Light the lamp, Twill. [*With forced gaiety.*] We'll have a jolly night, ha, ha, ha, ha!

Old King Cole was a jolly old soul, and a jolly old soul was he;
He called for his pipe, and he called for his bowl,
    And he called for his fiddlers three.

TWILL. Aye, master, that's the way to drown old care.

WIDGETTS. Drown who, sir? Do you mean sir, that any one is drowned in this establishment?

TWILL. Me sir, not I, sir—I only—

WIDGETTS. Go and lay the table for supper.

> [TWILL *picks up* MARY's *letter from the floor, twists it into an allumette, and, lighting it at the candle, lights with it the lamp on table at back.* WIDGETTS *walks about in a state of agitation and endeavours to sing.*

WIDGETTS. It's an awful business—but at all events they can't charge me with the deed. I have her letter to prove she made away with herself; *that* will clear me. [*Searches his pockets hastily.*] Where is it? What have I done with it? [*Looking about the floor.*] Eh! No, no! Twill, Twill, have you seen a letter lying about here?

TWILL. Letter! I found a piece of crumpled paper on the floor that I've lighted the lamp with; there's a bit of it left though.
        [*Gives him a fragment of the burnt letter.*

WIDGETTS. [*Glances hastily at it.*] Oh, heivings! You've lighted the lamp, and snuffed out the candle of my precious existence!

TWILL. Why, what's the matter, Mr. Widgetts? You are going to faint; stop till I'll fetch you a glass of water from the water-butt.

WIDGETTS. [*Interposing to prevent* TWILL *going to the kitchen.*] Water! Forbear!

TWILL. Bless me, how dreadful you look!

WIDGETTS. Do I? Ah, very likely! I've been seized with a sudden swimming in the water-butt—the head—the head, I mean.

TWILL. By my sowl—I see how it is: the murder's out.

WIDGETTS. [*Collaring him.*] Murder—what murder do you allude to? Who's done it, sir? Speak!

TWILL. Asy, Mr. Widgetts—asy, sir—sure I know you've been taking a drop too much.

WIDGETTS. A drop! [*Aside.*] The word puts me in a cold perspiration. Oh, aye—ha, ha, ha! You may go, Twill; I shan't want you any longer. Stop! You haven't had any enjoyment lately; there's an order for the Adelphi; go there my boy, and be happy. [*Gives him a card.*]

TWILL. Oh, thank you, sir, may be I'm not a lucky boy.
[*Exit hastily.*

WIDGETTS. Now he's gone, I can reflect upon my terrible situation. *She* must be removed—but how? That's the point.
[*He stands, buried in thought.*

Enter MARY, *disguised as a boy, wearing an old blouse.*

MARY. Aei—aei—yoo—

WIDGETTS. Eh! Who are you? What do you want?

MARY. E-eh? You must speak up; I'm rather hard of hearing.

WIDGETTS. [*Bawling.*] I say, what do you want?

MARY. I'm Mary White, the laundress's young man, and I'm come to carry home her basket of clothes.

WIDGETTS. The devil! [*Speaking very loud.*] She's gone, my good fellow; she's been gone these two hours.

MARY. Two hours! Well, I'm in no hurry; I can stop, but I may as well eat my supper while I'm waiting. I've got a plummy slice of ham in my pocket, [*Pulls a crust of bread and a slice of ham, wrapped in a play-bill, from her pocket.*] and a play-bill too, for a table-cloth. [*Spreading bill on table.*] I think that's coming it rather genteel. [*Takes a clasp knife out of her pocket.*] Fond of ham, old fellow?

WIDGETTS. Why, you impudent young vagabond, you don't mean to say you're going to sup here? Be off, and be damn'd to you.

MARY. Well, you *are* a regular brick, and I don't mind if I do take some of your pickles.

WIDGETTS. [*Bawls.*] Zounds! I say, you mustn't sup here.

MARY. Mustn't sup here? Why didn't you say so at once? Never mind, I'll go into the kitchen and take it there.   [*Going.*

WIDGETTS. [*Alarmed.*] To the kitchen! [*Holds her.*] Not for the world; you quite misunderstood me—don't disturb yourself; sit down, do. [*Pushes her again into the chair—aside.*] What's to become of me? I'd pitch him into the street, only I'm afraid of making a disturbance. There's no making him hear. Ecod! I know what I'll do; I'll run and borrow the speaking-trumpet that I saw this morning hanging at Smith, the broker's, door, and speak to him through that. [*Going, returns.*] Stay, the devil might tempt him to peep into the kitchen; I'll lock the door.

> [*Locks the folding-door, goes through pantomime, expressive of sorrow for his victim in the water-butt, and exit.*

MARY. [*Jumping up and laughing.*] Ha, ha, ha, ha, ha! Ho, ho, ho, ho! Oh, dear, never was anything managed so cleverly. Ha, ha, ha, ha! [*Throwing off cap and neckerchief.*] To think that he didn't know me, and what a rage he was in. Well, now I'm ready for him in another character. [*Takes off her leggings and blouse, and appears dressed as a young man of fashion. Surveys herself in the cheval-glass.*] Yes, it will do—it will do—a very smart little fellow, not extensive, but uncommonly well got up. These were the clothes that poor Brown got to be married in; they fit me to a nicety. [*Knock at door.*] Come in.

Enter two WAITERS, *carrying tray with supper, covered dishes, plates, bottles, glasses, &c.*

WAITER. Supper, sir, ordered by Mr. Widgetts.

MARY. Supper! Oh, yes. All right. Mr. Widgetts is out, but he'll be back presently; leave it on this table if you please. [WAITER *places tray on table at back,* R.] There, that will do; plates, knives, and forks. All right—you need not wait, young man.

WAITER. Thank you, sir. Anything else, sir?

MARY. No; everything is beautiful, thank you.

WAITER. Thank you, sir. Good night, sir.

MARY. Good night. [*Exit* WAITERS. MARY *looks under the covers.*] Lobsters, roast fowl, kidneys. Ah! the ungrateful

wretch never asked me to such a supper, but never mind.
Hark, I hear him returning.

[*She throws the blouse, hat, and gaiters, into the clothes-basket
and carries all into the chamber.*

Enter WIDGETTS.

WIDGETTS. [*Shouting through speaking-trumpet.*] Now young
fell—low I sa—a—ay! Hey! he's gone and the coast's clear.
[*Sees supper-tray.*] Oh! What! They've sent the supper from
the tavern. I quite forgot it. Dear me, this dreadful affair has
so upset me and given me such a turn that I doubt I'll never
come straight again. What will Ma'amselle Cheri Bounce
think of me? I dare say she's been here and gone? Everybody's
gone but my interesting victim. Ah! She's still there, standing
with all her imperfections on her head in the water-butt. Well,
I suppose every one has his lot, but mine's a lot I don't know
how to dispose of. I must remove the body from the establishment at all events, and I'll do it now while the house is still.
[*Goes to folding-doors and puts key in the lock.*] Oh! I haven't
strength to open the door with them green boots kicking at
my conscience. Courage, Widgetts, courage! Be a man—
though you are but a tailor. Stay, I'll take a thimbleful of
brandy first. [*Takes bottle from table and pours out a glass which
he drinks.*] Ah, that's a reviver. [*Drinks and comes down.*] Betts
has raised the standard of British spirit in my heart. [*Drinks.*]
Well, we all want comfort in this miserable world. [*Drinks.*]
There's poor Mary White gone on a weeping and *wailing*
voyage to that bourne from whence no traveller gets a return
ticket. [MARY *laughs in room.*] Ah, what's that? A laugh—it
had a hollow and inhuman sound—could it be *she?* [*Points to
folding-doors.*] Mary—a—a—a—how do I know—she may
have been turned into something horrible. The fiend of the
water-butt, perhaps. She may come to me at night; she said
she would. Oh, Lord! The idea of the ghost of a damp laundress at your back. [*Shudders.*] W—h—h—h—hew! [MARY
laughs.] There, there it is again, that demoniac laugh. I wish
I could peep into the kitchen, but I daren't lest I should see
her glaring at me with one eye through the bung-hole of the
water-butt. Bless me, how my knees keep giving double
knocks upon each other! [MARY *sings in room.*] Ah! Surely

that's singing. [*Listens.*] Ghosts haven't got a singing license. Hark! 'Tis somebody committing vocal violence in my bed-room. [*Goes to door of bed-chamber and looks in.*] Hey! there's a young fellow making himself quite at home in my establish-ment. I am not aware I ever saw him before. What had I better do? Go in and ask him what he wants—no—that might be dangerous; 'twill be safer in my present peculiar position to appear as a stranger. Let me see—I have it—capital idea—the waiter from the tavern with the supper—I think I could do a waiter; it's only, 'Coming, sir, in *one* minute, coming; two brandies and water, coming, sir.' [*He ties one of the supper napkins round his neck for a white cravat, changes his coat for an old black one that hangs on the back of a chair; while doing so he looks into the room now and again.*] There goes my Macassar oil and my Circassian cream. There, my *eau de cologne* too, that cost me half-a-guinea a bottle. An impudent rascal! D——n me if he's not rummaging my drawers! That's free and easy at all events. Come, I think I'm pretty well disguised now. [*Looks at himself in the cheval-glass.*] No, confound it! This face of mine will never do—it might be known—I want a pair of whiskers to hide it. Ecod, I've hit it again; this chair —[*Takes knife from table and cuts open the stuffed seat of the chair.*] there's enough hair in it to whisker a regiment of Turks.

[*Pulls a handful of the hair out of the chair-seat, goes to the chimney-glass and arranges it round his chin so as to look like a pair of large whiskers.*]

Enter MARY, *still dressed as a young man, and drying her hands with a towel.*

MARY. [*Aside and laughing.*] Heavens, what a figure!

WIDGETTS. Hem! A—I beg your pardon—but you seem—a—eh?

MARY. Exactly. And who are you?

WIDGETTS. Me—I—a—ah—I'm—a—the waiter—from the tavern.

MARY. Perhaps, then, you can tell me where I can find Mr. Widgetts?

WIDGETTS. Not exactly. You've particular business with him?

MARY. Rather. In fact—I don't mind telling you—I'm one of the detective police.

WIDGETTS. [*Alarmed.*] You! A gentleman?

MARY. Oh yes, we go about in all manner of disguises when we want to pick up a shy bird. Now, I'm looking for Widgetts, and I shouldn't mind giving five pounds if you could tell me where to lay my hand upon him.
> [*Lays her hand on* WIDGETTS*'s shoulder, who starts.*

WIDGETTS. Ah! Ha, ha, ha! Five pounds! Is it a—very serious business, eh?

MARY. Merely a hanging matter.

WIDGETTS. Nothing more? [*Aside.*] The dreadful deed's discovered. I'll be off. Hem! Well, I'll go and look after Mr. Widgetts.

MARY. No, no, you must stop here; I've no doubt I shall want you presently.

Enter MADEMOISELLE CHERI BOUNCE.

CHERI. I beg pardon.

WIDGETTS. [*Aside.*] Zounds, Ma'amselle Cheri Bounce!

CHERI. I expected to meet a gent—Mr. Widgetts.

MARY. Who invited you to supper.

WIDGETTS. [*Aside.*] How did the fellow know that?

MARY. My friend Widgetts has been obliged to leave home rather suddenly, but he has left me here to perform the agreeable for him. Supper, you see, is waiting, ma'amselle.

WIDGETTS. [*Coming forward.*] Allow me to observe—

MARY. Lay the table.

WIDGETTS. [*Aside.*] The rascal's not going to eat my supper!
> [*Lays the table.*

CHERI. [*Aside.*] Really a very nice young man.

MARY. My name is Spraggs—Spraggs, ma'amselle—like my friend Widgetts I'm dotingly fond of the girls—aw—pawsitive fact—can't help it, never could, and don't think I ever shall. Let me take your shawl. [*Takes off* CHERI BOUNCE*'s shawl.*] A divine figure—demme!

WIDGETTS. [*Coming between them.*] Allow me to observe—

MARY. Lay the table, *waiter.*

WIDGETTS. [*Aside.*] D—n the table.
  [*Lays the plates and dishes and places the chairs.* MARY *gallants* CHERI BOUNCE *apart.*

WIDGETTS. [*Polishing a plate; furiously.*] Here's a pleasant situation: waiter at my own supper, and afraid to open my mouth. The rascal's making love to her, and she likes it— hang 'em, I wish I could strangle them.
                    [MARY *and* CHERI BOUNCE *laugh.*

CHERI. Oh, you droll wretch, you're ten times funnier than that stupid Widgetts.

MARY. Hang Widgetts.

WIDGETTS. [*Coming between them.*] I beg your pardon.

MARY. What d'ye want? Is the table laid?

WIDGETTS. [*Aside.*] D—n the table. [*Returns to table, and bawls out.*] Supper's ready!

MARY. Ah! [*To* CHERI BOUNCE.] Come, my dear.
                    [WIDGETTS *seats himself at table.*
  What!

WIDGETTS. [*Jumps up.*] Beg pardon—I vacate.
                    [MARY *and* CHERI BOUNCE *seat themselves.*

MARY. Now, my dear ma'amselle, here are fowl, and lobster, and kidneys.

WIDGETTS. [*Aside.*] I wish they were sticking in his gizzard.

MARY. Now then, waiter, be alive, and take your tin.
  [*Claps one of the dish covers on* WIDGETTS's *head, who snatches it off and flings it away in a rage.*

WIDGETTS. Allow me to observe—

MARY. There's no bread, my good fellow.

WIDGETTS. Coming. [*Aside.*] D—n the bread.
  [*Goes to a table at back, on which is a loaf of bread and rolls.*

MARY. What part of the fowl shall I send you, ma'amselle?

CHERI. The funny idea, Mr. Spraggs, if you please.

MARY. The funny idea; well, I never!

CHERI. The merry thought, you know.

MARY. Oh, to be sure, yes, the funny idea. [*Cutting the fowl.*

WIDGETTS. Bread.

[*Claps the loaf of bread on the dish before* MARY, *who throws it at him.*

MARY. Roll, stupid. Plates, waiter. [WIDGETTS *puts the roll under his arm, and hands plates to* MARY.] Allow me to add a kidney; they look beautiful.

CHERI. Thank you.

[MARY *puts some fowl and a sausage on the plate, which she gives to* WIDGETTS *for* CHERI BOUNCE, *and then helps herself.*

WIDGETTS. [*Comes down with the plate in his hand.*] How uncommon savoury it smells! He's not looking.

[*Takes the kidney off the plate, and puts it in his pocket.*

MARY. Waiter.

[WIDGETTS *lays the plate before* CHERI BOUNCE.

Open that champagne, waiter.

WIDGETTS. [*Aside.*] My champagne, too!

[*Opening a bottle of champagne.*

MARY. [*Helps* CHERI BOUNCE.] I hope you liked your kidney.

CHERI. What kidney, Mr. Spraggs?

WIDGETTS. [*Snatching the kidney out of his pocket, and putting it, unperceived, on* CHERI BOUNCE'S *plate.*] Why, *that* kidney.

CHERI. Dear me, I didn't perceive it before.

[WIDGETTS *places champagne on the table.*

MARY. Celery, waiter.

[WIDGETTS *goes to table at back for celery.* MARY *fills two glasses of champagne, and drinks with* CHERI BOUNCE. WIDGETTS *returns with stalks of celery in his coat pocket, and without being perceived takes the champagne bottle, fills a glass for himself, comes down and drinks.*

I say, ma'amselle, this is rare fun.

CHERI. Glorious!

MARY. I'll give you, the absent Widgetts.

CHERI. I've no objection to drink poor Widgetts' health, but I don't at all wish for his company; he's such a particularly conceited fool.

WIDGETTS. [*Aside, and scarcely able to restrain himself.*] Do I look like a fool?   [*They drink.* WIDGETTS *comes to the table.*

As the sole surviving friend of Mr. Widgetts, will you allow me to say—

[*Presses the plate to his breast. Knock at door.*

MARY. Hold your tongue, and open the door.

CHERI. Perhaps 'tis Widgetts.

WIDGETTS. No it isn't; Widgetts is—elsewhere.

[*Knocking at door.*

BROWN. [*Outside.*] Open the door! I must come in.

CHERI. [*Alarmed.*] Heavens! That's Brown's voice. If he finds me here I shall be ruined.

WIDGETTS. Don't let him in.   [*Runs to door.*

CHERI. Where on earth can I conceal myself? Ah, here!
[*Throws open folding doors.* WIDGETTS *stands transfixed with terror;* CHERI BOUNCE *screams in a state of dreadful alarm.*]
Oh, oh, oh! There's a woman drowned in the water-butt!

MARY. 'Tis Mary White, the laundress—Widgetts murdered her.

WIDGETTS. I'll be d——d if he did!

MARY. Never mind, he'll be hanged for it all the same.
          [*Exit through folding doors which she closes after her.*

WIDGETTS. Widgetts hanged! You might as well hang me.

CHERI. Good heavens! What a horrid place I've got into.
[*Knocking at door.* BROWN *outside calling,* 'Let me in! Open the door.'] Oh! That Brown will make another victim of *me*.
          [*Runs into chamber.*

Enter BROWN.

BROWN. Where is she? Where's Mademoiselle Cheri Bounce? I know she's here.

WIDGETTS. I beg your pardon—she left here half an hour ago. I called the cab for her myself, a patent hansom, No. 749.

BROWN. Where's Widgetts then? Where's the villain Widgetts, the destroyer of my happiness?

WIDGETTS. My good fellow, don't be outrageous! Mr. Widgetts is unfortunately absent—he's gone to close the eyes of a dying uncle, and won't be back to-night.

Enter TWILL.

TWILL. Oh, please, sir, they wouldn't admit the order at the Adelphi. [*Sees* WIDGETTS *and bursts into a fit of laughter.*] Ha, ha, ha, ha! Why, surely this ain't Guy Faux day, Mr. Widgetts?

BROWN. Widgetts!

CHERI. [*At door.*] Widgetts? [*Retires.*

TWILL. Of course! That's Mr. Widgetts, my master—I'll never deny him.

WIDGETTS. [*Aside.*] Then I've nothing for it but a bolt—out of my bed-room window.
[*Rushes into chamber.* CHERI BOUNCE *screams inside.* WIDGETTS *rushes out again followed by* CHERI BOUNCE *beating him with her umbrella.*

CHERI. Stop him! Don't let him escape—he has murdered a woman!

TWILL. Murdered a woman? Oh, the dirty blackguard! What a taste he had!
[BROWN *attempts to seize him, but* WIDGETTS *strikes his hat over his eyes, runs round the table, and runs to door,* L., *against which* TWILL *has placed his back.*
[*In a boxing attitude.*] No, you don't!
[BROWN *now collars him, and* CHERI BOUNCE *beats him with her umbrella.*

BROWN. Ha, have I got you at last—[*Shaking him.*] villain!

WIDGETTS. Help! Murder—police—help!

TWILL. [*Dancing at door.*] Police! Here's an illigant row—go it, little one—fire away, umbrella! She don't lay it into him at all.

WIDGETTS. Stop—stop—stop! Spare the remnant of an injured tailor's life. You think I cut off Mary White's thread, but I didn't; the horrid act was her own deed. She got jealous of me and mixed her proud spirit with too much water; she'd tell you so herself, poor soul, if she could.

MARY. [*Speaking inside folding doors, in a solemn voice.*] No, she wouldn't.

WIDGETTS. Angels and bannisters support me. [*Drops on his knees.* CHERI BOUNCE *throws herself into the arms of* BROWN. *General consternation.*] 'Tis her voice—her ghost is come back to walk the earth in them green boots. Injured shade—speak for me, if ghosts have parts of speech, and tell them I'm innocent.

MARY. You caused my death by your falsity.

WIDGETTS. O-oh! I know it; but sooner than you should have made an object of yourself, I'd have married you ten times over.

MARY. And would you marry me now, if I was living?

WIDGETTS. I would—to-morrow morning.   [MARY *runs out.*

MARY. Then, Whittington, I'm your loving Mary again!

WIDGETTS. [*Jumps up and tries to avoid her; she follows him.*] Hollo! No—keep off. [*She embraces him.*] Hey! Bless me; you're neither damp or dead! On the contrary, you're remarkably warm and lively. But are you sure you're not a water nymph, and that you have not got private apartments in the Thames or the New River?

MARY. No, Widgy, don't be afraid; 'twas only a trick of mine to plague you for your inconstancy. [*Pointing to water-butt.*] She's not *me*, but the dummy figure dressed up in some of my clothes.

WIDGETTS. Ah! I've been finely hoaxed. And where's the detective policeman that eat my lobster and drank my wine?

MARY. Why, of course, he's here.   [*Points to herself.*

WIDGETTS. Oh, you villain! But what's to be done with Brown? [BROWN *and* CHERI BOUNCE, *who have been conversing at the back during the latter part of the dialogue, come down.*

BROWN. Ask ma'amselle here, for she's consented to be Mrs. Brown next Monday, and as for this little affair of the supper, I was in the plot with Mary.

WIDGETTS. I hope you were not in the water-butt with her; but, never mind, I don't want any further explanation. I've had my lesson—[*To audience.*] and I hope you have all profited by it. Now, if there's any single, good-looking young fellow here wants a bit of advice—eh, there's my friend, Smith. Smith, my dear boy, when you invite a female friend to a quiet bit of supper, mind there's no water-butt on the premises; and—I mention this confidentially to all you bachelors—if your laundress is young and pretty, you had better pay your washing bills regularly; and don't, like me, get yourself into a scrape by not knowing HOW TO SETTLE ACCOUNTS WITH YOUR LAUNDRESS.

BOX AND COX

A ROMANCE OF REAL LIFE IN ONE ACT

BY

JOHN MADDISON MORTON (1811–1891)

—————

First performed at the Lyceum Theatre
1 November 1847

—————

CAST

JOHN BOX, a journeyman printer	Mr. Buckstone
JAMES COX, a journeyman hatter	Mr. Harley
MRS. BOUNCER, a lodging-house keeper	Mrs. Macnamara

PREFACE TO *BOX AND COX*

THE playwriting career of John Maddison Morton spanned half a century: his first play, a pantomime, was performed in 1833, and the last one produced in his lifetime, a farce, in 1885. His considerable output—over 125 attributed pieces—made him the busiest and easily the most popular farce-writer of the century; a hundred of these pieces are farces. Morton was the great farceur of the people; he dramatized the comic peccadillos and imbroglios of a wide range of working- and lower-middle-class characters, as well as placing his farces in more respectable middle-class settings when he chose. Wherever he set them and whatever class material he used, his work is cozily familiar and strongly domestic. Titles like *My Husband's Ghost*, *My Wife's Second Floor*, *My Precious Betsy*, *Who's my Husband?*, *Friend Waggles*, *My Wife's Come, How Stout You're Getting*, *An Englishman's House is his Castle*, *Wooing one's Wife*, and *My Wife's Bonnet* are plentiful. Unusually genteel and restrained is *Atchi* (1868),[1] set in the gardens of a country house where Lord Adonis Fickleton and Lady Mayduke engage in a battle of wits and stratagems, his objective being to secure the hand of her husband's sister Emily, and hers to frustrate him and expose him as a roué. The battle ends in deadlock; in the final scene she secretly puts sneezing powder into his snuffbox and he begins to sneeze as he proposes to Emily. He retaliates by sprinkling the powder onto a rose he presents her as an emblem of peace; Emily and the husband sniff it too, and at the curtain all four characters are sneezing uncontrollably. Much more typical of Morton is *Slasher and Crasher* (1848). Faced with the seemingly insurmountable difficulty of proving their non-existent courage in order to win their ladies, Slasher and Crasher concoct a plot in which they will insult each other, come to blows, fight a duel with unloaded pistols, and finish it off with swords. Contrary to plan the timid Slasher refuses to be provoked and ignores Crasher's desperate signals; after drinking

---

[1] The fact that *Atchi* was written for the Bancrofts' Prince of Wales's and not for Morton's usual market at the Adelphi, Princess's, and Olympic would explain its refinement.

freely, however, he grows bold, attacks Crasher in earnest, fights the duel, pursues Crasher around the room knocking the furniture about, smashes up the greenhouse, runs his sword through the upholstery, and engages Crasher in a melodramatic broadsword combat.

Box and Cox, perhaps the most popular of all nineteenth-century farces, certainly the one to stay in print the longest, and still played by amateurs, was adapted, like so many of Morton's farces, from the French. In this case Morton mixed plots from two different pieces: *Une Chambre pour Deux* (1839) by E. F. Prieur and A. Letorzec (performed in 1847 as *Une Chambre à Deux Lits*), and *Frisette* (1846), by Labiche and A. Lefranc. The former contains the plot of two strangers occupying the same room without each other's knowledge, the latter the extra complication of what became Penelope Ann in *Box and Cox*. Morton had already used *Une Chambre pour Deux* in *The Double-Bedded Room* (1843), in which the organist Dulcimer Pipes and the hot-blooded Major Minus, who is running away with Mrs. Lomax and pursued by Mr. Lomax, have unknown to each other taken the only room left in a York inn. In the final dark scene Pipes and Mrs. Lomax, each believing that no-one else is in the room, discover the other bed occupied. She is frightened by a thunderstorm, and throws herself in fear upon the miserable Pipes; the Major creeps into the room out of the rain and believes Pipes to be Mrs. Lomax; Pipes in turn thinks that the Major is Mrs. Lomax—in short there is much comic business of vacating and returning to the beds and an armchair whose occupants rapidly alternate, and a series of misunderstandings and surprise discoveries.

The pattern of construction and dialogue in *Box and Cox* is highly symmetrical, with an elaborate internal counterpoint that proves remarkably complex upon detailed analysis. The play is also an extensive parody of melodramatic speeches, situations, climaxes, emotions, sentiments, and plot machinery; the title-page description, 'A Romance of Real Life', suggests as much. Box and Cox themselves are not only—as in much good farce—perfectly ordinary and serious people who treat absolutely ludicrous situations with profound gravity, but they are also intense and highly emotional characters whose scenes are punctuated by excellent comic anti-climaxes partly dependent for effect upon immediately previous melodramatic build-ups.

Thus the play operates on more than one level of comedy, and is all the more effective because it is solidly grounded in that humble domestic reality and materiality of daily existence of which Morton was such a master; the comic contrast between homely normality and the absurd situation is therefore even sharper.

In its first season at the Lyceum *Box and Cox* received 114 performances. Four acting editions were collated to establish the present text: *Lacy's Acting Edition of Plays*, v. 5; *Duncombe's British Theatre*, v. 60; *Dicks' Standard Plays*, no. 1059; and *Heywood's Original Dramas, Farces, Operettas*, no. 190. Of these the earlier *Lacy* and *Duncombe* are more authoritative; actually the four texts are virtually the same. The *Lacy* text turns up again in the American *French's Minor Drama*, v. 21. The Lord Chamberlain's copy, also used in collation, is slightly shorter than the printed texts, but there are no changes of substance. The acting editions contain more jokes and elegant turns of phrase than the manuscript, and Box's occupation is altered from baker to printer. *Box and Cox* has also been translated into French, Spanish, German, Dutch, Russian, and Esperanto. F. C. Burnand adapted it as a comic opera, *Cox and Box* (1867), with music by Sullivan (Bouncer becomes a military gentleman); it was also 'africanized' by E. B. Christy, 'adapted to the Ethiopian stage', as he put it, for a New York company, and appeared in a series entitled *The Darkey Drama* (*c.* 1867).

PLATE 3

Box and Cox. John Harley as Cox and J. B. Buckstone as Box.
The Harvard Theatre Collection

SCENE. *A room decently furnished; at* C. *a bed with curtains closed; at* L. C. *a door; at* L. *a door; at* L. *a chest of drawers; at back,* R., *a window; at* R. *a door; at* R. *fire-place, with mantelpiece; table and chairs; a few common ornaments on chimney-piece.* COX, *dressed with the exception of his coat, is looking at himself in a small looking-glass, which he holds in his hand.*

COX. I've half a mind to register an oath that I'll never have my hair cut again! [*His hair is very short.*] I look as if I had been just cropped for the Militia, and I was particularly emphatic in my instructions to the hairdresser only to cut the ends off. He must have thought I meant the other ends. Never mind; I shan't meet anybody to care about so early. Eight o'clock! I declare I haven't a moment to lose. Fate has placed me with the most punctual, particular and peremptory of hatters, and I must fulfil my destiny. [*Knock at door.*] Open locks, whoever knocks!

Enter MRS. BOUNCER.

MRS. BOUNCER. Good-morning, Mr. Cox. I hope you slept comfortably, Mr. Cox.

COX. I can't say I did, Mrs. Bouncer. I should feel obliged to you if you could accommodate me with a more protuberant bolster, Mrs. B. The one I've got now seems to me to have about a handful and a half of feathers at each end, and nothing whatever in the middle.

MRS. BOUNCER. Anything to accommodate you, Mr. Cox.

COX. Thank you. Then perhaps you'll be good enough to hold this glass while I finish my toilet.

MRS. BOUNCER. Certainly. [*Holding glass before* COX, *who ties on his cravat.*] Why, I do declare, you've had your hair cut!

COX. Cut! It strikes me I've had it mowed! It's very kind of you to mention it, but I'm sufficiently conscious of the absurdity of my personal appearance already. [*Puts on his coat.*] Now for my hat. [*Puts on his hat, which comes over his eyes.*] That's the effect of having one's hair cut. This hat fitted me quite tight before. Luckily I've got two or three more. [*Goes in and returns with three hats of different shapes, and puts them on, one after the other, all of which are too big for him.*] This is pleasant! Never mind. This one appears to me to wabble about rather less than the others—[*Puts on hat.*] and now I'm off! By the bye, Mrs. Bouncer, I wish to call your attention to a fact that has been evident to me for some time past—and that is, that my coals go remarkably fast——

MRS. BOUNCER. Lor, Mr. Cox!

COX. It is not only the case with the coals, Mrs. Bouncer, but I've lately observed a gradual and steady increase of evaporation among my candles, wood, sugar, and lucifer matches.

MRS. BOUNCER. Lor, Mr. Cox! You surely don't suspect me?

COX. I don't say I do, Mrs. B.; only I wish you distinctly to understand that I don't believe it's the cat.

MRS. BOUNCER. Is there anything else you've got to grumble about, sir?

COX. Grumble! Mrs. Bouncer, do you possess such a thing as a dictionary?

MRS. BOUNCER. No, sir.

COX. Then I'll lend you one—and if you turn to the letter G, you'll find 'Grumble, verb neuter—to complain without a cause.' Now that's not my case, Mrs. B. And now that we are upon the subject, I wish to know how it is that I frequently find my apartment full of smoke?

MRS. BOUNCER. Why, I suppose the chimney——

COX. The chimney doesn't smoke tobacco. I'm speaking of tobacco smoke, Mrs. B. I hope, Mrs. Bouncer, *you're* not guilty of cheroots or Cubas?

MRS. BOUNCER. Not I, indeed, Mr. Cox!

COX. Nor partial to a pipe?

MRS. BOUNCER. No, sir.

COX. Then how is it that——

MRS. BOUNCER. [*Confused.*] Why, I suppose—yes—that must be it——

COX. At present I am entirely of your opinion—because I haven't the most distant particle of an idea what you mean.

MRS. BOUNCER. Why, the gentleman who has got the attic is

hardly ever without a pipe in his mouth; and there he sits with his feet on the mantelpiece——

cox. The mantelpiece! That strikes me as being a considerable stretch, either of your imagination, Mrs. B., or the gentleman's legs. I presume you mean the fender, or the hob.

MRS. BOUNCER. Sometimes one, sometimes t'other. Well, there he sits for hours, and puffs away into the fireplace.

cox. Ah, then you mean to say that this gentleman's smoke, instead of emulating the example of all other sorts of smoke, and going *up* the chimney, thinks proper to affect a singularity by taking the contrary direction.

MRS. BOUNCER. Why——

cox. Then I suppose the gentleman you are speaking of is the same individual that I invariably meet coming up stairs when I'm going down, and going down when I'm coming up?

MRS. BOUNCER. Why—yes—I——

cox. From the appearance of his outward man, I should unhesitatingly set him down as a gentleman connected with the printing interest.

MRS. BOUNCER. Yes, sir, and a very respectable young gentleman he is.

cox. Well, good morning, Mrs. Bouncer.

MRS. BOUNCER. You'll be back at your usual time, I suppose, sir?

cox. Yes—nine o'clock. You needn't light my fire in future, Mrs. B.; I'll do it myself. Don't forget the bolster! [*Going—stops.*] A halfpenny worth of milk, Mrs. Bouncer, and be good enough to let it stand—I wish the cream to accumulate.

[*Exit.*

MRS. BOUNCER. He's gone at last! I declare I was all in a tremble for fear Mr. Box should come in before Mr. Cox went out. Luckily they've never met yet, and what's more, they're not very likely to do so; for Mr. Box is hard at work at a newspaper office all night, and doesn't come home till the morning, and Mr. Cox is busy making hats all day long, and doesn't come home till night; so that I'm getting double rent for my room, and neither of my lodgers are any wiser for it.

It was a capital idea of mine, that it was! But I haven't an instant to lose. First of all, let me put Mr. Cox's things out of Mr. Box's way. [*She takes the three hats,* cox's *dressing gown and slippers, opens door at* L *and puts them in; then shuts door and locks it.*] Now then, to put the key where Mr. Cox always finds it. [*Puts the key on the ledge of the door.*] I really must beg Mr. Box not to smoke so much. I was dreadfully puzzled to know what to say when Mr. Cox spoke about it. Now then, to make the bed, and don't let me forget that what's the head of the bed for Mr. Cox becomes the foot of the bed for Mr. Box; people's tastes do differ so. [*Goes behind the curtains of the bed, and seems to be making it; then appears with a very thin bolster in her hand.*] The idea of Mr. Cox presuming to complain of such a bolster as this!

[*She disappears again behind curtains.*

BOX. [*Without.*] Pooh, pooh! Why don't you keep your own side of the staircase, sir?

Enter BOX, *dressed as a printer.*

[*Puts his head out of door again, shouting.*] It was as much your fault as mine, sir. I say, sir, it was as much your fault as mine, sir!

MRS. BOUNCER. [*Emerging from behind the curtains of bed.*] Lor, Mr. Box, what is the matter?

BOX. Mind your own business, Bouncer.

MRS. BOUNCER. Dear, dear, Mr. Box, what a temper you are in, to be sure! I declare you are quite pale in the face.

BOX. What colour would you have a man be who has been setting up long leaders for a daily paper all night?

MRS. BOUNCER. But then, you've all the day to yourself.

BOX. [*Looking significantly at* MRS. BOUNCER.] So it seems. Far be it from me, Bouncer, to hurry your movements, but I think it right to acquaint you with my immediate intention of divesting myself of my garments and going to bed.

MRS. BOUNCER. Oh, Mr. Box!   [*Going.*

BOX. Stop! Can you inform me who the individual is that I invariably encounter going down stairs when I'm coming up, and coming up stairs when I'm going down?

MRS. BOUNCER. [*Confused.*] Oh—yes—the gentleman in the attic, sir.

BOX. Oh! There's nothing particularly remarkable about him, except his hats. I meet him in all sorts of hats—white hats and black hats—hats with broad brims, and hats with narrow brims, hats with naps, and hats without naps—in short, I have come to the conclusion that he must be individually and professionally associated with the hatting interest.

MRS. BOUNCER. Yes, sir. And by the bye, Mr. Box, he begged me to request of you, as a particular favour, that you would not smoke quite so much.

BOX. Did he? Then you may tell the gentle hatter, with my compliments, that if he objects to the effluvia of tobacco he had better domesticate himself in some adjoining parish.

MRS. BOUNCER. [*Pathetically.*] Oh! Mr. Box, you surely wouldn't deprive me of a lodger.

BOX. It would come to precisely the same thing, Bouncer, because if I detect the slightest attempt to put my pipe out, I at once give you warning that I shall give you warning at once.

MRS. BOUNCER. Well, Mr. Box, do you want anything more of me?

BOX. On the contrary—I've had quite enough of you.

MRS. BOUNCER. Well, if ever! What next, I wonder?
[*Exit, slamming door after her.*

BOX. It's quite extraordinary, the trouble I always have to get rid of that venerable female. She knows I'm up all night, and yet she seems to set her face against my indulging in a horizontal position by day. Now, let me see—shall I take my nap before I swallow my breakfast, or shall I take my breakfast before I swallow my nap—I mean, shall I swallow my nap before—no—never mind! I've got a rasher of bacon somewhere. [*Feeling in his pockets.*] I've the most distinct and vivid recollection of having purchased a rasher of bacon. Oh, here it is—[*Produces it, wrapped in paper, and places it on table.*] and a penny roll. The next thing is to light the fire. Where are my lucifers? [*Looking on mantelpiece, and taking*

box, opens it.] Now, 'pon my life, this is too bad of Bouncer—
this is by several degrees too bad! I had a whole box full
three days ago, and now there's only one! I'm perfectly aware
that she purloins my coals and my candles and my sugar, but
I did think—oh, yes, I did think that my lucifers would be
sacred! [*Takes candlestick off the mantelpiece, in which there is a
very small end of candle—looks at it.*] Now I should like to ask
any unprejudiced person or persons their opinion touching
this candle. In the first place, a candle is an article that I don't
require, because I'm only at home in the daytime—and I
bought this candle on the first of May—Chimney-sweepers'
Day—calculating that it would last me three months, and
here's one week not half over, and the candle three parts
gone! [*Lights the fire—then takes down a gridiron, which is
hanging over fire-place.*] Mrs. Bouncer has been using my
gridiron! The last article of consumption that I cooked upon it
was a pork chop, and now it is powerfully impregnated with
the odour of red herrings! [*Places gridiron on fire, and then
with a fork lays rasher of bacon on the gridiron.*] How sleepy I
am, to be sure! I'd indulge myself with a nap if there was
anybody here to superintend the turning of my bacon.
[*Yawning again.*] Perhaps it will turn itself. I must lie down—
so here goes.

[*He lies down on the bed, closing the curtains around him.*

After a short pause, enter COX, *hurriedly.*

COX. Well, wonders will never cease! Conscious of being eleven
minutes and a half behind time, I was sneaking into the shop
in a state of considerable excitement, when my venerable
employer, with a smile of extreme benevolence on his aged
countenance, said to me—'Cox, I shan't want you to-day—
you can have a holiday.' Thoughts of 'Gravesend and back—
fare One Shilling,' instantly suggested themselves, inter-
mingled with visions of 'Greenwich for Fourpence.' Then came
the Twopenny Omnibuses, and the Halfpenny Boats—in
short, I'm quite bewildered! However, I must have my
breakfast first—that'll give me time to reflect. I've bought a
mutton chop, so I shan't want any dinner. [*Puts chop on
table.*] Good gracious! I've forgot the bread. Holloa, what's
this? A roll, I declare. Come that's lucky! Now, then, to light

the fire. Holloa—[*Seeing the lucifer box on table.*] who presumes
to touch my box of lucifers? Why, it's empty! I left one in it—
I'll take my oath I did. Heyday! Why the fire *is* lighted!
Where's the gridiron? *On* the fire, I declare. And what's that
on it? Bacon? Bacon it is! Well, now, 'pon my life, there's a
quiet coolness about Mrs. Bouncer's proceedings that's
almost amusing. She takes my last lucifer—my coals, and my
gridiron, to cook her breakfast by. No, no—I can't stand this!
Come out of that! [*Pokes fork into bacon, and puts it on a plate on
the table; then places his chop on the gridiron, which he puts on the
fire.*] Now, then, for my breakfast things.

    [*Taking key, opens door, L., and goes out, slamming the door
after him with a loud noise.*

BOX. [*Suddenly showing his head from behind curtains.*] Come in!
If it's you, Mrs. Bouncer, you needn't be afraid. I wonder how
long I've been asleep? [*Suddenly recollecting.*] Goodness
gracious—my bacon! [*Leaps off bed and runs to fire-place.*]
Holloa, what's this? A chop? Whose chop? Mrs. Bouncer's,
I'll be bound! She thought to cook her breakfast while I was
asleep—with my coals, too, and my gridiron! Ha, ha! But
where's my bacon? [*Seeing it on the table.*] Here it is. Well,
'pon my life, Bouncer's going it! And shall I curb my
indignation? Shall I falter in my vengeance? No! [*Digs the
fork into the chop—opens window and throws chop out—shuts
window again.*] So much for Bouncer's breakfast, and now for
my own! [*With fork he puts the bacon on the gridiron again.*] I
may as well lay my breakfast things.

    [*Goes to mantelpiece, takes key out of one of the ornaments,
opens door, R. and exit, slamming door after him.*

COX. [*Putting his head in quickly at door, L.*] Come in, come in!
[*Opens door and enters with a small tray, on which are tea-
things, etc., which he places on drawers, and suddenly recollects.*]
Oh, goodness, my chop! [*Running to fireplace.*] Holloa—
what's this! The bacon again! Oh, pooh! Zounds—confound
it—dash it—damn it—I can't stand this! [*Pokes fork into
bacon, opens window and flings it out—shuts window again and
returns to drawers for tea-things; encounters* BOX *coming from
his cupboard with his tea-things—they walk down stage together.*]
Who are you, sir?

BOX. If you come to that—who are *you?*

COX. What do you want here, sir?

BOX. If you come to that—what do *you* want?

COX. [*Aside.*] It's the printer!   [*Puts tea-things on the drawers.*

BOX. [*Aside.*] It's the hatter!   [*Puts tea-things on table.*

COX. Go to your attic, sir.

BOX. *My* attic, sir? *Your* attic, sir!

COX. Printer, I shall do you a frightful injury if you don't instantly leave my apartment.

BOX. *Your* apartment? You mean *my* apartment, you contemptible hatter, you!

COX. *Your* apartment? Ha, ha! Come, I like that! Look here, sir—[*Produces a paper out of his pocket.*] Mrs. Bouncer's receipt for the last week's rent, sir!

BOX. [*Produces a paper and holds it close to* COX's *face.*] Ditto, sir!

COX. [*Suddenly shouting.*] Thieves!

BOX. Murder!

BOX *and* COX. Mrs. Bouncer! Mrs. Bouncer!
              [*Each running to door, calling.*

MRS. BOUNCER *runs in.*

MRS. BOUNCER. What is the matter?
    [COX *and* BOX *seize* MRS. BOUNCER *by the arm, and drag her forward.*

BOX. Instantly remove that hatter!

COX. Immediately turn out that printer!

MRS. BOUNCER. Well, but gentlemen——

COX. Explain!   [*Pulling her round to him.*

BOX. Explain! [*Pulling her round to him.*] Whose room is this?

COX. Yes, woman, whose room is this?

BOX. Doesn't it belong to me?

MRS. BOUNCER. No!

COX. There! You hear, sir—it belongs to me.

MRS. BOUNCER. No—it belongs to both of you!   [*Sobbing.*

BOX *and* COX. Both of us?

MRS. BOUNCER. Oh, dear gentlemen, don't be angry; but you see, this gentleman—[*Pointing to* BOX.] only being at home in the daytime, and that gentleman—[*Pointing to* COX.] at night, I thought I might venture—until my little back second-floor room was ready——

BOX *and* COX [*Eagerly.*] When will your little back second-floor room be ready?

MRS. BOUNCER. Why, to-morrow——

COX. I'll take it!

BOX. So will I!

MRS. BOUNCER. Excuse me, but if you both take it, you may just as well stop where you are.

BOX *and* COX. True.

COX. I spoke first, sir!

BOX. With all my heart, sir! The little back second-floor room is yours, sir—now go!

COX. Go? Pooh, pooh!

MRS. BOUNCER. Now, don't quarrel, gentlemen. You see, there used to be a partition here——

BOX *and* COX. Then put it up!

MRS. BOUNCER. Nay, I'll see if I can't get the other room ready this very day. Now, do keep your tempers.   [*Exit.*

COX. What a disgusting position!

[*Walking rapidly round the stage.*

BOX. [*Sitting down on chair at one side of table, and following* COX'*s movements.*] Will you allow me to observe, if you have not had any exercise to-day, you'd better go out and take it?

COX. I shall not do anything of the sort, sir.

[*Seating himself at the table opposite* BOX.

BOX. Very well, sir!

COX. Very well, sir! However, don't let me prevent *you* from going out.

BOX. Don't flatter yourself, sir. [COX *is about to break a piece of the roll off.*] Holloa! That's my roll, sir.

[*Snatches it away, puts a pipe in his mouth, and lights it with a piece of tinder. Puffs smoke across the table towards* COX.

cox. Holloa! What are you about, sir?

box. What am I about? I'm about to smoke.

cox. Wheugh!   [*Goes to the window and flings it open.*

box. Holloa! [*Turning round.*] Put down that window, sir!

cox. Then put your pipe out, sir!

box. There!   [*Puts pipe on the table.*

cox. There!   [*Slams down window and re-seats himself.*

box. I shall retire to my pillow.

    [*Gets up, takes off his jacket, then goes towards bed and sits upon it.*

cox. [*Jumps up, goes to bed and sits down.*] I beg your pardon, sir—I cannot allow anyone to rumple my bed.

box. *Your* bed? Hark ye, sir—can you fight?

cox. No, sir.

box. No? Then come on.   [*Sparring at* cox.

cox. Sit down, sir, or I'll instantly vociferate 'Police!'

box. [*Seats himself;* cox *does the same.*] I say, sir——

cox. Well, sir?

box. Although we are doomed to occupy the same room for a few hours longer, I don't see any necessity for our cutting each other's throat, sir.

cox. Not at all. It's an operation that I should decidedly object to.

box. And after all, I've no violent animosity against you, sir.

cox. Nor have I any rooted antipathy to you, sir.

box. Besides, it was all Mrs. Bouncer's fault, sir.

cox. Entirely, sir.   [*Gradually approaching chairs.*

box. Very well, sir!

cox. Very well, sir!   [*Pause.*

box. Take a bit of roll, sir?

cox. Thank ye, sir.   [*Breaking a bit off.* **Pause.**

box. Do you sing, sir?

cox. I sometimes join in a chorus.

BOX. Then give us a chorus. [*Pause.*] Have you seen the Bosjesmans, sir?

COX. No, sir; my wife wouldn't let me.

BOX. Your *wife*?

COX. That is—my *intended* wife.

BOX. Well, that's the same thing. I congratulate you.

[*Shaking hands.*

COX. [*With a deep sigh.*] Thank ye. [*Seeing* BOX *about to get up.*] You needn't disturb yourself, sir; she won't come here.

BOX. Oh! I understand. You've got a snug little establishment of your own here—on the sly—cunning dog. [*Nudging* COX.

COX. [*Drawing himself up.*] No such thing, sir—I repeat, sir, no such thing, sir; but my wife—I mean my *intended* wife—happens to be the proprietress of a considerable number of bathing machines——

BOX. [*Suddenly.*] Ha! Where?   [*Grasping* COX's *arm.*

COX. At a favourite watering place. How curious you are!

BOX. Not at all. Well?

COX. Consequently, in the bathing season—which luckily is rather a long one—we see but little of each other; but as that is now over I am daily indulging in the expectation of being blessed with the sight of my beloved. [*Very seriously.*] Are *you* married?

BOX. Me? Why—not exactly.

COX. Ah, a happy bachelor?

BOX. Why—not precisely.

COX. Oh, a—widower?

BOX. No—not absolutely.

COX. You'll excuse me, sir—but at present I don't exactly understand how you can help being one of the three.

BOX. Not help it?

COX. No, sir—not you, nor any other man alive!

BOX. Ah, that may be—but I'm not alive!

COX. [*Pushing back his chair.*]—You'll excuse me, sir—but I don't like joking upon such subjects.

BOX. But I am perfectly serious, sir; I've been defunct for the last three years.

COX. [*Shouting.*] Will you be quiet, sir?

BOX. If you won't believe me, I'll refer you to a very large, numerous, and respectable circle of disconsolate friends.

COX. My very dear sir—my *very* dear sir—if there does exist any ingenious contrivance whereby a man on the eve of committing matrimony can leave this world, and yet stop in it, I shouldn't be sorry to know it.

BOX. Oh, then I presume I'm not to set you down as being frantically attached to your intended?

COX. Why, not exactly; and yet at present I'm only aware of one obstacle to my doting upon her—and that is, that I can't abide her.

BOX. Then there's nothing more easy. Do as I did.

COX. [*Eagerly.*] I will! What was it?

BOX. Drown yourself.

COX. [*Shouting again.*] Will you be quiet, sir?

BOX. Listen to me. Three years ago it was my misfortune to captivate the affections of a still blooming, though somewhat middle-aged widow, at Ramsgate.

COX. [*Aside.*] Singular enough—just my case three months ago at Margate!

BOX. Well, sir, to escape her importunities, I came to the determination of enlisting into the Blues or Life Guards.

COX. [*Aside.*] So did I. How very odd!

BOX. But they wouldn't have me; they actually had the effrontery to say I was too short——

COX. [*Aside.*] And I wasn't tall enough!

BOX. So I was obliged to content myself with a marching regiment. I enlisted!

COX. [*Aside.*] So did I. Singular coincidence!

BOX. I'd no sooner done so than I was sorry for it.

COX. [*Aside.*] So was I.

BOX. My infatuated widow offered to purchase my discharge on condition that I'd lead her to the altar.

cox. [*Aside.*] Just my case!

box. I hesitated; at last I consented.

cox. [*Aside.*] I consented at once!

box. Well, sir, the day fixed for the happy ceremony at length drew near—in fact, too near to be pleasant—so I suddenly discovered that I wasn't worthy to possess her, and I told her so; when, instead of being flattered by the compliment, she flew upon me like a tiger of the female gender. I rejoined, when suddenly something whizzed past me within an inch of my ear, and shivered into a thousand fragments against the mantelpiece. It was the slop-basin. I retaliated with a tea cup. We parted, and the next morning I was served with a notice of action for breach of promise.

cox. Well, sir?

box. Well, sir, ruin stared me in the face; the action proceeded against me with gigantic strides. I took a desperate resolution. I left my home early one morning, with one suit of clothes on my back and another tied up in a bundle under my arm. I arrived on the cliffs, opened my bundle, deposited the suit of clothes on the very verge of the precipice, took one look down in the yawning gulf beneath me—and walked off in the opposite direction.

cox. Dear me! I think I begin to have some slight perception of your meaning. Ingenious creature! You disappeared—the suit of clothes was found——

box. Exactly; and in one of the pockets of the coat, or waistcoat, or the pantaloons—I forget which—there was also found a piece of paper with these affecting farewell words: 'This is thy work, oh Penelope Ann!'

cox. Penelope Ann! [*Starts up, takes* box *by the arm, and leads him slowly to front of stage.*] Penelope Ann?

box. Penelope Ann.

cox. Originally widow of William Wiggins?

box. Widow of William Wiggins.

cox. Proprietor of bathing machines?

box. Proprietor of bathing machines.

COX. At Margate?

BOX. And Ramsgate.

COX. It must be she! And you, sir—you are Box—the lamented,
long-lost Box?

BOX. I am!

COX. And I was about to marry the interesting creature you so
cruelly deceived.

BOX. Ah, then you are Cox!

COX. I am!

BOX. I heard of it. I congratulate you—I give you joy! And now
I think I'll go and take a stroll.   [*Going.*

COX. No you don't! [*Stopping him.*] I'll not lose sight of you till
I've restored you to the arms of your intended.

BOX. *My* intended? You mean *your* intended.

COX. No, sir—yours!

BOX. How can she be *my* intended now that I am drowned?

COX. You're no such thing, sir, and I prefer presenting you to
Penelope Ann.

BOX. I've no wish to be introduced to your intended.

COX. *My* intended? How can that be, sir? You proposed to her
first!

BOX. What of that, sir? I came to an untimely end, and you
popped the question afterwards.

COX. Very well, sir!

BOX. Very well, sir!

COX. You are much more worthy of her than I am, sir. Permit
me, then, to follow the generous impulse of my nature—I
give her up to you.

BOX. Benevolent being! I wouldn't rob you for the world!
[*Going.*] Good-morning, sir.

COX. [*Seizing him.*] Stop!

BOX. Unhand me, hatter, or I shall cast off the lamb and assume
the lion!

COX. Pooh!   [*Snapping his fingers in* BOX's *face.*

BOX. An insult to my very face—under my very nose! [*Rubbing it.*] You know the consequences, sir—instant satisfaction, sir!

COX. With all my heart, sir!

[*They begin ringing bells violently, and pull down bell pulls.*

BOX *and* COX. Mrs. Bouncer! Mrs. Bouncer!

MRS. BOUNCER *runs in.*

MRS. BOUNCER. What is it, gentlemen?

BOX. Pistols for two!

MRS. BOUNCER. Yes, sir.   [*Going.*

COX. Stop! You don't mean to say, thoughtless and imprudent woman, that you keep loaded firearms in the house?

MRS. BOUNCER. Oh, no—they're not loaded.

COX. Then produce the murderous weapons instantly!

[*Exit* MRS. BOUNCER.

BOX. I say, sir.

COX. Well, sir?

BOX. What's your opinion of duelling, sir?

COX. I think it's a barbarous practice, sir.

BOX. So do I, sir. To be sure, I don't so much object to it when the pistols are not loaded.

COX. No, I dare say that *does* make some difference.

BOX. And yet, sir—on the other hand—doesn't it strike you as rather a waste of time for two people to keep firing pistols at one another, with nothing in 'em.

COX. No, sir—not more than any other harmless recreation.

BOX. Hark ye! Why do you object to marry Penelope Ann?

COX. Because, as I have observed already, I can't abide her. You'll be very happy with her.

BOX. Happy? Me? With the consciousness that I have deprived *you* of such a treasure? No, no, Cox!

COX. Don't think of me, Box—I shall be sufficiently rewarded by the knowledge of my Box's happiness.

BOX. Don't be absurd, sir!

COX. Then don't you be ridiculous, sir!

BOX. I won't have her!

COX. No more will I!

BOX. I have it! Suppose we draw lots for the lady—eh, Mr. Cox?

COX. That's fair enough, Mr. Box.

BOX. Or what say you to dice?

COX. [*Eagerly.*] With all my heart! Dice by all means.

BOX. [*Aside.*] That's lucky! Mrs. Bouncer's nephew left a pair here yesterday. He sometimes persuades me to have a throw for a trifle, and as he always throws sixes, I suspect they are good ones.   [*Goes to cupboard and brings out dice-box.*

COX. [*Aside.*] I've no objection at all to dice. I lost one pound seventeen and sixpence at last Barnet Races to a very gentlemanly looking man who had a most peculiar knack of throwing sixes. I suspected they were loaded, so I gave him another half-crown, and he gave me the dice.

    [*Takes dice out of his pocket.*

BOX. Now then, sir.

COX. I'm ready, sir. [*They seat themselves at opposite sides of the table.*] Will you lead off, sir?

BOX. As you please, sir. The lowest throw, of course, wins Penelope Ann?

COX. Of course, sir.

BOX. Very well, sir!

COX. Very well, sir!

BOX. [*Rattling dice and throwing.*] Sixes!

COX. That's not a bad throw of yours, sir. [*Rattling dice—throws.*] Sixes!

BOX. That's a pretty good one of yours, sir. [*Throws.*] Sixes!

COX. [*Throws.*] Sixes!

BOX. Sixes!

COX. Sixes!

BOX. Sixes!

COX. Sixes!

BOX. Those are not bad dice of yours, sir.

COX. Yours seem pretty good ones, sir.

BOX. Suppose we change?

COX. Very well, sir.   *[They change dice.*

BOX. [*Throwing.*] Sixes!

COX. Sixes!

BOX. Sixes!

COX. Sixes!

BOX. [*Flinging down the dice.*] Pooh! It's perfectly absurd your going on throwing sixes in this sort of way, sir!

COX. I shall go on till my luck changes, sir!

BOX. Let's try something else. I have it! Suppose we toss for Penelope Ann?

COX. The very thing I was going to propose!
    [*They each turn aside and take out a handful of money.*

BOX. [*Aside, examining money.*] Where's my tossing shilling? Here it is.

COX. [*Aside, examining money.*] Where's my lucky sixpence? I've got it.

BOX. Now then, sir, heads wins?

COX. Or tails lose, whichever you prefer.

BOX. It's the same to me, sir.

COX. Very well, sir—heads I win; tails you lose.

BOX. Yes. [*Suddenly.*] No—heads wins, sir.

COX. Very well—go on.

BOX. [*Tossing.*] Heads!

COX. [*Tossing.*] Heads!

BOX. [*Tossing.*] Heads!

COX. [*Tossing.*] Heads!

BOX. Ain't you rather tired of turning up heads, sir?

COX. Couldn't you vary the monotony of our proceedings by an occasional tail, sir?

BOX. [*Tossing.*] Heads!

COX. [*Tossing.*] Heads!

BOX. Heads? Stop, sir! Will you permit me? [*Taking* COX's *sixpence.*] Holloa, your sixpence has got no tail, sir!

COX. [*Seizing* BOX's *shilling.*] And your shilling has got two heads!

BOX. Cheat!

COX. Swindler!
[*They are about to rush upon each other, then retreat to some distance and commence sparring and striking fiercely at one another.*

Enter MRS. BOUNCER.

BOX *and* COX. Is the little back second-floor room ready?

MRS. BOUNCER. Not quite, gentlemen. I can't find the pistols, but I have brought you a letter—it came by the General Post yesterday. I am sure I don't know how I came to forget it, for I put it carefully in my pocket.

COX. And you've kept it carefully in your pocket ever since?

MRS. BOUNCER. Yes, sir. I hope you'll forgive me, sir. [*Going.*] By the bye, I paid twopence for it.

COX. Did you? Then I *do* forgive you. [*Exit* MRS. BOUNCER.] 'Margate.' The postmark decidedly says 'Margate.'

BOX. Oh, doubtless a tender epistle from Penelope Ann.

COX. Then read it, sir. [*Handing letter to* BOX.

BOX. Me, sir?

COX. Of course. You don't suppose I'm going to read a letter from your intended.

BOX. *My* intended? Pooh! It's addressed to you—C.O.X.

COX. Do you think that's a C? It looks to me like a B.

BOX. Nonsense! Fracture the seal.

COX. [*Opens letter—starts.*] Goodness gracious!

BOX. [*Snatching letter—starts.*] Gracious goodness!

COX. [*Taking letter again.*] 'Margate, May the 4th. Sir—I hasten to convey to you the intelligence of a melancholy accident, which has bereft you of your intended wife.' He means *your* intended.

BOX. No, *yours*! However, it's perfectly immaterial—but she unquestionably was yours.

COX. How can that be? You proposed to her first.

BOX. Yes, but then you—now don't let us begin again. Go on.

COX. [*Resuming letter.*] 'Poor Mrs. Wiggins went out for a short excursion in a sailing boat. A sudden and violent squall soon after took place, which it is supposed upset her, as she was found two days afterwards, keel upwards.'

BOX. Poor woman!

COX. The boat, sir! [*Reading.*] 'As her man of business, I immediately proceeded to examine her papers, amongst which I soon discovered her will, the following extract from which will, I have no doubt, be satisfactory to you: "I hereby bequeath my entire property to my intended husband." ' Excellent, but unhappy creature!   [*Affected.*

BOX. Generous ill-fated being!   [*Affected.*

COX. And to think that I tossed up for such a woman!

BOX. When I remember that I staked such a treasure on the hazard of a die!

COX. I'm sure, Mr. Box, I can't sufficiently thank you for your sympathy.

BOX. And I'm sure, Mr. Cox, you couldn't feel more if she had been your own intended.

COX. *If* she'd been *my own* intended! She *was* my own intended.

BOX. *Your* intended? Come, I like that! Didn't you very properly observe just now, sir, that I proposed to her first?

COX. To which you very sensibly replied that you'd come to an untimely end.

BOX. I deny it!

COX. I say you have!

BOX. The fortune's mine!

COX. Mine!

BOX. I'll have it!

COX. So will I!

BOX. I'll go to law!

COX. So will I!

BOX. Stop; a thought strikes me. Instead of going to law about the property, suppose we divide it.

COX. Equally?

BOX. Equally. I'll take two-thirds.

COX. That's fair enough, and I'll take three-fourths.

BOX. That won't do. Half and half.

COX. Agreed! There's my hand upon it.

BOX. And mine.

> [*About to shake hands. A postman's knock heard at street door.*

COX. Holloa! Postman again?

BOX. Postman yesterday—postman to-day.

Enter MRS. BOUNCER.

MRS. BOUNCER. Another letter, Mr. Cox—twopence more.

COX. I forgive you again. [*Taking letter. Exit* MRS. BOUNCER.]
Another trifle from Margate. [*Opens letter—starts.*] Goodness gracious!

BOX. [*Snatching letter—starts.*] Gracious goodness!

COX. [*Snatching letter again—reads.*] 'Happy to inform you, false alarm.'

BOX. [*Overlooking.*] 'Sudden squall—boat upset—Mrs. Wiggins, your intended——'

COX. 'Picked up by a steamboat——'

BOX. 'Carried into Boulogne——'

COX. 'Returned here this morning——'

BOX. 'Will start by early train to-morrow——'

COX. 'And be with you at ten o'clock exact.'

> [*Both simultaneously pull out their watches.*

BOX. Cox, I congratulate you!

COX. Box, I give you joy!

BOX. I'm sorry that most important business at the Colonial Office will prevent my witnessing the truly happy meeting between you and your intended. Good morning! [*Going.*

COX. [*Stopping him.*] It's obviously for me to retire. Not for worlds would I disturb the rapturous meeting between you and your intended. Good morning!

BOX. You'll excuse me, sir, but our last arrangement was that she was *your* intended.

COX. No, yours!

BOX. Yours!

BOX *and* COX. Yours! [*Ten o'clock strikes—noise of an omnibus.*

BOX. Ha, what's that? A cab's drawn up at the door! [*Running to window.*] No, it's a twopenny omnibus!

COX. [*Leaning over* BOX's *shoulder.*] A lady's got out——

BOX. There's no mistaking that majestic person—it's Penelope Ann!

COX. Your intended!

BOX. Yours!

COX. Yours!   [*Both run to door, and eagerly listen.*

BOX. Hark! She's coming upstairs!

COX. Shut the door!
     [*They slam the door, and both lean against it with their backs.*

MRS. BOUNCER. [*Without, and knocking.*] Mr. Cox! Mr. Cox!

COX. [*Shouting.*] I've just stepped out!

BOX. So have I!

MRS. BOUNCER. [*Without.*] Mr. Cox! [*Pushing at the door;* COX *and* BOX *redouble their efforts to keep the door shut.*] Open the door! It's only me, Mrs. Bouncer!

COX. Only you? Then where's the lady?

MRS. BOUNCER. Gone!

COX. Upon your honour?

BOX. As a gentleman?

MRS. BOUNCER. Yes, and she's left a note for Mr. Cox.

COX. Give it to me.

MRS. BOUNCER. Then open the door!

COX. Put it under. [*A letter is put under the door;* COX *picks up the letter and opens it.*] Goodness gracious!

BOX. [*Snatching letter.*] Gracious goodness!
                              [COX *snatches the letter.*

COX. [*Reading.*] 'Dear Mr. Cox, pardon my candour——'

BOX. [*Looking over and reading.*] 'But being convinced that our feelings, like our ages, do not reciprocate——'

COX. 'I hasten to apprise you of my immediate union——'

BOX. 'With Mr. Knox.'

cox. Huzza!

box. Three cheers for Knox. Ha, ha, ha!
   [*Tosses the letter in the air and begins dancing;* cox *does the same.*

mrs. bouncer. [*Putting her head in at door.*] The little second-floor back room is quite ready.

cox. I don't want it!

box. No more do I!

cox. What shall part us?

box. What shall tear us asunder?

cox. Box!

box. Cox! [*About to embrace;* box *stops, seizes* cox's *hand, and looks eagerly in his face.*] You'll excuse the apparent insanity of the remark, but the more I gaze on your features, the more I'm convinced that you're my long-lost brother.

cox. The very observation I was going to make to you!

box. Ah, tell me—in mercy tell me—have you such a thing as a strawberry mark on your left arm?

cox. No!

box. Then it is he!   [*They rush into each other's arms.*

cox. Of course we stop where we are?

box. Of course!

cox. For, between you and me, I'm rather partial to this house.

box. So am I—I begin to feel quite at home in it.

cox. Everything so clean and comfortable——

box. And I'm sure the mistress of it, from what I have seen of her, is very anxious to please.

cox. So she is—and I vote, Box, that we stick by her.

box. Agreed! There's my hand upon it—join but yours—agree that the house is big enough to hold us both, then Box——

cox. And Cox——

box *and* cox. Are satisfied!   [*Curtain.*

THE AREA BELLE

AN ORIGINAL FARCE IN ONE ACT

BY

WILLIAM BROUGH (1826–1870) and ANDREW HALLIDAY
(1830–1877)

───

First performed at the Adelphi Theatre
7 March 1864

───

CAST

PITCHER, in the Police	Mr. J. L. Toole
TOSSER, in the Grenadiers	Mr. Paul Bedford
WALKER CHALKS, a milkman	Mr. Robert Romer
MRS. CROAKER, the Missus	Mrs. Lewis
PENELOPE, the Area Belle	Mrs. Alfred Mellon

PREFACE TO *THE AREA BELLE*

BROUGH AND HALLIDAY between them wrote thirteen one-act farces and a drama in the brief period of their collaboration; these were all acted between 1861 and 1865, eight of them at the Adelphi. Before they came together Brough had been a journalist, co-author with his brother Robert of a series of burlesques, and author in his own right of a number of farces, extravaganzas, and burlesques. He began his career as a dramatist with a burlesque of *The Tempest, The Enchanted Isle, or 'Raising the Wind' on the Most Approved Principles* (1848), and ended it with another maritime burlesque, *The Flying Dutchman, or The Demon Seaman and the Lass that Loved a Sailor* (1869). Of some sixty plays he wrote on his own or with other playwrights he was best known for the burlesques and extravaganzas. Halliday, whose full name was Andrew Halliday Duff, was born in Scotland and had been an essayist and journalist in London in the 1850s. After collaborating with Brough he was chiefly known for a drama, *The Great City* (1867), and several adaptations of Scott and Dickens: *Little Emily* (1869), *Amy Robsart* (1870), *Little Nell* (1870), *The Lady of the Lake* (1872), and *Nicholas Nickleby* (1875).

The names of characters in the Brough–Halliday farces are completely expressive of their amiably plebeian, pie-and-sausage content: Fidge, Boodle, Toddles, Figgs, Marrowbone, Podge, Spout, Lollipop, Dollop, Lolliboy, Nobbler, Snipper, Clipper, Snatcher, Taters, Crusher, Pumps, Pouncer, Groggins, Muggins, etc. The world of these farces is the world of servants, lesser tradesmen, the working and lower-middle class; the occasional representatives of a more elevated class level are usually quite indistinguishable in character and conduct from their social inferiors. Peter Familias, the bumbling houseowner of *The Census* (1861),[1] obsessed with filling out his census forms correctly, summons the household at six in the morning for this

---

[1] Several of the Brough–Halliday farces (and many other nineteenth-century farces), like *The Census*, are immediately topical: *A Shilling Day at the Great Exhibition* (1862), *Doing Banting, Upstairs and Downstairs* (1865), and *The Mudborough Election*.

purpose in order to be quite ready for the census-taker. He experiences great difficulty in doing the job properly, since his niece is about to elope with Albert, who conceals himself in the china-closet. Discovered, he too must be put down on the forms, as must the policeman who arrives to arrest him and who is engaged to the maid, as must Albert's drunken cabman who is hauled into the house. Albert's words of love to the niece are typical of the domestic materialism of even the sentiments of these farces:

The cab is in waiting round the corner which will convey us at the moderate charge of sixpence per mile—luggage extra—to happiness and the Great Northern Railway. . . . once safe in an Edinburgh hotel, we have but to call in the boots and chambermaid, and taking one another by the hand, exclaim, 'If you loves me as I loves you, no knife shall cut our loves in two.' . . . let us away to where joy, bliss, and happiness—not forgetting the cabman, who will charge for time—are awaiting us.

In *My Heart's in the Highlands* (1863), two cockneys, Walker and Muggins, greengrocer and hairdresser respectively, take an excursion train to Scotland and make fools of themselves at the house of John O'Groat, a retired tobacconist. O'Groat, smitten with Scottish ways and the Scottish character, takes them for genuine Highlanders. Dressed in *'extravagant Highland costume'*, they indulge in equally extravagant physical business, which includes getting drunk, fumbling with guns (their bag of game consists of O'Groat's turkey and pig), and being so puzzled by the uses of the enormous caber, putting stone, and hammer with which their host expects them to practise that they begin to break up the stone with the hammer, thus thinking to be helpful and mend O'Groat's road. *Doing Banting* (1864) exploits the publicity given to William Banting's *A Lecture on Corpulence* (1863) and depicts the attempt of the obese Alderman Podge (a retired tallow-chandler) and his equally obese sister and butler to slim so that they can appear in genteel society. To do this they accept 'treatment' from a fraudulent scientific lecturer, Pankey, who has not enjoyed a square meal for a week. The most comic scenes, concerned entirely with food, show Pankey denying the family an excellent meal while eating it all himself, and then the aftermath when the starving Podges and their butler raid the larder, in the dark, of a knuckle of ham and a pigeon pie; they hide from each other and from a policeman who takes them for housebreakers. The waiter Veskit of *The Mudborough Election* (1865) is persuaded to disguise himself and stand as a candidate in the forthcoming election because otherwise there will be no contest to stimulate free spending on the electors of the borough. Pursued by a landlady whom he has promised to marry in payment of six weeks' rent and his laundry bill, Veskit avoids her for a time by going up and down in a dumb waiter. At last he is bribed to retire from the election, pays the landlady what he owes her, and claims the waitress for his bride. Aside from the physical business of the chase and the dumb waiter, the best moments of the piece occur when Veskit, making his acceptance speech to the electors dressed up in false whiskers, a white hat, and an eyeglass—taken locally to be the correct dress of a member of Parliament—keeps jumping down to answer a customer's call for service and has to be stopped each time from revealing his real identity.

These examples should suffice to illustrate the work of Brough and Halliday; *The Area Belle* is thoroughly representative of their farces and also the best of them. This kind of farce had been popular since the late 1830s, but was soon to pass from the West End stage. Its jolly vulgarity and lower-class matey domesticity did not entirely disappear, but had little place in three-act adaptations of French boulevard farce and the middle-class refinements of Pinero's Court Theatre farces.

The Area Belle was acted 128 times in its first season. The text is that of *Lacy's Acting Edition of Plays*, v. 62, collated with the only other edition of the play, the American *De Witt's Acting Plays*, no. 93, and the Lord Chamberlain's copy. Except for a few variants and slight differences in punctuation, the printed texts are identical; they add to and subtract from the Lord Chamberlain's manuscript, but not to any significant extent. The song that J. L. Toole as Pitcher sang over the supper table was 'A Norrible Tale' by E. L. Blanchard.

PLATE 4

The Area Belle. The kitchen setting

SCENE. *A Kitchen. Area steps from street seen through window,* c; *kitchen door from area,* R. c.; *practicable copper,* R.; *pantry door,* L.; *cupboard,* L. c.; *table, chairs, dresser, &c.*

PENELOPE. [*Cleaning dish covers and singing.*] 'I'd choose to be a daisy, if I might be a flower.' If I might be a flower, indeed! Why, everybody says I *am* a flower! Pitcher says I'm like the rose. Tosser calls me his tulip. Chalks says my breath's like butter cups, while the baker's young man came in the other day while I was making pies, and said I was flour all over. [*Sticks up cover over dresser.*] Oh, it's very nice to be so universally admired; [*Looking at herself in the cover.*] not, perhaps, that it's much to be wondered at. And yet it's rather puzzling to have so many sweethearts! One doesn't know how to choose amongst 'em; and I'm obliged to keep a book, what fine folks call a *dairy*, for fear I should forget whose turn it is to come and visit me. Let me see—there's Pitcher in the police, and Tosser in the Grenadiers, and there's Dobbs the baker, and Chumps the butcher—they all come by turns. And there's the milkman: he, I believe, is rather sweet upon me, but I have never put the milkman in the dairy yet. [*Looks at book.*] Now then, whose turn is it tonight? Missus is going out, and I shall have a nice long evening. [*Reads.*] 'Pitcher.' Ah, he is a nice young man! I do think, if I have a preference, it's Pitcher. [*Looks at book, and starts.*] What's this? Good gracious, if I haven't asked Tosser too! Now, if there is another man in the world besides Pitcher that I adore, it's Tosser! What am I to do? If Pitcher or Tosser meet tonight there will be bloodshed. I must forego the happiness of receiving either, and have recourse to the pepper box. [*Puts pepper box on window sill.*] There, that's our signal—that's the red light on our railway, and means 'danger.' Whosoever's turn it is to come, that signal in the window informs him that missus or some other heavy luggage train is in the way, and he shunts off accordingly.

CHALKS. [*Without.*] Milk below.

PENELOPE. There's the milkman, but he only comes professionally. He's not upon my private visiting list yet.

[CHALKS *comes down steps, and enters.*

PENELOPE. Don't want any this afternoon, Mr. Chalks; don't trouble yourself to come down the steps.

CHALKS. It's no trouble, thank you, ma'am. Ah! it ain't all milk that brings me down them steps, Miss Penelope.

PENELOPE. I have long suspected it, sir; it strikes me there's a certain quantity of water, with a modicum of chalk.

CHALKS. No, Miss Penelope, my milk is as genuine as my feelings. Listen to me, Penelope—I'm a plain man.

PENELOPE. Yes, you *are* rather plain, Mr. Chalks.

CHALKS. I don't mean that, Miss Penelope; I mean that I'm a straight-forward man, a honest man, and I have nine cows as gives ten quarts a day each; and I have a horse and cart, Miss Penelope, and a first-rate milk walk. Yes, and I have a 'eart, Miss Penelope; and all them worldly goods, the 'eart included I'm willing to share with——

PENELOPE. [*Turning away and sentimentally.*] With some one in your own walk of life which will 'ave you, Mr. Chalks, and very proper too. Good afternoon.

CHALKS. I see what it is. It's that policeman, or that soldier, that I have seen lounging round about the area; it's the uniform. But let me tell you, Miss Penelope, fine feathers don't make fine birds.

PENELOPE. Which I despise the imputation, Mr. Chalks; there's the steps, sir.

CHALKS. I'm going, Miss Penelope, but let me tell you that this smock frock covers a 'eart as warm as ever beat under a red jacket, Miss Penelope.

PENELOPE. None of your imperence, sir.

CHALKS. Or under a swallow-tailed blue with pewter buttons, Miss Penelope.

PENELOPE. You are a low person, Mr. Chalks.

CHALKS. I may be low, but Penelope, this 'eart—[*Slaps his breast.*] broken, by Jove!

PENELOPE. Your heart?

CHALKS. No; but the new-laid egg that under happier circumstances I should have made you a present of, but which like my prospects is gone all to smash—and a nice mess my feelings and my pockets is in, in consequence! Farewell, Penelope! Pockets will wash, but feelings won't—we only gets them *mangled*.   [*Exit up steps.*

PENELOPE. Well, after all, Chalks is not a bad sort; but what is he compared to Pitcher or to Tosser?

Enter MRS. CROAKER, *calling* PENELOPE.

MRS. CROAKER. Hasn't the postman been, Penelope?

PENELOPE. Not yet, mum. [*Aside.*] Ah! there's another of my admirers. Now if it wasn't for my admiration for Pitcher and Tosser, I do think I should like that postman.

MRS. CROAKER. Then those orders for the play won't come. Go and make up the drawing-room fire, Penelope.

PENELOPE. La, mum, I thought you were going out.

MRS. CROAKER. What right have you to think, pray? I've changed my mind.

PENELOPE. [*Aside.*] How lucky I put up the pepper box!

MRS. CROAKER. Will you be good enough to see about that fire?

PENELOPE. Yes, mum, I'm going. But for that preserving pepper box, the fat would indeed have been in the fire!
                                                        [*Exit.*

MRS. CROAKER. This comes of trusting to play actors! There's a man I used to think my friend promised me orders for the play tonight, and now, when I have set my heart on going, he deceives me. [*Looking round the kitchen.*] Everything in disorder as usual! Those servant girls, they are really more trouble than they are worth; there's that dish cover—I've distinctly told Penelope a hundred times, on the lowest calculation, to hang that dish cover on the middle hook over the chimney piece; instead of that, she's got it over the dresser. [*Puts it in its place.*] The shovel on the wrong side of the fireplace, of course. [*Shifts it.*] And here now, I ask any one if that is a becoming place for a pepper box? [*Removes the pepper box.*] There! I'm not sorry that the orders didn't come, for I am just in a humour to stop at home and make myself disagreeable. [*Postman's knock.*] The postman! I shouldn't wonder if that's the orders after all. [*Goes to the area door.*] Throw it down here, postman. [*Re-enters with letter.*] It *is* the orders; I knew he'd send them. That's all right—I wouldn't have been kept at home this evening for the world.

Enter PENELOPE.

PENELOPE. I've lighted the fire, ma'am, and the room's all comfortable.

MRS. CROAKER. What nonsense you are talking, girl! I'm going out—I told you so.

PENELOPE. No, ma'am, you said——

MRS. CROAKER. Don't answer me, Penelope.

PENELOPE. [*Aside.*] Good gracious! Some one has moved the pepper box—Pitcher and Tosser will be here together!
[*Tries to put pepper box back in the window unperceived.*

MRS. CROAKER. What are you fidgeting about there for? Fetch me my boots.

PENELOPE. Yes, mum. [*Puts pepper box back in window—aside.*] I breathe again. [*Exit.*

MRS. CROAKER. [*Going to window to read order.*] 'Admit two to the pepper boxes.' Pepper boxes! Oh, I see—'the upper boxes.' How badly these actors write—pepper boxes, indeed! [*Sneezes.*] Why, I declare, there *is* a pepper box. Now, I could have sworn I put that pepper box in its place. I know I meant to, but I suppose the postman's knock hammered it out of my head. There—there's no mistake about it this time. [*Puts pepper box on dresser.*] Now for the theatre.

Enter PENELOPE, *with boots.*

PENELOPE. Here's your Badmorals, mum.

MRS. CROAKER. Very well; you come and help me to dress.
[*Exit.*

PENELOPE. Yes, mum. Oh, what a chance, if I hadn't made that dreadful error in my dairy! Missus is going out, and I might have had a whole evening of bliss with Pitcher, or of paradise with Tosser; but Pitcher and Tosser both together! Oh, earthquakes would be nothing to it!

MRS. CROAKER. [*Without.*] Penelope!

PENELOPE. Oh! I'm a coming, mum! What a nuisance missusses are—they're really more trouble than they're worth. [*Exit.*
[*A whistle is heard outside, and* TOSSER *is seen cautiously coming down area steps—examines window.*

TOSSER. All right, all right; no pepper box to-night—[*Enters.*] so, in the absence of pepper—we'll take the citadel by assault. [*Looking about.*] Familiar, though subterraneous scene of comfort and cold mutton! How oft at that happy fireside have I breathed the hardent vow, and sipped the surreptitious gin and water! In this old chair how many a time has this 'ere son of Mars sat courting of Venus—which her name is Penelope—vile the cold pigeon pie has been a heating up in that there hoven! On such blissful occasions, when I have seen Penelope preparing of a tart, how my 'eart has beat at the spectacle of her loveliness; and how my mouth has watered when I see her a spooning out the jam! Yes— and that commodious cupboard, whose friendly shelter I have so often shared with the black-beetles and the blacking bottles, when old Mother Croaker has dropped in upon us inopportunely and promiscuously! Where can Penelope be? I am longing to embrace her; and I dined at half-past one, which until the present period of the evening p.m. is a many hours. However, as I know old Mother Croaker ain't at home this evening——

MRS. CROAKER. [*Without.*] Penelope!

TOSSER. The devil! She *is* at home; and yet no pepper box in the window gave warning of the untoward circumstance. The old un's coming down stairs. I'll seek the more congenial society of the beetles and the blacking bottles.
[*Exit into cupboard.*
[PITCHER *is seen coming down the area steps—whistles— approaches cautiously.*

PITCHER. No pepper box in the window—it's all right. The missus is gone out, and the dear creature is all alone. Hollo, not here! Why has the divinity deserted her shrine? I dare say she's gone up stairs to titivate, in order to appear charming in the eyes of her devoted Pitcher. [*Looks around.*] Talk about Bowers of Bliss and Caves of Harmony. Give me a snug kitchen, where the cook is susceptible, and the family up stairs is such as require small joints and has 'em frequent. What a proud thing it is to be entrusted with the duty of watching over the hearths and homes of one's native country —to be the guardian spirit which protects these scenes of peace and plenty from the foot of the spoiler. Here is peace, and in that there pantry there is plenty. May the two combined ever reign in the households of that West Central District of the town in which it has pleased the Fates and Sir Richard Mayne to allot the beat of that active and intelligent officer, Pitcher! Where can Penelope be? The absence of the pepper box denotes that the missus is out. [*Bell rings.*] Why, that's the old girl's dressing-room bell—she's not gone yet. I'll bolt—no I won't—I'll hide until I receive further information! This cupboard: many's the time it has sheltered me before. [*Opens cupboard door.*] What, occupied! Just you come out of this!   [*Dragging* TOSSER *forward.*

TOSSER. I beg your pardon, sir, I'll go quietly; I won't offer no resistance.

PITCHER. What are you doing here, sir?

TOSSER. Not with the slightest intention to commit a felony, sir, I assure you.

PITCHER. What are you doing here, sir?

TOSSER. Well, I suppose you know; the old girl sent you to lug me out, of course.

PITCHER. Old girl? Nothing of the sort!

TOSSER. She didn't! Then allow me in my turn to ask you what *you* do here?

PITCHER. [*Aside.*] Horrible suspicion! If he should be a rival!

TOSSER. [*Aside.*] Terrible surmise! If he should be a sweetheart of Penelope's!

PITCHER. Who are you, sir?

TOSSER. Sir, I repeat the question—who are you?

PITCHER. I am a policeman, sir.

TOSSER. So I perceive, and I am a soldier.

PITCHER. The fact is sufficiently apparent, sir—a full private— a very full private, I should say.

PLATE 5

The Area Belle. Paul Bedford as Tosser and J. L. Toole as Pitcher

TOSSER. I see it all; you are here, sir, as a lover of the cook.

PITCHER. Yes, sir, and you're another.

TOSSER. I own it. I love Penelope.

PITCHER. Penelope is loved by me.

TOSSER. By you—you bloated bluebottle!

PITCHER. Bluebottle! Who are you calling bluebottle? You scarlet runner!

TOSSER. Insult a military man! Nothing but blood can wipe out the insult!   [*Threatening him.*

PITCHER. Assault a policeman in the execution of his duty! Fine and imprisonment!

TOSSER. I'll have satisfaction, sir!

PITCHER. So shall I.

TOSSER. There's my card.   [*Giving a directed envelope.*

PITCHER. [*Points to the number on his collar.*] There's mine. Weapons?

TOSSER. Bayonets.

PITCHER. Truncheons.

TOSSER. I won't have truncheons.

PITCHER. Nor I bayonets.

TOSSER. Then what do you say to belts?

PITCHER. With buckles?

TOSSER. With buckles.

PITCHER. I'd rather not.

TOSSER. Then what's the use of talking about fighting?

PITCHER. None whatever. I suppose you think yourself a very fine fellow in that red coat? How much do you get now for making such a object of yourself?

TOSSER. Thirteen pence a day, and find my own victuals. What do you get?

PITCHER. Nineteen shillings a week and find my own cooks, and I must say I think the public get their civil and military protection cheap at the money. Do you know, I feel uncommon hungry?

TOSSER. Well, I should have no objection to a snack myself. I wish that girl would come. I feel a longing at my heart.

PITCHER. So do I, and also somewhere else in the immediate neighbourhood. [*Placing hand on his stomach.*

Enter PENELOPE.

PENELOPE. Missus is gone at last, and the coast is clear. What do I see? Pitcher and Tosser both together!

TOSSER. Penelope, where do you keep the knives?

PENELOPE. The knives! Oh, don't, for pity's sake!

TOSSER. Where do you keep the knives?

PITCHER. And the forks?

PENELOPE. One word, for mercy's sake—do you mean murder or cold mutton?

TOSSER. Well, cold mutton to begin with.

PITCHER. Cut near the knuckle, with a little currant jelly if you've got it. Them's my sentiments.

PENELOPE. Stop; let me first see you're friends. Shake hands! Come, Pitcher! Tosser, do now!

PITCHER. Tosser, my friend, your hand!

TOSSER. Yours, my friend—and Pitcher! [*They shake hands.*

PENELOPE. That's right; and now for supper.

TOSSER. I second the motion.

PITCHER. [*Who has gone to pantry, and enters with cold mutton.*] Carried unanimously!

PENELOPE. [*Laying the cloth.*] Now, Tosser, go and get the plates; look sharp! [*Exit* TOSSER.] And you, Pitcher, run into the pantry for the cold gammon of bacon.

PITCHER. Yes, dear; but in the absence of the military, let me take the hopportunity of telling you as there's no one loves you like your faithful Pitcher——

Enter TOSSER.

TOSSER. [*Putting down jar on table.*] Pickles!

PENELOPE. Now then, the bacon and the plates—make haste!
[*Exit* PITCHER.

TOSSER. One moment: while the bobby's out of sight, let me lay bare my buzzum to you, Penelope. The only man in the whole universe that loves you for yourself alone is Tosser!

Enter PITCHER, *with dish.*

PITCHER. Gammon and spinach!   [*Puts it down on table.*

PENELOPE. Now come; pretty waiters you are—where are the plates and knives and forks?

TOSSER. Plates in an instant!

PITCHER. Knives and forks in a jiffy!   [*Both go to dresser.*

PENELOPE. Oh, how delightful to think that, after all my fears, Pitcher and Tosser should have met so comfortable—just like lambs! Missus is safe for the next six hours—shan't we have a jolly evening?

TOSSER. All right, my tulip; here's the crockery.

PITCHER. Come on, my rosebud; here's the cutlery, Mappin's best.

PENELOPE. Now then, sit down; I'm sure I don't know which to help first.

TOSSER. [*Sitting* R. *of table.*] Me, my dear, if you please.
    [*Taking plate.*

PITCHER. [*Sitting* L. *of table.*] Certainly not, sir; the civil force takes precedence of the military in time of peace.
    [*Snatches away plate.*

PENELOPE. Well, don't let us have war, now. [*Gives* TOSSER *a plate of meat.*] Let's have peace——

PITCHER. [*Cutting himself another slice.*] And plenty!

PENELOPE. That's right—I like harmony.

PITCHER. Do you? You shall have some—I'll sing you a song.

PENELOPE. Oh, do; but don't sing with your mouth full.

TOSSER. Order, ladies and gentlemen; Pitcher, 444 B., will oblige.   [PITCHER *sings.*

PENELOPE. Bravo—a very good song, and very well sung! What will you allow us to say after it, Mr. Pitcher?

PITCHER. Say! I'll say a little bit more off the knuckle, cut thick.

PENELOPE. [*Helping him.*] Oh, isn't this delightful—shan't we have a pleasant evening? [*Knocking and ringing heard.*] What's that? [*Runs back to area steps.*] Good gracious! Missus!

PITCHER *and* TOSSER. The missus!

[*They drop knives and forks.*

PENELOPE. What on earth can have brought her back. [*Knocking heard.*] Do be quick—get in here. [*Both run to cupboard.*] No, there's no room for both of you. You go in there!

[*Pushing* TOSSER *into cupboard—another knock.*

PITCHER. And what's to become of me? Do put me somewhere!

PENELOPE. I have it; here—get in—she's coming down the area steps!

[*Puts him into copper and puts lid over him—knocking and ringing repeated outside.*

PENELOPE. [*Picking up knives, forks, &c.*] I'm a coming, mum! Oh, what a state the place is in! And if missus sees this terrible circumstantial evidence, there will be a regular havalanche!

MRS. CROAKER. [*Coming down steps.*] Where's that girl? Why don't she answer the door? Oh, here you are! Pretty thing indeed for a respectable housekeeper to have to get into her own house like an area sneak!

PENELOPE. Oh, mum, I didn't think you would be back so soon, and——

MRS. CROAKER. So soon! No, I should think not! The impertinence of that man at the theatre! He actually refused to admit me, because it was past seven o'clock. Pretty thing if respectable people are to hurry themselves to death to suit *their* whims! I didn't want to go to their rubbishing theatre, and if anybody thinks I'm angry or disappointed, they're very much mistaken! [*Kicks off clogs, bangs down her fan and bonnet.*] There, take those things up stairs, Penelope.

PENELOPE. Yes, mum, but——

MRS. CROAKER. But what?

PENELOPE. Nothing, mum, only I thought you'd like to sit up in the drawing room; it's so damp down here to-night, mum, and the black beetles is running about like anythink.

MRS. CROAKER. Go when I tell you, girl! Eh, what's this? Meat on the table!

PENELOPE. Oh, please, mum, I thought you would like to sit down in the kitchen, and have your supper—it's so cold in the drawing room, and the chimney smokes awful!

MRS. CROAKER. Well, just go and see to it. [*Puts meat and supper things on dresser, leaving only the cloth on the table.*

PENELOPE. Yes, mum. [*Going towards cupboard, and aside to him.*] Keep quiet, Tosser, if you love me.

MRS. CROAKER. Are you going?

PENELOPE. Yes, mum; directly, mum. [*Sidling over to copper —aside.*] Pitcher, be still, if you have the least regard for me.

MRS. CROAKER. Do you hear, girl?

PENELOPE. [*Starts.*] Yes, mum, I'm going. [*Aside.*] If Tosser should cough or Pitcher sneeze, there'll be a resurrection in the house!   [*Exit.*

MRS. CROAKER. Now, how shall I pass the evening? A good idea—as I'm not to enjoy myself this evening, no one else shall. Penelope shall begin her wash to-night instead of to-morrow morning. I'll light the copper at once. [*Goes to copper and lights fire.*] That's so far good. Now to give out the soap and soda.   [*Exit.*

PITCHER. [*Putting his head out.*] It's getting rather warm! It strikes me I stand a decent chance of being roasted—by Jove, here's the missus!

Enter MRS. CROAKER. PITCHER *disappears in copper.*

MRS. CROAKER. Good gracious, if I haven't lit the fire without turning on the water! [*Turns on tap—noise of water heard.*] And now for the collars and pocket handkerchiefs.   [*Exit.*

PITCHER. [*Looking out.*] Hollo, it's getting rather damp here! It strikes me I stand a decent chance of being drowned—the water's coming in! However, with the aid of my truncheon, I've stopped the pipe up with my pocket handkerchief. Hollo, by Jove, the water's forced it out! I can't stand this—the coast is clear—I'll bolt! [*Jumps out and puts lid on copper.*]

There's somebody coming, and I've left my hat behind me—I
can't go through the streets in this state! Oh here, this table.
　　　[Hides under the table—the cloth reaches the ground.

Enter PENELOPE.

PENELOPE. Now then, while missus is up stairs, I'll just get
them safe away. [*Seeing copper alight.*] What do I see? The
fire lighted under the copper! [*Takes off lid of copper—steam
rises.*] Pitcher is boiled! [*Fishes with copper stick, and brings out
a pocket handkerchief wet and ragged.*] Done all to rags!
[*Bringing out his hat.*] And this is all that is left of my
Pitcher! [*Going to cupboard.*] Oh, Tosser, Tosser!

PITCHER. [*Peeping out under table cloth.*] Eh, it's Penelope! She's
calling Tosser! I'll listen and see what she has to say to him.

PENELOPE. Tosser, dear Tosser!

PITCHER. [*Aside.*] Dear Tosser—ah!

PENELOPE. [*Opening cupboard door.*] Good gracious, he's
asleep! Asleep! To think that Tosser should indulge in
slumber while Pitcher was being biled like—like beef! Tosser,
dear Tosser, wake!

TOSSER. [*Waking and rubbing his eyes.*] What is it—what is it,
Penelope?

PENELOPE. Pitcher!

TOSSER. I like him, Penelope—no unfriendliness towards him
whatever—he's a broth of a boy.

PENELOPE. He is indeed! Look here, stewed down to this.
　　　　　　　　　　　　[Showing hat and handkerchief.

TOSSER. What do you mean?

PENELOPE. A haccident—boiled alive in the copper, like—like
a raw lobster!

TOSSER. Who done it, Penelope?

PENELOPE. All of us, we had all a hand in it—missus and you
and me; we're all guilty in the eye of the law.

TOSSER. Then let me be off.　　　　　　　　　　　*[Going.*

PENELOPE. Not without me, Tosser, I can never leave you
now. Come, let us fly together to the ends of the earth!

PITCHER. [*Overturning table, and getting up with the table cloth round him.*] Never! I forbid the banns!

TOSSER *and* PENELOPE. Good gracious, it's his ghost!

TOSSER. Worthy, but disembodied Pitcher——

PENELOPE. Beloved, but much injured ghost——

PITCHER. [*Aside.*] By Jove, they take me for a ghost! I'll keep it up.   [*Rolls his eyes and groans fearfully.*

PENELOPE. Rest, perturbed spirit!

TOSSER. What's your little game?

PITCHER. My game—ha, ha, to warm you! [*Sees mutton on dresser and seizes it.*] Behold the bait that lured me on to my destruction!   [*Gnaws at mutton.*

TOSSER. Ah, would you! Oh, nonsense, ghosts can't eat cold mutton!

PITCHER. Avaunt! Don't touch me! I'm a *gobblin'*.

TOSSER. [*Boldly.*] I'll lay him, Penelope! I'll lay him before he eats up all the joint.

PENELOPE. No, let him be, it may appease his angry spirit.

PITCHER. It do—it do.

PENELOPE. Would you like anything to drink with it?

PITCHER. I should.   [*Groans.*

TOSSER. Oh, don't do that; eat your victuals quietly, like a good ghost.

PENELOPE. Will you take it hot or cold?

PITCHER. Hot—hot—hot—with sugar and a little bit of lemon.

PENELOPE. I'll fetch it; but you'll promise that you'll vanish then?

PITCHER. No, never; no power can move me from this spot.

MRS. CROAKER. [*Without.*] Penelope!

Enter MRS. CROAKER.

MRS. CROAKER. Hollo! Upon my word——

PITCHER. The missus, by Jove!   [*Rushes to area steps.*

TOSSER. The missus, by jingo!   [*Rushes to area steps.*

MRS. CROAKER. [*Running after them.*] Stop thief—murder—thieves!

PENELOPE. Oh, don't, ma'am, it's the ghost of him you biled!

MRS. CROAKER. Ghost indeed—what are you talking about? I'll ghost them!

PENELOPE. 'Orrors upon 'orrors' 'ed!

CHALKS. [*Seen on area steps arresting their flight.*] Ah! so I've caught you, have I—come along.

MRS. CROAKER. Bring 'em this way, my good man!

Enter CHALKS, *driving them before him into the kitchen.*

CHALKS. I've got 'em, mum—I've got 'em! Just caught 'em bolting up the area steps.

MRS. CROAKER. With my best table cloth!

PENELOPE. Table cloth! Then it's not a ghost?

PITCHER. No—I give up the ghost.   [*Drops cloth.*

TOSSER. Perhaps you'll give up the mutton too.
                                        [*Seizes mutton.*

MRS. CROAKER. My mutton! [*Seizing mutton from* TOSSER.] So this is the way you take care of the place in my absence! You leave the house this moment, without warning, and without a character!

PENELOPE. Pitcher—Tosser!   [*Crying.*

MRS. CROAKER. Oh, no doubt they'll stand your friends.

TOSSER. [*Aside.*] The dear creature's got the sack—no more nice suppers. Penelope, your conduct is disgraceful.
                                        [*Turning away.*

PENELOPE. Oh, Tosser!

TOSSER. I resign you to Pitcher.

PENELOPE. Pitcher!

PITCHER. Penelope, you have brought a blight upon this domestic hearth; I resign you to Tosser.

MRS. CROAKER. And these, girl, are your true lovers!

CHALKS. No, mum, they're not; but I can tell you where to find the article.

MRS. CROAKER. Where, I should like to know?

CHALKS. Here! [*Slaps his breast.*] By Jove, broke that other egg that was to have made it up!

PENELOPE. Oh, Mr. Chalks, something always whispered to me that you loved me for myself alone.

CHALKS. [*To* MRS. CROAKER.] I'm no cupboard lover, mum—I never had a bite or sup in your house, mum. I've a comfortable home of my own which I can offer to Penelope, and——

PITCHER. Well, you needn't bounce; I'd do the same myself if I had one.

TOSSER. Of course, but not having homes of our own we had to make ourselves at home here, mum, the best way we could.

PENELOPE. Pitcher and Tosser, I despise you both! Walker Chalks, you're a trump!

CHALKS. Penelope, you're a lily of the valley!

TOSSER. That's all right.

PITCHER. Now we're all friends at last.

MRS. CROAKER. Friends indeed! I'll have no more of this—be off, all of you!

TOSSER. Halt—attention! Pitcher, do your duty!

PITCHER. [*Drawing staff and to audience.*] Don't anybody move on! I take you all into custody—for one moment. This old lady says she'll have no more of this—what do you say? We leave it entirely to you; if you say you'll have more of it to-morrow night and the night after, and for many nights to come, it won't be missuses, nor milkmen, nor pepper boxes in the window that will prevent Pitcher——

TOSSER. And Tosser——

PITCHER. From paying their devoirs to——

PENELOPE. The Area Belle. [*Curtain.*

TOM COBB

OR FORTUNE'S TOY

AN ENTIRELY ORIGINAL FARCICAL COMEDY
IN THREE ACTS

BY

WILLIAM SCHWENCK GILBERT (1836–1911)

———

*First performed at the St. James's Theatre
24 April 1875*

———

CAST

COLONEL O'FIPP, an Irish adventurer	Mr. Clifford Cooper
TOM COBB ⎫ young surgeons	Mr. E. W. Royce
WHIPPLE ⎭	Mr. Edgar Bruce
MATILDA O'FIPP, the Colonel's daughter	Miss Edith Challis
MR. EFFINGHAM ⎫	Mr. De Vere
MRS. EFFINGHAM ⎪ a romantic	Mrs. Chippendale
BULSTRODE EFFINGHAM ⎬ family	Mr. W. J. Hill
CAROLINE EFFINGHAM ⎭	Miss Litton
FOOTMAN	Mr. Russell
BIDDY	Miss E. Doyne

Three Months are supposed to elapse between each Act

PREFACE TO *TOM COBB*

ALTHOUGH of all nineteenth-century dramatists Gilbert, together with Shaw and Oscar Wilde, had the most mature and
sophisticated sense of the absurd, he was not a farceur in the
style of Morton, Coyne, or Brough and Halliday. In fact, when
he tried his hand at the conventional farce, as in *A Medical Man*
(1872), he wrote it badly. Much more suited to his abilities and
creative powers were the ironies of the German Reed burlesques,
the fairy comedies such as *The Palace of Truth* (1870), the operas,
and the 'farcical comedy' of *Tom Cobb* and *Engaged*. Before
writing these last two plays Gilbert had successfully adapted
Un Chapeau de Paille d'Italie (1851), by Eugène Labiche and
Marc Michel, as *The Wedding March* (1873), but after that did
not participate in the fashionable vogue of adaptation from
French farce, except for *On Bail* (1877), a reworking of an
earlier farce, *Committed for Trial* (1874). Before he surrenders
himself for assaulting a ticket-collector, Lovibond of *On Bail*
goes off to a supper party at a theatre whose manager, reveng-
ing himself for a practical joke that Lovibond previously played
upon him, has invited not only burlesque actresses but also the
governor of the prison to whom Lovibond must report the next
morning: each man is unaware of the other's identity and each
poses ridiculously as a baronet. Back at Lovibond's house, his
wife's admirer has been mistakenly arrested in his place. In the
last act Lovibond, suffering miserably from a hangover, turns
up at the prison to find that he is already there; disguised as
a barrister he interviews the other Lovibond and with growing
fury realizes that he is talking to an ardent worshipper of his
wife. At the last moment all complications are resolved and the
play ends on a note of general domestic harmony. The plot is
promising, but since *On Bail* deals in mistaken identities, conventional farce misunderstandings, extravagant physical business, and not in Gilbert's natural areas of strength, the ironic
and absurd, it is a weak play. The most felicitous moment
happens to be the most ironic, when Lovibond, dressed in
immaculate evening clothes for his supper party, comforts his
distressed wife, who believes that he is going straight to prison;

as he embraces her he calmly pulls on his gloves behind her back.

Since Gilbert called both *Tom Cobb* and *Engaged* 'farcical comedy', I should explain why the former is included in the farce volume and the latter assigned to the comedy volume. Of course the two plays have strong resemblances, and I have pointed out that farce and comedy in the nineteenth century were not entirely dissimilar. Both plays treat ludicrous situations with apparently the greatest seriousness; indeed, Gilbert insisted on this kind of treatment from actors. His prefatory note to *Engaged*, in which he demanded that 'it should be played with the most perfect earnestness and gravity throughout . . . the characters, one and all, should appear to believe, throughout, in the perfect sincerity of their words and actions', could just as well be applied to *Tom Cobb*.[1] That Gilbert was acutely conscious of this particular problem of performance style is also evident from his note to the acting edition of *The Wedding March*; here he also warned against exaggeration and declared that the actors 'should rely for the fun of their parts on the most improbable things being done in the most earnest manner *by persons of every-day life*'.

Both *Tom Cobb* and *Engaged* regard life and human motives with extreme irony; in both of them romantic love combines happily with love of money, and characters betray each other equally happily. Both plays contain a mock-tragic heroine with great passions and lofty romantic ideals. Obviously the difference between them does not lie here, nor in the fact that utterly humourless characters respond to profoundly ridiculous situations with imperturbable normality, for this is true of both. What seems to me to make *Tom Cobb* a farce and *Engaged* a comedy is not so much that the latter is cooler and more poised, a more mature work, but that in *Tom Cobb* the hero (or anti-hero) suffers those extraordinary pressures an individual can be subjected to in farce, and in *Engaged* he does not; *Tom Cobb* is more metaphysically akin to farce. It is true that Cheviot Hill of *Engaged* does not know whether he is legally married, but although this agitates him he seems perfectly able to cope almost indefinitely, and loving three women simultaneously does not

---

[1] Gilbert actually directed, in the modern sense of the word, the first production of *Engaged*, so was aware of the acting problems at first hand.

strike him as abnormal. Indeed, no character in *Engaged* is especially conscious of abnormality. But the absurdity of his situation drives Tom Cobb almost mad; he is quite aware of it, and it renders him absolutely helpless. It even makes him doubt his own identity. At the end of Act II he says, 'You say I'm engaged to you. I dare say I am. If you said I was engaged to your mother, I'd dare say it too. I've no idea who I am, or where I am, or what I am saying or doing.' Here in desperation speaks the true farce hero, and his predicament is thoroughly characteristic of the genre.

Tom Cobb was performed fifty-three times before the close of the St. James's season. The text used here is that in Gilbert's *Original Plays*, Second Series (1881), published by Chatto and Windus and collated with *Lacy's Acting Edition of Plays*, v. 117 (the later *French's Acting Edition*, no. 1752 is identical) and the Lord Chamberlain's copy. The *Lacy* has fuller scene descriptions than the text in *Original Plays*, and these have been used; otherwise the two editions are virtually the same; there are corruptions in the *Lacy*. The Examiner of Plays licensed *Tom Cobb* for the Royal Court in November 1874, under the title of *Buried Alive*. The printed texts make some cuts in the manuscript copy and a few minor alterations; Mrs. O'Fipp and Ben Isaacs appear briefly in the licenser's copy but were eliminated by the time the play reached the stage.

ACT I

SCENE. *A shabby but pretentious sitting-room in* COLONEL
O'FIPP's *house. Doors* R. *and* C. *Fireplace* R., *table* C. *Breakfast laid.*

Enter TOM COBB, *with open letter in his hand.*

TOM. I haven't a penny—I haven't the ghost of a prospect of a
penny. In debt everywhere, and now I'm told that judgment's
been signed against me for £250 by the cruellest Jew in
Christendom. Upon my soul, it's enough to make a fellow shy
things about; I swear it is! But everything always *did* go
wrong with me, even before I was born, for I was always expected to be a girl, and turned out something quite different,
and no fault of mine, I'm sure! [*Producing pistol.*] Oh, if I was
only quite, quite sure I knew how to load it, I'd blow my
brains out this minute! I would, upon my word and honour.

Enter MATILDA.

MATILDA. Eh! and what good 'ld that do, dear?

TOM. It would rid the world of an unhappy wretch. The world's
a beast, and I hate it.

MATILDA. Then if you hate it, what d'ye want to be doing it a
good turn for? Sure it would be a bad bargain, lovey, for
you'd lose the world, whereas the world 'ld only lose *you.*
                    [*Takes pistol away from him.*

TOM. There's truth in that.

MATILDA. If I was you, dear, I'd go on living to spite it.

TOM. Oh, ain't that small! Oh, ain't that like a woman!

MATILDA. And after all, ye're not so badly off. Don't ye board
and lodge on nominal turr'ms with a rale cornel?

TOM. Yes, that's true enough.

MATILDA. And ain't ye engaged to a rale cornel's daughter?
And isn't *that* something to live for?
                    [*Goes to table and cuts bread and butter.*

TOM. Oh, I've plenty to live *for,* but I've nothing to live *on.*

Upon my word, Matilda, when you come to think of it, it *is* a most extraordinary thing that I can't get any patients! I'm a qualified practitioner, right enough. I've passed the College of Surgeons.

MATILDA. So have I, dear, often.

TOM. You can't be more a surgeon than I am, put it how you will; but nobody seems to know it, and I'm sure I don't know how to tell 'em. I can't send sandwich men about with advertisements—the College wouldn't like that. I can't hang placards out from a real colonel's balcony: 'Walk up, walk up, this is the Shop for Amputations!' or 'To married couples and others'—the Horse Guards wouldn't like that. [*Taking up carving-knife.*] Upon my word, Matilda, when I look at you and reflect that there isn't an operation in the whole range of practical surgery that I shouldn't be delighted to perform upon you at five minutes' notice for nothing, why, it *does* seem a most extraordinary thing that I can't get any patients!

Enter COLONEL O'FIPP, *in seedy, showy dressing-gown.*

O'FIPP. Good mornin', Thomas; Matilda, my own, the mornin' to ye. [*Kisses her.*] Breakfast ready? That's well. Good appetite, Thomas?   [*They sit to breakfast.*

TOM. Tremendous.   [*Taking an egg.*

O'FIPP. [*Aside.*] Then I'll spile it for ye. [*Aloud.*] Don't crack that egg till you're sure ye'll want it. [*Takes it from him.*] Thomas Cobb, I'm goin' to have a wurr'd or two with ye about your prospects, sorr.

TOM. Oh, Lord!   [*Turns away from his breakfast.*

O'FIPP. When I gave my consint to yer engagement with me beautiful and beloved daughter—— don't cry, my child.

MATILDA. No, pa.   [*Takes an egg.*

O'FIPP. Ye tould me ye were about to purchase a practice, and like a simple ould soldier I believed ye.

MATILDA. Sure, and so he was. Didn't ye introduce him to Ben Isaacs, and didn't he lend him the money to do it?

TOM. Which your papa immediately exchanged for bills.

O'FIPP. Which is another turr'm for money.

TOM. Another term for money?

MATILDA. Papa has always been accustomed to regard his I.O.U.'s as currency.

TOM. Why, who do you suppose would sell me a practice for a bundle of your I.O.U.'s?

O'FIPP. My name, sorr, is considered in the City to be as good for a thousand pounds as for a hundred.

MATILDA. Papa's is one of the oldest names in the kingdom.

O'FIPP. Yes, sorr. And let me tell ye it's on some of the oldest bills in the kingdom, too. Such is the value of my name that I suppose I have renewed oftener than any man aloive! And it isn't every man that can say *that*!

TOM. But when I try to discount your paper, capitalists always say, 'Who's O'Fipp?' And when I tell 'em he's a colonel, they say, 'What's he a colonel of?'

O'FIPP. Colonel of a ridgment, to be sure.

TOM. Yes, but in what service?

O'FIPP. Never mind the surrvice, sorr. It was the 27th ridgment of it. That's enough for any man. There's many a surrvice besides the British surrvice, I believe, sorr?

TOM. Oh, I believe there's a good many.

O'FIPP. There's the Spanish surrvice, sorr—and the Hungarian surrvice—and the Italian surrvice, and the French surrvice, and the——

MATILDA. And the dinner surrvice.

TOM. And the Church Service.

O'FIPP. No, sorr. When a gintleman asks me my ridgment, he has a right to know it, and I tell him at once. But when he asks me in what surrvice, sorr, why, that's a piece of impertinent curiosity, and I ask him what the devil he means by it.

TOM. Oh, I'm sure *I* don't care; the regiment's quite enough for *me*. But then I ain't a capitalist.

O'FIPP. Well, sorr, let us come to the p'int. For two months ye've been engaged to my lovely and accomplished daughter —— don't cry, my love.

MATILDA. No, pa.   [*Takes an egg.*

o'fipp. And ye're as far from marrying her as iver. Now during the last two months my poor child's been wastin' the best years of her loife, and she can't wait much longer. Can ye, Matilda?

matilda. 'Deed, and I can't then. I'm twenty-noine and a bit.

o'fipp. She's twenty-noine—and a bit! Now it's roight to tell ye, and you too, Matilda, that a gintleman of good birth, irreproachable morals, and a considerable command of ready money, has done me the honour to propose for me daughter's hand. I say no more, sorr. As a man of honour there's two courses open to ye, and I leave ye to decide which of 'em ye'll take.　　　　　　　　　　　　　　　　　　　　　[*Exit.*

tom. [*In great grief.*] Matilda, did you hear that?

matilda. Yes, Tom, I heard that.

tom. [*Furious.*] Who is the scoundrel who has dared to aspire to your hand?

matilda. 'Deed, and I don't know, but it'll be some one who's lendin' money to papa. I ginerally go with the bills.

tom. [*Aghast.*] What!

matilda. When a body falls in love with me, papa ginerally borrows money of him, and he gives bills, and I go with 'em. It's a rule of the family.

tom. But surely you'll never countenance such a bargain?

matilda. 'Deed, and I don't want to, Tom dear, but I've countenanced it for thirteen years, and sure it 'ld look odd to refuse now. Besides, dear, I'm not as young as I was.

tom. No, but then you're not as old as you might be.

matilda. No, but I'm as old as I mean to be. There's razin for ye, Tom, and ye want it.

tom. Well, I'm sure I don't know what to do; I'm at my wits' end.

matilda. Then it's the beginning end, and there's hope for ye yet.　　　　　　　　　　　　　　　　　　　　　　　[*Knock.*

tom. Who's that?

matilda. There, now, if it ain't your friend Whipple's carriage.

TOM. Whipple! Whipple with a carriage! A fool, an impostor, a quack, with a carriage! What does he want to come flaunting his one-horse fly in my face for? There, I actually did that man's botany papers for him at the College, and now he's rolling in fever patients—literally *rolling* in fever patients—while I haven't one to my back!

MATILDA. Well, maybe he'll help ye if ye ask him. He's a pleasant man.

TOM. Pleasant, is he? I don't know what you call pleasant. Why, there's a squalid old pauper idiot, a patient of his, who's got no name of his own, and Whipple christened him Tom Cobb because he says he's the ugliest old lunatic he ever saw and reminds him of me. And all the boys in the neighbourhood have taken it up, and he's been known as Tom Cobb for the last two years. That's pleasant of Whipple.

MATILDA. Sure, it's his joke.

TOM. Yes, I know it's his joke, but I don't like his joke. One Tom Cobb's enough at a time, and [*Taking out pistol.*] if I was only quite, quite sure I knew how to load it, I'd snuff one of 'em out this minute. I would; upon my word and honour, I would!   [*Exit.*

MATILDA. Poor Tom! He's an innocent boy and he's fond of me, and I like him too, and it's a pity he ain't rich. And now who's the gintleman with the command of ready money who's proposed for me, I'd like to know?

Enter BIDDY.

BIDDY. Mr. Whipple.   [*Exit.*

Enter WHIPPLE.

WHIPPLE. Miss Matilda, don't think me premature for calling, but I came because I really couldn't wait any longer.

MATILDA. And ye did right; sit ye down.

WHIPPLE. I couldn't help it; you're not angry?

MATILDA. Not I! If ye couldn't help it, what were ye to do?

WHIPPLE. I declare I haven't slept a wink all night from anxiety.

MATILDA. Would ye like to take a snooze on the sofa?

WHIPPLE. A snooze? Miss Matilda, hasn't your father told you?

MATILDA. Told me—told me what?

WHIPPLE. Why, that I——

MATILDA. Ye niver mean to sit there and tell me ye're the young gintleman of high family, unblemished morals, and considerable command of ready money?

WHIPPLE. That's me—he *has* told you. Yes, Miss Matilda, I have dared——

MATILDA. But don't ye know I'm engaged to your friend, Tom Cobb?

WHIPPLE. Tom Cobb! Yes, I know you are. A mule, a clod, an unsuccessful clod! Yes, I know he's tied to you as a log is tied to the leg of a runaway donkey. I beg your pardon—I don't mean that; but you can't really love him?

MATILDA. 'Deed, and I like him very well then. He's a good boy. But tell me now—is it bills?

WHIPPLE. [*Rather taken aback.*] Well, yes; since you put it like that, it *is* bills.

MATILDA. Then I tell ye what, Mr. Whipple: I'm tired of being handed over with stamped paper.

WHIPPLE. [*Earnestly.*] There was *no* stamp on it; indeed, there was no stamp on it. It was an I.O.U.

MATILDA. It's the same thing. I like Tom Cobb better than I like you, and if he'll marry me in a month I'll have him, and if he won't, why I'll talk to you. There's your answer now, and don't bother again.

WHIPPLE. In a month! [*Aside.*] In a month! He *shan't* marry her in a month! If I can only manage to get him out of the way, and keep him there for a few weeks! [*Suddenly.*] I'll do it! It'll cost money, but I'll do it.

Enter TOM COBB.

Ah, Tom, my boy, I'm delighted to see you; how uncommonly jolly you're looking, to be sure!

TOM. [*Very miserably.*] Yes, I should say I was looking uncommonly jolly.

WHIPPLE. Why, what's the matter?

TOM. Why, a good many things; and look here, Whipple, I wish next time you want a godfather for a nameless pauper you'd choose somebody else.

WHIPPLE. Oh, you mean ugly old Tom Cobb. I beg your pardon—but he was so like you I couldn't help it. But there, that needn't distress you—for he died last night, and there's an end of him. Never mind, old boy, I'll make it up to you some day.

TOM. [*Suddenly.*] Will you? Whipple, I'm in an awful fix about Ben Isaacs' bills; now you're well off—I did your botany paper for you at the College. Will you lend me £250 on my personal security? I want a plain answer—yes or no.

WHIPPLE. My dear boy, of course; with pleasure.

TOM. [*Delighted and surprised.*] My dear Whipple!

WHIPPLE. You shall have it, of course.

TOM. When?

WHIPPLE. Why, now if you like.

TOM. What—the money?

WHIPPLE. No, the plain answer. I haven't a penny at my bankers. I've lent it all—to the Colonel. What have you done with the money?

TOM. Well, *I* lent it all to—the Colonel. He borrowed it the very day he agreed to my engagement with Matilda; didn't he, dear?

MATILDA. [*Clearing away breakfast things.*] Just that very same day, dear. Directly after I told him ye were going to propose for me, and immediately before ye did it.

WHIPPLE. Good soldier, the Colonel.

TOM. Oh, he didn't borrow it because he wanted it; he borrowed it to prevent my wasting it in foolishness. He said so; but I *should* like to have a go in at some foolishness now and then, if it was only a pair of trousers or half a dozen socks.

MATILDA. Yes, ye want socks.

[*Exit* MATILDA *with breakfast things.*

TOM. But what's the use of socks to a man who's going to blow his brains out? Whipple, I do assure you on my honour, if I knew a safe and perfectly painless way of popping out of this world into comfortable quarters in the next, I'd adopt it— upon my word and honour, I'd adopt it!

WHIPPLE. [*Suddenly.*] Do you mean that?

TOM. Yes, I mean that.

WHIPPLE. Then I'll help you. Now, observe: my old pauper patient, Tom Cobb, died last night. He hasn't a friend or relation in the world to claim him. Well, I certify to his death, and he's comfortably buried, and there's an end of old Tom Cobb.

TOM. The ugly one?

WHIPPLE. The ugly one, of course.

TOM. I don't see what you're driving at.

WHIPPLE. Don't you? Why, if Tom Cobb's dead and buried, what becomes of the bill Tom Cobb gave Ben Isaacs?

TOM. But the ugly Tom Cobb never gave a bill. [*A light breaks upon him.*] Oh, you cunning devil!

WHIPPLE. Now then, what d'ye say to dying by deputy?

TOM. By Jove, it's worth thinking of.

WHIPPLE. Worth thinking of? It's worth jumping at without stopping to think at all.

TOM. I believe you're right. [*After a pause.*] I'll do it! I'm a dead man! I can come to life again, I suppose, when I like?

WHIPPLE. Oh, yes, under another name. But you'll have to hide away for a few months.

TOM. Oh, ah; but [*Turning out his pockets.*] how about burial fees?

WHIPPLE. Will five and twenty pounds do it?

TOM. Five and twenty pounds will just do it.

WHIPPLE. Then come along at once to my house, and take leave of this life.

TOM. But you'll let me take a last farewell of Matilda?

WHIPPLE. No, no; bother Matilda!   [*Taking his arm.*

TOM. Oh, but you mustn't bother Matilda!

WHIPPLE. Now, now, do come along.

TOM. Hang it all, let me see her before the tomb closes over me for three months!

WHIPPLE. No, you can write to her; now come at once, or I won't help you.

TOM. Then farewell, Matilda; I go to my doom. Whipple, during my decease I confide her to you. Be a mother to her. [*Kissing photograph.*] Farewell, unhappy Matilda; be true to my memory, for I'm as good as dead, and you're engaged to a body!   [*He staggers out wildly, followed by* WHIPPLE.

Enter MATILDA.

MATILDA. Now, where's he gone with Whipple, I'd like to know? That Whipple's up to some bedevilment with him, I'll go bail.

Enter BIDDY.

BIDDY. Please, miss, here's a young lady as says she must see you, and won't take no denial.

MATILDA. A young lady?

Enter CAROLINE, *in great agitation. She is a romantic-looking young lady, with long curls and gushing, poetical demeanour. She pauses melodramatically.*

CAROLINE. Matilda! Don't ye know me?

MATILDA. 'Deed, and I don't. Why, if it isn't my old school-fellow, Carrie Effingham! It's Carrie, as I'm a living sinner!

CAROLINE. Yes, I came to town yesterday; and though ten long weary years have flown since last we met, I could not pass my dear old friend's abode without one effort to awake those slumbering chords that, struck in unison, ever found ready echoes in our sister hearts.

MATILDA. Why, ye talk nonsense as well as ever, dear; but I'm glad to see ye.

CAROLINE. How well—how very well you're looking—and heavens, how lovely!

MATILDA. Yes, dear. Ye're lookin' older. Ye're not married yet, I suppose?

CAROLINE. Alas, no!   [*Wiping her eyes.*

MATILDA. Don't fret, dear; it'll come.

CAROLINE. Oh, Matilda, a maiden's heart should be as free as the summer sun itself; and it's sad when, in youth's heyday, its trilling gladness has been trodden underfoot by the iron-shod heel of a serpent.

MATILDA. Yes, it's sad when that's happened. Tell me all about it.

CAROLINE. Swear that, come what may, no torture shall ever induce you to reveal the secret I am going to confide to you.

MATILDA. Oh, I'll swear that with pleasure.

CAROLINE. Will you believe me when I tell you that—I have loved?

MATILDA. Oh, yes!

CAROLINE. And that I have been loved in return?

MATILDA. Well, ye—es. Oh, yes; it's possible.

CAROLINE. He was a poet-soldier, fighting the Paynim foe in India's burning clime—a glorious songster, who swept the lute with one hand while he sabred the foe with the other!

MATILDA. Was he in the band?

CAROLINE. The band! He was a major-general!

MATILDA. Oh! Handsome?

CAROLINE. I know not. I never saw him.

MATILDA. Ye never saw him?

CAROLINE. I never saw his face; but—I have seen his soul!

MATILDA. What's his soul like?

CAROLINE. Like? Like the frenzied passion of the antelope! Like the wild fire of the tiger-lily! Like the pale earnestness of some lovesick thunder-cloud that longs to grasp the fleeting lightning in his outstretched arms!

MATILDA. Was he often like that?

CAROLINE. Always!

MATILDA. A pleasant man in furnished lodgings! And where did ye see his soul?

CAROLINE. He poured it into the columns of the *Weybridge Watchman*, the local paper of the town that gave him birth. Dainty little poems, the dew of his sweet soul, the tender frothings of his soldier brain. In them I read him, and in them I loved him! I wrote to him for his autograph—he sent it. I sent him my photograph, and directly he saw it he proposed in terms that cloyed me with the sweet surfeit of their choice exuberance, imploring me at the same time to reply by telegraph. Then, maiden-like, I longed to toy and dally with his love. But Anglo-Indian telegraphic rates are high; so, much against my maiden will, I answered in one word—that one word, yes!

MATILDA. And ye've engaged yerself to a man whose face ye've niver seen?

CAROLINE. I've seen his soul!

MATILDA. And when d'ye think ye'll see his body?

CAROLINE. Alas, never, for (pity me) he is faithless! We corresponded for a year, and then his letters ceased; and now, for eighteen months, no crumb nor crust of comfort has appeased my parched and thirsting soul! Fortunately my solicitor has all his letters.

MATILDA. Oh, I see. And when does the action come off?

CAROLINE. I know not. We have advertised for him right and left. Twenty men of law are on his track, and my brother Bulstrode, an attorney's clerk, carries a writ about him night and day. Thus my heart-springs are laid bare that every dolt may gibe at them—the whole county rings with my mishap— its gloomy details are on every bumpkin's tongue! This— this is my secret. Swear that you will never reveal it!

[*Kneeling at her feet.*

MATILDA. Oh, but ye'll get thumping damages when ye *do* find him.

CAROLINE. It may be so. The huckstering men of law appraise my heart-wreck at five thousand pounds.

MATILDA. Well, and I wish ye may get it, dear.

CAROLINE. Thank you, oh, thank you for that wish!

[*Rises and shakes her hand heartily.*

MATILDA. Ye're not goin'?

CAROLINE. No, I have come to spend a long, long day. I'm going to take my bonnet off. [*Solemnly.*] Dear Matilda, we have not met for many many years, and I long—I cannot tell you, Matilda, how earnestly I long—to see all your new things!   [*Exeunt together, arms round waists.*

Enter O'FIPP.

O'FIPP. There's an ungrateful daughter to refuse Whipple, and me pinched for money till I can hardly raise an egg for breakfast. But she shan't have Tom Cobb, anyhow. I'll see to that! A pretty kettle of fish I'm boiling for myself! When I've sent Tom Cobb about his business, what'll the ongrateful villain do? Why, he'll sue on them bills o' mine, as if I'd never bin the next thing to a father-in-law to him! But that's the way with mean and thankless naturs. Do 'em an injustice and they're never satisfied till they've retaliated.

Enter MATILDA *with letter, and pretending to cry.*

MATILDA. Papa dear, I've bad news for you.

O'FIPP. Bad news? At whose suit?

MATILDA. It ain't that, dear; it's my Tom.

O'FIPP. And what's the scamp been doin' now?

MATILDA. The scamp's bin dyin'.

O'FIPP. Dying? What d'ye mean?

MATILDA. I mean Tom's dead.

O'FIPP. [*Looking at her sternly.*] Matilda, are ye in earnest, or have ye bin at the Eau de Cologne?

MATILDA. Oh, I'm in earnest. Tom's dead.

O'FIPP. Who's killed him?

MATILDA. Faith, an' he killed himself. He's written to say so. Here's his letter. He encloses yer two bills and app'ints ye his executor.

O'FIPP. Ye pain and surproise me more than I can tell ye. Poor Tom! He was a koind and ginerous lad, and I'd hoped to have met these bills under happier circumstances. Well, his executor deals with them now—that's me; and the question is whether, in the interests of Tom's estate, it would be worth while to proceed against the acceptor—that's me again; and, on the whole, I don't recommend it. [*Tears them up.*] Now tell me all about it; don't cry, my child.

MATILDA. No, pa. Well, it's loike this—Ben Isaacs was over-pressin', and poor Tom was bothered, and thought he'd make an end of himself; and just then he heard that the ould man that Whipple called Tom Cobb from the loikeness had just died. So Tom thought he'd make one death do for the two. Sure, he's been economically brought up.

O'FIPP. What! Am I to onderstand that Thomas Cobb has been troiflin' with the most sacred feelings of an old soldier's grey-headed ould harrut?

MATILDA. Well, he's shamming dead, if ye mean that, and he hopes you'll go to the funeral.

O'FIPP. Shamming dead, is he! Shamming dead! Let me come across him, and by the blood of the O'Fipps, I'll make him sham dead in rale earnest!

MATILDA. But papa dear, the boy's hard pressed.

O'FIPP. Don't interrupt an honest burst of feelin' in an ould military officer. For months I've looked forward loike a simple ould soldier to meetin' those bills, and now I've destroyed them, and deproived meself of a pleasure which might have lasted me the next twenty years! But I'll expose him. It's a croime of some sort, pretendin' to be dead when ye're not. It's obtainin' burial under false pretences, if it's nothing else! What's that?

MATILDA. [*With paper in her hand.*] It's his will.   [*Laughing.*

O'FIPP. [*Indignantly.*] His will!

MATILDA. Yes; would ye have a gintleman doi without a will?

O'FIPP. A gintleman! A beggarly scoundrel! [*Opens it.*] Ha, ha! He leaves ye everything, Matilda. It's duly signed and witnessed, all quite in form. By my soul, I congratulate ye on yer accession to fortune and prosperity!

MATILDA. It's just done to give colour to his death. Don't be hasty, dear. It's the first time I've been mentioned in a will, and maybe it'll be the last.   [*Laughing.*

O'FIPP. [*Furious.*] Mentioned in a will! It's an outrage—a sacrilege I tell ye—an insult to a simple ould officer and his deluded gyurl, to mention them in a swindlin' document that's not worth the ink it's written with! This is how I treat it,

Matilda. [*Crumpling it up.*] This is how I treat it; [*Throws it in the fire.*] and if that thief Tom Cobb was here, I'd crumple him too and send him after it!

Enter WHIPPLE, *breathless and much excited.*

WHIPPLE. Oh, Colonel!

O'FIPP. Well, sorr?

WHIPPLE. Here's news! My old man, the ugly old man who always went by the name of Tom Cobb——

O'FIPP. Well, sorr?

WHIPPLE. He died last night! Poor ugly old Tom Cobb died last night.

MATILDA. We know all about it; we knew it half an hour ago.

WHIPPLE. Yes, Matilda, but you don't know this: I went to his cottage this morning, and on the bed I found a hasty scrawled note written by the old man just before he died. [O'FIPP *becomes interested.*] It contained these words, 'Look under the fireplace.' I got a crowbar, raised the hearth, and under it I found gold—gold, silver, and bank-notes in profusion! No end of gold—you could roll in it; you could roll in it! And he hasn't a friend or relation in the world!

[O'FIPP, *during the last few lines, has hurriedly snatched the will out of the fire, and smoothed it out, unobserved. He produces it with a dignified air.*

WHIPPLE. What's that?

O'FIPP. This, sorr, is the poor old gintleman's will, in which he leaves everything to my beloved daughter.

WHIPPLE. But that's not *old* Tom Cobb's will! That's the will *young* Tom Cobb made in fun just now!

O'FIPP. Sorr, old Tom Cobb's dead, and here's a will signed 'Tom Cobb.' Put that and that together, and what d'ye make of it?

[WHIPPLE *falls into a chair amazed. Tableau.*

ACT II

SCENE. *The same room in* COLONEL O'FIPP'*s house, but very handsomely furnished. Pictures, busts, etc. Tables* R. C. *and* L. C.*; writing materials on latter, sherry and glasses on former.*

MATILDA *discovered working,* WHIPPLE *on a stool at her feet.*

WHIPPLE. My darling Matilda, who was it who said the course of true love never did run smooth? Are not our loves true? And could anything be smoother than their course during the last three months?

MATILDA. No, dear, savin' that when ye proposed for me, papa kicked ye out of the house.

WHIPPLE. He did, in the effusion of the moment, and I honour him for it. On his unexpected accession to wealth he naturally looked for a wealthy and well-born son-in-law, and I honour him for it. But the doughty old soldier was open to reason, and when I proved to him that his wealth depended on my secrecy, he admitted his error at once, like a frank old warrior as he is, and I honour him for it.

MATILDA. Poor Tom! I wonder what's come of him all this while? It's three months since he——

WHIPPLE. Died.

MATILDA. Died, and I've never heard a word from him since.

WHIPPLE. Then he can't complain if you've been inconstant.

MATILDA. 'Deed, and he can't. It's clear a young girl must marry somebody. It's nature.

Enter O'FIPP.

WHIPPLE. Of course it is, and if he truly loves you—really and truly loves you as I do, he ought to be delighted when he comes back to find that you've engaged yourself to a gentleman in every way his superior.

O'FIPP. Deloighted when he comes back? Divil a bit! By razin that he won't come back any more!

MATILDA. Won't come back any more?

O'FIPP. Not he. Isn't he dead, and haven't we buried him, and paid his debts, and proved his will, and stuck up a tombstone that he'd blush to read? Sure, it'll be in the highest degree ondacent in him to give the lie to a tombstone!

WHIPPLE. But Tom never had any tact—and if he *should* be guilty of the indiscretion of turning up——

O'FIPP. Well, sorr, if he should, I shall be prepared to admit that I've acted under a misconception. But sorr, before I yield possession of the estate which has so miraculously come into my hands, I shall satisfy meself beyond all doubt that I am not dealin' with an imposthor. Any one who assumes to be the late Tom Cobb will have to establish his identity beyond all manner of doubt. And as I've paid Mr. Ben Isaacs and his other creditors conditionally on his being dead, he may find that difficult, sorr—he may find that difficult.   [*Exit.*

MATILDA. Well, Tom Cobb may be dead, but when he finds out the use that's been made of his will, he'll not rest in his grave, I'm thinking, that's all!

WHIPPLE. But if he *should* return—if Tom Cobb's shade *should* take it into his ghostly head to revisit the scenes of his earthly happiness—promise me that you will treat him with the cold respect due to a disembodied spirit.

MATILDA. But when d'ye think he'll come?

WHIPPLE. Well, between ourselves, I think we may look for his apparition at an early date. Unless the necessaries of life are considerably cheaper in the other world than in this, Tom Cobb's five and twenty pounds must be as shadowy as himself by this time.

MATILDA. But if he comes to life, who's to kill him again?

WHIPPLE. Oh, your papa will have to kill him; it's his turn. Besides, it's a colonel's business to kill people.

MATILDA. And a doctor's, too.

WHIPPLE. Yes, Matilda. But we don't *pay* people to die; they pay us to kill 'em. It's the rule of the profession.

[*Exeunt.*

Enter TOM COBB, *preceded by* FOOTMAN. TOM *is very seedy and dirty, and his boots are in holes.*

FOOTMAN. If you'll take a seat, sir, I'll tell the Colonel you want to see him. What name shall I say?

TOM. [*Aside.*] If I give him my real name he'll faint. [*Aloud.*] The Duke of Northumberland. [*Aside.*] That'll draw him. [*Aloud.*] I haven't a card. [FOOTMAN *is incredulous. He is about to go, but returns and removes tray with sherry; then exit.*] Well, nicely the old scoundrel's feathered his nest, upon my word! Real Axminster, satin furniture, ancestors, busts! And this has been going on for three months, and I only heard of it yesterday. Why, he's made me accessory to a forgery, and I'm being advertised for in every paper in the kingdom! Why, it's penal servitude! Who'd think an Irish colonel could be such a scoundrel! Well, you never know when you're safe in this world; upon my soul, you don't. I never met a man in my life whose manner and appearance inspired me with so much confidence.

Enter O'FIPP.

Well, upon my word, Colonel O'Fipp, you're a nice officer, you are! I make a will more by way of a joke than anything else, and you have the face to apply it to the property of a friendless old man who went by my name! Why, it's robbery; it's forgery; and Docket and Tape are offering £50 reward to any one who can give information about me! Now look here—destroy that will and restore the property, or I'll answer this advertisement this very minute. I will; upon my soul and honour, I will—there!

O'FIPP. I believe I have the honour of addressin' the Jook of Northumberland.

TOM. Oh, don't talk nonsense, Colonel; you know me well enough.

O'FIPP. Am I to onderstand, sorr, that ye're not the distinguished nobleman you represented yerself to be?

TOM. Oh, haven't I been deceived in you! Oh, Colonel, Colonel, you *have* turned out treacherous; upon my soul, you have!

O'FIPP. I'm at a loss to comprehend your meanin', sorr. Will ye oblige me by informing me whom I have the honour of addressin'?

TOM. You've the honour of addressing a miserable, poor devil who'll be standing alongside of you at the Old Bailey bar in about three weeks, if he's not very much mistaken.

O'FIPP. Upon my wurrd, sorr, ye've got the advantage of me.

TOM. Have I? Then I'm the only man that ever did. I don't think Tom Cobb is the sort of man to get any advantage out of Colonel O'Fipp. [O'FIPP *falls sobbing into chair*.] What's the matter now?

O'FIPP. Ye mentioned the name of Tom Cobb, sorr. I had a dear, dear friend of that name once. He was to have married me daughter, sorr, but he's gone!

TOM. Well, if that's what you're crying for—cheer up, because he's come back again.

O'FIPP. [*Seizing his hand.*] Me dear friend, me very dear friend, if ye can only assure me that poor, dear, dead and gone Tom Cobb is aloive, me gratitude shall know no bounds! Maybe you're his brother?

TOM. His brother! Get out!

O'FIPP. No? I thought ye moight be; I seem to see a loikeness.

TOM. I should think you did!

O'FIPP. A distant loikeness, sorr.

TOM. A mere suggestion, I suppose?

O'FIPP. A faint shadowy indication of a remote family resemblance; that's all, sorr, I give ye my honour. And now tell me where is he, that I may embrace him.

TOM. Well, he's here; but don't embrace him.

O'FIPP. Sorr, d'ye mean to sit there and tell me to me very face that you're me beloved ould friend Tom Cobb?

TOM. Well, if the marks on my linen are to be trusted——

O'FIPP. Ah, sorr, beware of jumpin' at conclusions on insufficient grounds. Depend upon it, ye're mistaken, sorr.

TOM. Well, upon my honour, I begin to think I am!

O'FIPP. Tom Cobb, sorr, is dead and buried. I had the melancholy satisfaction of following him to his grave—me dear friend Tim Whipple accompanied me, and he's at the present moment engaged in comforting my bereaved and inconsolable daughter.

TOM. I'm sure I'm very much obliged to him! Perhaps I could do that better than he?

O'FIPP. I think not, sorr. He's doing it very well—very well indeed.

TOM. Now once for all, Colonel, this won't do. There are plenty of people who know me if you don't. Here's my card—'T. Cobb, 6' in red cotton, [*Showing mark on pocket-handkerchief.*] and I've several other marks of the same character about me, which I shall be happy to show you at a more convenient opportunity.

O'FIPP. Sorr, documentary evidence in red cotton isn't worth the cambric it's stitched upon. Ye'll have to find some better proof of yer identity than that.

Enter MATILDA.

MATILDA. Papa dear, Tim's goin' to take me to the theayter. [*Sees* TOM.] Oh!

TOM. My darlin' Matilda! My beloved Matilda! I'm so, so, *so* glad to see you again, dear! Why, it's three months since we met. [*Kissing and hugging her.*] What a fool I've been to cut myself out of this sort of thing for three months! [*Kisses her.*] How very, very well you're looking!   [*Kisses her.*

MATILDA. Will ye koindly leave off kissin' me till I've had the pleasure of bein' inthrojuiced to ye?

TOM. Why, you don't mean to tell me *you* don't know me?

MATILDA. 'Deed, and I don't then. And yet I seem to have seen yer face before.

TOM. 'Deed, and you have, and you've kissed it before.

MATILDA. I don't rimimber kissin' it.

O'FIPP. You observe, sorr. She don't rimimber kissin' it.

MATILDA. Oh, papa!   [*Crying.*

O'FIPP. What's the matter, my dear?

MATILDA. There's somethin' about him that remoinds me of poor Tom!

O'FIPP. There's a faint resemblance; I remarked it meself.
                                        [*Wipes his eyes.*

TOM. Now, Matilda, don't *you* deny me. I've loved you so long
   in spite of your not having any money, and although you *do*
   go with the bills, and although you *are* older than I am, don't
   turn against me now. Oh, you *do* look so pretty!
                          [*Puts his arm round her and kisses her.*

Enter WHIPPLE. *He seizes* TOM *by the collar and whirls him away*
                          from MATILDA.

TOM. [*Seizing his hand.*] My dear Tim—my very dear Tim—
   you're the very man I wanted to see! I am most unaffectedly
   delighted to see you. [*Shaking his hand heartily.*] How well—
   how remarkably well you're looking, to be sure!

WHIPPLE. [*Shaking his hand with a great show of welcome.*] Yes,
   uncommonly well—never better. And how have *you* been?

TOM. Very well, but rather dull. I say, I've got into a nice scrape!
   They're after me—they're advertising for me!

WHIPPLE. No!

TOM. Fact! £50 is offered for me! What do you say to that?

WHIPPLE. Well, I should close with it.

TOM. Why?

WHIPPLE. Because I should think it's a good deal more than
   you're worth.

TOM. Ha, ha!

WHIPPLE. Ha, ha!

TOM. What a fellow you are! Same old Whipple! I say, the
   Colonel's a cool hand. What d'ye think he says now?

WHIPPLE. Nothing worth repeating, I should imagine.

TOM. What a caustic fellow you are! He says I'm dead!

WHIPPLE. Oh, he's an Irishman.

TOM. Ha, ha! Oh, that's very good; that's so like you.

WHIPPLE. *He's* not dead, Colonel.   [*Feeling* TOM's *pulse.*

TOM. There, Matilda, you hear that!   [*About to embrace her.*

WHIPPLE. What are you about? How dare you embrace that
   young lady?   [*Stopping him.*

TOM. You said I was alive.

WHIPPLE. But bless my heart, you don't suppose every man alive is privileged to embrace Miss O'Fipp?

MATILDA. A nice time I'd have of it.

O'FIPP. I tell ye, sorr, Tom Cobb is dead and buried.

WHIPPLE. Yes, poor Tom; he's dead.   [*Wipes his eyes.*

TOM. But you just said I was alive.

WHIPPLE. Yes, old chap, you're alive.

TOM. [*Puzzled.*] I see: your theory is that I'm alive, but I'm not Tom Cobb.

WHIPPLE. Yes, that's my theory.

TOM. But I'm like him, ain't I?

WHIPPLE. Well, now you mention it, you *are* like him.

TOM. Matilda—once more, I implore you——

     [*Seizing her hand.*

WHIPPLE. Matilda, leave the room! [*Takes her to door.*] Sir, misled by a resemblance which I admit to be striking, you have come here under the impression that you are my departed friend. I can excuse the error; but now that it's been pointed out to you, if ever you attempt to embrace this young lady again, I'll break your leg and set it myself.   [*Exit.*

TOM. Colonel O'Fipp, I——

O'FIPP. Stop, sorr. If this conversation is to continue, I must be informed whom I have the pleasure of addressing. Up to the present moment we have only learnt who you are *not*. Let us now proceed to ascertain who ye *are*.

TOM. Colonel, I'm in that state of mental confusion, that I declare I don't know who I am. Give me a little breathing time. When a young man believes he's been Tom Cobb for twenty-five years, and then suddenly finds himself kicked out of Tom Cobb, with nowhere to go to, he *wants* a little breathing time to look about him and find a name to let.

O'FIPP. Well, sorr, for the purpose of this interview one name's as good as another. Here's the *Toimes* newspaper. Ye'll find many a good name goin' beggin' in that. Choose yer name.

Here's a gintleman who was hanged this mornin'. Would ye like *his* name? He's done with it.

TOM. Don't be unpleasant, Colonel.

O'FIPP. Well, put your finger down; take the first that comes. [*Puts* COBB'S *finger on the newspaper at random.*] Here's one—the Bishop of Bath and Wells.

TOM. Nonsense! Who'd take me for a bishop?

O'FIPP. Then try again. Mr. and Mrs. German Reed.

TOM. Don't be absurd.

O'FIPP. Well, once more. Major-Gineral Arthur Fitzpatrick. What d'ye say to that?

TOM. But I don't look like a major-general.

O'FIPP. Well, sorr, and what of that? I don't look like a lieutenant-colonel, do I?

TOM. No, you don't, but a major-general in broken boots!

O'FIPP. Sure it's where yer corns have been shootin' through. Ye wouldn't have a major-gineral with corns that couldn't shoot, I suppose?

TOM. No!

O'FIPP. Now, sorr, it'll take a mighty deal of argument to pursuade me that you're not Major-Gineral Arthur Fitzpatrick in broken boots. Now, I've the credit of the surrvice at stake, and when I see a major-gineral in broken boots me harrut bleeds for him, and I long to allow him a pound a week, sorr—a pound a week—to keep up his military position.

TOM. A pound a week?

O'FIPP. No less, sorr. Now, as long as Major-Gineral Arthur Fitzpatrick chooses to claim a pound a week of me, it's here at his service. But on the onderstanding that he resumes his name and rank, and ceases for ever the dishonourable and unsoldierlike practice of masquerading under a false name. D'ye onderstand me, sorr?

TOM. Yes—I understand you.

O'FIPP. Do ye agree?

TOM. I'm so hungry and seedy and wretched that I'd agree to

anything. You couldn't oblige me with the first week in advance?

O'FIPP. Sorr, it has always been Terence O'Fipp's maxim to pay everything in advance. I'll go and get ye a pound, and ye can amuse yeself by writing out the receipt while I'm gone.

TOM. Colonel, I don't know whether to be very much obliged to you, or to look upon you as the coolest scamp unhung.

O'FIPP. Sorr, take my word for it, ye've every reason to do both.
[*Exit* O'FIPP.

TOM. Now that man's commanded a regiment for years—he's enjoyed the unlimited confidence of his sovereign (whoever that may be), and a thousand men have looked up to him with reverence and esteem. And it's been left to me (who am not naturally sharp) to find out that he's an atrocious scoundrel!

Enter FOOTMAN, *followed by* MR. EFFINGHAM, MRS. EFFING-HAM, BULSTRODE EFFINGHAM, *and* CAROLINE. TOM *takes up newspaper and sits.*

FOOTMAN. The Colonel will be here directly, ma'am.
[*Exit* FOOTMAN. *The others pose themselves in a group, as if being photographed:* MR. EFFINGHAM *seated,* MRS. EFFING-HAM *leaning on his left shoulder,* CAROLINE *seated in a picturesque attitude at her feet, and* BULSTRODE *standing gloomily behind.*

MRS. EFFINGHAM. Adolphus, what a sweet spot! A rural paradise, indeed. How balmy, and yet how cheap!

EFFINGHAM. I am an old, old man, and I have learnt the hollowness of outward splendours. The house is indeed well enough, and (it may be) cheap—but, after all, what *is* the house?

TOM. [*Politely.*] Seventy-five pounds a year, on a three years' agreement, I believe.

EFFINGHAM. [*Not heeding him.*] After all, what *is* the house but the outer husk? Let us rather learn to value the fruit within. The shell, truly, is goodly, but where, oh where is the kernel?

TOM. [*Politely.*] He will be here in one minute. [*All turn to look at him.*] I beg your pardon. [*They all turn slowly back again.*

BULSTRODE. [*Gloomily.*] To the soaring soul, fettered by stern destiny to the office stool of an obscure attorney, the contemplation of such a paradise opens a new vista of Life's Possibilities.

MRS. EFFINGHAM. My crushed and broken boy!

BULSTRODE. In such a home as this I feel I could lay the warp and woof of a Great Life. In the dingy purlieus of Somers Town life has no warp—no woof.

TOM. A kind of shoddy.

ALL. Sir!

TOM. Nothing—I didn't speak. [*They turn back as before.*] [*Aside.*] Extraordinary family!

MRS. EFFINGHAM. If there is one class of young men I detest beyond another, it is the class of young men who see a humorous side to everything.

CAROLINE. In the eyes of such a one the doughtiest deeds are the subject of a sneer—the noblest thoughts the peg on which to hang a parody.

BULSTRODE. Go to, sir—go to.

EFFINGHAM. [*To* MRS. EFFINGHAM.] I am an aged man—let me play the peacemaker. Remember, you are not as others are—you are a thing of thought—an abstraction. You must not expect the young man of average tastes to grasp you.

MRS. EFFINGHAM. I do *not* expect any young man to grasp *me*.

TOM. And she's right.

EFFINGHAM. We pity you, young man, but do not despise you. Read the master thoughts of mighty minds. Withdraw yourself within yourself. Soar. Be abstract. Think long and largely. Study the incomprehensible. Revolve. So will you learn at last to detach yourself from the sordid world, and float, as we float, in thoughts of empyrean purity.

CAROLINE. Oh, sir, my father is an aged man, and his words are wise. Be led by him and you will prosper.

MRS. EFFINGHAM. The young man is not of those who *can* detach themselves from the sordid world.

TOM. I beg your pardon. The young man is one of those who have detached themselves from the sordid world so completely that he can't get back again!

Enter O'FIPP.

O'FIPP. Now, if you've got the receipt——Mrs. Effingham! I'm rejoiced to see ye! Miss Caroline—Bulstrode—Mr. Effingham, my aged friend! Allow me to inthrojuice ye to a very particular friend and ould comrade—Major-Gineral Arthur Fitzpatrick. [TOM *bows.*] Foightin' Fitz we called him.

ALL. What!

O'FIPP. Major-Gineral Arthur Fitzpatrick.   [TOM *bows.*

MRS. EFFINGHAM. Of the 29th Madras Native Infantry?

TOM. [*Puzzled.*] I have no doubt that was my regiment.

MRS. EFFINGHAM. Viper!
                     [CAROLINE *faints in her father's arms.*
TOM. What!

MRS. EFFINGHAM. Viper! Deliberate and systematic viper!
                                    [*Goes to* CAROLINE.

BULSTRODE. Poetic fiend in human shape, despair!

EFFINGHAM. Blighter of fond and faithful hopes, behold your handiwork!

TOM. Why, what have I done?

O'FIPP. [*Turning up his sleeves.*] Ay, sorr, what have ye done? Answer me that. [*Turning up sleeves.*] Come, Gineral, no evasion, or by the blood of the O'Fipps——
     [CAROLINE *revives, and* EFFINGHAM *and* BULSTRODE *turn up their sleeves.*

CAROLINE. No, no—don't hurt him. I am better now. [*To* BULSTRODE, *who is turning up his sleeves and advancing in a threatening attitude.*] Brother, stand off! [*Throws herself between* TOM *and the others.*] Stand off—father, mother, brother, all! I have loved this man—ay, and I love him still. [*To* TOM.] Arthur—my poet-soldier—by our old vows—by the old poetic fire that burns in *your* heart and kindled mine, tell them—tell *me*—that you can explain everything.
                          [*Falls on her knees to him.*

TOM. Upon my word, I shouldn't like to undertake to do that. Why, I never saw you before in all my life.

MRS. EFFINGHAM. Despair that plea—it cannot serve you, sir. Your letters bind you—we are so advised.

TOM. But it can't be—it's impossible.

CAROLINE. Oh, Arthur, I am told by those who understand these things that you have indeed compromised yourself to the extent required by our common law. But you will not— oh, you will *not* compel me to bring our sacred loves into Court. You are a poet—a great, great poet—you will be faithful—you will be true.

EFFINGHAM. [*Kneels.*] Oh, sir, do not compel us to lay bare the workings of her young affections—do not force us to bring her very heartstrings into Court, that ribald minds may play upon them!

BULSTRODE. [*Gloomily.*] To the tune of £5,000.

Enter WHIPPLE.

O'FIPP. [*Brandishing a big stick.*] Gineral, do not blight this young lady's harrut. Give her your sacred promise, or by the blood of the O'Fipps, [*Sees that* TOM *has taken up a chair and looks threatening.*] my son-in-law elect shall teach you your forgotten duty! [*Hands stick to* WHIPPLE, *and retires.*]

WHIPPLE. [*Brandishing stick.*] Yes, sir. Promise at once, or nothing shall prevent me from [*Same business.*] urging this young lady's natural protector to inflict on you the condign punishment you so richly deserve.
[*Hands the stick to* EFFINGHAM, *and retires.*

EFFINGHAM. [*Brandishing stick.*] You speak nobly, sir. I am an old, old man, but I am yet hale and tough as hickory. [*Same business.*] I have a brave and stalwart son, and it is to his hand I confide the task of avenging the insult offered to his outraged family! [*Hands the stick to* BULSTRODE.

BULSTRODE. [*Gloomily.*] What prevents me from flying at his throat? What prevents me from whipping him as I would whip a cur? Tell me, somebody, what is it holds me back?

CAROLINE. *I* will tell you—it is mercy.

BULSTRODE. It is! [*Throwing away stick.*] I give you your life!

MRS. EFFINGHAM. My lion-hearted boy!

TOM. Do you know that you are labouring under some surprising and unaccountable delusion?

MRS. EFFINGHAM. Delusion, sir!

BULSTRODE. Delusion! Ha, ha!

CAROLINE. No, Arthur, no—this is no delusion, for see, I have your letters. [*Feeling for them.*] No, they are with my solicitor.

BULSTRODE. They are. I am his clerk, and at my broken-hearted sister's suit, cold calculating man of war, I serve you with this writ.

> [BULSTRODE *presents writ, which* CAROLINE, *kneeling at* TOM's *feet, reaches and hands to him, kissing his hand as she places the writ in it.*

TOM. [*Looking at writ.*] Breach of promise! [*Wildly.*] Don't bring any actions; don't resort to any violent measures. You say I'm engaged to you. I dare say I am. If you said I was engaged to your mother I'd dare say it too. I've no idea who I am, or what I am, or where I am, or what I am saying or doing, but you are very pretty, and you seem fond of me. I've no objection. I think I should rather like it: at least—*I'll try!*

CAROLINE. [*Flinging herself into his arms.*] My poet-soldier, and my minstrel boy!

> [EFFINGHAM, BULSTRODE, *and* MRS. EFFINGHAM *group themselves about* CAROLINE *and* TOM. *Tableau.*

ACT III

SCENE. *A drawing-room, shabbily furnished, in* EFFINGHAM's *house.* TOM *is discovered smoking a pipe on balcony with* CAROLINE. *The* EFFINGHAM *family is discovered grouped:* MRS. EFFINGHAM *seated; old* EFFINGHAM *leaning on her chair, with his arm round her neck, and* BULSTRODE *standing moodily behind. Two french windows in flat, leading on to balcony. Doors* R. *and* L.; *upper part of houses in street seen through windows.*

As curtain rises CAROLINE *enters from balcony, and throws herself at her mother's feet.*

MRS. EFFINGHAM. Where is your poet-lover, Caroline?

CAROLINE. I left him basking on the balcony, in deep communion with his inner self.

MRS. EFFINGHAM. Ah, what a priceless destiny is yours, my babe—to live a lifetime in the eternal sunlight of his poet brain!

CAROLINE. It is, but you shall share it—father—mother—brother—all! We will all share it, alway! I would not rob you of one ray that emanates from that divine face, for all the wealth of earth!

MRS. EFFINGHAM. My unselfish girl!

BULSTRODE. How nobly he looks when, sickened with the world, he turns his eyes inward to gaze upon his hidden self!

EFFINGHAM. None but Apollo ever looked as he looks then.

CAROLINE. Truly. Yet—shall I confess that when I saw him first my idiot heart sank deep within me, because, in the expression of his thoughts, I did *not* recognize Apollo's stamp?

BULSTRODE. Fie, Caroline! Would you have a poet carry his muse pick-a-back, for daws to pick at? Fie, Caroline—oh, fie!

MRS. EFFINGHAM. Some thoughts are too deep for utterance.

CAROLINE. And some too precious. Why should he scatter such gems broadcast? My poet-warrior thinks them to himself.

PLATE 6

Tom Cobb. The Effingham family. Act III

BULSTRODE. He does. It is his weird and warlike way.

CAROLINE. He comes. His fancy-flight has ended for the nonce. My soldier-minstrel has returned to earth!

Enter TOM *from balcony.* CAROLINE *goes to meet him, and brings him forward lovingly. His appearance is somewhat altered. He parts his hair in the centre, and allows it to grow long. He wears a very low lie-down collar in order to look Byronic. He sits.* CAROLINE *throws herself at his feet, and* MR. *and* MRS. EFFINGHAM *cross and group themselves about him.* MRS. EFFINGHAM *kneels,* BULSTRODE *standing moodily behind his mother.*

EFFINGHAM. Arthur, ennoble us. Raise us one step towards the Empyrean. Give us a Great Thought!

BULSTRODE. From the vast treasures of your poet brain, we beg some spare small change.

TOM. Well, I really don't know; I haven't anything just now.

CAROLINE. We are the bees, and you the flower. We beg some honey for our little hives.

TOM. [*With a desperate effort to be brilliant.*] Talking of bees— [*All take out note-books and write down what follows.*] talking of bees, have you ever remarked how the busy little insect avails herself of the sunshine to gather her sweet harvest from— from every opening flower?

EFFINGHAM. [*Writing.*] We have, we have. How true to fact!

BULSTRODE. [*Writing.*] You said 'her sweet harvest,' I think?

TOM. Her sweet harvest.

BULSTRODE. [*Writing.*] Her sweet harvest.
                              [*All shake their heads and sigh.*

TOM. Her honey, you know.

BULSTRODE. Thank you.
          [*Sighs. All finish writing and put up their note-books.*

MRS. EFFINGHAM. You are a close student of nature, sir.

TOM. Yes, I do a good deal in that way.

MRS. EFFINGHAM. How simple are his words, and yet what priceless pearls of thought lie encased beneath their outer crust!

TOM. Yes, I always wrap them in an outer crust, to keep them from the cold.   [*All take out note-books and write this down.*

CAROLINE. [*Writing.*]

> He wraps them in an outer crust
> To keep them from the cold!

And once I sneered at these grand utterances, just as we continually sneer at shapeless clods upon the road, which on inspection turn out to be jewelled bracelets of exceeding price.

TOM. Nothing more common. It's the old story. The superficial mind—[*All take out books and write.*] the superficial mind looks for cream upon the surface of the milk, but the profound philosopher dives down deep below. [*Aside.*] Much more of this and my mind will give way!

MRS. EFFINGHAM. You are a deep thinker, sir. I can fancy Shakespeare to have been such another.

CAROLINE. Shakespeare? Shakespeare never said anything like that! How—how do you do it?

TOM. I don't know. It comes. I shut my eyes and it comes.
[*All shut their eyes and try.*

CAROLINE. I cannot do it. Ah me! I shall never learn to talk like that.

MRS. EFFINGHAM. Bulstrode, had you had communion with the Major-General in earlier life, he might have helped to shape your destiny to some nobler end.

BULSTRODE. No, it might not be. I am fated. Destiny has declared against me. Fettered to the desk of an obscure attorney—forced to imprison my soaring soul within the left-off garments of a father whose figure has but little in common with my own, who can wonder that my life is one protracted misfit?

EFFINGHAM. My boy, sneer not at those clothes. They have been worn for many, many years by a very old, but very upright man. Be proud of them. No sordid thought has ever lurked behind that waistcoat. That hat has never yet been doffed to vicious wealth. Those shoes have never yet walked into the parlours of the sinful.

MRS. EFFINGHAM. [*Embracing him.*] I am sure of that, Adolphus—I am very, very sure of that.

BULSTRODE. It may be as you say. I *do* respect these clothes, but not even a father's eloquence can gloze over the damning fact that they are second-hand!

[*Exit on to balcony, as* MR. *and* MRS. EFFINGHAM *exeunt lovingly.*

CAROLINE. A blessing on him. Is he not benevolent?

TOM. Yes, he looks so. Why do benevolent people have such long hair? Do they say to themselves, 'I am a benevolent person, so I will let my hair grow,' or do they let it grow because they are too benevolent to cut it off?

CAROLINE. There are thousands of such questions that appear at every turn to make us marvel at Nature's strange decrees. Let us not pry into these dark secrets. Let us rather enquire whether you have any chance of getting anything to do?

TOM. No; there's no opening for major-generals just now.

CAROLINE. And yet how nobly you would lead your troops into action, caracolling at their head on a proud Arabian barb, and rousing them to very frenzy by shouting forth martial songs of your own composition! Oh, it would madden them!

TOM. Yes, I think it would! But at present I've only my half-pay—a pound a week—and we can't marry on that.

CAROLINE. Why not? It is ten shillings a week each. I am content if you are. Say, Arthur, shall we be made one?

TOM. My dear Caroline, it's nonsense to talk about being made one. [*She takes out her note-book.*] It's my experience that when poor people marry, they're made half a dozen, at least, in no time!

CAROLINE. Arthur! [*Shuts up book.*] Well, I must wait and hope. Oh for a war! [TOM *much alarmed.*] A vast, vast, vast war! Oh for the clash of steel-clad foemen! Oh for the deadly cannon-ade! And loud above the din of battle, I hear my Arthur's voice, as, like a doughty Paladin of old, he cleaves his path where'er the fight is thickest! Oh, I think I see him doing it!
[*Exit.*

TOM. Yes. I think I see myself doing it! Poor, dear girl, it's a shame to deceive her, but what can I do in the face of this confounded advertisement, which still appears in all the

papers every day! [*Reads.*] ' £50 reward will be paid to any
one who will give any information concerning the where-
abouts of Thomas Cobb, M.R.C.S. Apply to Docket and Tape,
27, Paragon, Somers Town!' For just six months this blight-
ing paragraph has appeared in every paper in London. Every
one is talking about it; a Christmas annual has been published, *How We Found Tom Cobb*, and a farce called *Tom
Cobb Found at Last* is playing at a principal theatre.

Enter WHIPPLE.

Whipple, you here?

WHIPPLE. Yes, how de do? I'm quite well. So's Matilda.

TOM. That name!

WHIPPLE. She's downstairs, with Miss Effingham.

TOM. Downstairs! And does she—don't think I ask from an
improper motive—does she ever talk about me?

WHIPPLE. Never mentions you by any chance. But she often
drops a tear to the memory of poor dead-and-gone Tom Cobb.

TOM. Oh, she does *that*, does she? That's rather nasty for you,
isn't it?

WHIPPLE. Not a bit. It does her credit, and I honour her for it.
The poor fellow's dead, and there's an end to him. I loved
him as a brother! [*Wiping his eye.*] He did my botany papers
for me at the College. But it's no use repining. No power on
earth can bring him to life again, now. How she loved that
man!

TOM. [*Half sobbing.*] Oh, Matilda! Be good to her, Whipple.

WHIPPLE. I will, General; trust me.

TOM. Is she—is she as fond of the theatre as ever?

WHIPPLE. Quite. We go every night.

TOM. She used to call it the 'theayter.'

WHIPPLE. [*Much moved.*] She does still!

TOM. Bless her for it. And does she still like oysters after the
play?

WHIPPLE. Always. She bargains for 'em—stout and oysters.

TOM. She used to call them 'histers.'

WHIPPLE. She does still.

TOM. Oh, thank you for this news of her. Oh, Whipple, make that woman happy!

WHIPPLE. Trust me—I will, for poor dear Tom Cobb's sake. How she loved that man! [*Wipes his eye.*] But this is not business. The Colonel, who is downstairs with Mr. Effingham, begged me to give you this—your weekly screw. Allow me, Major-General.   [*Gives him a sovereign.*

TOM. Thank you. The Colonel is always regular and punctual with my little pension.

WHIPPLE. The Colonel is extremely punctilious about money matters. Oh, I quite forgot—he further desires me to say that from this moment he proposes to discontinue your weekly payment.

TOM. [*Aghast.*] What!

WHIPPLE. From this moment your little pension dries up.

TOM. Do you mean to tell me that he intends deliberately to break his plighted word?

WHIPPLE. That is precisely what I intended to convey.

TOM. And cut off my only source of sustenance?

WHIPPLE. Absolutely.

TOM. But hang it, man, don't he know that his liberty and wealth are at my mercy?

WHIPPLE. Yes, he knows that, but he's prepared to risk it. You see, General, Messrs. Docket and Tape are looking out for Tom Cobb. Tom Cobb's wanted. I don't know what he's done, but people talk about a forged will. He's advertised for every day. You may have noticed it.

TOM. Yes, I've remarked it.

WHIPPLE. Well, if Tom Cobb is alive this advertisement is quite enough to keep him quiet. The Colonel, having this fact strongly before his eyes, considers that as he has no further interest in Major-General Fitzpatrick's existence, he does not see why he should be called upon to contribute to his support.

TOM. But it's ruin! Hang it—it's starvation! Whipple, you used to be a nice man once—ask him to see me—ask him to speak to me for five minutes! By your old niceness, I implore you!

WHIPPLE. I can't resist that appeal! I'll ask him, but I'm not sanguine. You see, he's been in the constant practice of breaking his promise for the last sixty-five years, and it's degenerated into a habit. [*Exit.*

TOM. And I did that man's———. [*Furious.*] But I'll be even with them all. I don't care now. I've nothing to lose, and I'm a desperate man. My mind's made up. I'll write to Docket and Tape, and tell the whole truth! [*Sits down to write.*] Now, Colonel O'Fipp, tremble, and you, Whipple, tremble, and Matilda—[*Throws down pen.*] I would spare Matilda! But no, let *her* tremble too! [*Finishes letter; about to ring bell.*] Now, now, I shall soon know the worst!

Enter BULSTRODE *from balcony.*

BULSTRODE. The Major-General seems moody. On what is he thinking? On the sacking of towns, perchance?

TOM. Bulstrode, you're a lawyer's clerk, aren't you?

BULSTRODE. Cursed be my lot, I am!

TOM. Do you happen to know Docket and Tape?

BULSTRODE. I do!

TOM. Who are they?

BULSTRODE. My loathed employers!

TOM. What! Why, then, you know all about this Tom Cobb whom they are advertising for, and whose name is on every tongue?

BULSTRODE. I should rather say I did.

TOM. [*Excited.*] A—what is he wanted for?

BULSTRODE. Much.

TOM. Yes, but what—what?

BULSTRODE. It is a weird tale. Wild horses shouldn't drag it from me.

TOM. But, hang it, you can trust *me*.

BULSTRODE. [*Takes his hand.*] General, I think I can—but I'm sure I won't.

TOM. But why do you object?

BULSTRODE. Major-General Fitzpatrick, had you the password of some leaguered town, and an enemy, armed to the teeth, demanded that word at the pistol's mouth, what would you do?

TOM. Tell him at once without a moment's hesitation.

BULSTRODE. Then am I made of doughtier stuff. Sir, I hate my employers, I loathe their unholy practices, but—I respect their secrets. Good day; I go to them.   [*Exit.*

TOM. So it seems I've had my head in the lion's mouth for the last three months without knowing it! Well, well—there is a grim justice in the fact that my punishment will be brought about through the employers of the son of the husband of the mother of the young woman to whom I was to have been married.

Enter O'FIPP.

O'FIPP. Now, sorr, ye've expressed a wish for an audience. On consideration I have resolved to grant it.

TOM. You're very good, Colonel.

O'FIPP. You may say that, sorr, for I have discovered that ye're an imposthor. An out and out imposthor, sorr! Ye're no more a gineral officer than I'm a gineral postman.

TOM. But I never said I was. *You* said I was a major-general, and you ought to know. It isn't for me to set up my opinion on a military matter against a lieutenant-colonel's.

O'FIPP. Sorr, I'm a soft-hearted, simple ould fool, and at first your military bearing deceived me practised oi, and I was moved to pity by yer plausible tale and yer broken boots. I was touched by yer sorrows, and I was disposed to try and heal them.

TOM. The boots?

O'FIPP. The sorrows. Now, sorr, a lie has ever been me scorrn and aversion, and an imposture me deepest abhorrence.

TOM. Colonel, I respect your sentiments, for they are my own. You discontinue my allowance, and you are quite right. Your hand.

o'FIPP. [*Rather surprised.*] Sorr, ye spake like a gintleman. Ye're not a gintleman, but ye spake like one. [*Sees note in* TOM's *hand.*] What's that?

TOM. It's a letter to Docket and Tape, in which I confess myself to be the Tom Cobb they're advertising for, and offering to give them all the information in my power.

o'FIPP. [*Amazed.*] But ye're niver goin' to send that?

TOM. I'm going to send it directly.

o'FIPP. Ye're doin' it to frighten me.

TOM. Frighten a colonel? I wouldn't presume to attempt it!

o'FIPP. But——oh, ye'll niver sind it—it would ruin ye.

TOM. It'll ruin us all.   [*Rings.*

o'FIPP. No, no—they can't touch me, mind that! I'm a simple ould man; it's well known, and aisy done. Don't send that, Tom Cobb, and I'll pay ye the pound a week; damme, I'll double it—treble it! I'm a simple ould soldier, and I'm fond of ye, Tom, and I'll not let ye ruin yeself for me!

TOM. Sir, a lie has ever been my scorn and aversion, and an imposture my deepest abhorrence.

Enter SERVANT.

Take this to the address at once.   [*Exit* SERVANT.

o'FIPP. [*Going to doors* R. *and* L.] Effingham—Mrs. Effingham —Matilda—Bulstrode—Whipple—all of ye—come here! [*To* TOM.] Ye've determined to inform on me grey hairs— I'll be first in the field anyhow—mind that now.

Enter all the characters from different doors: BULSTRODE *and* CAROLINE *holding back* TOM; WHIPPLE *and* MATILDA *holding back* o'FIPP.

MRS. EFFINGHAM. What—what is the clamour?

MATILDA. Papa, dear, what's he bin doin' to ye?

o'FIPP. This man—who has passed himself off as a major-gineral—he's a swindler—an imposthor—he's deceived us all —he's practised on our inexperience.

CAROLINE. Arthur—Arthur—speak—what, oh, what is this?

PLATE 7

Tom Cobb. E. W. Royce as Tom Cobb

MATILDA. Don't call him Arthur—his name's Tom—Tom.

CAROLINE. Tomtom? Impossible. Tell them, Arthur, that it is false. Tell them that you are not—you cannot be Tomtom!

O'FIPP. His name's Tom Cobb. Tom Cobb, Mr. Bulstrode— and he's a swindlin' apothecary—the man you've been advertising for these six months.

[CAROLINE *faints in* MR. *and* MRS. EFFINGHAM's *arms.*]

BULSTRODE. Amazement!

EFFINGHAM. Monster—once more behold your work!

MRS. EFFINGHAM. Viper! Creeping, crawling, unadulterated viper!

TOM. I am Tom Cobb, M.R.C.S.; there's my card—'Tom Cobb, 6.' [*Producing handkerchief.*] Lead me away.

BULSTRODE. This is a day of great events. We have sought you everywhere for six months.

TOM. I know you have. Your advertisement has been the nightmare of my life.

BULSTRODE. Amazement! There was a nameless old man, who bore so strong a resemblance to you that scoffers called him by your name. He died in squalor barely six months since.

TOM. All is over—lead me away!

BULSTRODE. He was supposed to have much money in the house, though not a penny could be found. But besides this untold gold, there was standing in his name a sum amounting to £12,000.

TOM. I know nothing about the £12,000. But I am amenable to the law. Take me to my dungeon!

BULSTRODE. No dungeon yawns for you, oh happy sir. Wealth —wealth waits you open-armed!

ALL. What!

BULSTRODE. You had a father once—that father yet another of his own, the aged man so strangely like yourself. That aged person had a son—that son another son—that son your father, and that other son yourself!

TOM. Then—I am the old man's grandson!

BULSTRODE. That is the same idea in vulgar phrase. You are his grandson and his heir-at-law.

CAROLINE. [*Reviving.*] My poet-surgeon, and my old, old love!
[*Embracing him.*

MRS. EFFINGHAM. My son!

BULSTRODE. My brother!

TOM. Well, Colonel, I must trouble you to hand over the property. If it's inconvenient——

O'FIPP. [*From behind his handkerchief.*] It is.

TOM. Well, I'm sorry, that's all.

O'FIPP. Maybe ye're sorry, sorr, but ye're not so sorry as I am, I'll go bail!

MATILDA. Papa dear, don't fret. Sure, I'm a poor penniless girl now, but ain't I goin' to marry a handsome and ginerous young gintleman of good fortune? [*Leaning on* TOM's *shoulder.*] And won't he be a son to ye, and give ye a home for the rest of yer days?
[WHIPPLE *appears to remonstrate with her.* CAROLINE *expresses indignation and clings to her mother.*

TOM. But I protest!

O'FIPP. Tom Cobb, ye spake like a gintleman. Ye're not a gintleman, but ye spake like one. I accept yer offer with pride and gratitude, my son! [*Seizes his hand.*

TOM. Get out! [*Shakes him off.*] Whipple, take this young lady. Matilda, go with the bills! [*Hands her to* WHIPPLE, *who takes her up, expostulating with her.*] Caroline, you loved me as a penniless but poetical major-general; can you still love me as a wealthy but unromantic apothecary?

CAROLINE. I can! I can love you as a wealthy anything!

MRS. EFFINGHAM. We all can!

BULSTRODE. All!
[*They group about him,* MR. *and* MRS. EFFINGHAM *on each side,* BULSTRODE *behind, and* CAROLINE *at his feet;* O'FIPP, WHIPPLE, *and* MATILDA *seated at table, with their heads buried in their arms. Curtain.*

THE MAGISTRATE

A FARCE IN THREE ACTS

BY

ARTHUR WING PINERO (1855–1934)

———

First performed at the Court Theatre
21 March 1885

———

CAST

Mr. Posket	magistrates of the Mulberry Street Police Court	Mr. Arthur Cecil
Mr. Bullamy		Mr. Fred Cape
Colonel Lukyn, from Bengal, retired		Mr. John Clayton
Captain Horace Vale, Shropshire Fusiliers		Mr. F. Kerr
Cis Farringdon, Mrs. Posket's son by her first marriage		Mr. H. Eversfield
Achille Blond, proprietor of the Hôtel des Princes		Mr. Chevalier
Isidore, a waiter		Mr. Deane
Mr. Wormington, chief clerk at Mulberry Street		Mr. Gilbert Trent
Inspector Messiter	Metropolitan Police	Mr. Albert Sims
Sergeant Lugg		Mr. Lugg
Constable Harris		Mr. Burnley
Wyke, servant at Mr. Posket's		Mr. Fayre
Agatha Posket, late Farringdon, *née* Verrinder		Mrs. John Wood
Charlotte, her sister		Miss Marion Terry
Beatie Tomlinson, a young lady reduced to teaching music		Miss Norreys
Popham		Miss La Coste

PREFACE TO *THE MAGISTRATE*

THE MAGISTRATE was the first of Pinero's successful run of farces at the Court Theatre under the management of John Clayton and Arthur Cecil. Together with its successors, *The Schoolmistress* (1886) and *Dandy Dick* (1887), *The Magistrate* brought Pinero his first real popularity and fame after nearly ten years of playwriting.[1] His best farce before those at the Court was *In Chancery* (1884), in which Marmaduke Jackson, having lost his memory in a railway accident, is on the brink of marriage to the buxom daughter of a blustery Irish hotelkeeper, McCafferty, when a detective arrives from London to arrest him, as one Montague Joliffe, for absconding with a ward of Chancery. Jackson believes that he *is* Joliffe, especially as the initials 'M.J.' are on his collars; when the real Joliffe, posing as a servant, and his bride turn up at the same hotel in flight from the law, Jackson assumes that Mrs. Joliffe is *his* wife and flees to London from the marriage ceremony with Miss McCafferty. Somehow he finds himself in his own home and regains his memory. His wife suspects him of infidelity, and her suspicions are confirmed when the angry McCafferty wedding party rush into the house. In order to escape the law the Joliffes have decided to humour Jackson's former delusion that Mrs. Joliffe is his wife, so that in the last act three women simultaneously claim the unfortunate Jackson as husband. *In Chancery* is a first-rate farce with excellent characterizations of the roaring McCafferty and the helplessly bewildered, harassed Jackson, and an admirable scheme of cumulative complication and mis-understanding.

Of Pinero's plays at the Court, *The Cabinet Minister* (1890) is an ironic comedy rather than a farce, and *The Amazons* (1893), entitled a 'Farcical Romance', is a very obvious anti-feminist satire upon a family whose three daughters have been brought up as members of the opposite sex and dressed like them at home. The plot concerns the successful and sometimes low-comedy efforts of three young men to break down this unnatural barrier

---

[1] For further comment on Pinero, see Volume One, pp. 247–50.

between the ladies and their essentially womanly and romantic selves.

Far superior as farce to both these plays are *The Schoolmistress* and *Dandy Dick*. The plot of the former is involved: Queckett, a middle-aged dandy newly married to the headmistress of Volumnia College for girls, Miss Dyott, is blackmailed into posing as uncle to one of the girls when they throw a secret party in their headmistress's absence (actually a 'holiday' to cover up her other career as Constance Delaporte, the star singer of a new comic opera) to celebrate the secret wedding of one of their number against her father's wishes. Complications multiply when Admiral Rankling, the tetchy father concerned, coincidentally joins the party but fails to recognize the daughter whom he has not seen for years. Comic tensions are intensified until the College is set on fire; the party escape by ladders, and several truths are revealed when Miss Dyott returns in her opera costume and the Admiral discovers his daughter. In the third act the characters shelter from the fire in the Admiral's house, bump into each other in the dark, and chase about in pursuit and avoidance. Characterization is influenced by the conception of ideal girlhood as depicted in Robertson's *School* and Albery's *Two Roses*, but such perfection is ironically tempered by another influence, the sweetly romantic, 'ideal', but ingeniously scheming females of Gilbert's *Engaged*. Indeed, the tone of *The Schoolmistress*, notably of the scenes between the Quecketts, is frequently Gilbertian. It is a clever farce, but has neither the humanity nor the feeling for farcical catastrophe of *Dandy Dick*, whose anti-hero, Dr. Jedd, the Dean of St. Marvell's, is cast in the same mould as the gentle and helpless Posket of *The Magistrate*. Like Posket, the Dean, once he has committed himself to a course of action that proves disastrous—attempting to administer a bolus to the horse Dandy Dick, upon which his financial hopes for the new steeple and his own solvency are riding in next day's race—finds himself the powerless victim of hostile chance. Comedy arises from the contrast between the Dean's mildness, courtesy, and respectability on the one hand, and on the other the coarse and cruel world of horses, gambling, crime, prison, and loss of dignity which is really so alien to him and in which he becomes so defencelessly and calamitously involved.

Dandy Dick and *The Magistrate* are the finest flowers of late nineteenth-century farce. In the latter Pinero skilfully manipulates the plot elements of French farce, especially the convergence of all parties on the private dining-room in the *scène à faire*, in a way that according to one critic struck out 'quite a new line' and was 'brimful of good honest fun, with all the briskness of the Palais-Royal pieces without any of their objectionable features'.[1] Pinero had learned his French lessons well, and *The Magistrate* uses French machinery in a characteristically warm-hearted and eccentrically English way: 'good honest fun', in fact, of native growth but foreign seed. Mr. Posket is one of those 'probable people placed in possible circumstances' whom Pinero believed should be the principal characters of farce,[2] and his utter middle-class respectability makes him the perfect farce victim. Like Dove of Boucicault's *Forbidden Fruit* Posket is a man of the law, except that where Dove is only a barrister Posket is invested with authority and has further to fall. Thus Pinero makes appropriately ironical use of his victims' professions: Posket is a pillar of the law, Dr. Jedd a pillar of the church. Both pillars crumble. Morally as well as physically Posket and Jedd—again like Dove—emerge tattered and besmirched from their struggle with darkness. Like the tragic hero, the anti-hero of farce suffers in order to be wise.

The Magistrate ran for 363 performances on its first appearance. It was revived at Terry's in 1892 with Edward Terry as Posket and Fanny Brough as Mrs. Posket, at the Arts in 1943, the St. Martin's in 1944, the Old Vic in 1959, and at Chichester in 1969 with Alistair Sim and Maggie Smith. The text used here is that of the first edition of 1892, published by Heinemann, collated with the *French* acting edition of 1936 and the Lord Chamberlain's copy; stage directions from the *French*, which are much the same as those in the licenser's copy, have been incorporated. There are a few variants between the 1892 and the *French*; corruptions in the former can be remedied from the licenser's text, which is slightly longer than the texts of the printed editions.

[1] *The Theatre* (April 1885), p. 199.
[2] Preface to *The Cabinet Minister* (1892), ed. M. C. Salaman.

ACT I

A well-furnished drawing-room in the house of MR. POSKET *in Bloomsbury.*

BEATIE TOMLINSON, *a pretty, simply dressed little girl of about sixteen, is playing the piano, as* CIS FARRINGDON, *a manly youth wearing an Eton jacket, enters the room.*

CIS. Beatie!

BEATIE. Cis dear! Dinner isn't over, surely?

CIS. Not quite. I had one of my convenient headaches and cleared out. [*Taking an apple and some cobnuts from his pocket and giving them to* BEATIE.] These are for you, dear, with my love. I sneaked 'em off the sideboard as I came out.

BEATIE. Oh, I mustn't take them!

CIS. Yes, you may—it's my share of dessert. Besides, it's a horrid shame you don't grub with us.

BEATIE. What, a poor little music mistress!

CIS. Yes. They're only going to give you four guineas a quarter. Fancy getting a girl like you for four guineas a quarter—why, an eighth of you is worth more than that! Now peg away at your apple. [*Produces a cigarette.*

BEATIE. There's company at dinner, isn't there?
[*Munching her apple.*

CIS. Well, hardly. Aunt Charlotte hasn't arrived yet, so there's only old Bullamy.

BEATIE. Isn't old Bullamy anybody?

CIS. Old Bullamy—well, he's only like the Guv'nor, a police magistrate at the Mulberry Street Police Court.

BEATIE. Oh, does each police court have two magistrates?

CIS. [*Proudly.*] All the best have two.

BEATIE. Don't they quarrel over getting the interesting cases? I should.

CIS. I don't know how they manage—perhaps they toss up who's to hear the big sensations. There's a Mrs. Beldam, who is rather a bore sometimes; I know the Guv always lets old Bullamy attend to her. But, as a rule, I fancy they go half and half, in a friendly way. [*Lighting cigarette.*] For instance, if the Guv'nor wants to go to the Derby he lets old Bullamy have the Oaks—and so on, see?

[*He sits on the floor, comfortably reclining against* BEATIE, *and puffing his cigarette.*

BEATIE. Oh, I say, Cis, won't your mamma be angry when she finds I haven't gone home?

CIS. Oh, put it on to your pupil. [*Kissing her.*] Say, I'm very backward.

BEATIE. I think you are extremely forward—in some ways. I do wish I could get you to concentrate your attention on your music lessons. But I wouldn't get you into a scrape.

CIS. No fear of that. Ma is too proud of me.

BEATIE. But there's your step-father.

CIS. The dear old Guv'nor! Why, he's too good-natured to say 'Bo!' to a goose. You know, Beatie, I was at a school at Brighton when ma got married—when she got married the second time, I mean—and the Guv'nor and I didn't make each other's acquaintance till after the honeymoon.

BEATIE. Oh, fancy your step-father blindly accepting such a responsibility! [*Gives him a cobnut to crack for her.*

CIS. Yes, wasn't the Guv'nor soft! I might have been a very indifferent sort of young fellow for all he knew.

[*Having cracked the nut with his teeth, he returns it to her.*

BEATIE. Thank you, dear.

CIS. Well, when I heard the new dad was a police magistrate, I *was* scared. Said I to myself, 'If I don't mind my P's and Q's, the Guv'nor—from force of habit—will fine me all my pocket-money.' But it's quite the reverse—he's the mildest, meekest— [*The door opens suddenly.*] Look out! Some one coming!

[*They both jump up,* BEATIE *scattering the nuts that are in her lap all over the floor.* CIS *throws his cigarette into the fireplace and sits at the piano, playing a simple exercise very badly.* BEATIE *stands behind him, counting.*

BEATIE. One—and two—and one—and two.

WYKE, *the butler, appears at the door, and mysteriously closes it after him.*

WYKE. [*In a whisper.*] Ssss! Master Cis! Master Cis!

CIS. Hallo—what is it, Wyke?

WYKE. [*Producing a decanter from under his coat.*] The port wine what you asked for, sir. I couldn't get it away before—the old gentlemen do hug port wine so.

CIS. Got a glass?

WYKE. Yes, sir. [*Producing wine-glass from his pocket, and pouring out wine.*] What ain't missed ain't mourned, eh, Master Cis?

CIS. [*Offering wine.*] Here you are, Beatie dear.

BEATIE. The idea of such a thing! I couldn't!

CIS. Why not?

BEATIE. If I merely sipped it I shouldn't be able to give you your music lesson properly. Drink it yourself, you dear thoughtful boy.

CIS. I shan't—it's for you.

BEATIE. I can't drink it!

CIS. You must.

BEATIE. I won't!

CIS. You're disagreeable!

BEATIE. Not half so disagreeable as you are.   [*They wrangle.*

WYKE. [*To himself, watching them.*] What a young gentleman it is, and only fourteen! Fourteen—he behaves like forty! [CIS *chokes as he is drinking the wine;* BEATIE *pats him on the back.*] Why, even Cook has made a 'ash of everything since he's been in the house, and as for Popham——! [*Seeing some one approaching.*] Look out, Master Cis!

     [CIS *returns to the piano,* BEATIE *counting as before.* WYKE *pretends to arrange the window curtains, concealing the decanter behind him.*

BEATIE. One and two—and one and two—and one, &c.

Enter POPHAM, *a smart-looking maid-servant.*

POPHAM. Wyke, where's the port?

WYKE. [*Vacantly.*] Port?

POPHAM. Port wine. Missus is furious.

WYKE. Port?

POPHAM. [*Pointing to the decanter.*] Why! There! You're carrying it about with you!

WYKE. Why, so I am! Carrying it about with me! Shows what a sharp eye I keep on the Guv'nor's wines. Carrying it about with me! Missus will be amused.   [*Goes out.*

POPHAM. [*Eyeing* CIS *and* BEATIE. *To herself.*] There's that boy with *her* again! Minx! Her two hours was up long ago. Why doesn't she go home? Master Cis, I've got a message for you.

CIS. For me, Popham?

POPHAM. Yes, sir. [*Quietly to him.*] The message is from a young lady who up to last Wednesday was all in all to you. Her name is Emma Popham.

CIS. [*Trying to get away.*] Oh, go along, Popham!

POPHAM. [*Holding his sleeve.*] Ah, it wasn't 'Go along, Popham' till that music girl came into the house. I will go along, but— cast your eye over this before you sleep tonight. [*She takes out of her pocket-handkerchief a piece of printed paper which she hands him between her finger and thumb.*] Part of a story in *Bow Bells* called 'Jilted; or, Could Blood Atone?' Wrap it in your handkerchief—it came round the butter.

[*She goes out;* CIS *throws the paper into the grate.*

CIS. Bother the girl! Beatie, she's jealous of you!

BEATIE. A parlour-maid jealous of *me*—and with a bit of a child of fourteen!

CIS. I may be only fourteen, but I feel like a grown-up man! You're only sixteen—there's not much difference—and if you will only wait for me, I'll soon catch you up and be as much a man as you are a woman. [*Lovingly.*] Will you wait for me, Beatie?

BEATIE. I can't—I'm getting older every minute!

CIS. [*Desperately.*] Oh, I wish I could borrow five or six years from somebody!

BEATIE. Many a person would be glad to lend them. [*Lovingly.*] And oh, I wish you could!

CIS. [*Putting his arm round her.*] You do! Why?

BEATIE. Because I—because——

CIS. [*Listening.*] Look out! Here's the mater!
[*They run to the piano; he resumes playing, and she counting as before.*

BEATIE. One and two—and one—and two, &c.

Enter AGATHA POSKET, *a handsome, showy woman, of about thirty-six, looking perhaps younger.*

AGATHA. Why, Cis child, at your music again?

CIS. Yes, ma, always at it. You'll spoil my taste by forcing it if you're not careful.

AGATHA. We have no right to keep Miss Tomlinson so late.

BEATIE. [*Nervously.*] Oh, thank you, it doesn't matter. I—I— am afraid we're not making—very—great—progress.

CIS. [*Winking at* BEATIE.] Well, if I play that again, will you kiss me?

BEATIE. [*Demurely.*] I don't know, I'm sure. [*To* AGATHA.] May I promise that, ma'am?
[*Sits in the window recess.* CIS, *joining her, puts his arm round her waist.*

AGATHA. [*Sharply.*] No, certainly not. [*To herself, watching them.*] If I could only persuade Æneas to dismiss this *protégée* of his, and to engage a music-master, it would ease my conscience a little. If this girl knew the truth, how indignant she would be! And then there is the injustice to the boy himself, and to my husband's friends who are always petting and foldling and caressing what they call 'a fine little man of fourteen!' Fourteen! Oh, what an idiot I have been to conceal my child's real age! [*Looking at the clock.*] Charlotte is late; I wish she would come. It will be a relief to worry her with my troubles.

POSKET. [*Outside.*] We smoke all over the house, Bullamy, all over the house.

AGATHA. I will speak to Æneas about this little girl, at any rate.

Enter POSKET, *a mild gentleman of about fifty, smoking a cigarette, followed by* BULLAMY, *a fat, red-faced man with a bronchial cough and general huskiness.*

POSKET. Smoke anywhere, Bullamy—smoke anywhere.

BULLAMY. Not with my bronchitis, thank ye.

POSKET. [*Beaming at* AGATHA.] Ah, my darling!

BULLAMY. [*Producing a small box from his waistcoat pocket.*] All I take after dinner is a jujube—sometimes two. [*Offering the box.*] May I tempt Mrs. Posket?

AGATHA. No, thank you. [*Treading on one of the nuts which have been scattered over the room.*] How provoking—who brings nuts into the drawing-room?

POSKET. Miss Tomlinson still here? [*To* BEATIE.] Don't go, don't go. Glad to see Cis so fond of his music. Your sister Charlotte is behind her time, my darling.

AGATHA. Her train is delayed, I suppose.

POSKET. You must stay and see my sister-in-law, Bullamy.

BULLAMY. Pleasure—pleasure!

POSKET. *I* have never met her yet; we will share first impressions. In the interim, will Miss Tomlinson delight us with a little music?

BULLAMY. [*Bustling up to the piano.*] If this young lady is going to sing she might like one of my jujubes.

    [BEATIE *sits at the piano with* CIS *and* BULLAMY *on each side of her.* POSKET *treads on a nut as he walks over to his wife.*

POSKET. Dear me—how come nuts into the drawing-room? [*To* AGATHA.] Of what is my darling thinking so deeply? [*Treads on another nut.*] Another! My pet, there are nuts on the drawing-room carpet!

AGATHA. [*Rousing herself.*] Yes. I want to speak to you, Æneas.

POSKET. About the nuts?

AGATHA. No—about Miss Tomlinson—your little *protégée*.

POSKET. Ah, nice little thing.

AGATHA. Very. But not old enough to exert any decided influence over the boy's musical future. Why not engage a master?

POSKET. What, for a mere child?

AGATHA. A mere child—oh!

POSKET. A boy of fourteen!

AGATHA. [*To herself.*] Fourteen!

POSKET. A boy of fourteen, not yet out of Czerny's exercises.

AGATHA. [*To herself.*] If we were alone now, I might have the desperation to tell him all!

POSKET. Besides, my darling, you know the interest I take in Miss Tomlinson; she is one of the brightest little spots on my hobby-horse. Like all our servants, like everybody in my employ, she has been brought to my notice through the unhappy medium of the Police Court over which it is my destiny to preside. Our servant, Wyke, a man with a beautiful nature, is the son of a person I committed for trial for marrying three wives. To this day, Wyke is ignorant as to which of those three wives he is the son of! Cook was once a notorious dipsomaniac, and has even now not entirely freed herself from early influences. Popham is the unclaimed charge of a convicted baby-farmer. Even our milkman came before me as a man who had refused to submit specimens to the analytic inspector. And this poor child, what is she?

AGATHA. Yes, I know.

POSKET. The daughter of a superannuated General, who abstracted four silk umbrellas from the Army and Navy Stores—and on a fine day too!   [BEATIE *ceases playing.*

BULLAMY. Very good—very good!

POSKET. Thank you—thank you!

BULLAMY. [*To* POSKET, *coughing and laughing and popping a jujube into his mouth.*] My dear Posket, I really must congratulate you on that boy of yours—your step-son. A most wonderful lad. So confoundedly advanced too.

POSKET. Yes, isn't he? Eh!

BULLAMY. [*Confidentially.*] While the piano was going on just now, he told me one of the most humorous stories I've ever heard. [*Laughing heartily and panting, then taking another jujube.*] Ha, ha! Bless me, I don't know when I have taken so many jujubes!

POSKET. My dear Bullamy, my entire marriage is the greatest possible success. A little romantic too. [*Pointing to* AGATHA.] Beautiful woman!

BULLAMY. Very, very. [*Looking at her through eyeglass.*] I never committed a more stylish, elegant creature.

POSKET. [*Warmly.*] Thank you, Bullamy—we met abroad, at Spa, when I was on my holiday.

Enter WYKE, *with tea-tray, which he hands round.*

BULLAMY. I shall go there next year.

POSKET. She lost her first husband about twelve months ago in India. He was an army contractor.

BEATIE. [*To* CIS *at the piano.*] I must go now—there's no excuse for staying any longer.

CIS. [*To her disconsolately.*] What the deuce shall *I* do?

POSKET. [*Pouring out milk.*] Dear me, this milk seems very poor. When he died, she came to England, placed her boy at a school in Brighton, and then moved about quietly from place to place, drinking——   [*Sips tea.*

BULLAMY. [*With concern.*] Drinking?

POSKET. The waters—she's a little dyspeptic. [WYKE *goes out.*] We encountered each other at the *Tours des Fontaines*—by accident I trod upon her dress——

BEATIE. Good-night, Cis dear.

CIS. Oh!

POSKET. I apologised. We talked about the weather, we drank out of the same glass, discovered that we both suffered from the same ailment, and the result is complete happiness.
                    [*He bends over* AGATHA *gallantly.*

AGATHA. Æneas!

[*He kisses her; then* CIS *kisses* BEATIE, *loudly.* POSKET *and* BULLAMY *both listen puzzled.*

POSKET. Echo?

BULLAMY. Suppose so!
[*He kisses the back of his hand experimentally;* BEATIE *kisses* CIS.
Yes.

POSKET. Curious. [*To* BULLAMY.] Romantic story, isn't it?

BEATIE. Good-night, Mrs. Posket. I shall be here early to-morrow morning.

AGATHA. I am afraid you are neglecting your other pupils.

BEATIE. [*Confused.*] Oh, they're not so interesting as Cis— [*Correcting herself.*] Master Farringdon. Good-night.

AGATHA. Good-night, dear.   [BEATIE *goes out quietly.*

POSKET. [*To* BULLAMY.] We were married abroad without consulting friends or relations on either side. That's how it is I have never seen my sister-in-law, Miss Verrinder, who is coming from Shropshire to stay with us—she ought to——

Enter WYKE.

WYKE. Miss Verrinder has come, ma'am.

POSKET. Here she is.

AGATHA. Charlotte!

Enter CHARLOTTE, *a fine handsome girl, followed by* POPHAM *with hand luggage.*

AGATHA. [*Kissing her.*] My dear Charley.   [WYKE *goes out.*

CHARLOTTE. Aggy darling, aren't I late! There's a fog on the line—you could cut it with a knife. [*Seeing* CIS.] Is that your boy?

AGATHA. Yes.

CHARLOTTE. Good gracious! What is he doing in an Eton jacket at his age?

AGATHA. [*Softly to* CHARLOTTE.] Hush! Don't say a word about my boy's age yet awhile.

CHARLOTTE. Oh!

AGATHA. [*About to introduce* POSKET.] There is my husband.

CHARLOTTE. [*Mistaking* BULLAMY *for him.*] Oh, how could she! [*To* BULLAMY, *turning her cheek to him.*] I congratulate you—I suppose you ought to kiss me.

AGATHA. No, no!

POSKET. Welcome to my house, Miss Verrinder.

CHARLOTTE. Oh, I beg your pardon. How do you do?

BULLAMY. [*To himself.*] Mrs. Posket's an interfering woman.

POSKET. [*Pointing to* BULLAMY.] Mr. Bullamy.
                    [BULLAMY, *aggrieved, bows stiffly.*

AGATHA. Come upstairs, dear; will you have some tea?

CHARLOTTE. No, thank you, pet, but I should like a glass of soda water.

AGATHA. Soda water!

CHARLOTTE. Well, dear, you can put what you like at the bottom of it.
        [AGATHA *and* CHARLOTTE *go out,* POPHAM *following.*

POPHAM. [*To* CIS.] Give me back my *Bow Bells* when you have read it, you imp.   [*Goes out.*

CIS. By Jove, Guv, isn't Aunt Charlotte a stunner?

POSKET. Seems a charming woman.

BULLAMY. [*To himself.*] Posket's got the wrong one! That comes of marrying without first seeing the lady's relations.

CIS. Come along, Guv—let's have a gamble—Mr. Bullamy will join us.   [*Opens the card-table, arranges chairs and candles.*

BULLAMY. A gamble?

POSKET. Yes—the boy has taught me a new game called 'Fireworks'; his mother isn't aware that we play for money, of course, but we do.

BULLAMY. Ha, ha, ha! Who wins?

POSKET. He does now—but he says I shall win when I know the game better.

BULLAMY. What a boy he is!

POSKET. [*Delighted.*] Isn't he a wonderful lad? And only fourteen, too. I'll tell you something else—perhaps you had better not mention it to his mother.

BULLAMY. No, no, certainly not.

POSKET. He's invested a little money for me.

BULLAMY. What in?

POSKET. Not *in*—*on*—on Sillikin for the Lincolnshire Handicap. Sillikin to win and Butterscotch one, two, three.

BULLAMY. Good Lord!

POSKET. Yes, the dear boy said, 'Guv, it isn't fair you should give me all the tips; I'll give you some'—and he did—he gave me Sillikin and Butterscotch. He'll manage it for you, if you like. 'Plank it down', he calls it.

BULLAMY. [*Chuckling and choking.*] Ha, ha! Ho, ho! [*Taking a jujube.*] This boy will ruin me in jujubes.

CIS. All ready. Look sharp! Guv, lend me a sov to start with?

POSKET. A sov to start with? [*They sit at the table upstage.* AGATHA *and* CHARLOTTE *come into the room.*] We didn't think you would return so soon, my darling.

AGATHA. Go on amusing yourselves, I insist; only don't teach my Cis to play cards.

BULLAMY. Ho, ho!

POSKET. [*To* BULLAMY.] Hush! Hush!

AGATHA. [*To* CHARLOTTE.] I'm glad of this—we can tell each other our miseries undisturbed. Will you begin?

CHARLOTTE. Well, at last I am engaged to Captain Horace Vale.

AGATHA. Oh! Charley, I'm so glad!

CHARLOTTE. Yes—so is he—he says. He proposed to me at the Hunt Ball—in the passage—Tuesday week.

AGATHA. What did he say?

CHARLOTTE. He said, 'By Jove, I love you awfully.'

AGATHA. Well—and what did you say?

CHARLOTTE. Oh, I said, 'Well, if you're going to be as eloquent as all that, by Jove, I can't stand out.' So we settled it in the passage. He bars flirting till after we're married. That's my misery. What's yours, Aggy?

AGATHA. Something awful!

CHARLOTTE. Cheer up, Aggy! What is it?

AGATHA. Well, Charley, you know I lost my poor dear first husband at a very delicate age.

CHARLOTTE. Well, you were five-and-thirty, dear.

AGATHA. Yes, that's what I mean. Five-and-thirty is a very delicate age to find yourself single. You're neither one thing nor the other. You're not exactly a two-year-old, and you don't care to pull a hansom. However, I soon met Mr. Posket at Spa—bless him!

CHARLOTTE. And you nominated yourself for the Matrimonial Stakes. Mr. Farringdon's The Widow, by Bereavement, out of Mourning, ten pounds extra.

AGATHA. Yes, Charley, and in less than a month I went triumphantly over the course. But, Charley dear, I didn't carry the fair weight for age—and that's my trouble.

CHARLOTTE. Oh, dear!

AGATHA. Undervaluing Æneas' love, in a moment of, I hope, not unjustifiable vanity, I took five years from my total, which made me thirty-one on my wedding morning.

CHARLOTTE. Well, dear, many a misguided woman has done that before you.

AGATHA. Yes, Charley, but don't you see the consequences? It has thrown everything out. As I am now thirty-one, instead of thirty-six as I ought to be, it stands to reason that I couldn't have been married twenty years ago, which I was. So I have had to fib in proportion.

CHARLOTTE. I see—making your first marriage occur only fifteen years ago.

AGATHA. Exactly.

CHARLOTTE. Well then, dear, why worry yourself further?

AGATHA. Well, dear, don't you see? If I am only thirty-one now, my boy couldn't have been born nineteen years ago, and if he could, he oughtn't to have been, because on my own showing I wasn't married till four years later. Now you see the result!

CHARLOTTE. Which is, that that fine strapping young gentleman over there is only fourteen.

AGATHA. Precisely. Isn't it awkward! And his moustache is becoming more and more obvious every day.

CHARLOTTE. What does the boy himself believe?

AGATHA. He believes his mother, of course, as a boy should. As a prudent woman, I always kept him in ignorance of his age—in case of necessity. But it is terribly hard on the poor child, because his aims, instincts, and ambitions are all so horribly in advance of his condition. His food, his books, his amusements are out of keeping with his palate, his brain, and his disposition; and with all this suffering—his wretched mother has the remorseful consciousness of having shortened her offspring's life.

CHARLOTTE. Oh, come, you haven't quite done that.

AGATHA. Yes, I have—because, if he lives to be a hundred, he must be buried at ninety-five.

CHARLOTTE. That's true.

AGATHA. Then there's another aspect. He's a great favourite with all our friends—women friends especially. Even his little music mistress and the girl-servants hug and kiss him because he's such an engaging boy, and I can't stop it. But it's very awful to see these innocent women fondling a young man of nineteen.

CHARLOTTE. The women don't know it.

AGATHA. But they'd like to know it. They ought to know it! The other day I found my poor boy sitting on Lady Jenkins's lap, and in the presence of Sir George. I have no right to compromise Lady Jenkins in that way. And now, Charley, you see the whirlpool in which I am struggling—if you can throw me a rope, pray do.

CHARLOTTE. What sort of a man is Mr. Posket, Aggy?

AGATHA. The best creature in the world. He's a practical philanthropist.

CHARLOTTE. Um—he's a police magistrate, too, isn't he?

AGATHA. Yes, but he pays out of his own pocket half the fines he inflicts. That's why he has had a reprimand from the Home Office for inflicting such light penalties. All our servants have graduated at Mulberry Street. Most of the pictures in the dining-room are genuine Constables.

CHARLOTTE. Take my advice—tell him the whole story.

AGATHA. I dare not!

CHARLOTTE. Why?

AGATHA. I should have to take such a back seat for the rest of my married life. [*The party at the card-table breaks up.*

BULLAMY. [*Grumpily.*] No, thank ye, not another minute. What is the use of talking about revenge, my dear Posket, when I haven't a penny piece left to play with?

POSKET. [*Distressed.*] I'm in the same predicament! Cis will lend us some money, won't you, Cis?

CIS. Rather!

BULLAMY. No, thank ye, that boy is one too many for me. I've never met such a child. Good-night, Mrs. Posket. [*Treads on a nut.*] Confound the nuts!

AGATHA. Going so early?

CIS. I hate a bad loser, don't you, Guv?

AGATHA. Show Mr. Bullamy down stairs, Cis.

BULLAMY. Good-night, Posket. Oh! I haven't a shilling left for my cabman.

CIS. I'll pay the cab.

BULLAMY. No, thank ye! I'll walk. [*Opening jujube box.*] Bah! Not even a jujube left and on a foggy night, too! Ugh!

[*Goes out.*

Enter WYKE, *with four letters on salver.*

CIS. Any for me?

WYKE. One, sir.

CIS. [*To himself.*] From Achille Blond; lucky the mater didn't see it.

[*Goes out.* WYKE *hands letters to* AGATHA, *who takes two, then to* POSKET, *who takes one.*

AGATHA. This is for you, Charley—already. [WYKE *goes out.*

CHARLOTTE. Spare my blushes, dear—it's from Horace, Captain Vale. The dear wretch knew I was coming to you. Heigho! Will you excuse me?

POSKET. Certainly.

AGATHA. Excuse me, please?

CHARLOTTE. Certainly, my dear.

POSKET. Certainly, my darling. Excuse me, won't you?

CHARLOTTE. Oh, certainly.

AGATHA. Certainly, Æneas.
[*Simultaneously they all open their letters, and lean back and read.*

Lady Jenkins is not feeling very well.

CHARLOTTE. [*Angrily.*] If Captain Horace Vale stood before me at this moment, I'd slap his face!

AGATHA. Charlotte!

CHARLOTTE. [*Reading.*] 'Dear Miss Verrinder—Your desperate flirtation with Major Bristow at the Meet on Tuesday last, three days after our engagement, has just come to my knowledge. Your letters and gifts, including the gold-headed hair-pin given me at the Hunt Ball, shall be returned to-morrow. By Jove, all is over! Horace Vale.' Oh, dear!

AGATHA. Oh, Charley, I'm so sorry! However, you can deny it.

CHARLOTTE. [*Weeping.*] That's the worst of it; I can't.

POSKET. [*To* AGATHA.] My darling, you will be delighted. A note from Colonel Lukyn.

AGATHA. Lukyn—Lukyn? I seem to know the name.

POSKET. An old schoolfellow of mine who went to India many years ago. He has just come home. I met him at the club last night and asked him to name an evening to dine with us. He accepts for to-morrow.

AGATHA. Lukyn, Lukyn?

POSKET. Listen. [*Reading.*] 'It will be especially delightful to me, as I believe I am an old friend of your wife and of her first husband. You may recall me to her recollection by reminding her that I am the Captain Lukyn who stood sponsor to her boy when he was christened at Baroda.'

AGATHA. [*Giving a loud scream.*] Oh!

POSKET. My dear!

AGATHA. I—I've twisted my foot.

POSKET. How *do* nuts come into the drawing-room?
[*Picks up nut and puts it on the piano.*

CHARLOTTE. [*Quietly to* AGATHA.] Aggy?

AGATHA. [*To* CHARLOTTE.] The boy's godfather.

CHARLOTTE. When was the child christened?

AGATHA. A month after he was born. They always are.

POSKET. [*Reading the letter again.*] This is *very* pleasant.

AGATHA. Let—let me see the letter, I—I may recognize the handwriting.

POSKET. [*Handing her the letter.*] Certainly, my pet. [*To himself.*] Awakened memories of Number One. [*Sighing.*] That's the worst of marrying a widow; somebody is always proving her previous convictions.

AGATHA. [*To* CHARLOTTE.] 'No. 19a, Cork Street.' Charley, put on your things and come with me.

CHARLOTTE. Agatha, you're mad!

AGATHA. I'm going to shut this man's mouth before he comes into this house to-morrow.

CHARLOTTE. Wait *till* he comes.

AGATHA. Yes, till he stalks in here with his 'How d'ye do, Posket? Haven't seen your wife since the year '66, by Gad, sir!' Not I! Æneas!

POSKET. My dear.

AGATHA. Lady Jenkins—Adelaide—is very ill; she can't put her foot to the ground with neuralgia.
[*Taking the letter from her pocket, and giving it to him.*

POSKET. Bless me!

AGATHA. We have known each other for six long years.

POSKET. Only six weeks, my love.

AGATHA. Weeks *are* years in close friendship. My place is by her side.

POSKET. [*Reading the letter.*] 'Slightly indisposed, caught trifling cold at the Dog Show. Where do you buy your handkerchiefs?' There's nothing about neuralgia or putting her foot to the ground here, my darling.

AGATHA. No, but can't you read between the lines, Æneas? That is the letter of a woman who is not at all well.

POSKET. All right, my darling, if you are bent upon going I will accompany you.

AGATHA. Certainly not, Æneas—Charlotte insists on being my companion; we can keep each other warm in a closed cab.

POSKET. But can't I make a third?

AGATHA. Don't be so forgetful, Æneas—don't you know that in a four-wheeled cab, the fewer knees there are the better?

[AGATHA *and* CHARLOTTE *go out.*

Enter CIS *hurriedly.*

CIS. What's the matter, Guv?

POSKET. Your mother and Miss Verrinder are going out.

CIS. Out of their minds? It's a horrid night.

POSKET. Yes, but Lady Jenkins is ill.

CIS. Oh! Is ma mentioned in the will?

POSKET. [*Shocked.*] Good gracious, what a boy! No, Cis, your mother is merely going to sit by Lady Jenkins's bedside, to hold her hand, and to tell her where one goes to—to buy pocket-handkerchiefs.

CIS. [*Struck with an idea.*] By Jove! The mater can't be home again till half-past twelve or one o'clock.

POSKET. Much later if Lady Jenkins's condition is alarming.

CIS. Hurray! [*He takes the watch out of* POSKET'S *pocket.*] Just half-past ten. Greenwich mean, eh Guv?

[*He puts the watch to his ear, pulling* POSKET *towards him by the chain.*

POSKET. What an extraordinary lad!

CIS. [*Returning watch.*] Thanks. They have to get from here to

Campden Hill and back again. I'll tell Wyke to get them the worst horse on the rank.

POSKET. My dear child!

CIS. Three-quarters of an hour's journey from here at least. Twice three-quarters, one hour and a half. An hour with Lady Jenkins—when women get together, you know, Guv, they do talk—that's two hours and a half. Good. Guv, will you come with me?

POSKET. [*Horrified.*] Go with you! Where?

CIS. Hôtel des Princes, Meek Street. A sharp hansom does it in ten minutes.

POSKET. Meek Street, Hôtel des Princes! Child, do you know what you're talking about?

CIS. Rather. Look here, Guv, honour bright—no blab if I show you a letter.

POSKET. I won't promise anything.

CIS. You won't! Do you know, Guv, you are doing a very unwise thing to check the confidence of a lad like me?

POSKET. Cis, my boy!

CIS. Can you calculate the inestimable benefit it is to a youngster to have some one always at his elbow, some one older, wiser, and better off than himself?

POSKET. Of course, Cis, of course, I *want* you to make a companion of me.

CIS. Then how the deuce can I do that if you won't come with me to Meek Street?

POSKET. Yes, but deceiving your mother!

CIS. *Deceiving* the mater would be to tell her a crammer—a thing, I hope, we're both of us much above.

POSKET. Good boy, good boy.

CIS. *Concealing* the fact that we're going to have a bit of supper at the Hôtel des Princes is doing my mother a great kindness, because it would upset her considerably to know of the circumstances. You've been wrong, Guv, but we won't say anything more about that. Read the letter.

[*Gives* POSKET *the letter.*

POSKET. [*Reading in a dazed sort of a way.*] 'Hôtel des Princes, Meek Street, W. Dear Sir—Unless you drop in and settle your arrears, I really cannot keep your room for you any longer. Yours obediently, Achille Blond. Cecil Farringdon, Esq.' Good heavens! You have a room at the Hôtel des Princes!

CIS. A room! It's little better than a coop.

POSKET. You don't occupy it?

CIS. But my friends do. When I was at Brighton I was in with the best set—hope I always shall be. I left Brighton—nice hole I was in. You see, Guv, I didn't want my friends to make free with your house.

POSKET. [*Weakly.*] Oh, didn't you?

CIS. So I took a room at the Hôtel des Princes—when I want to put a man up he goes there. You see, Guv, it's *you* I've been considering more than myself.

POSKET. [*Beside himself.*] But you are a mere child!

CIS. A fellow is just as old as he feels. I feel no end of a man. Hush, they're coming down! I'm off to tell Wyke about the rickety four-wheeler.

POSKET. Cis, Cis! Your mother will discover I have been out.

CIS. Oh, I forgot, you're married, aren't you?

POSKET. Married!

CIS. Say you are going to the club.

POSKET. But that's not the truth, sir!

CIS. Yes it is. We'll pop in at the club on our way, and you can give me a bitters.   [*Goes out.*

POSKET. Good gracious, what a boy! Hôtel des Princes, Meek Street! What shall I do? Tell his mother? Why, it would turn her hair grey. If I could only get a quiet word with this Mr. Achille Blond, I could put a stop to everything. That is my best course, not to lose a moment in rescuing the child from his boyish indiscretion. Yes, I must go with Cis to Meek Street.

Enter AGATHA *and* CHARLOTTE, *elegantly dressed.*

AGATHA. Have you sent for a cab, Æneas?

POSKET. Cis is looking after that.

AGATHA. Poor Cis! How late we keep him up.

Enter CIS.

CIS. Wyke has gone for a cab, ma dear.

AGATHA. Thank you, Cis darling.

CIS. If you'll excuse me, I'll go to my room. I've another bad headache coming on.

AGATHA. [*Kissing him.*] Run along, my boy.

CIS. Good-night, ma. Good-night, Aunt Charlotte.

CHARLOTTE. Good-night, Cis.

AGATHA. [*To herself.*] I wish the cab would come.
                [AGATHA *and* CHARLOTTE *look out of the window.*

CIS. [*At the door.*] Ahem! Good-night, Guv.

POSKET. You've told a story—two, sir! You said you were going up to your room.

CIS. So I am—to dress.

POSKET. You said you had a bad headache coming on.

CIS. So I have, Guv. I always get a bad headache at the Hôtel des Princes.   [*Goes out.*

POSKET. Oh, what a boy!

AGATHA. [*To herself.*] When will that cab come?

POSKET. Ahem! My pet, the idea has struck me that as you are going out, it would not be a bad notion for me to pop into my club.

AGATHA. The club! You were there last night.

POSKET. I know, my darling. Many men look in at their clubs every night.

AGATHA. A nice example for Cis, truly! I particularly desire that you should remain at home to-night, Æneas.

POSKET. [*To himself.*] Oh, dear me!

CHARLOTTE. [*To* AGATHA.] Why not let him go to the club, Agatha?

AGATHA. He might meet Colonel Lukyn there.

CHARLOTTE. If Colonel Lukyn is there we shan't find him in Cork Street.

AGATHA. Then we follow him to the club.

CHARLOTTE. Ladies never call at a club.

AGATHA. Such things have been known.

Enter WYKE.

WYKE. [*Grinning behind his hand.*] The cab is coming, ma'am.

AGATHA. Coming? Why didn't you bring it with you?

WYKE. I walk quicker than the cab, ma'am. It's a good horse, slow, but very certain.

AGATHA. We will come down.

WYKE. [*To himself.*] Just what the horse has done. [*To* AGATHA.] Yes, ma'am. [*Goes out.*

AGATHA. Good-night, Æneas.

POSKET. [*Nervously.*] I wish you would allow me to go to the club, my pet.

AGATHA. Æneas, I am surprised at your obstinacy. It is so very different from my first husband.

POSKET. [*Annoyed.*] Really, Agatha, I am shocked. I presume the late Mr. Farringdon occasionally used his clubs?

AGATHA. Indian clubs. Indian clubs are good for the liver; London clubs are not. Good-night!

POSKET. I'll see you to your cab, Agatha.

AGATHA. No, thank you.

POSKET. Upon my word!

CHARLOTTE. [*To* AGATHA.] Why not?

AGATHA. He would want to give the direction to the cabman!

CHARLOTTE. The first tiff. Good-night, Mr. Posket.

POSKET. Good-night, Miss Verrinder.

AGATHA. Have you any message for Lady Jenkins?

POSKET. Confound Lady Jenkins!

AGATHA. I will deliver your message in the presence of Sir

George, who, I may remind you, is the Permanent Secretary at the Home Office.

[AGATHA *and* CHARLOTTE *go out;* POSKET *paces up and down excitedly.*

POSKET. Gurrh! I'm not to go to the club! I set a bad example to Cis! Ha, ha! I am different from her first husband. Yes, I am—I'm alive for one thing. I—I—I—I—I'm dashed if I don't go out with the boy.

CIS. [*Putting his head in at the door.*] Coast clear, Guv? All right.

Enter CIS, *in fashionable evening dress, carrying* POSKET'S *overcoat and hat.*

Here are your hat and overcoat.

POSKET. [*Recoiling.*] Where on earth did you get that dress suit?

CIS. Mum's the word, Guv. Brighton tailor—six months' credit. He promised to send in the bill to you, so the mater won't know. [*Putting* POSKET'S *hat on his head.*] By Jove, Guv, don't my togs show you up?

POSKET. [*Faintly.*] I won't go, I won't go. I've never met such a boy before.

CIS. [*Proceeds to help him with his overcoat.*] Mind your arm, Guv. You've got your hand in a pocket. No, no—that's a tear in the lining. That's it.

POSKET. I forbid you to go out!

CIS. Yes, Guv. And I forbid you to eat any of those devilled oysters we shall get at the Hôtel des Princes. Now you're right!

POSKET. I am not right!

CIS. Oh, I forgot! [*He pulls out a handful of loose money.*] I found this money in your desk, Guv. You had better take it out with you; you may want it. Here you are—gold, silver, and coppers. [*He empties the money into* POSKET'S *overcoat pocket.*] One last precaution, and then we're off.

[*Goes to the writing-table, and writes on a half-sheet of note-paper.*

PLATE 8

The Magistrate. Harry Eversfield as Cis and Arthur Cecil as Posket. Act I

POSKET. I shall take a turn round the Square, and then come home again! I will not be influenced by a mere child! A man of my responsible position—a magistrate—supping slily at the Hôtel des Princes in Meek Street—it's horrible.

CIS. Now then—we'll creep downstairs quietly so as not to bring Wyke from his pantry. [*Giving* POSKET *a paper.*] You stick that up prominently, while I blow out the candles.

[CIS *blows out the candles on the piano.*

POSKET. [*Reading.*] 'Your master and Mr. Cecil Farringdon are going to bed. Don't disturb them.' I will not be a partner to any written document. This is untrue.

CIS. No, it isn't—we are going to bed when we come home. Make haste, Guv.

POSKET. Oh, what a boy! [*Pinning the paper on to the curtain.*

CIS. [*Turning down the lamp, and watching* POSKET.] Hallo, Guv, hallo! You're an old hand at this sort of game, are you?

POSKET. How dare you!

CIS. [*Taking* POSKET'*s arm.*] Now then, don't breathe.

POSKET. [*Quite demoralised.*] Cis! Cis! Wait a minute—wait a minute!

CIS. Hold up, Guv.

Enter WYKE.

Oh, bother!

WYKE. Going out, sir?

POSKET. [*Struggling to be articulate.*] No—yes—that is—partially—half round the Square, and possibly—er—um—back again. [*To* CIS.] Oh, you bad boy!

WYKE. [*Coolly going up to the paper on curtain.*] Shall I take this down now, sir?

POSKET. [*Quietly to* CIS.] I'm in an awful position! What am I to do?

CIS. Do as I do—tip him.

POSKET. What!

CIS. Tip him.

POSKET. Oh, yes—yes. Where's my money?

[CIS *takes two coins out of* POSKET'S *pocket and gives them to him without looking at them.*

CIS. Give him that.

POSKET. Yes.

CIS. And say—'Wyke, you want a new umbrella—buy a very good one. Your mistress has a latch-key, so go to bed.'

POSKET. Wyke!

WYKE. Yes, sir.

POSKET. [*Giving him money.*] Go to bed—buy a very good one. Your mistress has a latch-key—so—so you want a new umbrella!

WYKE. [*Knowingly.*] All right, sir. You can depend on me. Are you well muffled up, sir? Mind you take care of him, Master Cis.

CIS. [*Supporting* POSKET, *who groans softly.*] Capital, Guv, capital. Are you hungry?

POSKET. Hungry! You're a wicked boy. I've told a falsehood.

CIS. No, you haven't, Guv—he really does want a new umbrella.

POSKET. Does he, Cis? Does he? Thank heaven! [*They go out.*

WYKE. [*Looking at money.*] Here! What, twopence! [*Throws the coins down in disgust.*] I'll tell the missus. [*Curtain.*

ACT II

A supper-room at the Hôtel des Princes, Meek Street, with two doors—the one leading into an adjoining room, the other into a passage—and a window opening on to a balcony.

ISIDORE, *a French waiter, is showing in* CIS *and* POSKET, *who is still very nervous and reluctant.*

CIS. Come on, Guv—come on. How are you, Isidore?

ISIDORE. I beg your pardon—I am quite well, and so are you, zank you.

CIS. I want a pretty little light supper for myself and my friend, Mr. Skinner.

ISIDORE. Mr. Skinner.

POSKET. [*To* CIS.] Skinner! Is some one else coming?

CIS. No, no. You're Skinner.

POSKET. Oh! [*Wanders round the room.*

CIS. Mr. Skinner, of the Stock Exchange. What have you ready?

ISIDORE. [*In an undertone to* CIS.] I beg your pardon—very good—but Monsieur Blond he say to me, 'Isidore, listen now; if Mr. Farringdon he come here, you say, I beg your pardon, you are a nice gentleman, but will you pay your little account when it is quite convenient, before you leave the house at once.'

CIS. Quite so; there's no difficulty about that. What's the bill?

ISIDORE. [*Gives the bill.*] I beg your pardon. Eight pounds four shillings.

CIS. Phew! Here go my winnings from old Bullamy and the Guv. [*Counting out money.*] Two pounds short. [*Turning to* POSKET, *who is carefully examining the scratches on the mirrors.*] Skinner! Skinner!

POSKET. Visitors evidently scratch their names on the mirrors. Dear me! Surely this is a spurious title—'Lottie, Duchess of Fulham!' How very curious!

CIS. Skinner, got any money with you?

POSKET. Yes, Cis, my boy.   [*Feels for his money.*

CIS. You always keep it in that pocket, Skinner.

POSKET. [*Taking out money.*] Oh, yes.
> [CIS *takes two sovereigns from* POSKET *and gives the amount of his bill to* ISIDORE, *who goes to the sideboard to count out change.*

CIS. No putting the change to bed, Isidore.

POSKET. What's that?

CIS. Putting the change to bed! Isidore will show you. [*To* ISIDORE, *who comes to them with the change and the bill on a plate.*] Isidore, show Mr. Skinner how you put silver to bed.

ISIDORE. Oh, Mr. Farringdon, I beg your pardon—no, no!

POSKET. It would be most instructive.

ISIDORE. Very good. [*Goes to the table, upon which he puts plate.*] Say I have to give you change sixteen shillings.

POSKET. Certainly.

ISIDORE. Very good, Before I bring it to you I slip a little half-crown under the bill—so. Then I put what is left on the top of the bill, and I say, 'I beg your pardon, your change.' You take it, you give me two shillings for myself, and all is right.

POSKET. [*Counting the silver on the bill with the end of his glasses.*] Yes, but suppose I count the silver; it is half-a-crown short!

ISIDORE. Then I say, 'I beg your pardon, how dare you say that?' Then I do so. [*He pulls the bill from the plate.*] Then I say, 'The bill is eight pounds four shillings, [*handing the plate*] count again.'

POSKET. Ah, of course, it's all right now.

ISIDORE. Very good, then you give me five shillings for doubting me. Do it, do it.

POSKET. [*In a daze, giving him the five shillings.*] Like this?

ISIDORE. Yes, like that. [*Slipping the money into his pocket.*] I beg your pardon—thank you. [*Handing* CIS *the rest of the change.*] Your change, Mr. Farringdon.

CIS. Oh I say, Isidore!

Enter BLOND, *a fat, middle-aged French hotel-keeper, with a letter in his hand.*

ISIDORE. Monsieur Blond.

BLOND. Good evening, Mr. Farringdon.

ISIDORE. [*Quietly to* BLOND.] Ze bill is all right.

CIS. Good evening. [*Introducing* POSKET.] My friend, Mr. Harvey Skinner, of the Stock Exchange.

BLOND. Very pleased to see you. [*To* CIS.] Are you going to enjoy yourselves?

CIS. Rather.

BLOND. You usually eat in this room, but you don't mind giving it up for to-night—now, do you?

CIS. Oh, Achille!

BLOND. Come, come, to please me. A cab has just brought a letter from an old customer of mine, a gentleman I haven't seen for over twenty years, who wants to sup with a friend in this room to-night. It's quite true.   [*Giving* CIS *a letter.*

CIS. [*Reading to himself.*] '19A, Cork Street. Dear Blond— Fresh, or rather, stale from India—want to sup with my friend, Captain Vale, to-night, at my old table in my old room. Must do this for Auld Lang Syne. Yours, Alexander Lukyn.' Oh, let him have it. Where will you put us?

BLOND. You shall have the best room in the house, the one next to this. This room—pah! Come with me. [*To* POSKET.] Have you known Mr. Farringdon for a long time?

POSKET. No, no. Not very long.

BLOND. Ah, he is a fine fellow—Mr. Farringdon. Now, if you please. You can go through this door.
     [*Wheels sofa away from before door and unlocks it.*

CIS. [*To* POSKET.] You'll look better after a glass or two of Pommery, Guv.

POSKET. No, no, Cis—now, no champagne.

CIS. No champagne, not for my friend, Harvey Skinner! Come, Guv—dig me in the ribs—like this. [*Digging him in the ribs.*] Chuck!

POSKET. [*Shrinking.*] Oh, don't!

CIS. And say, 'Hey!' Go on, Guv.

POSKET. I can't—I can't. I don't know what it may mean.

CIS. [*Digging him in the ribs again.*] Go on—ch-uck!

POSKET. What, like this? [*Returning the dig.*] Ch-uck.

CIS. That's it, that's it. Ha, ha! You are going it, Guv.

POSKET. [*Getting excited.*] Am I, Cis? Am I? [*Waving his arm.*] Hey!

CIS *and* POSKET. Hey!

CIS. Ha, ha! Come on! Serve the supper, Achille.

BLOND. Ah, he is a grand fellow, Mr. Farringdon! [CIS *and* POSKET *go into the other room. To* ISIDORE.] Replace the canapé.
> [*There is a sharp knock at the other door.* BLOND *follows* CIS *and* POSKET *into the other room, then locks the door on the inside.*

ISIDORE. Come in, please.

Enter COLONEL LUKYN *and* CAPTAIN VALE. LUKYN *is a portly, grey-haired, good-looking military man;* VALE *is pale-faced and heavy-eyed, while his manner is languid and dejected.*

LUKYN. This is the room. Come in, Vale. This is my old supper-room—I haven't set foot here for over twenty years. By George, I hope to sup here for another twenty.

VALE. [*Dejectedly.*] Do you? In less than that, unless I am lucky enough to fall in some foreign set-to, I shall be in Kensal Green.

LUKYN. [*Looking round the room sentimentally.*] Twenty years ago! Confound 'em, they've painted it.

VALE. My people have eight shelves in the Catacombs at Kensal Green.

LUKYN. Nonsense, man, nonsense. You're a little low. Waiter, take our coats.

VALE. Don't check me, Lukyn. My shelf is four from the bottom.

LUKYN. You'll forget the number of your shelf before you're half-way through your oysters.

VALE. [*Shaking his head.*] An oyster merely reminds me of my own particular shell. [ISIDORE *begins to remove* VALE'S *coat.*

LUKYN. Ha, ha! Ha, ha!

VALE. Don't, Lukyn, don't [*In an undertone to* LUKYN.] It's very good of you, but by Jove, my heart is broken. [*To* ISIDORE.] Mind my flower, waiter, confound you.
                    [*He adjusts flower in his button-hole.*

ISIDORE. You have ordered supper, sir?

LUKYN. Yes, on the back of my note to Mr. Blond. Serve it at once.

ISIDORE. I beg your pardon, sir, at once.   [*Goes out.*

LUKYN. So, you've been badly treated by a woman, eh, Vale?

VALE. Shockingly. Between man and man, a Miss Verrinder—Charlotte. [*Turning away.*] Excuse me, Lukyn.
    [*Produces a folded silk handkerchief, shakes it out, and gently blows his nose.*

LUKYN. [*Lighting a cigarette.*] Certainly—certainly—does you great credit. Pretty woman?

VALE. Oh, lovely! A most magnificent set of teeth. All real, as far as I can ascertain.

LUKYN. No!

VALE. Fact.

LUKYN. Great loss—have a cigarette.

VALE. [*Taking case from* LUKYN.] Parascho's?

LUKYN. Yes. Was she—full grown?

VALE. [*Lighting his cigarette.*] Just perfection. She rides eight stone fifteen, and I have lost her, Lukyn. Beautiful tobacco.

LUKYN. What finished it?

VALE. She gave a man a pair of worked slippers three days after our engagement.

LUKYN. No!

VALE. Fact. You remember Bristow—Gordon Bristow?

LUKYN. Perfectly. Best fellow in the world.

VALE. He wears them.

LUKYN. Villain! Will you begin with a light wine, or go right on to the champagne?

VALE. By Jove, it's broken my heart, old fellow. I'll go right on to the champagne, please. Lukyn, I shall make you my executor.

LUKYN. Pooh! You'll outlive me! Why don't they bring the supper? My heart has been broken like yours. It was broken first in Ireland in '55. It was broken again in London in '61, but in 1870 it was smashed in Calcutta, by a married lady that time.

VALE. A married lady?

LUKYN. Yes, my late wife. Talk about broken hearts, my boy, when you've won your lady, not when you've lost her.

Enter ISIDORE, *with a tray of supper things.*

The supper. [*To* VALE.] Hungry?

VALE. [*Mournfully.*] Very.

Enter BLOND, *with an envelope.*

BLOND. Colonel Lukyn.

LUKYN. Ah, Blond, how are you? Not a day older. What have you got there?

BLOND. [*Quietly to* LUKYN *in an undertone.*] Two ladies, Colonel, downstairs in a cab, must see you for a few minutes alone.

LUKYN. Good gracious! Excuse me, Vale. [*Takes the envelope from* BLOND *and opens it: reading the enclosed card.*] Mrs. Posket—Mrs. Posket! 'Mrs. Posket entreats Colonel Lukyn to see her for five minutes upon a matter of urgent necessity, and free from observation.' By George! Posket must be ill in bed—I thought he looked seedy last night. [*To* BLOND.] Of course—of course. Say I'll come down.

BLOND. It is raining outside. I had better ask them up.

LUKYN. Do—do. I'll get Captain Vale to step into another room. Be quick. Say I am quite alone.

BLOND. Yes, Colonel. [*Hurries out.*

CIS. [*In the next room, rattling glasses and calling.*] Waiter! Waiter! Waiter-r-r! Where the deuce are you?

ISIDORE. Coming, sir, coming. I beg your pardon. [*Bustles out.*

LUKYN. My dear Vale, I am dreadfully sorry to bother you. Two ladies, one the wife of a very old friend of mine, have followed me here and want half a dozen words with me alone. I am in your hands—how can I manage it?

VALE. My dear fellow, don't mention it. Let me go into another room.

LUKYN. Thank you very much. You're so hungry too. Where's the waiter? Confound him, he's gone!

VALE. All right. I'll pop in here.
[*He passes behind sofa and tries the door leading into the other room.*

CIS. [*Within.*] What do you want? Who's there?

VALE. Occupied—never mind—I'll find my way somewhere.
[*There is a knock;* VALE *draws back.*

BLOND. [*Without.*] Colonel, are you alone? The ladies.

LUKYN. One moment. Deuce take it, Vale! The ladies don't want to be seen. By George—I remember. There's a little balcony to that window; step out for a few moments—keep quiet—I shan't detain you—it's nothing important—husband must have had a fit or something.

VALE. Oh, certainly!

LUKYN. Good fellow—here's your hat.
[*In his haste he fetches his own hat.*

BLOND. [*Outside, knocking.*] Colonel, Colonel!

LUKYN. One moment. [*Giving his hat to* VALE.] Awfully sorry. You're so hungry too. [VALE *puts on the hat, which is much too large for him.*] Ah, that's my hat.

VALE. My dear Lukyn—don't mention it.
[*Opening the window and going out.*

LUKYN. [*Drawing the curtain over the recess.*] Just room for him to stand like a man in a sentry-box. Come in, Blond.

BLOND *shows in* AGATHA *and* CHARLOTTE,
both wearing veils.

AGATHA. [*Agitated.*] Oh, Colonel Lukyn!

LUKYN. Pray compose yourself, pray compose yourself!

AGATHA. What will you think?

LUKYN. [*Holding out his hand, gallantly.*] That I am perfectly enchanted.

AGATHA. Thank you. [*Pointing to* CHARLOTTE.] My sister.
　　　　　　　　　　　　[LUKYN *and* CHARLOTTE *bow.*

LUKYN. Be seated. Blond? [*Softly to him.*] Keep the waiter out till I ring—that's all.　　[*The loud pattering of rain is heard.*

BLOND. Yes, Colonel.

LUKYN. Good gracious, Blond! What's that?

BLOND. The rain outside. It is cats and dogs.

LUKYN. [*Horrified.*] By George, is it? [*To himself, looking towards window.*] Poor devil! [*To* BLOND, *anxiously.*] There isn't any method of getting off that balcony, is there?

BLOND. No—unless by getting on to it.

LUKYN. What do you mean?

BLOND. It is not at all safe. Don't use it.
　　　　[LUKYN *stands horror-stricken;* BLOND *goes out. Heavy rain is heard.*

LUKYN. [*After some nervous glances at the window, wiping perspiration from his forehead.*] I am honoured, Mrs. Posket, by this visit—though for the moment I can't imagine——

AGATHA. Colonel Lukyn, we drove to Cork Street to your lodgings, and there your servant told us you were supping at the Hôtel des Princes with a friend. No one will be shown into this room while we are here?

LUKYN. No—we—ah—shall not be disturbed. [*To himself.*] Good heavens, suppose I never see him alive again!

AGATHA. [*Sighing wearily.*] Ah!

LUKYN. I'm afraid you've come to tell me Posket is ill.

AGATHA. I—no—my husband is at home.
　　　　　　[*A sharp gust of wind is heard with the rain.*

LUKYN. [*Starts.*] Lord forgive me! I've killed him.

AGATHA. [*With horror.*] Colonel Lukyn!

LUKYN. [*Confused.*] Madam!

AGATHA. Indeed, Mr. Posket is at home.

LUKYN. [*Glancing at the window.*] Is he? I wish we all were.

AGATHA. [*To herself.*] Sunstroke, evidently. Poor fellow! [*To LUKYN.*] I assure you my husband is at home, quite well, and by this time sleeping soundly.

[CIS *and* POSKET *are heard laughing in the next room.*

ISIDORE. [*Within.*] You are two funny gentlemen, I beg your pardon.

AGATHA. [*Startled.*] What is that?

LUKYN. In the next room. [*Raps at the door.*] Hush—hush, hush!

CHARLOTTE. Get it over Aggy, and let us go home. I am so awfully hungry.

LUKYN. [*Peering through the curtains.*] It is still bearing him. What's his weight? Surely he can't scale over ten stone. Lord, how wet he is!

AGATHA. Colonel Lukyn!

LUKYN. Madam, command me!

AGATHA. Colonel Lukyn, we knew each other at Baroda twenty years ago.

LUKYN. When I look at you, impossible.

AGATHA. Ah, then you mustn't look at me.

LUKYN. Equally impossible.

CHARLOTTE. [*To herself.*] Oh, I feel quite out of this.

AGATHA. You were at my little boy's christening?

LUKYN. [*Absently.*] Yes—yes—certainly.

AGATHA. You remember what a fine little fellow he was.

LUKYN. [*Thoughtfully*]. Not a pound over ten stone.

AGATHA. Colonel Lukyn!

LUKYN. [*Recovering himself.*] I beg your pardon, yes—I was at the christening of your boy.

AGATHA. [*To herself.*] One of the worst cases of sunstroke I have ever known.

LUKYN. I remember the child very well. Has he still got that absurd mug?

AGATHA. Colonel Lukyn!

LUKYN. Madam!

AGATHA. My child is, and always was—perfect.

LUKYN. You misunderstand me! I was his godfather; I gave him a silver cup.

AGATHA. Oh, do excuse me. [*Wiping her eyes.*] How did I become acquainted with such a vulgar expression? I don't know where I pick up my slang. It must be through loitering at shop windows. Oh, oh, oh!

LUKYN. Pray compose yourself. I'll leave you for a moment.
[*Going to the window.*

AGATHA. How shall I begin, Charley?

CHARLOTTE. Make a bold plunge, do! The odour of cooking here, to a hungry woman, is maddening.
[VALE *softly opens the window and comes into the recess, but remains concealed by the curtain from those on the stage.*

VALE. [*To himself.*] This is too bad of Lukyn! I'm wet to the skin and frightfully hungry! Who the deuce are these women?

AGATHA. Colonel Lukyn!

LUKYN. Madam. [*Listening.*] No crash yet.

AGATHA. [*Impulsively laying her hand upon his arm.*] Friend of twenty years! I will be quite candid with you. You are going to dine with us to-morrow?

LUKYN. Madam, I will repay your candour as it deserves. I am.

AGATHA. My husband knows of your acquaintance with the circumstances of my first marriage. I know what men are. When the women leave the dinner-table, men become retrospective. Now, to-morrow night, over dessert, I beg you not to give my husband dates.

LUKYN. [*Astonished.*] Eh?

AGATHA. Keep anything like dates from him.

LUKYN. [*Puzzled.*] Mustn't eat stone fruit?

AGATHA. No, I mean years, months, days—dates connected with my marriage with Mr. Farringdon.

LUKYN. Dear me, sore subject!

AGATHA. I will be more than candid with you. My present husband, having a very short vacation in the discharge of his public duties, wooed me but for three weeks; you, who have in your time courted and married, know the material of which that happy period is made up. The future is all-engrossing to the man; the presents—I mean the present, a joyous dream to the woman. But in dealing with my past I met with more than ordinary difficulties.

LUKYN. Don't see why—late husband died a natural death—wasn't stood on a balcony or anything.

AGATHA. Colonel Lukyn, you know I was six-and-thirty at the time of my recent marriage!

LUKYN. You surprise me!

AGATHA. You know it! Be frank, Lukyn! Am I not six-and-thirty?

LUKYN. You are.

AGATHA. Very well, then. In a three weeks' engagement how was it possible for me to deal with the various episodes of six-and-thirty years? The past may be pleasant, golden, beautiful—but one may have too much of a good thing.

LUKYN. [*To himself.*] I am in that position now.

AGATHA. The man who was courting me was seeking relaxation from the discharge of multifarious responsibilities. How could I tax an already wearied attention with the recital of the events of thirty-six years?

LUKYN. What did you do?

AGATHA. Out of consideration for the man I loved, I sacrificed five years of happy girlhood—told him I was but one-and-thirty—that I had been married only fifteen years previously—that my boy was but fourteen!

LUKYN. By George, madam, and am I to subscribe to all this?

AGATHA. I only ask you to avoid the question of dates.

LUKYN. But at a man's dinner-table——

AGATHA. You need not spoil a man's dinner. [*Appealingly.*] Not only a man's—but a woman's! Lukyn, Lukyn! Promise!

LUKYN. Give me a second to think.

[LUKYN, *turning away, discovers* CHARLOTTE *in the act of lifting the covers from the dishes and inspecting the contents.*

LUKYN. Ah, devilled oysters!

CHARLOTTE. Oh!

[*Drops dish-cover with a crash, and runs over to the table and speaks to* AGATHA.

LUKYN. Don't go—pray look at 'em again—wish I could persuade you to taste them. [*To himself.*] What am I to do? Shall I promise? Poor Posket! If I don't promise, she'll cry and won't go home. The oysters are nearly cold—cold! What must *he* be! [*Drawing aside the curtain and not seeing* VALE, *he staggers back.*] Gone—and without a cry—brave fellow, brave fellow!

AGATHA. Colonel Lukyn.

LUKYN. [*To himself.*] Decay of stamina in the army—pah! The young 'uns are worthy of our best days.

AGATHA. Colonel Lukyn, will you promise?

LUKYN. Promise? Anything, my dear madam, anything.

AGATHA. Ah, thank you! May I ask you to see us to our cab?

LUKYN. Certainly! Thank heaven, they're going!

AGATHA. [*To* CHARLOTTE.] It's all right; come along.

CHARLOTTE. [*To* AGATHA.] Oh, those oysters look so nice.

LUKYN. [*To himself.*] Stop! In my trouble, I am forgetting even the commonest courtesies to these ladies. [*To* AGATHA.] You have a long journey before you. I am sure your husband would not forgive me for letting you face such weather unprepared. Let me recommend an oyster or two and a thimbleful of champagne.

AGATHA. No thank you, Colonel Lukyn.

CHARLOTTE. [*To* AGATHA.] Say yes. I'm starving.

LUKYN. As you please. [*To himself.*] I knew they'd refuse. I've done my duty.

CHARLOTTE. [*To* AGATHA.] I was in the train till seven o'clock. Wait till you're a bona fide traveller—accept.

AGATHA. Ahem! Colonel, the fact is my poor sister has been travelling all day and is a little exhausted.

LUKYN. [*Horrified.*] You don't mean to say you're going to give me the inestimable pleasure. [CHARLOTTE *looks across at him, nodding and smiling.*] I am delighted.
[CHARLOTTE *sits hungrily at table;* LUKYN *fetches a bottle of champagne from the sideboard.*

AGATHA. Charlotte, I am surprised.

CHARLOTTE. Nonsense, the best people come here. Some of them have left their names on the mirrors.

VALE. [*Behind the curtain.*] This is much too bad of Lukyn. What are they doing now? [LUKYN *draws the cork.*] Confound it, they're having my supper!   [LUKYN *pours out wine.*

CHARLOTTE. Why doesn't he give me something to eat?
[*There is a clatter of knives and forks heard from the other room, then a burst of laughter from* CIS.

AGATHA. [*Starting*]. Charley, hark! How strange!

CHARLOTTE. Very. This bread is beautiful.
[CIS *is heard singing the chorus of a comic song boisterously.*

AGATHA. Don't you recognise that voice?

CHARLOTTE. [*Munching.*] The only voice I recognise is the voice of hunger.

AGATHA. I am overwrought, I suppose.
[LUKYN, *with his head drooping, fetches the dish of oysters from the sideboard.*

VALE. [*Behind the curtain.*] He has taken the oysters. I've seen him do it.

LUKYN. The oysters.
[LUKYN *sinks into his chair at the table and leans his head upon his hand; the two women look at each other.*

CHARLOTTE. [*To* AGATHA.] Anything wrong?

AGATHA. [*Tapping her forehead.*] Sunstroke—bad case!

CHARLOTTE. Oh—poor fellow. [*She gently lifts the corner of the dish, sniffs, then replaces cover.*] No plates.

AGATHA. Ask for them.

CHARLOTTE. You ask.

AGATHA. You're hungry.

CHARLOTTE. You're married. Comes better from you.

VALE. [*Behind curtain.*] This silence is terrible.

AGATHA. [*To* LUKYN.] Ahem! Ahem!

LUKYN. [*Looking up suddenly.*] Eh?

AGATHA. [*Sweetly.*] There are no plates.

LUKYN. [*Rousing himself.*] No plates? No plates? It's my fault. Pardon me. Where are the plates?
> [VALE, *still invisible, stretches out his hand through the curtain, takes up the plates and presents them to* LUKYN, *who recoils.*

VALE. [*In a whisper.*] Here are the plates. Look sharp, Lukyn.

LUKYN. [*With emotion.*] Vale! Safe and sound! [*He takes the plates, then grasps* VALE's *extended hand.*] Bless you, old fellow. I'm myself again. [*Going gaily to the table with the plates.*] My dear ladies, I blush—I positively blush—I am the worst host in the world.

VALE. [*To himself.*] By Jove, that's true.

AGATHA. Not at all—not at all.

LUKYN. [*Helping the ladies.*] I'll make amends, by George! You may have noticed I've been confoundedly out of sorts. That's my temperament—now up, now down. I've just taken a turn, ha, ha! Oysters. [*Handing plate to* AGATHA.

AGATHA. Thank you.

LUKYN. Ah, I've passed many a happy hour in this room. The present is not the least happy.

CHARLOTTE. [*Trying to attract his attention.*] Ahem! Ahem!

LUKYN. [*Gazing up at the ceiling.*] My first visit to the Hôtel des Princes was in the year—the year—let me think.

CHARLOTTE. [*Tearfully whispering to* AGATHA.] Isn't he going to help me?

LUKYN. Was it in '55?

AGATHA. [*Quickly passing her plate over to* CHARLOTTE.] I'm not hungry.

CHARLOTTE. You're a dear.

PLATE 9

The Magistrate. Captain Vale discovered. Act II

LUKYN. [*Emphatically.*] It *was* in '55. I'm forgetful again—pardon me. [*He hands plate of oysters to* CHARLOTTE, *and is surprised to find her eating vigorously.*] Why, I thought I—— [*To* AGATHA.] My dear madam, a thousand apologies. [*He helps her and then himself.*] Pah! they're cold—icy—you could skate on 'em. There's a dish of something else over there.
 [*He goes to the sideboard;* VALE's *hand is again stretched forth with the other covered dish.*

VALE. I say, Lukyn.

LUKYN. [*Taking the dish*] Thanks, old fellow. [*He returns to the table and lifts the cover.*] Soles—they look tempting. If there are only some lemons! Surely they are not so brutal as to have forgotten the lemons. Where are they? [*He returns to the sideboard.*] Where are they? [*In an undertone to* VALE.] Have you seen any lemons?

AGATHA. Pray, think less of us, Colonel Lukyn. Let me take care of you.

LUKYN. You're very kind. I wish you would let me ring for some lemons.
 [VALE's *hand comes as before from behind the curtain to the sideboard, finds the dish of lemons, and holds it out at arm's length.*

VALE. [*In a whisper.*] Lemons.
 [AGATHA *is helping* LUKYN, *when suddenly* CHARLOTTE, *with her fork in the air, leans back open-mouthed, staring wildly at* VALE's *arm extended with the dish.*

CHARLOTTE. [*In terror.*] Agatha! Agatha!

AGATHA. Charlotte! What's the matter, Charley?

CHARLOTTE. Agatha!

AGATHA. You're ill, Charlotte! Surely you are not choking?

CHARLOTTE. [*Pointing to the curtain.*] Look, look!
 [*They both scream.*

LUKYN. Don't be alarmed—I——

CHARLOTTE *and* AGATHA. [*Together.*] Who's that?

LUKYN. I can explain. Don't condemn till you've heard. I—I——. Damn it, sir, put those lemons down!

CHARLOTTE. He calls him 'Sir'—it must be a man.

LUKYN. It is a man. I am not in a position to deny that.

AGATHA. Really, Colonel Lukyn!

LUKYN. It is my friend. He—he—he's merely waiting for his supper.

AGATHA. [*Indignantly.*] Your friend! [*To* CHARLOTTE.] Come home, dear.

LUKYN. Do, do hear me! To avoid the embarrassment of your encountering a stranger, he retreated to the balcony.

AGATHA. [*Contemptuously.*] To the balcony? You have shamefully compromised two trusting women, Colonel Lukyn.

LUKYN. [*Energetically.*] I would have laid down my life rather than have done so. I did lay down my friend's life.

AGATHA. He has overheard every confidential word I have spoken to you.

LUKYN. Hear his explanation. [*To the curtain.*] Why the devil don't you corroborate me, sir?

VALE. [*From behind the curtain.*] Certainly. I assure you I heard next to nothing.

CHARLOTTE. [*Grasping* AGATHA's *arm.*] Oh, Agatha!

VALE. I didn't come in till I was exceedingly wet.

LUKYN. [*To* AGATHA.] You hear that?

VALE. And when I did come in——

CHARLOTTE. [*Hysterically.*] Horace!

VALE. I beg your pardon.

CHARLOTTE. It's Horace, Captain Vale.

VALE. [*Coming from behind the curtain, looking terribly wet.*] Charlotte—Miss Verrinder.

CHARLOTTE. What are you doing here? What a fright you look.

VALE. What am I doing here, Miss Verrinder? Really, Lukyn, your conduct calls for some little explanation.

LUKYN. My conduct, sir?

VALE. You make some paltry excuse to turn me out in the rain while you entertain a lady who you know has very recently broken my heart.

LUKYN. I didn't know anything of the kind.

VALE. I told you, Colonel Lukyn—this isn't the conduct of an officer and a gentleman.

LUKYN. Whose isn't, yours or mine?

VALE. Mine. I mean yours.

LUKYN. You are in the presence of ladies, sir; take off my hat.

VALE. I beg your pardon. I didn't know I had it on.
[*He throws the hat away, and the two men exchange angry words.*

CHARLOTTE. He's a very good-looking fellow; you don't see a man at his best when he's wet through.

AGATHA. [*Impatiently.*] Colonel Lukyn, do you ever intend to send for a cab?

LUKYN. Certainly, madam.   [*Going.*

VALE. One moment. I have some personal explanation to exchange with Miss Verrinder.

CHARLOTTE. [*To* AGATHA.] The slippers. [*To* VALE.] I am quite ready, Captain Vale.

VALE. Thank you. Colonel Lukyn, will you oblige me by stepping out on to that balcony?

LUKYN. [*Hotly.*] Certainly not, sir.

VALE. You're afraid of the wet, Colonel Lukyn; you are no soldier.

LUKYN. You know better, sir. As a matter of fact, that balcony can't bear a man like me.

VALE. Which shows that inanimate objects have a great deal of common sense, sir.

LUKYN. You don't prove it in your own instance, Captain Vale.

VALE. That's a verbal quibble, sir.   [*They talk angrily.*

AGATHA. [*To* CHARLOTTE.] It's frightfully late. Tell him to write to you.

CHARLOTTE. I must speak to him to-night; life is too short for letters.

AGATHA. Then he can telegraph.

CHARLOTTE. Half-penny a word and he has nothing but his pay.

AGATHA. Very well, then, Lady Jenkins has a telephone. I'll take you there to tea to-morrow. If he loves you, tell him to ring up 1338091.

CHARLOTTE. You thoughtful angel!

LUKYN. Mrs. Posket—Miss Verrinder—ahem—we——

VALE. Colonel Lukyn and myself——

LUKYN. Captain Vale and I fear that we have been betrayed, in a moment of——

VALE. Natural irritation.

LUKYN. Natural irritation, into the atrocious impropriety of differing——

VALE. Before ladies.

LUKYN. Charming ladies——

VALE. We beg your pardon—Lukyn!

LUKYN. Vale! [*They grasp hands.*] Mrs. Posket, I am now going out to hail a cab.

AGATHA. Pray do.

LUKYN. Miss Verrinder, the process will occupy five minutes.

VALE. [*Giving his hat to* LUKYN.] Lukyn, I return your kindness—my hat.

LUKYN. Thank you, my boy.

[LUKYN *puts on* VALE's *hat, which is much too small for him. As he is going out there is a knock at the door; he opens it:* BLOND *is outside.*

BLOND. Colonel, it is ten minutes past the time of closing; may I ask you to dismiss your party?

LUKYN. Pooh! Isn't this a free country?   [*Goes out.*

BLOND. Yes, you are free to go home, Colonel. I shall get into trouble.   [*Following him out.*

CHARLOTTE. [*To* AGATHA.] I'll have the first word. Really, Captain Vale, I'm surprised at you.

VALE. There was a happy time, Miss Verrinder, when I might have been surprised at you.

CHARLOTTE. A few hours ago it was—'By Jove, all is over.' Now I find you with a bosom friend enjoying devilled oysters.

VALE. I beg your pardon; I find you enjoying devilled oysters.

CHARLOTTE. [*Haughtily.*] Horace Vale, you forget you have forfeited the right to exercise any control over my diet.

VALE. One would think I had broken off our engagement.

CHARLOTTE. If you have not, who has? I have your letter saying all is over between us. [*Putting her handkerchief to her eyes.*] That letter will be stamped tomorrow at Somerset House. [*With sobs.*] I know how to protect myself.

VALE. Charlotte, can you explain your conduct with Gordon Bristow?

CHARLOTTE. I could if I chose; a young lady can explain anything.

VALE. But he is showing your gift to our fellows all over the place.

CHARLOTTE. It was a debt of honour. He laid me a box of gloves to a pair of slippers about 'Forked Lightning' for the Regimental Cup, and 'Forked Lightning' went tender at the heel. I couldn't come to you with debts hanging over me. [*Crying.*] I'm too conscientious.

VALE. By Jove, I've been a brute.

CHARLOTTE. Y-y-yes.

VALE. Can you forget I ever wrote that letter?

CHARLOTTE. That must be a question of time. [*She lays her head on his shoulder and then removes it.*] How damp you are! [*She puts her handkerchief upon his shoulder, and replaces her head. She moves his arm gradually up and arranges it round her shoulder.*] If you went on anyhow every time I discharged an obligation, we should be most unhappy.

VALE. I promise you I won't mention Bristow's slippers again. By Jove, I won't—there.

CHARLOTTE. Very well, then, if you do that I'll give you my word I won't pay any more debts before our marriage.

VALE. My darling!

CHARLOTTE. [*About to embrace him, but remembering that he is wet.*] No—no—you are too damp.

ISIDORE. [*Outside.*] I beg your pardon; it is a quarter of an hour over our time.

[AGATHA *has been sitting on the sofa; suddenly she starts, listening intently.*]

POSKET. [*Outside.*] I know—I know. I'm going directly I can get the boy away.

AGATHA. [*To herself.*] Æneas!

CIS. [*Outside.*] All right, Guv, you finish your bottle.

AGATHA. My boy!

ISIDORE. [*Outside.*] Gentlemen, come—come.

AGATHA. [*To herself.*] Miserable deceiver! This, then, is the club, and the wretched man conspires to drag my boy down to his own awful level. What shall I do? I daren't make myself known here. I know; I'll hurry home, and if I reach there before Æneas, which I shall do, [*Clenching her fist.*] I'll sit up for him.

Enter LUKYN.

AGATHA. [*Excitedly.*] Is the cab at the door?

LUKYN. It is.

AGATHA. Charlotte! Charlotte! [*Drawing her veil down.*

CHARLOTTE. I'm ready dear. [*To* VALE.] Married sisters are always a little thoughtless.

VALE. [*Offering his arm.*] Permit me.

LUKYN. [*Offering his arm to* AGATHA.] My dear madam.

They are all four about to leave when BLOND *enters hurriedly.*

BLOND. [*Holding up his hand for silence.*] Hush! Hush!

LUKYN. What's the matter?

BLOND. The police!

ALL. [*In a whisper.*] The police!

BLOND. [*Quietly.*] The police are downstairs at the door. I told you so.

CHARLOTTE. [*Clinging to* VALE.] Oh, dear! Oh, dear!

AGATHA. Gracious powers!

BLOND. Keep quiet, please. They may be satisfied with Madame
Blond's assurances. I must put you in darkness; they can see
the light here if they go round to the back.
        [*Blows out candles, and turns down the other lights.*

AGATHA *and* CHARLOTTE. Oh!

BLOND. Keep quiet, please! My licence is once marked already.
Colonel Lukyn, thank you for this.   [*He goes out.*

AGATHA. [*Whimpering.*] Miserable men! What have you done?
Are you criminals?

CHARLOTTE. You haven't deserted or anything on my account,
have you, Horace?

LUKYN. Hush! Don't be alarmed. Our time has passed so agreeably that we have overstepped the prescribed hour for closing
the hotel. That's all.

AGATHA. What can they do to us?

LUKYN. At the worst, take our names and addresses, and sum-
mon us for being here during prohibited hours.

AGATHA. [*Faintly.*] Oh!

CHARLOTTE. Horace, can't you speak?

VALE. By Jove, I very much regret this.

Enter ISIDORE.

LUKYN. Well, well?

ISIDORE. I beg your pardon; the police have come in.

LUKYN. The devil! [*To* AGATHA.] My dear lady, don't faint at
such a moment.

Enter BLOND *quickly, carrying a rug.*

BLOND. They are going over the house! Hide!

AGATHA *and* CHARLOTTE. Oh!
        [*There is a general commotion.*

BLOND. They have put a man at the back. Keep away from the
window. [*They are all bustling, and everybody is talking in
whispers;* LUKYN *places* AGATHA *under the table, where she is
concealed by the cover; he gets behind the overcoats hanging from the*

pegs; VALE *and* CHARLOTTE *crouch down behind sofa.*] Thank you very much. I am going to put Isidore to bed on the sofa. That will explain the light which has just gone out. [ISIDORE *quietly places himself upon the sofa;* BLOND *covers him with the rug.*] Thank you very much.   [*He goes out.*

AGATHA. [*In a stifled voice.*] Charley! Charley!

CHARLOTTE. Yes.

AGATHA. Where are you?

CHARLOTTE. Here.

AGATHA. Oh, where is Captain Vale?

CHARLOTTE. I think he's near me.

VALE. By Jove, Charlotte, I am!

AGATHA. Colonel Lukyn!

LUKYN. [*From behind the coats.*] Here, madam!

AGATHA. Don't leave us.

LUKYN. Madam, I am a soldier.

CHARLOTTE. Oh, Horace, at such a moment what a comfort we must be to each other.

VALE. My dear Charlotte, it's incalculable.
     [ISIDORE *gently raises himself and looks over the back of sofa.*

CHARLOTTE. [*In terror.*] What's that?

ISIDORE. [*Softly.*] I beg your pardon.   [*He sinks back.*

Enter BLOND *quietly, followed by* CIS *and* POSKET *on tip-toe,* POSKET *holding on to* CIS.

BLOND. This way; be quick. Excuse me, the police are just entering the room in which these gentlemen were having supper. One of them is anxious not to be asked any questions. Please to hide him and his friend somewhere. They are both very nice gentlemen. [*He goes out, leaving* CIS *and* POSKET.

POSKET. Cis, Cis! Advise me, my boy, advise me.

CIS. It's all right, Guv, it's all right. Get behind something.

AGATHA. [*Peeps from under the tablecloth.*] Æneas, and my child!
     [POSKET *and* CIS *wander about, looking for hiding-places.*

VALE. [*To* CIS.] Go away.

CIS. Oh!

LUKYN. [*To* POSKET, *who is fumbling at the coats.*] No, no.

BLOND. [*Popping his head in.*] The police—coming!
[CIS *disappears behind the window-curtain.* POSKET *dives under the table.*

AGATHA. Oh!

POSKET. [*To* AGATHA *in a whisper.*] I beg your pardon. I think I am addressing a lady. I am entirely the victim of circumstances. Accept my apologies for this apparent intrusion. [*No answer.*] Madam, I applaud your reticence, though any statement made under the present circumstances would not be used against you. [*Looking out.*] Where is that boy? [*Disappearing suddenly.*] Oh! Madam, it may be acute nervousness on your part, but you are certainly pinching my arm.

There is the sound of heavy feet outside, then enter MESSITER, *a gruff matter-of-fact Inspector of Police, followed by* HARRIS, *a constable, and* BLOND.

BLOND. You need not trouble yourself—take my word for it.

MESSITER. No trouble, Mr. Blond, thank you. [*Sniffing.*] Candles—blown out—lately. This is where the light was.

BLOND. Perhaps. My servant, Isidore, sleeps here; he has only just gone to bed.

MESSITER. Oh! [*Taking a bull's-eye lantern from* HARRIS *and throwing the light on* ISIDORE, *who is apparently sleeping soundly.*] Dead tired, I suppose?

BLOND. I suppose so.

MESSITER. [*Slightly turning down the covering.*] He sleeps in his clothes?

BLOND. Oh, yes.

MESSITER. Always?

BLOND. Always—it is a rule of the hotel.

MESSITER. Oh—why's that?

BLOND. To be ready for the morning.

MESSITER. All right—all right. [*Throwing the rug and blanket aside.*] Isidore, go downstairs and give your full name and particulars to Sergeant Jarvis.

ISIDORE. [*Rising instantly.*] Yes, sir—very good.

BLOND. [*To* ISIDORE.] Why do you wake up so soon? Devil take you!

ISIDORE. I beg your pardon. [*Goes out.*

MESSITER. What is underneath that window, Mr. Blond?

BLOND. The skylight over the kitchen—devil take it!

MESSITER. Thank you—*you* can go down to the sergeant now, Mr. Blond.

BLOND. With pleasure—devil take me! [*Goes out.*

MESSITER. Now then, Harris.

HARRIS. Yes, sir.

MESSITER. Keep perfectly still and hold your breath as long as you can.

HARRIS. Hold my breath, Sir?

MESSITER. Yes—I want to hear how many people are breathing in this room. Are you ready?

HARRIS. Yes, sir.

MESSITER. Go! [HARRIS *stands still, tightly compressing his lips;* MESSITER *quickly examines his face by the light of the lantern, then walks round the room, listening, and nodding his head with satisfaction as he passes the various hiding-places.* HARRIS *writhes in agony; in the end he gives it up and breathes heavily.*] Harris!

HARRIS. [*Exhausted.*] Yes, sir!

MESSITER. You're breathing.

HARRIS. Oh lor', yes, sir!

MESSITER. You'll report yourself to-night!

HARRIS. I held on till I nearly went off, sir.

MESSITER. [*Giving him the bull's-eye.*] Don't argue, but light up. There are half a dozen people concealed in this room. [*There is a cry from the women.* CHARLOTTE *and* VALE *rise;* LUKYN *steps from behind the coats.*] I thought so.

[*As* MESSITER *turns,* AGATHA *and* POSKET *rise,* CIS *comes quickly, catches hold of* POSKET, *and drags him across to the window.*

CIS. Come on, Guv, Come on!

[*They disappear through the curtain as* HARRIS *turns up the lights. Then there is a cry and the sound of a crash.*

AGATHA [*Sinking into chair.*] They're killed!

MESSITER. [*Looks through the window.*] No, they're not; they've gone into the kitchen and the balcony with them. Look sharp, Harris.   [HARRIS *goes out quickly.*

LUKYN. [*To* MESSITER.] I shall report you for this, sir.

MESSITER. [*Taking out his note-book.*] Very sorry, sir; it's my duty.

LUKYN. Duty, sir! Coming your confounded detective tricks on ladies and gentlemen! How dare you make ladies and gentlemen suspend their breathing till they nearly have apoplexy? Do you know I'm a short-necked man, sir?

MESSITER. I didn't want you to leave off breathing, sir. I wanted you to breathe louder. Your name and address, sir.

LUKYN. Gur-r-r-h!

MESSITER. [*Coaxingly.*] Army gentleman, sir?

LUKYN. How do you know that?

MESSITER. Short style of speaking, sir. Army gentlemen run a bit brusquish when on in years.

LUKYN. Oh! [*Conquering himself.*] Alexander Lukyn—Colonel— Her Majesty's Cheshire Light Infantry, late 41st Foot, 3rd Battalion—Bengal—Retired.

MESSITER. [*Writing.*] Hotel or club, Colonel?

LUKYN. Neither. 19A, Cork Street—lodgings.

MESSITER. [*Writing.*] Very nice part, Colonel. Thank you.

LUKYN. Bah!

MESSITER. Other gentleman?

VALE. [*With languid hauteur.*] Horace Edmund Cholmeley Clive Napier Vale—Captain—Shropshire Fusiliers—Stark's Hotel, Conduit Street.

MESSITER. [*Writing.*] Retired, sir?

VALE. No, confound you—active!

MESSITER. Thank you, Captain. Ahem! Beg pardon. The—the ladies.

> [CHARLOTTE *clings to* VALE, AGATHA *to* LUKYN.

AGATHA *and* CHARLOTTE. No—no! No—no!

LUKYN. [*To* AGATHA.] All right—all right—trust to me! [*To* MESSITER.] Well, sir?

MESSITER. Names and addresses, please.

LUKYN. [*Pacifically.*] Officer—my good fellow—tell me now—er—um—at the present moment, [*putting his hand in his pocket*] what are you most in want of?

MESSITER. These two ladies' names and addresses, please. Be quick, Colonel. [*Pointing to* AGATHA.] That lady first.

LUKYN. [*With an effort.*] Christian names—er—ah—er—Alice Emmeline.

MESSITER. [*Writing.*] Alice Emmeline. Surname?

LUKYN. Er—um—Fitzgerald—101, Wilton Street, Piccadilly.

MESSITER. Single lady?

LUKYN. Quite.

MESSITER. Very good, sir.

AGATHA. [*To* LUKYN, *tearfully.*] Oh, thank you, such a nice address too.

MESSITER. [*To* VALE.] Now Captain, please—that lady.

VALE. [*Who has been reassuring* CHARLOTTE.] Haw—ah—this lady is—ah—um—the other lady's sister.

MESSITER. Single lady, sir?

VALE. Certainly.

MESSITER. [*Writing.*] Christian name, Captain?

VALE. Ah—um—Harriet.

MESSITER. [*Writing.*] Surname?

VALE. Er—Macnamara.

MESSITER. [*With a grim smile.*] Quite so. Lives with her sister, of course, sir?

VALE. Of course.

MESSITER. Where at, sir?

VALE. Albert Mansions, Victoria Street.

CHARLOTTE. [*To* VALE.] Oh, thank you, I always fancied that spot.

MESSITER. Very much obliged, gentlemen.

LUKYN. [*Who has listened to* VALE'*s answers in helpless horror.*] By George, well out of it!

    [*The two ladies give a cry of relief.* CHARLOTTE *totters across to* AGATHA, *who embraces her. Taking down the overcoats and throwing one to* VALE.

Vale, your coat.

Enter HARRIS.

HARRIS. [*To* MESSITER.] Very sorry, sir; the two other gentlemen got clean off, through the back scullery door—old hands, to all appearance.

    [MESSITER *stamps his foot, with an exclamation.*

AGATHA. [*To herself.*] My boy—saved!

LUKYN. [*To* HARRIS, *who stands before the door.*] Constable, get out of the way.

MESSITER. [*Sharply.*] Harris!

HARRIS. [*Without moving.*] Yes, sir.

MESSITER. You will leave the hotel with these ladies, and not lose sight of them till you've ascertained what their names *are*, and where they *do* live.

LUKYN *and* VALE. What!

AGATHA *and* CHARLOTTE. Oh!

MESSITER. Your own fault, gentlemen; it's my duty.

LUKYN. [*Violently.*] And it is *my* duty to save these helpless women from the protecting laws of my confounded country! Vale!

VALE. [*Putting his coat on the sofa.*] Active!

LUKYN. [*To* HARRIS.] Let these ladies pass! [*He takes* HARRIS *by the collar and flings him over to* VALE, *who throws him over towards the ladies, who push him away.* MESSITER *puts a whistle to his mouth and blows; there is an immediate answer from without.*] More of your fellows outside?

MESSITER. Yes, sir, at your service. Very sorry, gentlemen, but you and your party are in my custody.

LUKYN *and* VALE. What?

AGATHA *and* CHARLOTTE. Oh!

MESSITER. For assaulting this man in the execution of his duty.

LUKYN. You'll dare to lock us up all night?

MESSITER. It's one o'clock now, Colonel—you'll come on first thing in the morning.

LUKYN. Come on? At what Court?

MESSITER. Mulberry Street.

AGATHA. [*With a scream.*] Ah! The magistrate?

MESSITER. Mr. Posket, mum.

[AGATHA *sinks into a chair,* CHARLOTTE *at her feet;* LUKYN, *overcome, falls on* VALE'*s shoulders. Curtain.*

ACT III

SCENE I. *The Magistrate's room at Mulberry Street Police Court, with a doorway covered by curtains leading directly into the Court, and a door opening into a passage. It is the morning after the events of the last Act.*

POLICE SERGEANT LUGG, *a middle-aged man with a slight country dialect, enters with 'The Times' newspaper, and proceeds to cut it and glance at its contents while he hums a song.*

Enter MR. WORMINGTON, *an elderly, trim and precise man.*

WORMINGTON. Good morning, Lugg.

LUGG. Morning, Mr. Wormington.

WORMINGTON. Mr. Posket not arrived yet?

LUGG. Not yet, sir. Hullo! [*Reading.*] 'Raid on a West End Hotel. At an early hour this morning——'

WORMINGTON. Yes, I've read that—a case of assault upon the police.

LUGG. Why, these must be the folks who've been so precious rampageous all night.

WORMINGTON. Very likely.

LUGG. Yes, sir, protestin' and protestin' till they protested everybody's sleep away. Nice-looking women, too, though as I tell Mrs. Lugg, now-a-days there's no telling who's the lady and who isn't. Who's got this job, sir?

WORMINGTON. Inspector Messiter.

LUGG. [*With contempt.*] Messiter! That's luck! Why he's the worst elocutionist in the force, sir.* [*As he arranges the newspaper upon the table, he catches sight of* WORMINGTON'S *necktie, which is bright red.*] Well, I—excuse me, Mr.

---

* A City magistrate, censuring a constable for the indistinctness of his utterances in the witness-box, suggested that the police should be instructed in a method of delivering evidence articulately. AUTHOR'S NOTE.

Wormington, but all the years I've had the honour of knowin' you, sir, I've never seen you wear a necktie with, so to speak, a dash of colour in it.

WORMINGTON. [*Uneasily.*] Well, Lugg, no, that's true, but to-day is an exceptional occasion with me. It is, in fact, the twenty-fifth anniversary of my marriage, and I thought it due to Mrs. Wormington to vary, in some slight degree, the sombreness of my attire. I confess I am a little uneasy in case Mr. Posket should consider it at all disrespectful to the Court.

LUGG. Not he, sir.

WORMINGTON. I don't know. Mr. Posket is punctiliousness itself in dress, and his cravat's invariably black. However, it is not every man who has a silver wedding-day.

LUGG. It's not every man as wants one, sir.

[WORMINGTON *goes out.*

At the same moment POSKET *enters quickly, and leans on his chair as if exhausted. His appearance is extremely wretched; he is still in evening dress, but his clothes are muddy, and his linen soiled and crumpled, while across the bridge of his nose he has a small strip of black plaster.*

POSKET. [*Faintly.*] Good morning, Lugg.

LUGG. Good morning to you, sir. Regretting the liberty I'm taking, sir—I've seen you look more strong and hearty.

POSKET. I am fairly well, thank you, Lugg. My night was rather—rather disturbed. Lugg!

LUGG. Sir?

POSKET. [*Nervously.*] Have any inquiries been made about me this morning—any messenger from Mrs. Posket, for instance, to ask how I am?

LUGG. No, sir.

POSKET. Oh. My child, my stepson, young Mr. Farringdon has not called, has he?

LUGG. No, sir.

POSKET. [*To himself.*] Where can that boy be? [*To* LUGG.] Thank you, that's all.

PLATE 10

The Magistrate. Arthur Cecil as Posket. Act III, Scene i

LUGG. [*Who has been eyeing* POSKET *with astonishment, goes to the door, and then touches the bridge of his nose. Sympathetically.*] Nasty cut while shavin', sir?   [*Goes out.*

POSKET. Where can that boy have got to? If I could only remember how, when, and where we parted! I think it was at Kilburn. Let me think—first, the kitchen. [*Putting his hand to his side as if severely bruised.*] Oh! Cis was all right, because I fell underneath; I felt it was my duty to do so. Then what occurred? A dark room, redolent of onions and cabbages and paraffin oil, and Cis dragging me over the stone floor, saying, 'We're in the scullery, Guv; let's try and find the tradesmen's door.' Next, the night air—oh, how refreshing! 'Cis, my boy, we will both learn a lesson from to-night—never deceive.' Where are we? In Argyll Street. 'Look out, Guv, they're after us.' Then—then, as Cis remarked when we were getting over the railings of Portman Square—then the fun began. We over into the Square—they after us. Over again, into Baker Street. Down Baker Street. Curious recollections, whilst running, of my first visit, as a happy child, to Madame Tussaud's, and wondering whether her removal had affected my fortunes. 'Come on, Guv—you're getting blown.' Where are we? Park Road. What am I doing? Getting up out of a puddle. St. John's Wood. The cricket-ground. 'I say, Guv, what a run this would be at Lord's, wouldn't it? And no fear of being run out either, more fear of being run in.' 'What road is this, Cis?' Maida Vale. Good gracious! A pious aunt of mine once lived in Hamilton Terrace; she never thought I should come to this. 'Guv?' 'Yes, my boy.' 'Let's get this kind-hearted coffee-stall keeper to hide us.' We apply. 'Will you assist two unfortunate gentlemen?' 'No, blowed if I will,' 'Why not?' ''Cos I'm a goin' to join in the chase after you.' Ah! Off again, along Maida Vale! On, on, heaven knows how or where, 'till at last no sound of pursuit, no Cis, no breath, and the early Kilburn buses starting to town. Then I came back again, and not much too soon for the Court. [*Going up to the washstand and looking into the little mirror, with a low groan.*] Oh, how shockingly awful I look, and how stiff and sore I feel! [*Taking off his coat and hanging it on a peg, then washing*

his hands.] What a weak and double-faced creature to be
a magistrate! I really ought to get some member of Parliament
to ask a question about me in the House. Where's the soap?
I shall put five pounds and costs into the poor's box to-
morrow. But I deserve a most severe caution. Ah, perhaps
I shall get that from Agatha. [*He takes off his white tie, rolls
it up and crams it into his pocket.*] When Wormington arrives
I will borrow some money and send out for a black cravat.
All my pocket money is in my overcoat at the Hôtel des
Princes. If the police seize it there is some consolation in
knowing that that money will never be returned to me. [*There
is a knock at the door.*] Come in!

Enter LUGG.

LUGG. Your servant, Mr. Wyke, wants to see you, sir.

POSKET. [*Testily.*] Bring him in. [LUGG *goes out.*] Wyke! From
Agatha! From Agatha!

Re-enter LUGG, *with* WYKE.

WYKE. Ahem! Good morning, sir.

POSKET. Good morning, Wyke. Ahem! Is Master Farringdon
quite well?

WYKE. He hadn't arrived home when I left, sir.

POSKET. Oh! Where is that boy? [*To* WYKE.] How is your
mistress this morning, Wyke?

WYKE. Very well, I hope, sir; *she* 'ain't come home yet, either.

POSKET. Not returned—nor Miss Verrinder?

WYKE. No, sir—neither of them.

POSKET. [*To himself.*] Lady Jenkins is worse; they are still
nursing her! Good women, true women!

WYKE. [*To himself.*] That's eased his deceivin' old mind.

POSKET. [*To himself.*] Now if the servants don't betray me and
Cis returns safely, the worst is over. To what a depth I have
fallen when I rejoice at Lady Jenkins's indisposition!

WYKE. Cook thought you ought to know that the mistress
hadn't come home, sir.

POSKET. Certainly. Take a cab at once to Campden Hill and

bring me back word how poor Lady Jenkins is. Tell Mrs. Posket I will come on the moment the Court rises.

WYKE. Yes, sir.

POSKET. And Wyke. It is not at all necessary that Mrs. Posket should know of my absence with Master Farringdon from home last night. Mrs. Posket's present anxieties are more than sufficient. Inform Cook and Popham and the other servants that I shall recognise their discretion in the same spirit I have already displayed towards you.

WYKE. [*With sarcasm.*] Thank you, sir. I will. [*He produces from his waistcoat-pocket a small packet of money done up in newspaper, which he throws down upon the table.*] Meanwhile, sir, I thought you would like to count up the little present of money you gave me last night, and in case you thought you'd been over-liberal, sir, you might halve the amount. It isn't no good spoiling of us all, sir.

Enter LUGG.

POSKET. You are an excellent servant, Wyke; I am very pleased. I will see you when you return from Lady Jenkins's. Be quick.

WYKE. Yes, sir. [*To himself.*] He won't give me twopence again in a hurry.   [*He goes out;* LUGG *is about to follow.*

POSKET. Oh, Lugg, I want you to go to the nearest hosier's and purchase me a neat cravat.

LUGG. [*Looking inquisitively at* POSKET.] A necktie, sir?

POSKET. Yes. [*Rather irritably, turning up his coat collar to shield himself from* LUGG'*s gaze.*] A necktie—a necktie.

LUGG. What sort of a kind of one, sir?

POSKET. Oh, one like Mr. Wormington's.

LUGG. One like he's wearing this morning, sir?

POSKET. Of course, of course, of course.

LUGG. [*To himself.*] Fancy him being jealous of Mr. Wormington, now. Very good, sir—what price, sir?

POSKET. The best. [*To himself.*] There now, I've no money. [*Seeing the packet on table.*] Oh, pay for it with this, Lugg.

LUGG. Yes, sir.

POSKET. And keep the change for your trouble.

LUGG. [*Delighted.*] Thank you, sir; thank you, sir—very much obliged to you, sir. [*To himself.*] That's like a liberal gentleman.   [*Goes out.*

At the same moment WORMINGTON *enters through the curtains with the charge sheet in his hand.* WORMINGTON, *on seeing* POSKET, *uneasily tucks his pocket-handkerchief in his collar so as to hide his necktie.*

WORMINGTON. H'm! Good morning.

POSKET. Good morning, Wormington.

WORMINGTON. The charge sheet.

POSKET. Sit down.

[WORMINGTON *puts on his spectacles;* POSKET *also attempts to put on his spectacles, but hurts the bridge of his nose, winces, and desists.*

POSKET. [*To himself.*] My nose is extremely painful. [*To* WORMINGTON.] You have a bad cold I am afraid, Wormington—bronchial?

WORMINGTON. Ahem! Well—ah—the fact is—you may have noticed how very chilly the nights are.

POSKET. [*Thoughtfully.*] Very, very.

WORMINGTON. The only way to maintain the circulation is to run as fast as one can.

POSKET. To run—as fast as one can—yes—quite so.

WORMINGTON. [*To himself, looking at* POSKET's *shirt front.*] How very extraordinary—he is wearing no cravat whatever!

POSKET. [*Buttoning up his coat to avoid* WORMINGTON's *gaze.*] Anything important this morning?

WORMINGTON. Nothing particular after the first charge, a serious business arising out of the raid on the Hôtel des Princes.

POSKET. [*Starting.*] Hôtel des Princes?

WORMINGTON. Inspector Messiter found six persons supping there at one o'clock this morning. Two contrived to escape.

POSKET. Dear me—I am surprised—I mean, did they?

WORMINGTON. But they left their overcoats behind them, and it is believed they will be traced.

POSKET. Oh, do you—do you think it is worth while? The police have a great deal to occupy them just now.

WORMINGTON. But surely if the police see their way to capture anybody we had better raise no obstacle.

POSKET. No—no—quite so—never struck me.

WORMINGTON. [*Referring to charge sheet.*] The remaining four it was found necessary to take into custody.

POSKET. Good gracious! What a good job the other two didn't wait! I beg your pardon—I mean —you say we have four?

WORMINGTON. Yes, on the charge of obstructing the police. The first assault occurred in the supper-room—the second in the four-wheeled cab on the way to the station. There were five persons in the cab at the time—the two women, the two men, and the Inspector.

POSKET. Dear me, it must have been a very complicated assault. Who are the unfortunate people?

WORMINGTON. The men are of some position. [*Reading.*] 'Alexander Lukyn, Colonel——'

POSKET. Lukyn! I—I—know Colonel Lukyn; we are old schoolfellows.

WORMINGTON. Very sad! [*Reading.*] The other is 'Horace, &c. &c. Vale—Captain—Shropshire Fusiliers'.

POSKET. And the ladies?

WORMINGTON. Call themselves 'Alice Emmeline Fitzgerald and Harriet Macnamara'.

POSKET. [*To himself.*] Which is the lady who was under the table with me?

WORMINGTON. They are not recognised by the police at present, but they furnish incorrect addresses, and their demeanour is generally violent and unsatisfactory.

POSKET. [*To himself.*] Who pinched me—Alice or Harriet?

WORMINGTON. I mention this case because it seems to be one calling for most stringent measures.

POSKET. Wouldn't a fine, and a severe warning from the Bench to the two persons who have got away——

WORMINGTON. I think not. Consider, Mr. Posket, not only defying the licensing laws, but obstructing the police!

POSKET. [*Reflectively.*] That's true—it is hard, when the police are doing anything, that they should be obstructed.

Enter LUGG.

LUGG. [*Attempting to conceal some annoyance.*] Your necktie, sir.

POSKET. [*Sharply.*] S-ssh!

WORMINGTON. [*To himself.*] Then he *came* without one—dear me!

LUGG. [*Clapping down a paper parcel on the table.*] As near like Mr. Wormington's as possible—brighter if anything.

POSKET. [*Opening the parcel, and finding a very common, gaudy neckerchief.*] Good gracious! What a horrible affair!

LUGG. [*Stolidly.*] According to my information, sir—like Mr. Wormington's.

POSKET. Mr. Wormington would never be seen in such an abominable colour.

WORMINGTON. [*In distress.*] Well—really—I—[*Removing the handkerchief from his throat.*] I am extremely sorry.

POSKET. My dear Wormington!

WORMINGTON. I happen to be wearing something similar— the first time for five-and-twenty years.

POSKET. Oh, I beg your pardon. [*To himself.*] Everything seems against me.

LUGG. One-and-nine it come to, sir. [*Producing the paper packet of money and laying it upon the table.*] And I brought back all the money you give me, thinking you'd like to look over it quietly. Really, sir, I never showed up smaller in any shop in all my life!

POSKET. [*Out of patience.*] Upon my word. First one and then another! What *is* wrong with the money? [*Opens the packet.*] Twopence! [*To himself, aghast.*] That man Wyke will tell all to Agatha! Oh, everything is against me!

[LUGG *has opened the door, taken a card from some one outside, and handed it to* WORMINGTON.

WORMINGTON. From cell No. 3. [*Handing the card to* POSKET.

POSKET. [*Reading.*] 'Dear Posket, for the love of goodness see me before the sitting of the Court. Alexander Lukyn.' Poor dear Lukyn! What on earth shall I do?

WORMINGTON. Such a course would be most unusual.

POSKET. [*Despairingly.*] Everything is unusual. Your cravat is unusual. This prisoner is invited to dine at my house to-day— that's peculiar. He is my wife's first husband's only child's godfather—that's a little out of the ordinary.

WORMINGTON. The charge is so serious!

POSKET. But I am a man as well as a magistrate; advise me, Wormington, advise me!

WORMINGTON. Well—you can apply to yourself for permission to grant Colonel Lukyn's request.

POSKET. [*Hastily scribbling on* LUKYN's *card.*] I do—I do—and after much conflicting argument I consent to see Colonel Lukyn here immediately. [*Handing the card to* WORMINGTON, *who passes it to* LUGG, *who then goes out.*] Don't leave me, Wormington—you must stand by me to see that I remain calm, firm, and judicial. [*He hastily puts on the red necktie in an untidy manner; it sticks out grotesquely.*] Poor Lukyn! I must sink the friend in the magistrate, and in dealing with his errors apply the scourge to myself. Wormington, tap me on the shoulder when I am inclined to be more than usually unusual.   [WORMINGTON *stands behind him.*

LUGG *enters with* LUKYN. LUKYN's *dressclothes are much soiled and disordered, and he too has a small strip of plaster upon the bridge of his nose. There is a constrained pause;* LUKYN *and* POSKET *both cough uneasily.*

LUKYN. [*To himself.*] Poor Posket!

POSKET. [*To himself.*] Poor Lukyn!

LUKYN. [*To himself.*] I suppose he has been sitting up for his wife all night, poor devil! Ahem! How are you, Posket?
          [WORMINGTON *touches* POSKET's *shoulder.*

POSKET. [*Pulling himself together.*] I regret to see you in this terrible position, Colonel Lukyn.

LUKYN. By George, old fellow, I regret to find myself in it. [*Sitting, and taking up newspaper.*] I suppose they've got us in *The Times*, confound 'em!

[*While* LUKYN *is reading the paper,* POSKET *and* WORMING-TON *hold a hurried consultation respecting* LUKYN'*s behaviour.*

POSKET. [*With dignity.*] Hem! Sergeant, I think Colonel Lukyn may be accommodated with a chair.

LUGG. He's in it sir.

LUKYN. [*Rising and putting down paper.*] Beg your pardon; forgot where I was. I suppose everything must be formal in this confounded place?

POSKET. I am afraid, Colonel Lukyn, it will be necessary even here to preserve strictly our unfortunate relative positions. [LUKYN *bows.*] Sit down. [LUKYN *sits again.*] POSKET *takes up the charge sheet.*] Colonel Lukyn! In addressing you now, I am speaking, not as a man, but as an instrument of the law. As a man I may or may not be a weak, vicious, despicable creature.

LUKYN. Certainly—of course.

POSKET. But as a magistrate I am bound to say you fill me with pain and astonishment.

LUKYN. Quite right—every man to his trade; go on, Posket.

POSKET. [*Turning his chair to face* LUKYN.] Alexander Lukyn— when I look at you—when I look at you———. [*He attempts to put on his spectacles, but hurts his nose again. To himself.*] Ah— my nose. [*To* LUKYN, *holding his spectacles a little way from his nose.*] I say, when I look at you, Alexander Lukyn, I confront a most mournful spectacle. A military officer, trained in the ways of discipline and smartness, now, in consequence of his own misdoings, lamentably bruised and battered, shamefully disfigured by plaster, with his apparel soiled and damaged—all terrible evidence of a conflict with that power of which I am the representative.

LUKYN. [*Turning his chair to face* POSKET.] Well, Posket, if it comes to that, when I look at you, when I look at you—[*He attempts to fix his glass in his eye, and hurts his nose. To himself.*] confound my nose! [*To* POSKET.] When I look at you, *you* are not a very imposing object this morning.

POSKET. [*Uneasily.*] Lukyn!

LUKYN. You look quite as shaky as I do—and you're not quite innocent of court plaster.

POSKET. [*Rising.*] Lukyn! Really!

LUKYN. And as for our attire, we neither of us look as if we had slipped out of a bandbox.

POSKET. [*In agony.*] Don't, Lukyn, don't! Pray respect my legal status! [WORMINGTON *leads* POSKET *back to his seat.*] Thank you, Wormington. Alexander Lukyn, I have spoken. It remains for you to state your motive in seeking this painful interview.

LUKYN. Certainly! Hem! You know, of course, that I am not alone in this affair?

POSKET. [*Referring to charge sheet.*] Three persons appear to be charged with you.

LUKYN. Yes. Two others got away. Cowards! If ever I find them, I'll destroy them!

POSKET. [*Wiping his brow.*] Lukyn!

LUKYN. I will! Another job for you, Posket.

POSKET. [*With dignity.*] I beg your pardon; in the event of such a deplorable occurrence, I should not occupy my present position. Go on, sir.

LUKYN. Horace Vale and I are prepared to stand the brunt of our misdeeds. [*Seriously*]. But Posket, there are ladies in the case.

POSKET. In the annals of the Mulberry Street Police Court such a circumstance is not unprecedented.

LUKYN. Two helpless, forlorn ladies.

POSKET. [*Referring to charge sheet.*] Alice Emmeline Fitzgerald and Harriet Macnamara. [*Gravely shaking his head.*] Oh, Lukyn, Lukyn!

LUKYN. Pooh! I ask no favour for myself or Vale, but I come to you, Posket, to beg you to use your power to release these two ladies without a moment's delay.

[WORMINGTON *touches* POSKET's *shoulder.*

POSKET. Upon my word, Lukyn! Do you think I am to be undermined?

LUKYN. [*Hotly.*] Undermine the devil, sir! Don't talk to me! Let these ladies go, I say! Don't bring them into Court, don't see their faces—don't hear their voices—if you do, you'll regret it!

POSKET. Colonel Lukyn!

LUKYN. [*Leaning across the table and gripping* POSKET *by the shoulder.*] Posket, do you know that one of these ladies is a married lady?

POSKET. Of course I don't sir. I blush to hear it.

LUKYN. And do you know that from the moment this married lady steps into your confounded Court, the happiness, the contentment of a doting husband become a confounded wreck and ruin?

POSKET. [*Rising.*] Then, sir, let it be my harrowing task to open the eyes of this foolish doting man to the treachery, the perfidy, which nestles upon his very hearthrug!

LUKYN. [*Sinking back.*] Oh, lor'! Be careful, Posket! By George, be careful!

POSKET. Alexander Lukyn, you are my friend. Amongst the personal property taken from you when you entered these precincts may have been found a memorandum of an engagement to dine at my house to-night at a quarter to eight o'clock. But Lukyn, I solemnly prepare you, you stand in danger of being late for dinner! I go further—I am not sure, after this morning's proceedings, that Mrs. Posket will be ready to receive you.

LUKYN. I'm confoundedly certain she *won't*!

POSKET. Therefore, Lukyn, as an English husband and father it will be my duty to teach you and your disreputable companions, [*referring to charge-sheet*] Alice Emmeline Fitzgerald and Harriet Macnamara, some rudimentary notions of propriety and decorum.

LUKYN. [*Rising.*] Confound you, Posket—listen!

POSKET. [*Grandly.*] I am listening, sir, to the guiding voice of Mrs. Posket—that newly-made wife still blushing from the embarrassment of her second marriage, and that voice says, 'Strike for the sanctity of hearth and home, for the credit of the wives of England—no mercy!'

WORMINGTON. It is time to go into Court, sir. The charge against Colonel Lukyn is first on the list.

LUKYN. Posket, I'll give you one last chance! If I write upon a scrap of paper the real names of these two unfortunate ladies, will you shut yourself up for a moment, away from observation, and read these names before you go into Court?

POSKET. Certainly not, Colonel Lukyn! I cannot be influenced by private information in dealing with an offence which is, in my opinion, as black as—as my cravat! Ahem!

[WORMINGTON *and* POSKET *look at each other's necktie and turn up their collars hastily.*

LUKYN. [*To himself.*] There's no help for it. Then, Posket, you must have the plain truth where you stand, by George! The two ladies who are my companions in this affair are——

POSKET. Sergeant! Colonel Lukyn will now join his party.

[LUGG *steps up to* LUKYN *sharply.*

LUKYN. [*Boiling with indignation.*] What, sir? What?

POSKET. Lukyn, I think we both have engagements—will you excuse me?

LUKYN. [*Choking.*] Posket! You've gone too far! If you went down on your knees—which you appear to have been recently doing—and begged the names of these two ladies, you shouldn't have 'em! No sir, by George, you shouldn't.

POSKET. Good morning, Colonel Lukyn.

LUKYN. You've lectured me, pooh-poohed me, snubbed me—a soldier, sir—a soldier! But when I think of your dinner-party to-night, with my empty chair—like Banquo, by George, sir—and the chief dish composed of a well-browned, well-basted, family skeleton, served up under the best silver cover, I pity you, Posket! Good morning!

[*He marches out with* LUGG.

POSKET. Ah! Thank goodness that ordeal is passed. Now, Wormington, I think I am ready to face the duties of the day. Shall we go into Court?

WORMINGTON. Certainly, sir.

[WORMINGTON *gathers up papers from the table.* POSKET *with a shaking hand pours out water from carafe and drinks.*

POSKET. [*To himself.*] My breakfast. [*To* WORMINGTON.] I hope I defended the sanctity of the Englishman's hearth, Wormington?

WORMINGTON. You did, indeed. As a married man, I thank you.

POSKET. [*Unsteadily.*] Give me your arm, Wormington. I am not very well this morning, and this interview with Colonel Lukyn has shaken me. I think your coat-collar is turned up, Wormington.

WORMINGTON. So is yours, I fancy, sir.

POSKET. Ahem!

[*They turn their collars down;* POSKET *takes* WORMINGTON's *arm. They are going towards the curtains when* WYKE *enters hurriedly at the door.*

WYKE. [*Panting.*] Excuse me, sir.

WORMINGTON. Hush, hush! Mr. Posket is just going into Court.

WYKE. Lady Jenkins has sent me back to tell you that she hasn't seen the missis for the last week or more.

POSKET. Mrs. Posket went to Campden Hill with Miss Verrinder last night!

WYKE. They haven't arrived there, sir.

POSKET. Haven't arrived!

WYKE. No sir—and even a slow four-wheeler won't account for that.

POSKET. Wormington, there's something wrong! Mrs. Posket quitted a fairly happy home last night and has not been seen or heard of since!

WORMINGTON. [*Taking his arm again.*] Pray don't be anxious, sir, the Court is waiting.

POSKET. [*In a frenzy, shaking him off.*] But I am anxious! Tell Sergeant Lugg to look over the Accident-Book, this morning's Hospital Returns, List of Missing Children,

Suspicious Pledges, People left Chargeable to the Parish, Attend to your Window Fastenings——! I—I—Wormington, Mrs. Posket and I disagreed last night!

WORMINGTON. [*Soothingly.*] Don't think of it, sir; you should hear me and Mrs. Wormington. Pray do come into Court.

POSKET. [*Hysterically.*] Court! I'm totally unfit for business, totally unfit for business!

[WORMINGTON *hurries him off through the curtains.*]

Enter LUGG, *almost breathless.*

LUGG. We've got charge one in the Dock—all four of 'em. [*Seeing* WYKE.] Hallo, you back again!

WYKE. Yes—seems so. [*They stand facing each other, dabbing their foreheads with their handkerchiefs.*] Phew! You seem warm.

LUGG. Phew! You don't seem so cool.

WYKE. I've been lookin' after two ladies.

LUGG. So have I.

WYKE. I haven't found 'em.

LUGG. If I'd known, I'd 'a been pleased to lend you our two. [*From the other side of the curtains there is the sound of a shriek from* AGATHA *and* CHARLOTTE.

WYKE. Lor', what's that!

LUGG. That *is* our two. Don't notice them—they're hystericals. They're mild now to what they have been. I say, old fellow—is your Guv'nor all right in his head?

WYKE. I suppose so—why?

LUGG. I've a partickler reason for asking. Does he ever tell you to buy him anything and keep the change?

WYKE. What d'yer mean?

LUGG. Well, does he ever come down handsome for your extry exertion—do you ever get any tips?

WYKE. Rather. What do you think he made me a present of last night?

LUGG. Don't know.

WYKE. Twopence—to buy a new umbrella.

LUGG. Well, I'm blessed! And he gave me the same sum to get him a silk necktie. It's my opinion he's got a softenin' of the brain. [*Another shriek from the two women, a cry from* POSKET, *and then a hubbub are heard. Running up to the curtains and looking through.*] Hallo, what's wrong? Here! I told you so—he's broken out, he's broken out.

WYKE. Who's broken out?

LUGG. The lunatic. Keep back, I'm wanted. [*He goes through the curtains.*]

WYKE. [*Looking after him.*] Look at the Guv'nor waving his arms and going on anyhow at the prisoners! Prisoners! Gracious goodness—it's the missis!

Amid a confused sound of voices POSKET *is brought in through the curtains by* WORMINGTON. LUGG *follows.* POSKET *is placed in a chair.* WORMINGTON *holds a glass of water to his lips.*

POSKET. [*Wildly.*] Wormington, Wormington! The two ladies, the two ladies! I know them!

WORMINGTON. [*Soothingly.*] It's all right, sir, it's all right—don't be upset, sir!

POSKET. I'm not well; what shall I do?

WORMINGTON. Nothing further, sir. What you have done is quite in form.

POSKET. What I *have* done?

WORMINGTON. Yes, sir—you did precisely what I suggested—took the words from me. They pleaded guilty.

POSKET. Guilty!

WORMINGTON. Yes, sir—and you sentenced them.

POSKET. [*Starting up.*] Sentenced them! The ladies!

WORMINGTON. Yes, sir. You've given them seven days, without the option of a fine.

[POSKET *collapses into* WORMINGTON'S *arms.*

SCENE II. POSKET's *drawing-room, as in the first act.*

Enter BEATIE *timidly, dressed in simple walking-costume.*

BEATIE. How dreadfully early! Eleven o'clock, and I'm not supposed to come till four. I wonder why I want to instruct Cis all day. I'm not nearly so enthusiastic about the two little girls I teach in Russell Square.

Enter POPHAM. *Her eyes are red as if from crying.*

POPHAM. [*Drawing back on seeing* BEATIE.] That music person again. I beg your pardon—I ain't got no instructions to prepare no drawing-room for no lessons till four o'clock.

BEATIE. [*Haughtily.*] I wish to see Mrs. Posket.

POPHAM. She hasn't come home.

BEATIE. Oh, then—er—um—Master Farringdon will do.

POPHAM. [*In tears.*] He haven't come home either!

BEATIE. Oh, where is he?

POPHAM. No one knows! His wicked old stepfather took him out late last night and hasn't returned him. Such a night as it was, too, and him still wearing his summer under-vests.

BEATIE. Mr. Posket?

POPHAM. Mr. Posket—no, my Cis!

BEATIE. How dare you speak of Master Farringdon in that familar way?

POPHAM. How dare I? Because me and him formed an attachment before ever you darkened our doors. [*Taking a folded printed paper from her pocket.*] You may put down the iron 'eel too heavy, Miss Tomlinson. I refer you to *Bow Bells*— 'First Love is Best Love; or, The Earl's Choice.' [*Offers paper.*

Enter CIS, *looking very pale, wornout, and dishevelled.*

POPHAM *and* BEATIE. Oh!

CIS. [*Staggering to a chair.*] Where's the mater?

POPHAM. Not home yet.

CIS. [*Faintly.*] Thank giminy!

BEATIE. He's ill!

POPHAM. Oh!

[BEATIE, *assisted by* POPHAM, *quickly wheels the large arm-chair forward. They catch hold of* CIS *and place him in it; he submits limply.*

BEATIE. [*Taking* CIS's *hand.*] What is the matter, Cis dear? Tell Beatie.

POPHAM. [*Taking his other hand, indignantly.*] Well, I'm sure! Who's given you raisins and ketchup from the store cupboard? Come back to Emma!

[CIS, *with his eyes closed, gives a murmur.*

BEATIE. He's whispering!

[*They both bob their heads down to listen.*

POPHAM. He says his head's a-whirling.

BEATIE. Put him on the sofa.

[*They take off his boots, loosen his necktie, and dab his forehead with water out of a flower-vase.*

CIS. [*Indistinctly.*] I—I—I wish you two girls would leave off.

[*They bob their heads down as before.*

BEATIE. He's speaking again. He hasn't had any breakfast! He's hungry!

POPHAM. Hungry! I thought he looked thin. Wait a minute, dear. Emma Popham knows what her boy fancies!

[*She runs out of the room.*

CIS. Oh, Beatie, hold my head while I ask you something.

BEATIE. Yes, darling?

CIS. No lady would marry a gentleman who had been a convict, would she?

BEATIE. No; certainly not!

CIS. I thought not. Well, Beatie, I've been run after by a policeman.

BEATIE. [*Leaving him.*] Oh!

CIS. [*Rising unsteadily.*] Not caught, you know, only run after; and walking home from Hendon this morning I came to the conclusion that I ought to settle down in life. Beatie—could I write out a paper promising to marry you when I'm one-and-twenty?

BEATIE. Don't be a silly boy—of course you could.

CIS. Then I shall; and when I feel inclined to have a spree I shall think of that paper and say, 'Cis Farringdon, if you ever get locked up, you'll lose the most beautiful girl in the world.'

BEATIE. And so you will.

CIS. I'd better write it now, before my head gets well again.

[*He writes; she bends over him.*

BEATIE. [*Tenderly.*] You simple, foolish Cis! If your head is so queer, shall I tell you what to say?

Enter POPHAM, *carrying a tray with breakfast dishes.*

POPHAM. [*To herself.*] He won't think so much of *her* now. His breakfast is my triumph. [*To* CIS.] Coffee, bacon, and a tea-cake.

BEATIE. Hush! Master Farringdon is writing something very important.

POPHAM. [*Going to the window.*] That's a cab at our door.

CIS. It must be the mater—I'm off!

[*He picks up his boots and goes out quickly.*

BEATIE. [*Following him with the paper and inkstand.*] Cis, Cis! You haven't finished the promise! You haven't finished the promise!

LUGG. [*Outside.*] All right, sir—I've got you—I've got you.

[POPHAM *opens the door.*

POPHAM. The master and a policeman!

Enter LUGG, *supporting* POSKET, *who sinks into an armchair with a groan.*

Oh, what's the matter?

LUGG. All right, my good girl, you run downstairs and fetch a drop of brandy and water.   [POPHAM *hurries out.*

POSKET. [*Groaning again.*] Oh!

LUGG. Now don't take on so, sir. It's what might happen to any married gentleman. Now, you're all right now, sir. And I'll hurry back to the Court to see whether they've sent for Mr. Bullamy.

POSKET. My wife! My wife!

LUGG. [*Soothingly.*] Oh, come now, sir, what *is* seven days! Why, many a married gentleman in your position, sir, would have been glad to have made it fourteen.

POSKET. Go away—leave me.

LUGG. Certainly sir.

Re-enter POPHAM *with a small tumbler of brandy and water; he takes it from her and drinks it.*

It's not wanted. I'm thankful to say he's better.

POPHAM. [*To* LUGG.] If you please, Cook presents her compliments, and she would be glad of the pleasure of your company downstairs, before leavin'. [*They go out.*

POSKET. Agatha and Lukyn! Agatha and Lukyn supping together at the Hôtel des Princes, while I was at home and asleep—while I ought to have been at home and asleep! It's awful!

CIS. [*Looking in at the door.*] Hallo, Guv!

POSKET. [*Starting up.*] Cis!

Enter CIS.

CIS. Where did you fetch, Guv?

POSKET. Where did I fetch! You wretched boy! I fetched Kilburn, and I'll fetch you a sound whipping when I recover my composure.

CIS. What for?

POSKET. For leading me astray, sir. Yours is the first bad companionship I have ever formed! Evil communication with you, sir, has corrupted me! [*Taking* CIS *by the collar and shaking him.*] Why did you abandon me at Kilburn?

CIS. Because you were quite done, and I branched off to draw the crowd away from you after me.

POSKET. Did you, Cis, did you? *Putting his hand on* CIS's *shoulder.*] My boy—my boy! Oh Cis, we're in such trouble!

CIS. You weren't caught, Guv?

POSKET. No—but do you know who the ladies are who were supping at the Hôtel des Princes?

CIS. No—do you?

POSKET. Do I? They were your mother and Aunt Charlotte.

CIS. The mater and Aunt Charlotte! Ha, ha, ha! [*Laughing and dancing with delight.*] Ha, ha! Oh, I say, Guv, what a lark!

POSKET. A lark! They were taken to the police station!

CIS. [*Changing his tone.*] My mother?

POSKET. They were brought before the magistrate and sentenced.

CIS. Sentenced?

POSKET. To seven days' imprisonment.

CIS. Oh! [*He puts his hat on fiercely.*

POSKET. [*Alarmed.*] What are you going to do?

CIS. Get my mother out first, and then break every bone in that magistrate's body.

POSKET. Cis, Cis! He's an unhappy wretch and he did his duty.

CIS. His duty! To send another magistrate's wife to prison! Guv, I'm only a boy, but I know what professional etiquette is. Come along! Which is the police station?

POSKET. [*In agony.*] Mulberry Street.

CIS. [*Recoiling.*] Who's the magistrate?

POSKET. I am!

CIS. You! [*Seizing* POSKET *by the collar and shaking him.*] You dare to lock up my mother! Come with me and get her out!

He is dragging POSKET *towards the door, when* BULLAMY *enters breathlessly.*

BULLAMY. My dear Posket!

CIS. [*Seizing* BULLAMY *and dragging him with* POSKET *to the door.*] Come with me and get my mother out!

BULLAMY. Leave me alone, sir! She *is* out! [*Panting.*] I managed it.

CIS *and* POSKET. [*Together.*] How?

BULLAMY. Wormington sent to me when you were taken ill. When I arrived at the Court, he had discovered from your man-servant Mrs. Posket's awful position.

CIS. [*Warmly.*] You leave my mother alone! Go on!

BULLAMY. Said I to myself, 'This won't do; I must extricate these people somehow!' I'm not so damned conscientious as you are, Posket.

CIS. Bravo! Go on!

BULLAMY. [*Producing his jujube box.*] The first thing I did was to take a jujube.

CIS. [*Snatching the jujube box from him.*] Will you make haste?

BULLAMY. Then said I to Wormington, 'Posket was *non compos mentis* when he heard this case—I'm going to reopen the matter!'

CIS. Hurrah!

BULLAMY. And I did. And what do you think I found out from the proprietor of the hotel?

POSKET *and* CIS. What?

BULLAMY. That this young scamp, Mr. Cecil Farringdon, hires a room at the Hôtel des Princes.

CIS. I know that.

BULLAMY. And that Mr. Farringdon was there last night with some low stockbroker of the name of Skinner.

CIS. Go on—go on! [*Offering him the jujube box.*] Take a jujube.

BULLAMY. [*Taking a jujube.*] Now the law, which seems to me quite perfect, allows a man who rents a little apartment at an inn to eat and drink with his friends all night long.

CIS. Well?

BULLAMY. So said I from the bench, 'These ladies and gentlemen appear to be friends or relatives of a certain lodger in the Hôtel des Princes.'

CIS. So they are!

BULLAMY. 'They were all discovered in one room.'

POSKET. So we were—I mean, so they were!

BULLAMY. 'And I shall adjourn the case for a week to give Mr. Farringdon an opportunity of claiming these people as his guests.'

CIS. Three cheers for Bullamy!

BULLAMY. So I censured the police for their interference and released the ladies on their own recognisances.

POSKET. [*Taking* BULLAMY's *hand.*] And the men?

BULLAMY. Well, unfortunately, Wormington took upon himself to despatch the men to the House of Correction before I arrived.

POSKET. [*Violently.*] I'm glad of it! They are dissolute villains! I'm glad of it.

Enter POPHAM, *scared.*

POPHAM. Oh, sir! Here's the missis and Miss Verrinder! In such a plight!

CIS. The mater! Guv, you explain! [*He hurries out.* POSKET *rapidly retires into the window recess.*

Enter AGATHA *and* CHARLOTTE, *pale, red-eyed, and agitated. They carry their hats, or bonnets, which are much crushed.* POPHAM *goes out.*

AGATHA *and* CHARLOTTE. [*Falling on to* BULLAMY's *shoulders.*] O—o—h—h!

BULLAMY. My dear ladies!   [*They seize* BULLAMY's *hands.*

AGATHA. Preserver!

CHARLOTTE. Friend!

AGATHA. How is my boy?

BULLAMY. Never better.

AGATHA. [*Fiercely.*] And the man who condemned his wife and sister-in-law to the miseries of a jail?

BULLAMY. Ahem! Posket—oh—he——

AGATHA. Is he well enough to be told what that wife thinks of him?

BULLAMY. It might cause a relapse.

AGATHA. It is my duty to risk that.

CHARLOTTE. [*Raising the covers of the dishes on the table. With an hysterical cry.*] Food!

AGATHA. Ah!

[AGATHA *and* CHARLOTTE *begin to devour a teacake voraciously.*]

POSKET. [*Advancing with an attempt at dignity.*] Agatha Posket!

AGATHA. [*Rising, with her mouth full and a piece of teacake in her hand.*] Sir!

   [CHARLOTTE *takes the tray and everything on it from the table and goes towards the door.*]

BULLAMY. [*Going to the door.*] There's going to be an explanation.

CHARLOTTE. [*At the door.*] There's going to be an explanation.

   [CHARLOTTE *and* BULLAMY *go out quietly.*

POSKET. How dare you look me in the face, madam?

AGATHA. How dare you look at anybody in any position, sir? You send your wife to prison for pushing a mere policeman.

POSKET. I didn't know what I was doing.

AGATHA. Not when you requested two ladies to raise their veils and show their faces in the dock? We shouldn't have been discovered but for that.

POSKET. It was my duty.

AGATHA. Duty! You don't go to the Police Court again alone! I guess now, Æneas Posket, why you clung to a single life so long. *You liked it!*

POSKET. I wish I had.

AGATHA. Why didn't you marry till you were fifty?

POSKET. Perhaps I hadn't met a widow, madam.

AGATHA. Paltry excuse. You revelled in a dissolute bachelorhood!

POSKET. Hah! Whist every evening!

AGATHA. You can't play whist *alone.* You're an expert at hiding, too!

POSKET. If I were I should thrash your boy!

AGATHA. When you wished to conceal yourself last night, you selected a table with a lady under it.

POSKET. [*Rubbing his arm.*] Ah, did you pinch me, or did Charlotte?

AGATHA. I did—Charlotte's a single girl.

POSKET. I fancy, madam, you found my conduct under that table perfectly respectful?

AGATHA. I don't know—I was too agitated to notice.

POSKET. Evasion—you're like all the women.

AGATHA. Profligate! You oughtn't to know that.

POSKET. No wife of mine sups unknown to me, with dissolute military men; we will have a judicial separation, Mrs. Posket.

AGATHA. Certainly—I suppose you'll manage that at your Police Court, too?

POSKET. I shall send for my solicitor at once.

AGATHA. Æneas! Mr. Posket! Whatever happens, you shall not have the custody of my boy.

POSKET. Your boy! *I* take charge of *him*? Agatha Posket, he has been my evil genius! He has made me a gambler at an atrocious game called 'Fireworks'—he has tortured my mind with abstruse speculations concerning 'Sillikin' and 'Butter-scotch' for the St. Leger—he has caused me to cower before servants, and to fly before the police.

AGATHA. He! My Cis?

Enter CIS, *having changed his clothes.*

CIS. [*Breezily.*] Hallo, mater—got back?

AGATHA. You wicked boy! You dare to have apartments at the Hôtel des Princes!

POSKET. Yes—and it was to put a stop to that which induced me to go to Meek Street last night.

CIS. Don't be angry mater! I've got you out of your difficulties.

POSKET. But you got me into mine!

CIS. Well, I know I did—one can't be always doing the right thing. It isn't Guv's fault—there!

POSKET. Swear it!

AGATHA. No, he doesn't know the nature of an oath. I believe him. Æneas, I see now this is all the result of a lack of candour on my part. Tell me, have you ever particularly observed this child?

POSKET. [*Weakly.*] Oh!

AGATHA. Has it ever struck you he is a little forward?

POSKET. Sometimes.

AGATHA. You are wrong; he is awfully backward. [*Taking* POSKET'*s hand.*] Æneas, men always think they are marrying angels, and women would be angels if they never had to grow old. That warps their dispositions. I have deceived you, Æneas.

POSKET. [*Clenching his fists.*] Ah! Lukyn!

AGATHA. No—no—you don't understand! Lukyn was my boy's godfather in 1866.

POSKET. [*Starting.*] 1866?

CIS. 1866?

CIS *and* POSKET. [*Reckoning rapidly upon their fingers.*] 1866.

AGATHA. [*Quickly.*] S-s-s-h! Don't count! Cis, go away! [*To* POSKET.] When you proposed to me in the Pantheon at Spa, you particularly remarked, 'Mrs. Farringdon, I love you for yourself *alone*'.

POSKET. I know I did.

AGATHA. Those were terrible words to address to a widow with a son of nineteen. [CIS *and* POSKET *again reckon rapidly upon their fingers.*] Don't count, Æneas, don't count! Those words tempted me. I glanced at my face in a neighbouring mirror, and I said 'Æneas is fifty—why should I—a mere woman, compete with him on the question of age? He has already the advantage—I will be generous—I will add to it!' I led you to believe I had been married only fifteen years ago; I deceived you and my boy as to his real age, and I told you I was but one-and-thirty.

POSKET. It wasn't the truth?

AGATHA. Ah! I merely lacked woman's commonest fault, exaggeration.

POSKET. But—Lukyn?

AGATHA. Knows the real facts. I went to him last night to beg him not to disturb an arrangement which had brought happiness to all parties. Look. In place of a wayward, troublesome child, I now present you with a youth old enough to be a joy, comfort and support!

CIS. Oh, I say, mater, this is a frightful sell for a fellow.

AGATHA. Go to your room, sir.

CIS. I always thought there was something wrong with me. Blessed if I'm not behind the age!   [CIS *goes out.*

AGATHA. Forgive me, Æneas. Look at my bonnet! A night in Mulberry Street, without even a powder-puff, is an awful expiation.

POSKET. Agatha! How do I know Cis won't be five-and-twenty to-morrow?

AGATHA. No—no—you know the worst, and as long as I live, I'll never deceive you again—except in little things.

Enter LUKYN *and* VALE.

LUKYN. [*Boiling with rage.*] By George, Posket!

POSKET. My dear Lukyn!

LUKYN. Do you know I am a confounded jail-bird, sir?

POSKET. An accident!

LUKYN. And do you know what has happened to me in jail— a soldier, sir—an officer?

POSKET. No.

LUKYN. I have been washed by the authorities!

POSKET. Lukyn, no!

Enter CHARLOTTE; *she rushes across to* VALE.

CHARLOTTE. Horace! Horace! Not you, too?

VALE. By Jove, Charlotte, I would have died first.

Enter BULLAMY, *quickly.*

BULLAMY. Mr. Posket, I shall choke, sir! Inspector Messiter is downstairs and says that Isidore the waiter swears that you are the man who escaped from Meek Street last night.

LUKYN. What?

BULLAMY. This is a public scandal, sir!

LUKYN. Your game is up, sir!

BULLAMY. You have brought a stain upon a spotless Police Court.

LUKYN. And lectured me upon propriety and decorum.

POSKET. Gentlemen, gentlemen, when you have heard my story you will pity me.

LUKYN *and* BULLAMY. [*Laughing ironically.*] Ha, ha!

POSKET. You will find your old friend a Man, a Martyr, and a Magistrate!

Enter CIS, *pulling* BEATIE *after him.*

CIS. Come on, Beatie! Guv—mater! Here's news! Beatie and I have made up our minds to be married.

AGATHA. Oh!

Enter POPHAM, *with champagne and glasses.*

POSKET. What's this?

CIS. Bollinger—'74—extra dry—to drink our health and happiness.

CHARLOTTE. Champagne! It may save my life!

AGATHA. Miss Tomlinson, go home!

POSKET. [*Grimly.*] Stop! Cis Farringdon, my dear boy, you are but nineteen at present, but you were only fourteen yesterday, so you are a growing lad; on the day you marry and start for Canada, I will give you a thousand pounds!

POPHAM. [*Putting her apron to her eyes.*] Oh!

CIS. [*Embracing* BEATIE.] Hurrah! We'll be married directly.

AGATHA. He's an infant! I forbid it!

POSKET. I am his legal guardian. Gentlemen, bear witness. I solemnly consent to that little wretch's marriage!

[AGATHA *sinks into a chair as the curtain falls.*